TASC: Full Study Guide and Test Strategies for the Test Assessing Secondary Completion

To obtain permission(s) to use the material from this work for any purpose including workshops or seminars, please submit a written request to

Phone: 800-496-5994

Email: info@smarteditionmedia.com

Library of Congress Cataloging-in-Publication Data
Smart Edition Media.
TASC: Full Study Guide and Test Strategies for the Test Assessing Secondary Completion
ISBN: Print: 978-1-949147-59-9, 2nd edition

1. TASC Exam
2. Study Guides
3. Test Assessing Secondary Completion
4. High School Equivalency
5. Careers

Disclaimer:

The opinions expressed in this publication are the sole works of Smart Edition Media and were created independently from any National Evaluation Systems or other testing affiliates. Between the time of publication and printing, specific standards as well as testing formats and website information may change that are not included in part or in whole within this product. Smart Edition Media develops sample test questions, and they reflect similar content as on real tests; however, they are not former tests. Smart Edition Media assembles content that aligns with exam standards but makes no claims nor guarantees candidates a passing score.

Printed in the United States of America

TASC: Full Study Guide and Test Strategies for the Test Assessing Secondary Completion

ISBN: Print: 978-1-949147-59-9
    Ebook: 978-1-949147-60-5

Print and digital composition by Book Genesis, Inc.

HOW TO ACCESS THE ONLINE RESOURCES

To access your online resources, follow these instructions:

1. Go to www.smarteditionmedia.com.
2. Select Sign In in the website navigation at the top of the page .
3. Select your book.
4. Follow the instructions on the login page for locating the password in your book (the password is case sensitive, so be sure to include any capital letters at the beginning of the password).

 Practice tests

 Flashcards

 Videos

  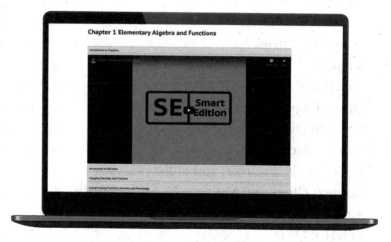

TABLE OF CONTENTS

INTRODUCTION

AN OVERVIEW OF THE TASC EXAM

The Test Assessing Secondary Completion (TASC) Exam is a national high school equivalency examination. The TASC assesses proficiency in the standard high school subjects of science, mathematics, reading, writing, and social studies. Considered to be an alternative to the GED Exam, the TASC is currently accepted by the following states: California, Colorado, Illinois, Indiana, Michigan, Mississippi, Nevada, New Jersey, New York, North Carolina, Ohio, Oklahoma, South Carolina, Texas, and West Virginia. The TASC is administered year round at testing centers within your state. Candidates are required to take the test in person at a recognized testing facility; and both online and paper-and-pencil versions of the test are available. See your local testing center for further details about scheduling your test.

ABOUT THIS BOOK

This book provides you with an accurate and complete representation of the TASC test and includes instructional content on the four core sections on the exam, plus a chapter on the writing section with practice essay prompts. The reviews in this book are designed to provide the information and strategies you need to do well on the exam. The full-length practice test in the book is based on the TASC and contains questions similar to those you can expect to encounter on the official test. A detailed answer key follows each practice quiz and test. These answer keys provide explanations designed to help you completely understand the test material. Each explanation references the book chapter to allow you to go back to that section for additional review, if necessary.

The Texas Instrument Model TI-30XS calculator is the preferred calculator of the TASC exam. This scientific calculator can be used for a portion of the Mathematics section of the test. Some states will also allow other scientific calculators to be used; however, these calculators must not have graphing capabilities. Refer to the list of accepted calculators on the official TASC website for your state. You should familiarize yourself with your calculator of choice before taking the actual exam. The practice test in this book does not have a separate calculator section. Instead, you should focus on knowing how to answer the math problems by hand as it will increase your confidence when taking the actual exam.

The TASC includes a reference guide of common math formulas that can be used during the test. As you work through the lessons in this study guide, create your own reference sheet that includes formulas for finding the area, perimeter, surface area, and volume of shapes; also include the formulas for mean, median, and algebraic calculations.

HOW TO USE THIS BOOK

Studies show that most people begin preparing for college-entry exams approximately 8 weeks before their test date. If you are scheduled to take your test in sooner than 8 weeks, do not despair! Smart Edition Media has designed this study guide to be flexible to allow you to concentrate on areas where you need the most support.

Whether you have 8 weeks to study – or much less than that – we urge you to take one of the online practice tests to determine areas of strength and weakness, if you have not done so already. These tests can be found in your online resources.

Once you have completed a practice test, use this information to help you create a study plan that suits your individual study habits and time frame. If you are short on time, look at your diagnostic test results to determine which subject matter could use the most attention and focus the majority of your efforts on those areas. While this study guide is organized to follow the order of the actual test, you are not required to complete the book from beginning to end, in that exact order.

HOW THIS BOOK IS ORGANIZED

Take a look at the Table of Contents. Notice that each **Section** in the study guide corresponds to a subtest of the exam. These sections are broken into **Chapters** that identify the major content categories of the exam.

Each chapter is further divided into individual **Lessons** that address the specific content and objectives required to pass the exam. Some lessons contain embedded example questions to assess your comprehension of the content "in the moment." All lessons contain a bulleted list called "**Let's Review.**" Use this list to refresh your memory before taking a practice quiz, test, or the actual exam. A **Practice Quiz**, designed to check your progress as you move through the content, follows each chapter.

Whether you plan on working through the study guide from cover to cover, or selecting specific sections to review, each chapter of this book can be completed in one sitting. If you must end your study session before finishing a chapter, try to complete your current lesson in order to maximize comprehension and retention of the material.

ONLINE SAMPLE TESTS

The purchase of this book grants you access to two additional full-length practice tests online. You can locate these exams on the Smart Edition Media website.

Go to the URL: https://smarteditionmedia.com/pages/tasc-online-resources and follow the password/login instructions.

STUDY STRATEGIES AND TIPS

MAKE STUDY SESSIONS A PRIORITY.

- Use a calendar to schedule your study sessions. Set aside a dedicated amount of time each day/week for studying. While it may seem difficult to manage, given your other responsibilities, remember that in order to reach your goals, it is crucial to dedicate the time now to prepare for this test. A satisfactory score on your exam is the key to unlocking a multitude of opportunities for your future success.
- Do you work? Have children? Other obligations? Be sure to take these into account when creating your schedule. Work around them to ensure that your scheduled study sessions can be free of distractions.

TIPS FOR FINDING TIME TO STUDY.
- Wake up 1-2 hours before your family for some quiet time
- Study 1-2 hours before bedtime and after everything has quieted down
- Utilize weekends for longer study periods
- Hire a babysitter to watch children

TAKE PRACTICE TESTS

- Smart Edition Media offers practice tests, both online and in print. Take as many as you can to help be prepared. This will eliminate any surprises you may encounter during the exam.

KNOW YOUR LEARNING STYLE

- Identify your strengths and weaknesses as a student. All students are different and everyone has a different learning style. Do not compare yourself to others.
- Howard Gardner, a developmental psychologist at Harvard University, has studied the ways in which people learn new information. He has identified seven distinct intelligences. According to his theory:

  "we are all able to know the world through language, logical-mathematical analysis, spatial representation, musical thinking, the use of the body to solve problems or to make things, an understanding of other individuals, and an understanding of ourselves. Where individuals differ is in the strength of these intelligences - the so-called profile of intelligences -and in the ways in which such intelligences are invoked and combined to carry out different tasks, solve diverse problems, and progress in various domains."

- Knowing your learning style can help you to tailor your studying efforts to suit your natural strengths.
- What ways help you learn best? Videos? Reading textbooks? Find the best way for you to study and learn/review the material.

WHAT IS YOUR LEARNING STYLE?

- **Visual-Spatial** – Do you like to draw, do jigsaw puzzles, read maps, daydream? Creating drawings, graphic organizers, or watching videos might be useful for you.
- **Bodily-kinesthetic** – Do you like movement, making things, physical activity? Do you communicate well through body language, or like to be taught through physical activity? Hands-on learning, acting out, role playing are tools you might try.
- **Musical** – Do you show sensitivity to rhythm and sound? If you love music, and are also sensitive to sounds in your environments, it might be beneficial to study with music in the background. You can turn lessons into lyricsor speak rhythmically to aid in content retention.
- **Interpersonal** – Do you have many friends, empathy for others, street smarts, and interact well with others? You might learn best in a group setting. Form a study group with other students who are preparing for the same exam. Technology makes it easy to connect, if you are unable to meet in person, teleconferencing or video chats are useful tools to aid interpersonal learners in connecting with others.
- **Intrapersonal** – Do you prefer to work alone rather than in a group? Are you in tune with your inner feelings, follow your intuition and possess a strong will, confidence and opinions? Independent study and introspection will be ideal for you. Reading books, using creative materials, keeping a diary of your progress will be helpful. Intrapersonal learners are the most independent of the learners.
- **Linguistic** – Do you use words effectively, have highly developed auditory skills and often think in words? Do you like reading, playing word games, making up poetry or stories? Learning tools such as computers, games, multimedia will be beneficial to your studies.
- **Logical-Mathematical** – Do you think conceptually, abstractly, and are able to see and explore patterns and relationships? Try exploring subject matter through logic games, experiments and puzzles.

CREATE THE OPTIMAL STUDY ENVIRONMENT

- Some people enjoy listening to soft background music when they study. (Instrumental music is a good choice.) Others need to have a silent space in order to concentrate. Which do you prefer? Either way, it is best to create an environment that is free of distractions for your study sessions.
- Have study guide – Will travel! Leave your house: Daily routines and chores can be distractions. Check out your local library, a coffee shop, or other quiet space to remove yourself from distractions and daunting household tasks will compete for your attention.
- Create a Technology Free Zone. Silence the ringer on your cell phone and place it out of reach to prevent surfing the Web, social media interactions, and email/texting exchanges. Turn off the television, radio, or other devices while you study.
- Are you comfy? Find a comfortable, but not *too* comfortable, place to study. Sit at a desk or table in a straight, upright chair. Avoid sitting on the couch, a bed, or in front of the TV. Wear clothing that is not binding and restricting.
- Keep your area organized. Have all the materials you need available and ready: Smart Edition study guide, computer, notebook, pen, calculator, and pencil/eraser. Use a desk lamp or overhead light that provides ample lighting to prevent eye-strain and fatigue.

HEALTHY BODY, HEALTHY MIND

- Consider these words of wisdom from Buddha, "To keep the body in good health is a duty – otherwise we shall not be able to keep our mind strong and clear."

KEYS TO CREATING A HEALTHY BODY AND MIND:

- Drink water – Stay hydrated! Limit drinks with excessive sugar or caffeine.
- Eat natural foods – Make smart food choices and avoid greasy, fatty, sugary foods.
- Think positively – You can do this! Do not doubt yourself, and trust in the process.
- Exercise daily – If you have a workout routine, stick to it! If you are more sedentary, now is a great time to begin! Try yoga or a low-impact sport. Simply walking at a brisk pace will help to get your heart rate going.
- Sleep well – Getting a good night's sleep is important, but too few of us actually make it a priority. Aim to get eight hours of uninterrupted sleep in order to maximize your mental focus, memory, learning, and physical wellbeing.

FINAL THOUGHTS

- Remember to relax and take breaks during study sessions.
- Review the testing material. Go over topics you already know for a refresher.
- Focus more time on less familiar subjects.

EXAM PREPARATION

In addition to studying for your upcoming exam, it is important to keep in mind that you need to prepare your mind and body as well. When preparing to take an exam as a whole, not just studying, taking practice exams, and reviewing math rules, it is critical to prepare your body in order to be mentally and physically ready. Often, your success rate will be much higher when you are *fully* ready.

Here are some tips to keep in mind when preparing for your exam:

SEVERAL WEEKS/DAYS BEFORE THE EXAM

- Get a full night of sleep, approximately 8 hours
- Turn off electronics before bed
- Exercise regularly
- Eat a healthy balanced diet, include fruits and vegetable
- Drink water

THE NIGHT BEFORE

- Eat a good dinner
- Pack materials/bag, healthy snacks, and water

- Gather materials needed for test: your ID and receipt of test. You do not want to be scrambling the morning of the exam. If you are unsure of what to bring with you, check with your testing center or test administrator.
- Map the location of test center, identify how you will be getting there (driving, public transportation, uber, etc.), when you need to leave, and parking options.
- Lay your clothes out. Wear comfortable clothes and shoes, do not wear items that are too hot/cold
- Allow minimum of ~8 hours of sleep
- Avoid coffee and alcohol
- Do not take any medications or drugs to help you sleep
- Set alarm

THE DAY OF THE EXAM

- Wake up early, allow ample time to do all the things you need to do and for travel
- Eat a healthy, well-rounded breakfast
- Drink water
- Leave early and arrive early, leave time for any traffic or any other unforeseeable circumstances
- Arrive early and check in for exam. This will give you enough time to relax, take off coat, and become comfortable with your surroundings.

Take a deep breath, get ready, go! You got this!

SECTION I. LANGUAGE ARTS – WRITING

CHAPTER 1 CONVENTIONS OF STANDARD ENGLISH

SPELLING

Spelling correctly is important to accurately convey thoughts to an audience. This lesson will cover (1) vowels and consonants, (2) suffixes and plurals, (3) homophones and homographs.

Vowels and Consonants

Vowels and **consonants** are different speech sounds in English.

The letters A, E, I, O, U and sometimes Y are **vowels** and can create a variety of sounds. The most common are short sounds and long sounds. Long **vowel** sounds sound like the name of the letter such as the *a* in late. Short **vowel** sounds have a unique sound such as the *a* in cat. A rule for **vowels** is that when two vowels are walking, the first does the talking as in pain and meat.

Consonants include the other twenty-one letters in the alphabet. **Consonants** are weak letters and only make sounds when paired with **vowels**. That is why words always must have a **vowel**. This also means that **consonants** need to be doubled to make a stronger sound like sitting, grabbed, progress. Understanding general trends and patterns for **vowels** and **consonants** will help with spelling. The table below represents the difference between short and long **vowels** and gives examples for each.

	Symbol	Example Words
Short a	a	Cat, mat, hat, pat
Long a	ā	Late, pain, pay, they, weight, straight
Short e	e	Met, said, bread
Long e	ē	Breeze, cheap, dean, equal
Short i	i	Bit, myth, kiss, rip
Long i	ī	Cry, pie, high
Short o	o	Dog, hot, pop
Long o	ō	Snow, nose, elbow
Short u	u	Run, cut, club, gum
Long u	ū	Duty, rule, new, food
Short oo	oo	Book, foot, cookie
Long oo	ōō	Mood, bloom, shoot

Suffixes and Plurals

A **suffix** is a word part that is added to the ending of a root word. A **suffix** changes the meaning and spelling of words. There are some general patterns to follow with **suffixes**.

- Adding -er, -ist, or -or changes the root to mean *doer* or *performer*

  - Paint → Painter
  - Abolition → Abolitionist
  - Act → Actor

- Adding -ation or -ment changes the root to mean *an action* or *a process*

  - Ador(e) → Adoration
  - Develop → Development

- Adding -ism changes the root to mean *a theory or ideology*

  - Real → Realism

- Adding -ity, -ness, -ship, or -tude changes the root to mean *a condition, quality, or state*

  - Real → Reality
  - Sad → Sadness
  - Relation → Relationship
  - Soli(tary) → Solitude

Plurals are similar to suffixes as letters are added to the end of the word to signify more than one person, place, thing, or idea. There are also general patterns to follow when creating **plurals**.

- If a word ends in -s,-ss,-z,-zz,-ch, or -sh, add -es.

  - Bus → Buses

- If a word ends in a -y, drop the -y and add -ies.

  - Pony → Ponies

- If a word ends in an -f, change the f to a v and add -es.

  - Knife → Knives

- For all other words, add an -s.

  - Dog → Dogs

Homophones and Homographs

A **homophone** is a word that has the same sound as another word, but does not have the same meaning or spelling.

- To, too, and two
- There, their, and they're
- See and sea

A **homograph** is a word that has the same spelling as another word, but does not have the same sound or meaning.

- Lead (to go in front of) and lead (a metal)
- Bass (deep sound) and bass (a fish)

Let's Review!

- Vowels include the letters A, E, I, O, U and sometimes Y and have both short and long sounds.
- Consonants are the other twenty-one letters and have weak sounds. They are often doubled to make stronger sounds.
- Suffixes are word parts added to the root of a word and change the meaning and spelling.
- To make a word plural, add -es, -ies, -ves, or -s to the end of a word.
- Homophones are words that have the same sound, but not the same meaning or spelling.
- Homographs are words that have the same spelling, but not the same meaning or sound.

CAPITALIZATION

Correct capitalization helps readers understand when a new sentence begins and the importance of specific words. This lesson will cover the capitalization rules of (1) geographic locations and event names, (2) organizations and publication titles, (3) individual names and professional titles, and (4) months, days, and holidays.

Geographic Locations and Event Names

North, east, south, and west are not capitalized unless they relate to a **definite region**.

- Go north on I-5 for 200 miles.
- The West Coast has nice weather.

Words like northern, southern, eastern, and western are also not capitalized unless they describe **people or the cultural and political activities of people**.

- There is nothing interesting to see in eastern Colorado.
- Midwesterners are known for being extremely nice.
- The Western states almost always vote Democratic.

These words are not capitalized when placed before a name or region unless it is part of the **official name**.

- She lives in southern California.
- I loved visiting Northern Ireland.

Continents, countries, states, cities, and **towns** need to be capitalized.

- Australia has a lot of scary animals.
- Not many people live in Antarctica.
- Albany is the capital of New York.

Historical events should be capitalized to separate the specific from the general.

- The bubonic plague in the Middle Ages killed a large portion of the population in Europe.
- The Great Depression took place in the early 1930s.
- We are living in the twenty-first century.

Organizations and Publication Titles

The **names of national organizations** need to be capitalized. Short prepositions, articles, and conjunctions within the title are not capitalized unless they are the first word.

- The National American Woman Suffrage Association was essential in passing the Nineteenth Amendment.
- The House of Representatives is one part of Congress.

- Most kids' favorite holiday is Christmas.
- The new school year usually starts after Labor Day.
- It is nice to go to the beach over Memorial Day weekend.

The **seasons** are not capitalized.

- It gets too hot in the summer and too cold in the winter.
- The flowers and trees bloom so beautifully in the spring.

Let's Review!

- Only capitalize directional words like north, south, east, and, west when they describe a definite region, people, and their political and cultural activities, or when it is part of the official name.
- Historical periods and events are capitalized to represent their importance and specificity.
- Every word except short prepositions, conjunctions, and articles in the names of national organizations are capitalized.
- The titles of publications follow the same rules as organizations.
- The names of individual people need to be capitalized.
- Professional titles are capitalized if they precede a name or are used as a direct address.
- All months of the year, days of the week, and holidays are capitalized.
- Seasons are not capitalized.

- The National Football League consists of thirty-two teams.

The **titles of books, chapters, articles, poems, newspapers, and other publications** should be capitalized.

- Her favorite book is *A Wrinkle in Time*.
- I do the crossword in *The New York Times* every Sunday.
- *The Jabberwocky* by Lewis Carroll has many silly sounding words.

Individual Names and Professional Titles

People's names as well as their **familial relationship title** need to be capitalized.

- Barack Obama was our first African American president.
- Uncle Joe brought the steaks for our Memorial Day grill.
- Aunt Sarah lives in California, but my other aunt lives in Florida.

Professional titles need to be capitalized when they precede a name, or as a direct address. If it is after a name or is used generally, titles do not need to be capitalized.

- Governor Cuomo is trying to modernize the subway system in New York.
- Andrew Cuomo is the governor of New York.
- A governor runs the state. A president runs the country.
- Thank you for the recommendation, Mr. President.
- I need to see Doctor Smith.
- I need to see a doctor.

Capitalize the **title of high-ranking government officials** when an individual is referred to.

- The Secretary of State travels all over the world.
- The Vice President joined the meeting.

With **compound titles**, the prefixes or suffixes do not need to be capitalized.

- George W. Bush is the ex-President of the United States.

Months, Days, and Holidays

Capitalize **all months of the year** (January, February, March, April, May, June, July, August, September, October, November, December) and **days of the week** (Sunday, Monday, Tuesday, Wednesday, Thursday, Friday, Saturday).

- Her birthday is in November.
- People graduate from college in May or June.
- Saturdays and Sundays are supposed to be fun and relaxing.

Holidays are also capitalized.

PUNCTUATION

Punctuation is important in writing to accurately represent ideas. Without correct punctuation, the meaning of a sentence is difficult to understand. This lesson will cover (1) periods, question marks, and exclamation points, (2) commas, semicolons, and colons, and (3) apostrophes, hyphens, and quotation marks.

Terminal Punctuation Marks: Periods, Question Marks, and Exclamation Points

Terminal punctuation is used at the end of a sentence. Periods, question marks, and exclamation points are the three types of terminal punctuation.

Periods (.) mark the end of a declarative sentence, one that states a fact, or an imperative sentence, one that states a command or request). Periods can also be used in abbreviations.

- Doctors save lives.
- She has a B.A. in Psychology.

Question Marks (?) signify the end of a sentence that is a question. Where, when, who, whom, what, why, and how are common words that begin question sentences.

- Who is he?
- Why is the sky blue?
- Where is the restaurant?

Exclamation Points (!) indicate strong feelings, shouting, or emphasize a feeling.

- Watch out!
- I hate you!
- That is incredible!

Internal Punctuation: Commas, Semicolons, and Colons

Internal punctuation is used within a sentence to help keep words, phrases, and clauses in order. These punctuation marks can be used to indicate elements such as direct quotations and definitions in a sentence.

A **comma** (,) signifies a small break within a sentence and separates words, clauses, or ideas.

Commas are used before conjunctions that connect two independent clauses.

- I ate some cookies, and I drank some milk.

Commas are also used to set off an introductory phrase.

- After the test, she grabbed dinner with a friend.

Short phrases that emphasis thoughts or emotions are enclosed by **commas**.

- The school year, thankfully, ends in a week.

Commas set off the words yes and no.

- Yes, I am available this weekend.
- No, she has not finished her homework.

Commas set off a question tag.

- It is beautiful outside, isn't it?

Commas are used to indicate direct address.

- Are you ready, Jack?
- Mom, what is for dinner?

Commas separate items in a series.

- We ate eggs, potatoes, and toast for breakfast.
- I need to grab coffee, go to the store, and put gas in my car.

Semicolons (;) are used to connect two independent clauses without a coordinating conjunction like *and* or *but*. A **semicolon** creates a bond between two sentences that are related. Do not capitalize the first word after the **semicolon** unless it is a word that is normally capitalized.

- The ice cream man drove down my street; I bought a popsicle.
- My mom cooked dinner; the chicken was delicious.
- It is cloudy today; it will probably rain.

Colons (:) introduce a list.

- She teaches three subjects: English, history, and geography.

Within a sentence, **colons** can create emphasis of a word or phrase.

- She had one goal: pay the bills.

More Internal Punctuation: Apostrophes, Hyphens, and Quotation Marks

Apostrophes (') are used to indicate possession or to create a contraction.

- Bob has a car - Bob's car is blue.
- Steve's cat is beautiful.

For plurals that are also possessive, put the **apostrophe** after the s.

- Soldiers' uniforms are impressive.

Make contractions by combining two words.

- I do not have a dog - I don't have a dog
- I can't swim.

Its and it's do not follow the normal possessive rules. Its is possessive while it's means "it is."

- It's a beautiful day to be at the park.
- The dog has many toys, but its favorite is the rope.

Hyphens (-) are mainly used to create compound words.

- The documentary was a real eye-opener for me.
- We have to check-in to the hotel before midnight.
- The graduate is a twenty-two-year-old woman.

Quotation Marks (") are used when directly using another person's words in your own writing. Commas and periods, sometimes question marks and exclamation points, are placed within **quotation marks**. Colons and semicolons are placed outside of the **quotation marks**, unless they are part of the quoted material. If quoting an entire sentence, capitalize the first word. If it is a fragment, do not capitalize the first word.

- Ernest Hemingway once claimed, "There is nothing noble in being superior to your fellow man; true nobility is being superior to your former self."
- Steve said, "I will be there at noon."

An indirect quote which paraphrases what someone else said does not need **quotation marks**.

- Steve said he would be there at noon.

Quotation marks are also used for the titles of short works such as poems, articles, and chapters. They are not italicized.

- Robert Frost wrote "The Road Not Taken."

Let's Review!

- **Periods (.)** signify the end of a sentence or are used in abbreviations.
- **Question Marks (?)** are also used at the end of a sentence and distinguish the sentence as a question.
- **Exclamation Points (!)** indicate strong feelings, shouting, or emphasis and are usually at the end of the sentence.
- **Commas (,)** are small breaks within a sentence that separate clauses, ideas, or words. They are used to set off introductory phrases, the words yes and no, question tags, indicate direct address, and separate items in a series.
- **Semicolons (;)** connect two similar sentences without a coordinating conjunctions such as and or but.
- **Colons (:)** are used to introduce a list or emphasize a word or phrase.
- **Apostrophes (')** indicate possession or a contraction of two words.
- **Hyphens (-)** are used to create compound words.
- **Quotation Marks (")** are used when directly quoting someone else's words and to indicate the title of poems, chapters, and articles.

CHAPTER 1 CONVENTIONS OF STANDARD ENGLISH
PRACTICE QUIZ

1. Which word(s) in the following sentence should NOT be capitalized?

   Can You Speak German?

   A. You and Speak

   B. Can and German

   C. Can, You, and Speak

   D. You, Speak, and German

2. Fill in the blank with the correctly capitalized form.

   Every week, they get together to watch _____.

   A. the bachelor   C. The bachelor

   B. The Bachelor   D. the Bachelor

3. Choose the correct sentence.

   A. They used to live in the pacific northwest.

   B. They used to live in the Pacific northwest.

   C. They used to live in the pacific Northwest.

   D. They used to live in the Pacific Northwest.

4. What is the sentence with the correct use of punctuation?

   A. Offcampus apartments are nicer.

   B. Off campus apartments are nicer.

   C. Off-campus apartments are nicer.

   D. Off-campus-apartments are nicer.

5. Which of the following sentences is correct?

   A. I asked Scott, How was your day?

   B. Scott said, it was awesome.

   C. He claimed, "My history presentation was great!"

   D. I said, That's wonderful!

6. What is the mistake in the following sentence?

   The highestranking officer can choose his own work, including his own hours.

   A. *Highestranking* needs a hyphen.

   B. There should be a comma after *officer*.

   C. There should be no comma after *work*.

   D. There should be a semicolon after *work*.

7. Which of the following spellings is correct?

   A. Busines   C. Buseness

   B. Business   D. Bussiness

8. What is the correct plural of morning?

   A. Morning   C. Morninges

   B. Mornings   D. Morningies

9. On Earth, _____ are seven continents.

   A. their   C. theer

   B. there   D. they're

CHAPTER 1 CONVENTIONS OF STANDARD ENGLISH
PRACTICE QUIZ – ANSWER KEY

1. A. *You and Speak.* Can is the first word in the sentence and needs to be capitalized. German is a nationality and needs to be capitalized. The other two words do not need to be capitalized. **See Lesson: Capitalization.**

2. B. *The Bachelor.* The names of TV shows are capitalized. *The* is capitalized here because it is the first word in the name. **See Lesson: Capitalization.**

3. D. *They used to live in the Pacific Northwest.* Specific geographic regions are capitalized. **See Lesson: Capitalization.**

4. C. *Off-campus apartments are nicer.* Hyphens are often used for compound words that are placed before the noun to help with understanding. **See Lesson: Punctuation.**

5. C. *He claimed, "My history presentation was great!"* Quotation marks enclose direct statements. **See Lesson: Punctuation.**

6. A. *Highestranking needs a hyphen.* Hyphens are used for compound words that describe a person or object. **See Lesson: Punctuation.**

7. B. *Business* is the only correct spelling. **See Lesson: Spelling.**

8. B. For most words ending in consonants, just add -s. **See Lesson: Spelling.**

9. B. *There* describes a place or position and is correctly spelled. **See Lesson: Spelling.**

CHAPTER 2 PARTS OF SPEECH

Nouns

In this lesson, you will learn about nouns. A noun is a word that names a person, place, thing, or idea. This lesson will cover (1) the role of nouns in sentences and (2) different types of nouns.

Nouns and Their Role in Sentences

A **noun** names a person, place, thing, or idea.

Some examples of nouns are:

- Gandhi
- New Hampshire
- garden
- happiness

A noun's role in a sentence is as **subject** or **object**. A subject is the part of the sentence that does something, whereas the object is the thing that something is done to. In simple terms, the subject acts, and the object is acted upon.

Look for the nouns in these sentences.

1. The Louvre is stunning. (subject noun: The Louvre)
2. Marco ate dinner with Sara and Petra. (subject noun: Marco; object nouns: dinner, Sara, Petra)
3. Honesty is the best policy. (subject noun: honesty; object noun: policy)
4. After the election, we celebrated our new governor. (object nouns: governor, election)
5. I slept. (0 nouns)

KEEP IN MIND . . .
The subjects *I* and *we* in the two sentences to the left are pronouns, not nouns.

Look for the nouns in these sentences.

1. Mrs. Garcia makes a great pumpkin pie. (subject noun: Mrs. Garcia; object noun: pie)
2. We really need to water the garden. (object noun: garden)
3. Love is sweet. (subject noun: love)
4. Sam loves New York in the springtime. (subject noun: Sam; object nouns: New York, springtime)
5. Lin and her mother and father ate soup, fish, potatoes, and fruit for dinner. (subject nouns: Lin, mother, father; object nouns: soup, fish, potatoes, fruit, dinner)

Why isn't the word *pumpkin* a noun in the first sentence? *Pumpkin* is often a noun, but here it is used as an adjective that describes what kind of *pie*.

Why isn't the word *water* a noun in the second sentence? Here, *water* is an **action verb**. To *water the garden* is something we do.

How is the word *love* a noun in the third sentence and not in the fourth sentence? *Love* is a noun (thing) in sentence 3 and a verb (action) in the sentence 4.

> **BE CAREFUL!**
> Words can change to serve different roles in different sentences. A word that is usually a noun can sometimes be used as an adjective or a verb. Determine a word's function in a sentence to be sure of its part of speech.

How many nouns can a sentence contain? As long as the sentence remains grammatically correct, it can contain an unlimited number of nouns.

Types of Nouns

Singular and Plural Nouns

Nouns can be **singular** or **plural**. A noun is singular when there is only one. A noun is plural when there are two or more.

- The book has 650 pages.

Book is a singular noun. *Pages* is a plural noun.

Often, to make a noun plural, we add *-s* at the end of the word: *cat/cats*. This is a **regular** plural noun. Sometimes we make a word plural in another way: *child/children*. This is an **irregular** plural noun. Some plurals follow rules, while others do not. The most common rules are listed here:

> **KEEP IN MIND . . .**
> **Some nouns are countable,** and others are not. For example, we eat *three blueberries*, but we **do not** drink *three milks*. Instead, we drink *three glasses of milk* or *some milk*.

Singular noun	Plural noun	Rule for making plural
star	stars	for most words, add *-s*
box	boxes	for words that end in *-j, -s, -x, -z, -ch* or *-sh*, add *-es*
baby	babies	for words that end in *-y*, change *-y* to *-i* and add *-es*
woman	women	irregular
foot	feet	irregular

Common and Proper Nouns

Common nouns are general words, and they are written in lowercase. **Proper nouns** are specific names, and they begin with an uppercase letter.

Examples:

Common noun	Proper noun
ocean	Baltic Sea
dentist	Dr. Marx
company	Honda
park	Yosemite National Park

Concrete and Abstract Nouns

Concrete nouns are people, places, or things that physically exist. We can use our senses to see or hear them. *Turtle, spreadsheet,* and *Australia* are concrete nouns.

Abstract nouns are ideas, qualities, or feelings that we cannot see and that might be harder to describe. *Beauty, childhood, energy, envy, generosity, happiness, patience, pride, trust, truth,* and *victory* are abstract nouns.

Some words can be either concrete or abstract nouns. For example, the concept of *art* is abstract, but *art* that we see and touch is concrete.

- We talked about *art*. (abstract)
- She showed me the *art* she had created in class. (concrete)

Let's Review!

- A noun is a person, place, thing, or idea.
- A noun's function in a sentence is as subject or object.
- Common nouns are general words, while proper nouns are specific names.
- Nouns can be concrete or abstract.

PRONOUNS

A pronoun is a word that takes the place of or refers to a specific noun. This lesson will cover (1) the role of pronouns in sentences and (2) the purpose of pronouns.

Pronouns and Their Role in Sentences

A **pronoun** takes the place of a noun or refers to a specific noun.

Subject, Object, and Possessive Pronouns

A pronoun's role in a sentence is as **subject**, **object**, or **possessive**.

Subject Pronouns	Object Pronouns	Possessive Pronouns
I	me	my, mine
you	you	your, yours
he	her	his
she	him	her, hers
it	it	its
we	us	ours
they	them	their, theirs

In simple sentences, subject pronouns come before the verb, object pronouns come after the verb, and possessive pronouns show ownership.

Look at the pronouns in these examples:

BE CAREFUL!

It is easy to make a mistake when you have multiple words in the role of subject or object.

- <u>She</u> forgot <u>her</u> coat. (subject: she; possessive: her)
- <u>I</u> lent <u>her</u> <u>mine</u>. (subject: I; object: her; possessive: mine)
- <u>She</u> left <u>it</u> at school. (subject: she; object: it)
- <u>I</u> had to go and get <u>it</u> the next day. (subject: I; object: it)
- <u>I</u> will never lend <u>her</u> something of <u>mine</u> again! (subject: I; object: her; possessive: mine)

Correct	Incorrect	Why?
John and I went out.	*John and me* went out.	*John and I* is a subject. *I* is a subject pronoun; *me* is not.
Johan took *Sam and me* to the show.	Johan took *Sam and I* to the show.	*Sam and me* is an object. *Me* is an object pronoun; *I* is not.

Relative Pronouns

Relative pronouns connect a clause to a noun or pronoun.

These are some relative pronouns:

who, whom, whoever, whose, that, which

- Steve Jobs, <u>*who founded Apple*</u>, changed the way people use technology.

The pronoun *who* introduces a clause that gives more information about Steve Jobs.

- This is the movie <u>*that Emily told us to see*</u>.

The pronoun *that* introduces a clause that gives more information about the movie.

Other Pronouns

Some other pronouns are:

this, that, what, anyone, everything, something

DID YOU KNOW?
Pronouns can sometimes refer to general or unspecified things.

Look for the pronouns in these sentences.

- What is that?
- There is something over there!
- Does anyone have a pen?

Pronouns and Their Purpose

The purpose of a pronoun is to replace a noun. Note the use of the pronoun *their* in the heading of this section. If we did not have pronouns, we would have to call this section *Pronouns and Pronouns' Purpose*.

What Is an Antecedent?

A pronoun in a sentence refers to a specific noun, and this noun called the **antecedent**.

- John Hancock signed the Declaration of Independence. <u>He</u> signed <u>it</u> in 1776.

The antecedent for *he* is John Hancock.
The antecedent for *it* is the Declaration of Independence.

BE CAREFUL!
Look out for unclear antecedents, such as in this sentence:

- Take the furniture out of the room and paint *it*.

What needs to be painted, the furniture or the room?

Find the pronouns in the following sentence. Then identify the antecedent for each pronoun.

Erin had an idea *that she* suggested to Antonio: "*I*'ll help *you* with *your* math homework if *you* help *me* with *my* writing assignment."

Pronoun	Antecedent
that	idea
she	Erin
I	Erin
you	Antonio
your	Antonio's
you	Antonio
me	Erin
my	Erin's

What Is Antecedent Agreement?

A pronoun must agree in **gender** and **number** with the antecedent it refers to. For example:

- Singular pronouns *I, you, he, she*, and *it* replace singular nouns.
- Plural pronouns *you, we*, and *they* replace plural nouns.
- Pronouns *he, she*, and *it* replace masculine, feminine, or neutral nouns.

Correct	Incorrect	Why?
<u>Students</u> should do <u>their</u> homework every night.	<u>A student</u> should do <u>their</u> homework every night.	The pronoun *their* is plural, so it must refer to a plural noun such as *students*.
When <u>an employee</u> is sick, <u>he or she</u> should call the office.	When <u>an employee</u> is sick, <u>they</u> should call the office.	The pronoun *they* is plural, so it must refer to a plural noun. *Employee* is not a plural noun.

Let's Review!

- A pronoun takes the place of or refers to a noun.
- The role of pronouns in sentences is as subject, object, or possessive.
- A pronoun must agree in number and gender with the noun it refers to.

ADJECTIVES AND ADVERBS

An **adjective** is a word that describes a noun or a pronoun. An **adverb** is a word that describes a verb, an adjective, or another adverb.

Adjectives

An **adjective** describes, modifies, or tells us more about a **noun** or a **pronoun**. Colors, numbers, and descriptive words such as *healthy, good,* and *sharp* are adjectives.

> **KEEP IN MIND . . .**
> Adjectives typically come **before the noun** in English. However, with **linking verbs** (non-action verbs such as *be, seem, look*), the adjective may come **after the verb** instead. Think of it like this: a linking verb **links** the adjective to the noun or pronoun.

Look for the adjectives in the following sentences:

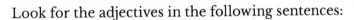

	Adjective	Noun or pronoun it describes
I rode the blue bike.	blue	bike
It was a long trip.	long	trip
Bring two pencils for the exam.	two	pencils
The box is brown.	brown	box
She looked beautiful.	beautiful	she
That's great!	great	that

Multiple adjectives can be used in a sentence, as can multiple nouns. Look at these examples:

	Adjectives	Noun or pronoun it describes
The six girls were happy, healthy, and rested after their long beach vacation.	six, happy, healthy, rested; long, beach	girls; vacation
Leo has a good job, but he is applying for a better one.	good; better	job; one

> **KEEP IN MIND . . .**
> Note comparative and superlative forms of adjectives, such as:
>
> fast, faster, fastest
>
> far, farther, farthest
>
> good, better, best
>
> bad, worse, worst

Articles: *A, An, The*

Articles are a unique part of speech, but they work like adjectives. An article tells more about a noun. *A* and *an* are **indefinite** articles. Use *a* before a singular **general** noun. Use *an* before a singular general noun that begins with a vowel.

The is a **definite** article. Use *the* before a singular or plural **specific** noun.

Look at how articles are used in the following sentences:

- I need *a* pencil to take *the* exam. (any pencil; specific exam)
- Is there *a* zoo in town? (any zoo)
- Let's go to *the* zoo today. (specific zoo)
- Can you get me *a* glass of milk? (any glass)
- Would you bring me *the* glass that's over there? (specific glass)

Adverbs

An **adverb** describes, modifies, or tells us more about a **verb**, an **adjective**, or another **adverb**. Many adverbs end in *-ly*. Often, adverbs tell when, where, or how something happened. Words such as *slowly, very,* and *yesterday* are adverbs.

Adverbs that Describe Verbs

Adverbs that describe verbs tell something more about the action.

Look for the adverbs in these sentences:

	Adverb	Verb it describes
They walked quickly.	quickly	walked
She disapproved somewhat of his actions, but she completely understood them.	somewhat; completely	disapproved; understood
The boys will go inside if it rains heavily.	inside; heavily	go; rains

Adverbs that Describe Adjectives

Adverbs that describe adjectives often add intensity to the adjective. Words like *quite, more,* and *always* are adverbs.

Look for the adverbs in these sentences:

	Adverb	Adjective it describes
The giraffe is very tall.	very	tall
Do you think that you are more intelligent than them?	more	intelligent
If it's really loud, we can make the volume slightly lower.	really; slightly	loud; lower

Adverbs that Describe Other Adverbs

Adverbs that describe adverbs often add intensity to the adverb.

Look for the adverbs in these sentences:

	Adverb	Adverb it describes
The mouse moved too quickly for us to catch it.	too	quickly
This store is almost never open.	almost	never
Those women are quite fashionably dressed.	quite	fashionably

Adjectives vs. Adverbs

Not sure whether a word is an adjective or an adverb? Look at these examples.

	Adjective	Adverb	Explanation
fast	You're a *fast* driver.	You drove *fast*.	The adjective *fast* describes *driver* (noun); the adverb *fast* describes *drove* (verb).
early	I don't like *early* mornings!	Try to arrive *early*.	The adjective *early* describes *mornings* (noun); the adverb *early* describes *arrive* (verb).
good/well	They did *good* work together.	They worked *well* together.	The adjective *good* describes *work* (noun); the adverb *well* describes *worked* (verb).
bad/badly	The dog is *bad*.	The dog behaves *badly*.	The adjective *bad* describes *dog* (noun); the adverb *badly* describes *behaves* (verb).

Let's Review!

- An **adjective** describes, modifies, or tells us more about a **noun** or a **pronoun**.
- An **adverb** describes, modifies, or tells us more about a **verb**, an **adjective**, or another **adverb**.

> **BE CAREFUL!**
>
> When an adverb ends in *-ly*, add *more* or *most* to make comparisons.
>
> **Correct:** The car moved *more slowly*.
>
> **Incorrect:** The car moved *slower*.

CONJUNCTIONS AND PREPOSITIONS

A **conjunction** is a connector word; it connects words, phrases, or clauses in a sentence. A **preposition** is a relationship word; it shows the relationship between two nearby words.

Conjunctions

A **conjunction** connects words, phrases, or clauses.

And, so, and *or* are conjunctions.

Types of Conjunctions

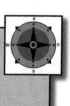

> **KEEP IN MIND . . .**
>
> A clause is a phrase that has a subject and a verb.
>
> Some clauses are **independent**. An independent clause can stand alone.
>
> Some clauses are **dependent**. A dependent clause relies on another clause in order to make sense.

- **Coordinating** conjunctions connect two words, phrases, or independent clauses. The full list of coordinating conjunctions is: *and, or, but, so, for, nor, yet.*
- **Subordinating** conjunctions connect a main (independent) clause and a dependent clause. The conjunction may show a relationship or time order for the two clauses. Some subordinating conjunctions are: *after, as soon as, once, if, even though, unless.*
- **Correlative** conjunctions are pairs of conjunctions that work together to connect two words or phrases. Some correlative conjunctions are: *either/or, neither/nor, as/as.*

Example	Conjunction	What it is connecting
Verdi, Mozart, **and** *Wagner* are famous opera composers.	and	three nouns
Would you like *angel food cake, chocolate lava cake,* **or** *banana cream pie* for dessert?	or	three noun phrases
I took the bus to work, **but** *I walked home.*	but	two independent clauses
It was noisy at home, **so** *we went to the library.*	so	two independent clauses
They have to clean the house **before** *the realtor shows it.*	before	a main clause and a dependent clause
Use **either** *hers* **or** *mine.*	either/or	two pronouns
After *everyone leaves,* make sure you lock up.	after	a main clause and a dependent clause
I'd **rather** *fly* **than** *take the train.*	rather/than	two verb phrases
As soon as *they announced the winning number,* she looked at her ticket and shouted, "Whoopee!"	as soon as	a main clause and a dependent clause

Prepositions

A **preposition** shows the relationship between two nearby words. Prepositions help to tell information such as direction, location, and time. *To, for,* and *with* are prepositions.

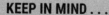

> **KEEP IN MIND . . .**
>
> Some prepositions are more than one word. *On top of* and *instead of* are prepositions.

Example	Preposition	What it tells us
The desk is in the classroom.	in	location
We'll meet you at 6:00.	at	time
We'll meet you at the museum.	at	place
The book is on top of the desk.	on top of	location

Prepositional Phrases

A preposition must be followed by an **object of the preposition**. This can be a noun or something that serves as a noun, such as a pronoun or a gerund.

DID YOU KNOW?

A gerund is the -*ing* form a verb that serves as a noun. *Hiking* is a gerund in this sentence:

I wear these shoes for *hiking*.

A **prepositional phrase** is a preposition plus the object that follows it.

Look for the prepositional phrases in the following examples. Note that a sentence can have more than one prepositional phrase.

Example	Preposition	Object of the preposition
The tiny country won the war *against all odds*.	against	all odds
Look *at us*!	at	us
Why don't we go swimming *instead of sweating in this heat?*	instead of; in	sweating; this heat
Aunt Tea kept the trophy *on a shelf of the cabinet between the sofas in the living room.*	on; of; between; in	a shelf; the cabinet; the sofas; the living room

> **BE CAREFUL!**
>
> Sometimes a word looks like a preposition but is actually part of the verb. In this case, the verb is called a phrasal verb, and the preposition-like word is called a particle. Here is an example:
>
> - *Turn on* the light. (*Turn on* has a meaning of its own; it is a phrasal verb. *On* is a particle here, rather than a preposition.)
> - Turn *on that street.* (*On that street* shows location; it is a prepositional phrase. *On* is a preposition here.)

Let's Review!

- A **conjunction** connects words, phrases, or clauses. *And, so,* and *or* are conjunctions.
- A **preposition** shows the relationship between two nearby words. *To, for,* and *with* are prepositions.
- A **prepositional phrase** includes a preposition plus the object of the preposition.

VERBS AND VERB TENSES

A **verb** is a word that describes a **physical or mental action** or a **state of being**. This lesson will cover the role of verbs in sentences, verb forms and tenses, and helping verbs.

The Role of Verbs in Sentences

A verb describes an action or a state of being. A complete sentence must have at least one verb.

Verbs have different tenses, which show time.

Verb Forms

Each verb has three primary forms. The **base form** is used for simple present tense, and the **past form** is used for simple past tense. The **participle form** is used for more complicated time situations. Participle form verbs are accompanied by a helping verb.

Base Form	Past Form	Participle Form
end	ended	ended
jump	jumped	jumped
explain	explained	explained
eat	ate	eaten
take	took	taken
go	went	gone
come	came	come

Some verbs are **regular**. To make the **past** or **participle** form of a regular verb, we just add *-ed*. However, many verbs that we commonly use are **irregular**. We need to memorize the forms for these verbs.

In the chart above, *end, jump,* and *explain* are regular verbs. *Eat, take, go,* and *come* are irregular.

Using Verbs

A simple sentence has a **subject** and a **verb**. The subject tells us who or what, and the verb tells us the action or state.

Example	Subject	Verb	Explanation/Time
They ate breakfast together yesterday.	They	ate	*happened yesterday*
I walk to school.	I	walk	*happens regularly*
We went to California last year.	We	went	*happened last year*
She seems really tired.	She	seems	*how she seems right now*
The teacher is sad.	teacher	is	*her state right now*

You can see from the examples in this chart that **past tense verbs** are used for a time in the past, and **present tense verbs** are used for something that happens regularly or for a state or condition right now.

Often a sentence has more than one verb. If it has a connector word or more than one subject, it can have more than one verb.

- The two cousins <u>live</u>, <u>work</u>, and <u>vacation</u> together. (3 verbs)
- The girls <u>planned</u> by phone, and then they <u>met</u> at the movies. (2 verbs)

BE CAREFUL!
When you have more than one verb in a sentence, make sure both verb tenses are correct.

Helping Verbs and Progressive and Perfect Tenses

Helping Verbs

A **helping verb** is a supporting verb that accompanies a main verb.

Questions, negative sentences, and certain time situations require helping verbs.

forms of helping verb "to be"	forms of helping verb "to have"	forms of helping verb "to do"	some modals (used like helping verbs)
am, are, is, was, were, be, being, been	have, has, had, having	do, does, did, doing	will, would, can, could, must, might, should

Here are examples of helping verbs in questions and negatives.

- Where *is* he *going*?
- *Did* they *win*?
- I *don*'t *want* that.
- The boys *can*'t go.

Progressive and Perfect Tenses

Helping verbs accompany main verbs in certain time situations, such as when an action is or was ongoing, or when two actions overlap in time. To form these tenses, we use a **helping verb** with the **base form plus *-ing*** or with the **participle form** of the main verb.

The **progressive tense** is used for an action that is or was ongoing. It takes base form of the main verb plus *-ing*.

Example sentence	Tense	*Explanation/Time*
I <u>am taking</u> French this semester.	Present progressive	*happening now, over a continuous period of time*
I <u>was working</u> when you stopped by.	Past progressive	*happened over a continuous period of time in the past*

The **perfect tense** is used to cover two time periods. It takes the *participle* form of the main verb.

Example sentence	Tense	Explanation/Time
I have lived here for three years.	Present perfect	*started in the past and continues to present*
I had finished half of my homework when my computer stopped working.	Past perfect	*started and finished in the past, overlapping in time with another action*

Sometimes we use both the **progressive** and **perfect** tenses together.

Example sentence	Tense	Explanation/Time
I have been walking for hours!	Present perfect progressive	*started in the past, took place for a period of time, and continues to present*
She had been asking for a raise for months before she finally received one.	Past perfect progressive	*started in the past, took place for a period of time, and ended*

Let's Review!

- A verb describes an action or state of being.
- Each verb has three primary forms: base form, past form, and participle form.
- Verbs have different tenses, which are used to show time.
- Helping verbs are used in questions, negative sentences, and to form progressive and perfect tenses.

CHAPTER 2 PARTS OF SPEECH PRACTICE QUIZ

1. **Select the part of speech of the underlined word in the following sentence.**

   She did <u>quite</u> well on the exam.

   A. Noun   C. Adjective

   B. Adverb   D. Preposition

2. **Select the noun that the underlined adjectives describe.**

   Two weeks after his surgery, Henry felt <u>strong</u> and <u>healthy</u>.

   A. weeks   C. surgery

   B. his   D. Henry

3. **Which word is an adverb that describes the underlined verb?**

   The man <u>spoke</u> to us wisely.

   A. man   C. us

   B. to   D. wisely

4. **Identify the conjunction in the following sentence.**

   He is sick, yet he came to work.

   A. is   C. came

   B. yet   D. to

5. **Which is <u>not</u> a prepositional phrase?**

   Keep me informed about the status of the problem throughout the day.

   A. Keep me informed

   B. about the status

   C. of the problem

   D. throughout the day

6. **How many prepositions are in the following sentence?**

   The athletes traveled from Boston to Dallas for the competition.

   A. 0   C. 2

   B. 1   D. 3

7. **Which words in the following sentence are proper nouns?**

   Matthew had a meeting with his supervisor on Tuesday.

   A. Matthew, meeting

   B. Matthew, Tuesday

   C. meeting, supervisor

   D. supervisor, Tuesday

8. **How many plural nouns are in the following sentence?**

   Marie's father's appendix was taken out.

   A. 0   C. 2

   B. 1   D. 3

9. **Which of the following words is an abstract noun?**

   A. Car   C. Ruler

   B. Tent   D. Health

10. **Which word in the following sentence is a pronoun?**

    To whom should the applicant address the letter?

    A. To   C. whom

    B. the   D. should

11. **Which pronoun correctly completes the following sentence?**

    Nigel introduced Van and ____ to the new administrator.

    A. I   C. she

    B. me   D. they

12. **Select the noun to which the underlined pronoun refers.**

    Greta Garbo, <u>who</u> performed in both silent and talking pictures, is my favorite actress.

    A. actress   C. performed

    B. pictures   D. Greta Garbo

13. **How many verbs are in the following sentence?**

    They toured the art museum and saw the conservatory.

    A. 0   C. 2

    B. 1   D. 3

14. **Which word in the following sentence is a helping verb?**

    They did not ask for our help.

    A. did   C. for

    B. ask   D. our

15. **Select the correct verb form to complete the following sentence.**

    William didn't think he would enjoy the musical, but he ____.

    A. do   C. liked

    B. did   D. would

Chapter 2 Parts of Speech
Practice Quiz – Answer Key

1. **B.** *Quite* is an adverb that describes the adverb *well*. **See Lesson: Adjectives and Adverbs.**

2. **D.** These adjectives describe *Henry*. **See Lesson: Adjectives and Adverbs.**

3. **D.** *Wisely* is an adverb that describes the verb *spoke*. **See Lesson: Adjectives and Adverbs.**

4. **B.** *Yet* is a conjunction. **See Lesson: Conjunctions and Prepositions.**

5. **A.** *Keep me informed* does not contain a preposition. *About, of,* and *throughout* are prepositions. **See Lesson: Conjunctions and Prepositions.**

6. **D.** *From, to,* and *for* are prepositions. **See Lesson: Conjunctions and Prepositions.**

7. **B.** *Matthew* and *Tuesday* are proper nouns. **See Lesson: Nouns.**

8. **A.** *Marie's* and *father's* are possessive; neither is plural. *Appendix* is a singular noun. **See Lesson: Nouns.**

9. **D.** *Health* is an abstract noun; it does not physically exist. **See Lesson: Nouns.**

10. **C.** *Whom* is a pronoun. **See Lesson: Pronouns.**

11. **B.** An object pronoun must be used here. **See Lesson: Pronouns.**

12. **D.** *Who* is a relative pronoun that refers to the subject *Greta Garbo*. **See Lesson: Pronouns.**

13. **C.** *Toured* and *saw* are verbs. **See Lesson: Verbs and Verb Tenses.**

14. **A.** *Did* is a helping verb; *ask* is the main verb. **See Lesson: Verbs and Verb Tenses.**

15. **B.** *Did* can be used here, for a shortened form of *did enjoy it*. **See Lesson: Verbs and Verb Tenses.**

CHAPTER 3 KNOWLEDGE OF LANGUAGE

TYPES OF SENTENCES

Sentences are a combination of words that communicate a complete thought. Sentences can be written in many ways to signal different relationships among ideas. This lesson will cover (1) simple sentences (2) compound sentences (3) complex sentences (4) parallel structure.

Simple Sentences

A **simple sentence** is a group of words that make up a **complete thought**. To be a complete thought, simple sentences must have one **independent clause.** An independent clause contains a single **subject** (who or what the sentence is about) and a **predicate** (a **verb** and something about the subject.)

Let's take a look at some simple sentences:

Simple Sentence	Subject	Predicate	Complete Thought?
The car was fast.	car	was fast (verb = was)	Yes
Sally waited for the bus.	Sally	waited for the bus (verb = waited)	Yes
The pizza smells delicious.	pizza	smells delicious (verb = smells)	Yes
Anton loves cycling.	Anton	loves cycling (verb = loves)	Yes

It is important to be able to recognize what a simple sentence is in order to avoid **run-ons** and **fragments**, two common grammatical errors.

A **run-on** is when two or more independent clauses are combined without proper punctuation:

FOR EXAMPLE

Gregory is a very talented actor he was the lead in the school play.

If you take a look at this sentence, you can see that it is made up of 2 independent clauses or simple sentences:

1. *Gregory is a very talented actor*
2. *he was the lead in the school play*

You <u>cannot</u> have two independent clauses running into each other without proper punctuation.

You can fix this run-on in the following way:

Gregory is a very talented actor. He was the lead in the school play.

A **fragment** is a group of words that looks like a sentence. It starts with a capital letter and has end punctuation, but when you examine it closely you will see it is not a complete thought.

Let's put this information all together to determine whether a group of words is a simple sentence, a run-on, or a fragment:

Group of Words	Category
Mondays are the worst they are a drag.	Run-On: These are two independent clauses running into one another without proper punctuation. FIX: *Mondays are the worst. They are a drag.*
Because I wanted soda.	Fragment: This is a dependent clause and needs more information to make it a complete thought. FIX: *I went to the store because I wanted soda.*
Ereni is from Greece.	Simple Sentence: YES! This is a simple sentence with a subject (*Ereni*) and a predicate (*is from Greece*), so it is a complete thought.
While I was apple picking.	Fragment: This is a dependent clause and needs more information to make it a complete thought. FIX: *While I was apple picking, I spotted a bunny.*
New York City is magical it is my favorite place.	Run-On: These are two independent clauses running into one another without proper punctuation. FIX: *New York City is magical. It is my favorite place.*

Compound Sentences

A **compound sentence** is a sentence made up of two independent clauses connected with a **coordinating conjunction**.

Let's take a look at the following sentence:

Joe waited for the bus, but it never arrived.

If you take a close look at this compound sentence, you will see that it is made up of two independent clauses:

1. *Joe waited for the bus*
2. *it never arrived*

The word *but* is the coordinating conjunction that connects these two sentences. Notice that the coordinating conjunction has a comma right before it. This is the proper way to punctuate compound sentences.

Here are other examples of compound sentences:

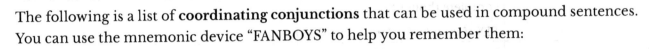

FOR EXAMPLE

I want to try out for the baseball team, and I also want to try out for track.

*Sally can play the clarinet in the band, **or** she can play the violin in the orchestra.*

*Mr. Henry is going to run the half marathon, **so** he has a lot of training to do.*

All these sentences are compound sentences since they each have two independent clauses joined by a comma and a coordinating conjunction.

The following is a list of **coordinating conjunctions** that can be used in compound sentences. You can use the mnemonic device "FANBOYS" to help you remember them:

For

And

Nor

But

Or

Yet

So

Think back to Section 1: Simple Sentences. You learned about run-ons. Another way to fix run-ons is by turning the group of words into a compound sentence:

RUN-ON:	*Gregory is a very talented actor he was the lead in the school play.*
FIX:	*Gregory is a very talented actor, **so** he was the lead in the school play.*

Complex Sentences

A **complex** sentence is a sentence that is made up of an independent clause and one or more dependent clauses connected to it.

Think back to Section 1 when you learned about fragments. You learned about a **dependent clause**, the part of a sentence that cannot stand by itself. These clauses need other information to make them complete.

You can recognize a dependent clause because they always begin with a **subordinating conjunction**. These words are a key ingredient in complex sentences.

Here is a list of **subordinating conjunctions**:

after	although	as	because	before
despite	even if	even though	if	in order to
that	once	provided that	rather than	since
so that	than	that	though	unless
until	when	whenever	where	whereas
wherever	while	why		

Let's take a look at a few complex sentences:

FOR EXAMPLE

Since the alarm clock didn't go off, I was late for class.

This is an example of a complex sentence because it contains:

A dependent clause:	*Since the alarm clock didn't go off*
An independent clause:	*I was late for class*
A subordinating conjunction:	*since*

Sarah studied all night for the exam even though she did not receive an A.

This is an example of a complex sentence because it contains:

A dependent clause:	*even though she did not receive an A*
An independent clause:	*Sarah studied all night*
A subordinating conjunction:	*even though*

*NOTE: To make a complex sentence, you can either start with the dependent clause or the independent clause. When beginning with the dependent clause, you need a comma after it. When beginning with an independent clause, you do not need a comma after it.

Parallel Structure

Parallel structure is the repetition of a grammatical form within a sentence to make the sentence sound more harmonious. Parallel structure comes into play when you are making a list of items. Stylistically, you want all the items in the list to line up with each other to make them sound better.

Let's take a look at when to use parallel structure:

1. Use parallel structure with verb forms:

   In a sentence listing different verbs, you want all the verbs to use the same form:

   Manuel likes hiking, biking, and mountain climbing.

   In this example, the words *hiking, biking* and *climbing* are all gerunds (having an -ing ending), so the sentence is balanced since the words are all using the gerund form of the verb.

   Manuel likes to hike, bike, and mountain climb.

In this example, the words *hike, bike* and *climb* are all infinitives (using the basic form of the verb), so the sentence is balanced.

You do not want to mix them up:

Manuel likes hiking, biking, and to mountain climb.

This sentence **does not** use parallel structure since *hiking* and *biking* use the gerund form of the verb and *to mountain climb* uses the infinitive form.

2. Use parallel structure with active and passive voice:

   In a sentence written in the **active voice**, the subject performs the action:

   Sally kicked the ball.

   Sally, the subject, is the one doing the action, kicking the ball.

   In a sentence written in the **passive voice**, the subject is acted on by the verb.

   The ball was kicked by Sally.

   When using parallel structure, you want to make sure your items in a list are either all in **active voice**:

   Raymond baked, frosted, and decorated the cake.

   Or all in **passive voice**:

   The cake was baked, frosted, and decorated by Raymond.

   You do not want to mix them up:

   The cake was baked, frosted, and Raymond decorated it.

   This sentence **does not** use parallel structure because it starts off with passive voice and then switches to active voice.

3. Use parallel structure with the length of terms within a list:

   When making a list, you should either have all short individual terms or all long phrases.

   Keep these consistent by either choosing short, individual terms:

   Cassandra is bold, courageous, and strong.

   Or longer phrases:

   Cassandra is brave in the face of danger, willing to take risks, and a force to be reckoned with.

   You do not want to mix them up:

   Cassandra is bold, courageous, and a force to be reckoned with.

This sentence **does not** use parallel structure because the first two terms are short, and the last one is a longer phrase.

Let's Review!

- A simple sentence consists of a clause, which has a single subject and a predicate.
- A compound sentence is made up of two independent clauses connected by a coordinating conjunction.
- A complex sentence is made up of a subordinating conjunction, an independent clause and one or more dependent clauses connected to it.
- Parallel structure is the repetition of a grammatical form within a sentence to make the sentence sound more harmonious.

TYPES OF CLAUSES

There are four types of clauses that are used to create sentences. Sentences with several clauses, and different types of clauses, are considered complex. This lesson will cover (1) independent clauses, (2) dependent clauses and subordinate clauses, and (3) coordinate clauses.

Independent Clause

An **independent clause** is a simple sentence. It has a subject, a verb, and expresses a complete thought.

- Steve went to the store.
- She will cook dinner tonight.
- The class was very boring.
- The author argues that listening to music helps productivity.

Two **independent clauses** can be connected by a semicolon. There are some common words that indicate the beginning of an **independent clause** such as: moreover, also, nevertheless, however, furthermore, consequently.

- I wanted to go to dinner; however, I had to work late tonight.
- She had a job interview; therefore, she dressed nicely.

Dependent and Subordinate Clauses

A **dependent clause** is not a complete sentence. It has a subject and a verb but does not express a complete thought. **Dependent clauses** are also called **subordinate clauses**, because they depend on the **independent or main clause** to complete the thought. A sentence that has both at least one **independent clause** and one **subordinate clause** are considered complex.

Subordinate clauses can be placed before or after the **independent clause**. When the **subordinate clause** begins the sentence, there should be a comma before the **main clause**. If the **subordinate clause** ends the sentence, there is no need for a comma.

Dependent clauses also have common indicator words. These are often called **subordinating conjunctions** because they connect a **dependent clause** to an **independent clause**. Some of these include: although, after, as, because, before, if, once, since, unless, until, when, whether, and while. Relative pronouns also signify the beginning of a **subordinate clause**. These include: that, which, who, whom, whichever, whoever, whomever, and whose.

- When I went to school...
- Since she joined the team...
- After we saw the play...
- *Because she studied hard*, she received an A on her exam.
- *Although the professor was late*, the class was very informative.
- I can't join you *unless I finish my homework*.

Coordinate Clause

A **coordinate clause** is a sentence or phrase that combines clauses of equal grammatical rank (verbs, nouns, adjectives, phrases, or independent clauses) by using a coordinating conjunction (and, but, for, nor, or so, yet). **Coordinating conjunctions** cannot connect a **dependent or subordinate clause** and an **independent clause.**

- She woke up, and he went to bed.
- We did not have cheese, so I went to the store to get some.
- Ice cream and candy taste great, but they are not good for you.
- Do you want to study, or do you want to go to Disneyland?

Let's Review!

- An **independent clause** is a simple sentence that has a noun, a verb, and a complete thought. Two **independent clauses** can be connected by a semicolon.
- A **dependent or subordinate clause** depends on the main clause to complete a thought. A **dependent or subordinate clause** can go before or after the **independent clause** and there are indicator words that signify the beginning of the **dependent or subordinate clause.**
- A **coordinate clause** connects two verbs, nouns, adjectives, phrases, or **independent clauses** using a **coordinating conjunction** (and, but, for, nor, or, so, yet).

SUBJECT AND VERB AGREEMENT

Every sentence must include a **subject** and a **verb**. The subject tells **who or what**, and the verb describes an **action or condition**. Subject and verb agree in number and person.

Roles of Subject and Verb

A complete sentence includes a **subject** and a **verb**. The verb is in the part of the sentence called the **predicate**. A predicate can be thought of as a verb phrase.

Simple Sentences

A sentence can be very simple, with just one or two words as the **subject** and one or two words as the **predicate**.

Sometimes, in a command, a subject is "understood," rather than written or spoken.

BE CAREFUL!

It's is a contraction of *it is*.

Its (without an apostrophe) is the possessive of the pronoun *it*.

Look at these examples of short sentences:

Sentence	Subject	Predicate, with main verb(s) underlined
I ate.	I	<u>ate</u>
They ran away.	They	<u>ran</u> away
It's OK.	It	<u>is</u> OK
Go and find the cat!	(You)	<u>go</u> and <u>find</u> the cat

Complex Sentences

Sometimes a subject or predicate is a long phrase or clause.

Some sentences have more than one subject or predicate, or even a predicate within a predicate.

Sentence	Subject(s)	Predicate(s), with main verb(s) underlined
My friend from work had a bad car accident.	My friend from work	<u>had</u> a bad car accident
John, his sister, and I plan to ride our bikes across the country this summer.	John, his sister, and I	<u>plan</u> to ride our bikes across the country this summer
I did so much for them, and they didn't even thank me.*	I; they	<u>did</u> so much for them; didn't even <u>thank</u> me
She wrote a letter that explained the problem.**	She	<u>wrote</u> a letter that explained the problem

*This sentence consists of two clauses, and each clause has its own subject and its own predicate.

**In this sentence, *that explained the problem* is part of the predicate. It is also a type of subordinate clause, called a relative clause, with its own subject and predicate.

Subject and Verb Agreement

Subjects and verbs must agree in **number** and **person**. This means that different subjects take different forms of a verb.

With **regular** verbs, simply add *-s* to the singular third person verb, as shown below:

	Singular		Plural	
	Subject	Verb	Subject	Verb
(first person)	I	play	we	play
(second person)	you	play	you	play
(third person)	he/she/it	plays	they	play

Some verbs are **irregular**, so simply adding *-s* doesn't work. For example:

Verb	Form for Third Person Singular Subject
have	has
do	does
fix	fixes

Look for subject-verb agreement in the following sentences:

- *I* usually <u>eat</u> a banana for breakfast.
- *Marcy* <u>does</u> well in school.
- The *cat* <u>licks</u> its fur.

Subject-Verb Agreement for the Verb *Be*

Present		Past	
I am	we are	I was	we were
you are	you are	you were	you were
he/she/it is	they are	they were	they were

Things to Look Out For

Subject-verb agreement can be tricky. Be careful of these situations:

- **Sentences with more than one subject:** If two subjects are connected by *and,* the subject is **plural**. When two singular subjects are connected by *neither/nor,* the subject is **singular**.

Sandra and Luiz <u>shop</u>. (plural)
Neither Sandra nor Luiz <u>has</u> money. (singular)

- **Collective nouns:** Sometimes a noun stands for a group of people or things. If the subject is **one group**, it is considered **singular**.

Those students <u>are</u> still on chapter three. (plural)
That class <u>is</u> still on chapter three. (singular)

- ***There is*** and ***there are***: With pronouns such as *there*, *what*, and *where*, the verb agrees with the noun or pronoun that follows it.

There<u>'s</u> a rabbit! (singular)
Where <u>are</u> my shoes? (plural)

- **Indefinite pronouns:** Subjects such as *everybody, someone,* and *nobody* are **singular**. Subjects such as *all, none,* and *any* can be either **singular or plural**.

Everyone in the band <u>plays</u> well. (singular)
All of the students <u>are</u> there. (plural)
All <u>is</u> well. (singular)

Let's Review!

- Every sentence has a subject and a verb.
- The predicate is the part of the sentence that contains the verb.
- The subject and verb must agree in number and person.
- The third person singular subject takes a different verb form.

MODIFIERS

A modifier is a word, phrase, or clause that adds detail or changes (modifies) another word in the sentence. Descriptive words such as adjectives and adverbs are examples of modifiers.

The Role of Modifiers in a Sentence

Modifiers make a sentence more descriptive and interesting.

Look at these simple sentences. Notice how much more interesting they are with modifiers added.

Simple sentence	With Modifiers Added
I drove.	I drove my family along snowy roads to my grandmother's house.
They ate.	They ate a fruit salad of blueberries, strawberries, peaches, and apples.
The boy looked.	The boy in pajamas looked out the window at the birds eating from the feeder.
He climbed.	He climbed the ladder to fix the roof.

Look at the modifiers in bold type in the following sentences. Notice how these words add description to the basic idea in the sentence.

	Modifier	Word It Modifies	Type
The hungry man ate **quickly**.	1. the; 2. hungry; 3. quickly	1. man 2. man; 3. ate	1. article 2. adjective; 3. adverb
The small child, **who had scraped his knee**, cried **quietly**.	1. the; 2. small; 3. who had scraped his knee; 4. quietly	1. child; 2. child; 3. child; 4. cried	1. article; 2. adjective; 3. adjective clause; 4. adverb
The horse **standing near the fence** is **beautiful**.	1. the; 2. standing near the fence; 3. beautiful	1. horse; 2. horse; 3. horse	1. article; 2. participle phrase; 3. adjective
Hana and Mario stood **by the lake** and watched **a gorgeous** sunset.	1. by the lake; 2. a; 3. gorgeous	1. stood; 2. sunset; 3. sunset	1. prepositional phrase; 2. article; 3. adjective
They tried **to duck out of the way as the large spider dangled from the ceiling**.	1. to duck out of the way; 2. as the large spider dangled; 3. from the ceiling	1. tried; 2. duck; 3. dangled	1. infinitive phrase; 2. adverb clause; 3. prepositional phrase

DID YOU KNOW?

Adjectives and adverbs are not the only modifiers. With a participle phrase, **an -ing verb** can act as a modifier. For example, *eating from the feeder* modifies *the birds*. With an infinitive, *to* **plus the main form of a verb** can act as a modifier. For example, *to fix the roof* modifies *climbed*.

43

Misplaced and Dangling Modifiers

A **misplaced modifier** is a modifier that is placed incorrectly in a sentence, so that it modifies the wrong word.

A **dangling modifier** is a modifier that modifies a word that should be included in the sentence but is not.

> **BE CAREFUL!**
> Sometimes there is a modifier within a modifier. For example, in the clause *as the large spider dangled,* *the* and *large* are words that modify *spider.*

Look at these examples.

- First, notice the modifier, in bold.
- Next, look for the word it modifies.

Incorrect	Problem	How to Fix It	Correct
Sam wore his new shirt to school, **which was too big for him.**	Misplaced modifier. Notice the placement of the modifier ***which was too big for him***. It is placed after the word *school,* which makes it seem like *school* is the word it describes. However, this was not the writer's intention. The writer intended for ***which was too big for him*** to describe the word *shirt*.	The modifier needs to be placed after the word *shirt,* rather than after the word *school.*	Sam wore his new shirt, **which was too big for him**, to school.
Running down the hallway, Maria's bag of groceries fell.	Dangling modifier. The modifier ***running down the hallway*** is placed before the phrase *Maria's bag of groceries,* which makes it seem this is what it describes. However, this was not the writer's intention; the *bag of groceries* cannot run! The correct reference would be the noun *Maria,* which was omitted from the sentence completely.	The modifier must reference *Maria,* rather than *Maria's bag of groceries.* This can be fixed by adding the noun *Maria* as a subject.	**Running down the hallway,** Maria dropped her bag of groceries.
With a leash on, my sister walked the dog.	Misplaced modifier. The modifier ***with a leash on*** is placed before *my sister,* which makes it seem like she is wearing a leash.	Move the modifier so that it is next to *the dog,* rather than *my sister.*	My sister walked the dog, **who had a leash on**.

Let's Review!

- A modifier is a word, phrase, or clause that adds detail by describing or modifying another word in the sentence.
- Adverbs, adjectives, articles, and prepositional phrases are some examples of modifiers.
- Misplaced and dangling modifiers have unclear references, leading to confusion about the meaning of a sentence.

> **BE CAREFUL!**
> A modifier should be placed next to the word it modifies. Misplaced and dangling modifiers lead to confusion about the meaning of a sentence.

DIRECT OBJECTS AND INDIRECT OBJECTS

A direct or indirect object has a relationship with the action verb that precedes it. A direct object directly receives the action of the verb. An indirect object indirectly receives the action.

Direct and Indirect Objects in a Sentence

An **object** in grammar is something that is acted on. The **subject** does the action; the **object** receives it.

An object is usually a noun or a pronoun.

There are three types of objects:

- direct object
- indirect object
- object of the preposition

KEEP IN MIND . . .
When there is an **indirect object**, it will be placed between the verb and the direct object.

Many sentences have a direct object. Some sentences also have an indirect object.

Look at these examples:

- Kim threw *the ball. The ball* is the direct object. *Ask yourself:* What did she throw?
- Kim threw *Tommy* the ball. *Tommy* is the indirect object. *Ask yourself:* Who did she throw it to?

Look for the objects in the sentences below.

Sentence	Direct Object	Indirect Object	Be Careful!
Her mom poured her a glass of milk.	a glass of milk (*ask:* what did she pour?)	her (*ask:* who did she pour it for?)	The indirect object, when there is one, can be found between the verb and the direct object.
They work hard.			Not all sentences have objects. Here, *hard* is not an object. It is not the recipient of *work*. Instead, it is a modifier; it describes the work.
Kazu bought Katrina a present.	a present (*ask:* what did he buy?)	Katrina (*ask:* whom did he buy it for?)	
Kazu bought a present for Katrina.	a present (*ask:* what did he buy?)		Don't confuse indirect objects with prepositional phrases. *For* is a preposition, so *Katrina* is the object of the preposition; it is not an indirect object.

BE CAREFUL!

Some verbs can never take **direct objects**. These are:

- **Linking verbs** such as *is* and *seem*.
- **Intransitive verbs** such as *snore, go, sit,* and *die*.
- *Ask yourself:* Can you *snore* something? No. Therefore, this verb cannot take a direct object.

Let's Review!

- A direct object directly receives the action of the verb.
- An indirect object indirectly receives the action of the verb.
- An indirect object comes between the verb and the direct object.

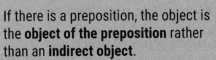

KEEP IN MIND . . .

If there is a preposition, the object is the **object of the preposition** rather than an **indirect object**.

Compare these two sentences:

- She made *me* dinner. (*Me* is an indirect object.)
- She made dinner *for me*. (*For me* is a prepositional phrase.)

Chapter 3 Knowledge of Language Practice Quiz

1. Identify the direct object in the following sentence.

   Paulo accidentally locked his keys in his car.

   A. Paulo   C. his keys

   B. accidentally   D. his car

2. Select the word that is an object of the underlined verb.

   The graduates <u>held</u> lit candles.

   A. The   C. lit

   B. graduates   D. candles

3. Select the verb that acts on the underlined direct object in the following sentence.

   We have no choice but to sit here and wait for these cows to cross <u>the road</u>!

   A. have   C. wait

   B. sit   D. cross

4. Which modifier, if any, modifies the underlined word in the following sentence?

   We always visit the <u>bakery</u> on the corner when we are in town.

   A. always

   B. on the corner

   C. when we are in town

   D. No modifier describes it.

5. Identify the dangling or misplaced modifier, if there is one.

   Having been repaired, we can drive the car again.

   A. Having been repaired

   B. we can drive

   C. the car again

   D. There is no dangling or misplaced modifier.

6. Which ending does <u>not</u> create a sentence with a dangling modifier?

   Trying to earn some extra money, ____.

   A. the new position paid more.

   B. he got a second job.

   C. the job was difficult.

   D. it was an extra shift.

7. Select the "understood" subject with which the underlined verb must agree.

   <u>Watch</u> out!

   A. You   C. I

   B. He   D. Out

8. How many verbs must agree with the underlined subject in the following sentence?

   <u>Kareem Abdul-Jabbar</u>, my favorite basketball player, dribbles, shoots, and scores to win the game!

   A. 0   C. 2

   B. 1   D. 3

9. Select the correct verb to complete the following sentence.

Our family ____ staying home for the holidays this year.

A. is   C. am

B. be   D. are

10. Fill in the blank with the correct subordinating conjunction.

You cannot go to the movies with your friends _____ you finish your homework.

A. If   C. Since

B. Once   D. Unless

11. Identify the dependent clause in the following sentence.

We decided to take our dog to the park although it was hot outside.

A. We decided to take our dog

B. to the park

C. although it was hot outside

D. to take our dog

12. Identify the independent clause in the following sentence.

After eating dinner, the couple went on a stroll through the park.

A. After eating dinner

B. The couple went on a stroll through the park

C. Through the park

D. Went on a stroll

13. Which of the following is an example of a simple sentence?

A. Tamara's sporting goods store.

B. Tamara has a sporting goods store in town.

C. Tamara has a sporting goods store it is in town.

D. Tamara's sporting goods store is in town, and she is the owner.

14. Which of the following uses a conjunction to combine the sentences below so the focus is on puppies requiring a lot of work?

Puppies are fun-loving animals. They do require a lot of work.

A. are fun-loving animals; they do require a lot of work.

B. Puppies are fun-loving animals, so they do require a lot of work.

C. Since puppies are fun-loving animals they do require a lot of work.

D. Although puppies are fun-loving animals, they do require a lot of work.

15. Which of the following options would complete the above sentence to make it a compound sentence?

The class of middle school students

_____.

A. served food at.

B. served food at a soup kitchen.

C. served food at a soup kitchen, and they enjoyed the experience.

D. served food at a soup kitchen even though they weren't required to.

CHAPTER 3 KNOWLEDGE OF LANGUAGE PRACTICE QUIZ – ANSWER KEY

1. C. *His keys* is the direct object of the verb *locked*. **See Lesson: Direct Objects and Indirect Objects.**

2. D. *Candles* is the direct object of the verb *held*. **See Lesson: Direct Objects and Indirect Objects.**

3. D. *The road* is a direct object of the verb *cross*. **See Lesson: Direct Objects and Indirect Objects.**

4. B. *On the corner* modifies *bakery*. **See Lesson: Modifiers, misplaced modifiers, dangling modifiers.**

5. A. *Having been repaired* is placed where it references *we*, but it should reference *the car*. **See Lesson: Modifiers, misplaced modifiers, dangling modifiers**

6. B. Of these choices, *trying to earn some extra money* can only reference *he*. **See Lesson: Modifiers, misplaced modifiers, dangling modifiers.**

7. A. In a command like this one, the "understood" subject is *you*. **See Lesson: Subject and Verb Agreement.**

8. D. The verbs *dribbles, shoots*, and *scores* must agree with the subject *Kareem Abdul-Jabbar*. **See Lesson: Subject and Verb Agreement.**

9. A. The subject *family* is singular and takes the verb *is*. **See Lesson: Subject and Verb Agreement.**

10. D. Unless. The word "unless" signifies the beginning of a dependent clause and is the only conjunction that makes sense in the sentence. **See Lesson: Types of Clauses.**

11. C. Although it was hot outside. It is dependent because it does not express a complete thought and relies on the independent clause. The word "although" also signifies the beginning of a dependent clause. **See Lesson: Types of Clauses.**

12. B. The couple went on a stroll through the park. It is independent because it has a subject, verb, and expresses a complete thought. **See Lesson: Types of Clauses.**

13. B. This is a simple sentence since it contains one independent clause consisting of a simple subject and a predicate. **See Lesson: Types of Sentences.**

14. D. The subordinate conjunction "although" combines the sentences and puts the focus on puppies requiring a lot of work. **See Lesson: Types of Sentences.**

15. C. This option would make the sentence a compound sentence. **See Lesson: Types of Sentences.**

CHAPTER 4 VOCABULARY ACQUISITION

Root Words, Prefixes, and Suffixes

A root word is the most basic part of a word. You can create new words by: adding a prefix, a group of letters placed before the root word; or a suffix, a group of letters placed at the end of a root word. In this lesson you will learn about root words, prefixes, suffixes, and how to determine the meaning of a word by analyzing these word parts.

Root Words

Root words are found in everyday language. They are the most basic parts of words. Root words in the English language are mostly derived from Latin or Greek. You can add beginnings (prefixes) and endings (suffixes) to root words to change their meanings. To discover what a root word is, simply remove its prefix and/or suffix. What you are left with is the root word, or the core or basis of the word.

At times, root words can be stand-alone words.

Here are some examples of stand-alone root words:

Stand-Alone Root Word	Meaning
dress	*clothing*
form	*shape*
normal	*typical*
phobia	*fear of*
port	*carry*

Most root words, however, are **not** stand-alone words. They are not full words on their own, but they still form the basis of other words when you remove their prefixes and suffixes.

Here are some common root words in the English language:

Root Word	Meaning	Example
ami, amic	*love*	amicable
anni	*year*	anniversary
aud	*to hear*	auditory
bene	*good*	beneficial
biblio	*book*	bibliography
cap	*take, seize*	capture
cent	*one hundred*	century
chrom	*color*	chromatic

Root Word	Meaning	Example
chron	*time*	chronological
circum	*around*	circumvent
cred	*believe*	credible
corp	*body*	corpse
dict	*to say*	dictate
equi	*equal*	equality
fract; rupt	*to break*	fracture
ject	*throw*	eject
mal	*bad*	malignant
min	*small*	miniature
mort	*death*	mortal
multi	*many*	multiply
ped	*foot*	pedestrian
rupt	*break*	rupture
sect	*cut*	dissect
script	*write*	manuscript
sol	*sun*	solar
struct	*build*	construct
terr	*earth*	terrain
therm	*heat*	thermometer
vid, vis	*to see*	visual
voc	*voice; to call*	vocal

Prefixes

Prefixes are the letters added to the **beginning** of a root word to make a new word with a different meaning.

Prefixes on their own have meanings, too. If you add a prefix to a root word, it can change its meaning entirely.

Here are some of the most common prefixes, their meanings, and some examples:

Prefix	Meaning	Example
auto	*self*	autograph
con	*with*	conclude
hydro	*water*	hydrate
im, in, non, un	*not*	unimportant
inter	*between*	international
mis	*incorrect, badly*	mislead

Prefix	Meaning	Example
over	*too much*	over-stimulate
post	*after*	postpone
pre	*before*	preview
re	*again*	rewrite
sub	*under, below*	submarine
trans	*across*	transcribe

Let's look back at some of the root words from Section 1. By adding prefixes to these root words, you can create a completely new word with a new meaning:

Root Word	Prefix	New Word	Meaning
dress (*clothing*)	un (*remove*)	**un**dress	*remove clothing*
sect (*cut*)	inter (*between*)	**inter**sect	*cut across or through*
phobia (*fear*)	hydro (*water*)	**hydro**phobia	*fear of water*
script (*write*)	post (*after*)	**post**script	*additional remark at the end of a letter*

Suffixes

Suffixes are the letters added to the **end** of a root word to make a new word with a different meaning.

Suffixes on their own have meanings, too. If you add a suffix to a root word, it can change its meaning entirely.

Here are some of the most common suffixes, their meanings, and some examples:

Suffix	Meanings	Example
able, ible	*can be done*	agreeable
an, ean, ian	*belonging or relating to*	European
ed	*happened in the past*	jogged
en	*made of*	wooden
er	*comparative (more than)*	stricter
est	*comparative (most)*	largest
ful	*full of*	meaningful
ic	*having characteristics of*	psychotic
ion, tion, ation, ition	*act, process*	hospitalization
ist	*person who practices*	linguist
less	*without*	artless
logy	*study of*	biology

Let's look back at some of the root words from Section 1. By adding suffixes to these root words, you can create a completely new word with a new meaning:

Root Word	Suffix	New Word	Meaning
aud (*to hear*)	logy (*study of*)	audio**logy**	*the study of hearing*
form (*shape*)	less (*without*)	form**less**	*without a clear shape*
port (*carry*)	able (*can be done*)	port**able**	*able to be carried*
normal (*typical*)	ity (*state of*)	normal**ity**	*condition of being normal*

Determining Meaning

Knowing the meanings of common root words, prefixes, and suffixes can help you determine the meaning of unknown words. By looking at a word's individual parts, you can get a good sense of its definition.

If you look at the word *transportation*, you can study the different parts of the word to figure out what it means.

If you were to break up the word you would see the following:

PREFIX: *trans = across*	ROOT: *port = carry*	SUFFIX: *tion = act or process*

If you put all these word parts together, you can define transportation as: *the act or process of carrying something across.*

Let's define some other words by looking at their roots, prefixes and suffixes:

Word	Prefix	Root	Suffix	Working Definition
indestructible	in (*not*)	struct (*build*)	able (*can be done*)	Not able to be "un" built (torn down)
nonconformist	non (*not*) con (*with*)	form (*shape*)	ist (*person who practices*)	A person who can not be shaped (someone who doesn't go along with the norm)
subterranean	sub (*under, below*)	terr (*earth*)	ean (*belonging or relating to*)	Relating or belonging to something under the earth

Let's Review!

- A root word is the most basic part of a word.
- A prefix is the letters added to beginning of a root word to change the word and its meaning.
- A suffix is the letters added to the end of a root word to change the word and its meaning.
- You can figure out a word's meaning by looking closely at its different word parts (root, prefixes, and suffixes).

CONTEXT CLUES AND MULTIPLE MEANING WORDS

Sometimes when you read a text, you come across an unfamiliar word. Instead of skipping the word and reading on, it is important to figure out what that word means so you can better understand the text. There are different strategies you can use to determine the meaning of unfamiliar words. This lesson will cover (1) how to determine unfamiliar words by reading context clues, (2) multiple meaning words, and (3) using multiple meaning words properly in context.

Using Context Clues to Determine Meaning

When reading a text, it is common to come across unfamiliar words. One way to determine the meaning of unfamiliar words is by studying other context clues to help you better understand what the word means.

Context means the other words in the sentences around the unfamiliar word.

You can look at these other words to find **clues** or **hints** to help you figure out what the word means.

FOR EXAMPLE

Look at the following sentence:

Some of the kids in the cafeteria _ostracized_ Janice because she dressed differently; they never allowed her to sit at their lunch table, and they whispered behind her back.

If you did not know what the word _ostracized_ meant, you could look at the **other words** for **clues** to help you.

Here is what we know based on the clues in the sentence:

- Janice dressed differently
- Some kids did not allow her to sit at their table
- They whispered behind her back

We know that the kids **never allowed her to sit at their lunch** table and that they **whispered behind her back**. If you put all these clues together, you can conclude that the other students were **mistreating** Janice by **excluding** her.

Therefore, based on these context clues, _ostracized_ means "excluded from the group."

Here's another example:

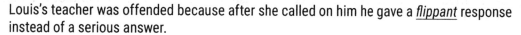

EXAMPLE 2

Look at this next sentence:

Louis's teacher was offended because after she called on him he gave a *flippant* response instead of a serious answer.

If you did not know what the word *flippant* meant, you could look at the **other words** for **clues** to help you.

Here is what we know based on the clues in the sentence:

- Louis's teacher was offended
- He gave a flippant response instead of a serious answer

We know that Louis said something that **offended** his teacher. Another keyword in this sentence is the word **instead**. This means that **instead of a serious answer** Louis gave the **opposite** of a serious answer.

Therefore, based on these context clues, *flippant* means "lacking respect or seriousness."

Multiple Meaning Words

Sometimes when we read words in a text, we encounter words that have **multiple meanings**.

Multiple meaning words are words that have **more than one definition** or meaning.

FOR EXAMPLE

The word **current** is a multiple meaning word. Here are the different definitions of *current*:
CURRENT:

1. adj: happening or existing in the present time
   Example: *It is important to keep up with* current *events so you know what's happening in the world.*
2. noun: the continuous movement of a body of water or air in a certain direction
   Example: *The river's* current *was strong as we paddled down the rapids.*
3. noun: a flow of electricity
   Example: *The electrical* current *was very weak in the house.*

Here are some other examples of words with multiple meanings:

Multiple Meaning Word	Definition #1	Definition #2	Definition #3
Buckle	noun: a metal or plastic device that connects one end of a belt to another	verb: to fasten or attach	verb: to bend or collapse from pressure or heat
Cabinet	noun: a piece of furniture used for storing things	noun: a group of people who give advice to a government leader	-
Channel	noun: a radio or television station	noun: a system used for sending something	noun: a long, narrow place where water flows
Doctor	noun: a person skilled in the science of medicine, dentistry, or one holding a PhD	verb: to change something in a way to trick or deceive	verb: to give medical treatment
Grave	noun: a hole in the ground for burying a dead body	adj: very serious	-
Hamper	noun: a large basket used for holding dirty clothes	verb: to slow the movement, action, or progress of	-
Plane	noun: a mode of transportation that has wings and an engine and can carry people and things in the air	noun: a flat or level surface that extends outward	noun: a level of though, development, or existence
Reservation	noun: an agreement to have something (such as a table, room, or seat) held for use at a later time	noun: a feeling of uncertainty or doubt	noun: an area of land kept separate for Native Americans to live an area of land set aside for animals to live for protection
Season	noun: one of the four periods in which a year is divided (winter, spring, summer, and fall)	noun: a particular period of time during the year	verb: to add spices to something to give it more flavor
Sentence	noun: a group words that expresses a statement, question, command, or wish	noun: the punishment given to someone by a court of law	verb: to officially state the punishment given by a court of law

From this chart you will notice that words with multiple meanings may have different **parts of speech**. A part of speech is a category of words that have the same grammatical properties. Some of the main parts of speech for words in the English language are: nouns, adjectives, verbs, and adverbs.

Part of Speech	Definition	Example
Noun	a person, place, thing, or idea	*Linda, New York City, toaster, happiness*
Adjective	a word that describes a noun or pronoun	*adventurous, young, red, intelligent*
Verb	an action or state of being	*run, is, sleep, become*
Adverb	a word that describes a verb, adjective, or other adverb	*quietly, extremely, carefully, well*

For example, in the chart above, *season* can be a **noun** or a **verb**.

Using Multiple Meaning Words Properly in Context

When you come across a **multiple meaning word** in a text, it is important to discern which meaning of the word is being used so you do not get confused.

You can once again turn to the **context clues** to clarify which meaning of the word is being used.

Let's take a look at the word *coach*. This word has several definitions:

COACH:
1. noun: a person who teaches and trains an athlete or performer
2. noun: a large bus with comfortable seating used for long trips
3. noun: the section on an airplane with the least expensive seats
4. verb: to teach or train someone in a specific area
5. verb: to give someone instructions on what to do or say in a certain situation

Since *coach* has so many definitions, you need to look at the **context clues** to figure out which definition of the word is being used:

The man was not happy that he had to sit in coach on the 24-hour flight to Australia.

In this sentence, the context clues **sit in** and **24-hour flight** help you see that *coach* means the least expensive seat on an airplane.

Let's look at another sentence using the word *coach*:

The lawyer needed to coach her witness so he would answer all the questions properly.

In this sentence, the context clues **so he would answer all the questions properly** help you see that the lawyer was giving the witness instructions on what to say.

Let's Review!

- When you come across an unfamiliar word in a text you can use context clues to help you define it.
- Context clues can also help you determine which definition of a multiple meaning word to use.

57

Synonyms, Antonyms, and Analogies

In order to utilize language to the best of your ability while reading, writing, or speaking, you must know how to interpret and use new vocabulary words, and also understand how these words relate to one another. Sometimes words have the same meaning. Sometimes words are complete opposites of each other. Understanding how the words you read, write, and speak with relate to each other will deepen your understanding of how language works. This lesson will cover (1) synonyms, (2) antonyms, and (3) analogies.

Synonyms

A **synonym** is a word that has the same meaning or close to the same meaning as another word. For example, if you look up the words *irritated* and *annoyed* in a dictionary, you will discover that they both mean "showing or feeling slight anger." Similarly, if you were to look up *blissful* and *joyful*, you will see that they both mean "extremely happy." The dictionary definition of a word is called its **denotation**. This is a word's literal or direct meaning.

When you understand that there are multiple words that have the same **denotation**, it will broaden your vocabulary.

It is also important to know that words with similar meanings have **nuances**, or subtle differences.

One way that words have nuances is in their **shades of meanings**. This means that although they have a similar definition, if you look closely, you will see that they have slight differences.

FOR EXAMPLE

If you quickly glance at the following words, you will see that they all have a similar meaning. However, if you look closely, you will see that their meanings have subtle differences. You can see their differences by looking at their various **levels** or **degrees**:

LEAST ⟶ MOST

---

nibble	bite	eat	devour
upset	angry	furious	irate
wet	soggy	soaked	drenched
good	great	amazing	phenomenal

Another way that words have nuance are in their **connotations**. A word's connotation is its **positive** or **negative** association. This can be the case even when two words have the same **denotations**, or dictionary definitions.

For example, the words *aroma* and *stench* both have a similar dictionary definition or **denotation**: "a smell." However, their **connotations** are quite different. *Aroma* has a **positive connotation** because it describes a *pleasant* smell. But *stench* has a **negative connotation** because it describes an unpleasant smell.

FOR EXAMPLE

Look at the following words. Although they have the same denotation, their connotations are very different:

Denotation	Positive Connotation	Negative Connotation
CLIQUE and *CLUB* both mean "a group of people."	*CLUB* has a positive connotation because it describes a group of people coming together to accomplish something.	*CLIQUE* has a negative connotation because it describes a group of people who exclude others.
INTERESTED and *NOSY* both mean "showing curiosity."	*INTERESTED* has a positive connotation because it means having a genuine curiosity about someone or something.	*NOSY* has a negative connotation because it describes who tries to pry information out of someone else to gossip or judge.
EMPLOY and *EXPLOIT* both mean "to use someone."	*EMPLOY* has a positive connotation because it means to use someone for a job.	*EXPLOIT* has a negative connotation because it means to use someone for one's own advantage.

Seeing that synonymous words have different **shades of meaning** and **connotations** will allow you to more precisely interpret and understand the nuances of language.

Antonyms

An **antonym** is a word that means the opposite or close to the opposite of another word. Think of an antonym as the direct opposite of a **synonym**. For example, *caring* and *apathetic* are antonyms because *caring* means "displaying concern and kindness for others" whereas *apathetic* means "showing no interest or concern."

Antonyms can fall under three categories:

Graded Antonyms:	Word pairs whose meanings are opposite and lie on a spectrum or continuum; there are many other words that fall between the two words. If you look at *hot* and *cold*, there are other words on this spectrum: *scalding,* **hot***, warm, tepid, cool,* **cold**
Relational Antonyms:	Word pairs whose opposites make sense only in the context of the relationship between the two meanings. These two words could not exist without the other: **open - close**
Complementary Antonyms:	Word pairs that have no degree of meaning at all; there are only two possibilities, one or the other: **dead - alive**

Here are some more examples of the three types of antonyms:

Graded Antonyms	Relational Antonyms	Complementary Antonyms
hard - soft	front - back	day - night
fast - slow	predator - prey	sink - float
bad - good	top - bottom	input - output
wet - dry	capture - release	interior - exterior
big - small	on - off	occupied - vacant

There are also common **prefixes** that help make antonyms. The most common prefixes for antonyms of words are: **UN**, **NON**, and **IN**. All these prefixes mean "not" or "without."

FOR EXAMPLE

UN:

likely – **un**likely
fortunate – **un**fortunate

IN:

tolerant – **in**tolerant
excusable – **in**excusable

NON:

conformist – **non**conformist
payment – **non**payment

Analogies

An **analogy** is a simple comparison between two things. Analogies help us understand the world around us by seeing how different things relate to one another.

In looking closely at words, analogies help us understand how they are connected.

In word analogies, they are usually set up using colons in the following way:

Pleasure: Smile :: Pain: _____

This can be read as: Pleasure **IS TO** Smile **AS** Pain **IS TO** _____

The answer: "grimace"

Sometimes you see analogies written out like this:

Pleasure is to Smile as Pain is to _____

These are the common types of word analogies that illustrate how different words relate to one another:

Type of Analogy	Relationship	Example
Synonyms	Two words with the same meaning	Beginner : Novice:: Expert : Pro
Antonyms	Two words with the opposite meaning	Hot : Cold :: Up : Down
Part/Whole	One word is a part of another word	Stars : Galaxy :: Pages : Book
Cause/Effect	One word describes a condition or action, and the other describes an outcome	Tornado : Damage :: Joke : Laughter
Object/Function	One word describes something, and the other word describes what it's used for	Needle : Sew :: Saw : Cut

Category/Type	One word is a general category, and the other is something that falls in that category	Music : Folk :: Dance : Ballet
Performer/Related Action	One word is a person or object, and the other words is the action he/she/it commonly performs	Thief : Steal :: Surgeon : Operate
Degree of Intensity	These words have similar meanings, but one word is stronger or more intense than the other	Glad : Elated :: Angry : Furious

By recognizing the type of analogy two words have, you then can explore how they are connected.

Let's Review!

- Synonyms are words that have the same meaning. Synonyms also have nuances.
- Analogies are words that have an opposite meaning. There are three types of antonyms.
- Analogies show how words relate to each other. There are different types of analogy relationships to look for.
- Understanding how words relate to each other will help you better understand language, pull meaning from texts, and write and speak with a wider vocabulary.

CHAPTER 4 VOCABULARY ACQUISITION PRACTICE QUIZ

1. Select the word from the following sentence that has more than one meaning.

   Cassandra's voice has a much different pitch than her brother's, so they sound great when they sing together.

   A. Voice   C. Pitch

   B. Different   D. Sing

2. Select the correct definition of the underlined word that has multiple meanings in the sentence.

   When the young boy saw his angry mother coming toward him, he made a bolt for the door.

   A. A large roll of cloth

   B. A quick movement in a particular direction

   C. A sliding bar that is used to lock a window or door

   D. A bright line of light appearing in the sky during a storm

3. Select the meaning of the underlined word in the sentence based on the context clues.

   When visiting the desert, the temperature tends to fluctuate, so you need to bring a variety of clothing.

   A. Rise   C. Change

   B. Drop   D. Stabilize

4. The use of the suffix *ous* in the word parsimonious indicates what about a person?

   A. He/she is full of stinginess

   B. He/she is against stinginess

   C. He/she is supportive of stinginess

   D. He/she is a person who studies stinginess

5. Which of the following prefixes means incorrect?

   A. un-   C. mis-

   B. non-   D. over-

6. What is the best definition of the word pugnacious?

   A. Rude   C. Deceiving

   B. Harmful   D. Combative

7. The following words have the same denotation. Which word has a negative connotation?

   A. Poised   C. Arrogant

   B. Assured   D. Confident

8. Whisk : Mix :: Flashlight: _____

   A. Hike   C. Camp

   B. Light   D. Travel

9. Which word in the list of synonyms shows the strongest degree of the word?

   A. Amusing   C. Uproarious

   B. Comical   D. Entertaining

CHAPTER 4 VOCABULARY ACQUISITION PRACTICE QUIZ – ANSWER KEY

1. **C**. The word "pitch" has more than one meaning. **See Lesson: Context Clues and Multiple Meaning Words.**

2. **B**. The meaning of <u>bolt</u> in the context of this sentence is "a quick movement in a particular direction. **See Lesson: Context Clues and Multiple Meaning Words.**

3. **C**. The meaning of <u>fluctuate</u> in the context of this sentence is "change." **See Lesson: Context Clues and Multiple Meaning Words.**

4. **A**. The suffix *ous* means "full of or possessing" so a parsimonious person is one who is full of stinginess. See **Lesson: Root Words, Prefixes, and Suffixes.**

5. **C**. The prefix that means "incorrect" is *mis*. See **Lesson: Root Words, Prefixes, and Suffixes.**

6. **D**. The root *pug* means "war," or "fight," so pugnacious means combative. See **Lesson: Root Words, Prefixes, and Suffixes.**

7. **C**. Arrogant has a negative connotation. **See Lesson: Synonyms, Antonyms, and Analogies.**

8. **B**. A whisk is a tool used to mix in the same way that a flashlight is a tool used to light. **See Lesson: Synonyms, Antonyms, and Analogies.**

9. **C**. Uproarious is the word that shows the strongest degree in the list of synonyms. **See Lesson: Synonyms, Antonyms, and Analogies.**

SECTION II. LANGUAGE ARTS: READING

CHAPTER 5 KEY IDEAS AND DETAILS

MAIN IDEAS, TOPIC SENTENCES, AND SUPPORTING DETAILS

To read effectively, you need to know how to identify the most important information in a text. You must also understand how ideas within a text relate to one other.

Main Ideas

The central or most important idea in a text is the **main idea**. As a reader, you need to avoid confusing the main idea with less important details that may be interesting but not central to the author's point.

The **topic** of a text is slightly different than the main idea. The topic is a word or phrase that describes roughly what a text is about. A main idea, in contrast, is a complete sentence that states the topic and explains what an author wants to say about it.

All types of texts can contain main ideas. Read the following informational paragraph and try to identify the main idea:

> The immune system is the body's defense mechanism. It fights off harmful bacteria, viruses, and substances that attack the body. To do this, it uses cells, tissues, and organs that work together to resist invasion.

The topic of this paragraph is the immune system. The main idea can be expressed in a sentence like this: "This paragraph defines and describes the immune system." Ideas about organisms and substances that invade the body are not the central focus. The topic and main idea must always be directly related to every sentence in the text, as the immune system is here.

Read the persuasive paragraph below and consider the topic and main idea:

> Football is not a healthy activity for kids. It causes head injuries that harm the ability to learn and achieve. It causes painful bodily injuries that can linger into adulthood. It teaches aggressive behavioral habits that make life harder for players after they have left the field.

The topic of this paragraph is youth football, and the main idea is that kids should not play the game. Note that if you are asked to state the main idea of a persuasive text, it is your job to be objective. This means you should describe the author's opinion, not make an argument of your own in response.

Both of the example paragraphs above state their main idea explicitly. Some texts have an implicit, or suggested, main idea. In this case, you need to figure out the main idea using the details as clues.

FOR EXAMPLE

The following fictional paragraph has an implicit main idea:

Daisy parked her car and sat gripping the wheel, not getting out. A few steps to the door. A couple of knocks. She could give him the news in two words. She'd already decided what she was going to do, so it didn't matter what he said, not really. Still, she couldn't make her feet carry her to the door.

The main idea here is that Daisy feels reluctant to speak to someone. This point is not stated outright, but it is clear from the details of Daisy's thoughts and actions.

Topic Sentences

Many paragraphs identify the topic and main idea in a single sentence. This is called a **topic sentence**, and it often appears at the beginning of a paragraph. However, a writer may choose to place a topic sentence anywhere in the text.

Some paragraphs contain an introductory sentence to grab the reader's attention before clearly stating the topic. A paragraph may begin by asking a rhetorical question, presenting a striking idea, or showing why the topic is important. When authors use this strategy, the topic sentence usually comes second:

> Have you ever wondered how your body fights off a nasty cold? **It uses a complex defense mechanism called the immune system.** The immune system fights off harmful bacteria, viruses, and substances that attack the body. To do this, it uses cells, tissues, and organs that work together to resist invasion.

Here, the first sentence grabs the attention, and the second, **boldfaced** topic sentence states the main idea. The remaining sentences provide further information, explaining what the immune system does and identifying its basic components.

COMPARE!

The informational paragraph above contains a question that grabs the attention at the beginning. The writer could convey the same information with a little less flair by omitting this device. The version you read in Section 1 does exactly this. (The topic sentence below is **boldfaced**.)

The immune system is the body's defense mechanism. It fights off harmful bacteria, viruses, and substances that attack the body. To do this, it uses cells, tissues, and organs that work together to resist invasion.

Look back at the football paragraph from Section 1. Which sentence is the topic sentence?

Sometimes writers wait until the end of a paragraph to reveal the main idea in a topic sentence. When you're reading a paragraph that is organized this way, you may feel like you're reading a bit of a puzzle. It's not fully clear what the piece is about until you get to the end:

> It causes head injuries that harm the ability to learn and achieve. It causes painful bodily injuries that can linger through the passage of years. It teaches aggressive behavioral habits that make life harder for players after they have left the field. **Football is not a healthy activity for kids.**

Note that the topic—football—is not actually named until the final, **boldfaced** topic sentence. This is a strong hint that this final sentence is the topic sentence. Other paragraphs with this structure may contain several examples or related ideas and then tie them together with a summary statement near the end.

Supporting Details

The **supporting details** of a text develop the main idea, contribute further information, or provide examples.

All of the supporting details in a text must relate back to the main idea. In a text that sets out to define and describe the immune system, the supporting details could explain how the immune system works, define parts of the immune system, and so on.

> **Main Idea:** The immune system is the body's defense mechanism.

> **Supporting Detail:** It fights off harmful bacteria, viruses, and substances that attack the body.

> **Supporting Detail:** To do this, it uses cells, tissues, and organs that work together to resist invasion.

The above text could go on to describe white blood cells, which are a vital part of the body's defense system against disease. However, the supporting details in such a text should *not* drift off into descriptions of parts of the body that make no contribution to immune response.

Supporting details may be facts or opinions. A single text can combine both facts and opinions to develop a single main idea.

> **Main Idea:** Football is not a healthy activity for kids.

> **Supporting Detail:** It teaches aggressive behavioral habits that make life harder for players after they have left the field.

> **Supporting Detail:** In a study of teenage football players by Dr. Sophia Ortega at Harvard University, 28% reported involvement in fights or other violent incidents, compared with 19% of teenage boys who were not involved in sports.

The first supporting detail above states an opinion. The second is still related to the main idea, but it provides factual information to back up the opinion. Further development of this paragraph could contain other types of facts, including information about football injuries and anecdotes about real players who got hurt playing the game.

Let's Review!

- The main idea is the most important piece of information in a text.
- The main idea is often expressed in a topic sentence.
- Supporting details develop the main idea, contribute further information, or provide examples.

SUMMARIZING TEXT AND USING TEXT FEATURES

Effective readers need to know how to identify and restate the main idea of a text through summary. They must also follow complex instructions, figure out the sequence of events in a text that is not presented in order, and understand information presented in graphics.

Summary Basics

A **summary** is a text that restates the ideas from a different text in a new way. Every summary needs to include the main idea of the original. Some summaries may include information about the supporting details as well.

The content and level of detail in a summary vary depending on the purpose. For example, a journalist may summarize a recent scientific study in a newspaper profile of its authors. A graduate student might briefly summarize the same study in a paper questioning its conclusions. The journalist's version would likely use fairly simple language and restate only the main points. The student's version would likely use specialized scientific vocabulary and include certain supporting details, especially the ones most applicable to the argument the student intends to make later.

The language of a summary must be substantially different from the original. It should not retain the structure and word choice of the source text. Rather, it should provide a completely new way of stating the ideas.

Read the passage below and the short summary that follows:

Original: There is no need for government regulations to maintain a minimum wage because free market forces naturally adjust wages on their own. Workers are in short supply in our thriving economy, and businesses must offer fair wages and working conditions to attract labor. Business owners pay employees well because common sense dictates that they cannot succeed any other way.

Effective Summary: The author argues against minimum wage laws. He claims free market forces naturally keep wages high in a healthy economy with a limited labor supply.

The effective summary above restates the main ideas in a new but objective way. Objectivity is a key quality of an effective summary. A summary does not exaggerate, judge, or distort the author's original ideas.

Not a Summary: The author makes a wild and unsupportable claim that minimum wage laws are unnecessary because market forces keep wages high without government intervention.

Although the above text might be appropriate in persuasive writing, it makes its own claims and judgments rather than simply restating the original author's ideas. It would not be an effective sentence in a summary.

In some cases, particularly dealing with creative works like fiction and poetry, summaries may mention ideas that are clearly implied but not stated outright in the original text. For example, a mobster in a thriller novel might turn to another character and say menacingly, "I wouldn't want anything to happen to your sweet little kids." A summary of this passage could objectively say the mobster had threatened the other character. But everything in the summary needs to be clearly supportable in the text. The summary could not go on to say how the other character feels about the threat unless the author describes it.

KEY POINT!

Many ineffective summaries attempt to imitate the structure of the original text and change only individual words. This makes the writing process difficult, and it can lead to unintentional plagiarism.

Ineffective Summary (Plagiarism): It is unnecessary for government regulations to create a minimum wage because capitalism adjusts wages without help. Good labor is rare in our excellent economy, and businesses need to offer fair wages and working conditions in order to attract workers.

The above text is an example of structural plagiarism. Summary writing does not just involve rewriting the original words one by one. An effective summary restates the main ideas of the text in a wholly original way.

Attending to Sequence and Instructions

Events happen in a sequence. However, many written texts present events out of order to create an effect on the reader. Nonfiction writers such as journalists and history writers may use this strategy to create surprise or bring particular ideas to the forefront. Fiction writers may interrupt the flow of a plot to interweave bits of a character's history or to provide flashes of insight into future events. Readers need to know how to untangle this presentation of events and figure out what actually happened first, second, and third. Consider the following passage:

> The man in dark glasses was looking for something. He checked his pockets. He checked his backpack. He walked back to his car, unlocked the doors, and inspected the area around the seats. Shaking his head, he re-locked the doors and rubbed his forehead in frustration. When his hand bumped his sunglasses, he finally realized where he had put them.

This passage does not mention putting the sunglasses on until the end, but it is clear from context that the man put them on first, before beginning his search. You can keep track of sequence by paying attention to time words like *when* and *before*, noticing grammatical constructions *he had* that indicate when events happened, and making common sense observations like the fact that the man is wearing his dark glasses in the first sentence.

Sequence is also an important aspect of reading technical and functional documents such as recipes and other instructions. If such documents present many steps in a large text block without illustrations or visual breaks, you may need to break them down and categorize them yourself. Always read all the steps first and think about how to follow them before jumping in.

To see why, read the pancake recipe below:

Combine flour, baking powder, sugar, and salt. Break the eggs into a separate bowl. Add milk and oil to the beaten eggs. Combine dry and liquid ingredients and stir. While you are doing the above, put a small amount of oil into a pan and heat it on medium heat. When it is hot, spoon batter onto the pan.

To follow directions like these effectively, a reader must break them down into categories, perhaps even rewriting them in a numbered list and noting when to start steps like heating the pan, which may be worth doing in a different order than it appears above.

Interpreting Graphics

Information is often presented in pictures, graphs, or diagrams. These **graphic elements** may provide information to back up an argument, illustrate factual information or instructions, or present key facts and statistics.

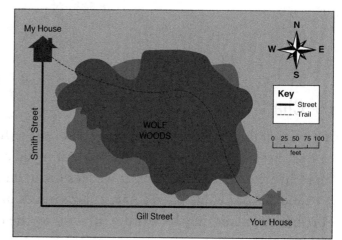

When you read charts and graphs, it is important to look carefully at all the information presented, including titles and labels, to be sure that you are interpreting the visuals correctly.

Diagram

A diagram presents a picture with labels that shows the parts of an object or functions of a mechanism. The diagram of a knee joint below shows the parts of the knee. Like many diagrams, it is placed in relation to a larger object—in this case, a leg—to clarify how the labeled parts fit into a larger context.

Flowchart

A flowchart shows a sequence of actions or decisions involved in a complex process. A flowchart usually begins with an oval-shaped box that asks a yes-no question or gives an instruction. Readers follow arrows indicating possible responses. This helps readers figure out how to solve a problem, or it illustrates how a complex system works.

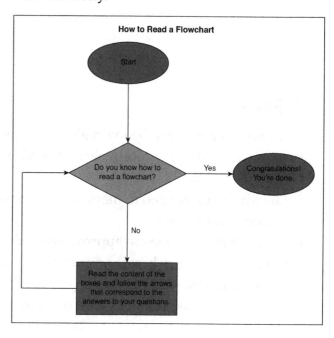

Bar Graph

A bar graph uses bars of different sizes to represent numbers. Larger bars show larger numbers to convey the magnitude of differences between two numeric values at a glance. In this case, each rectangle shows the number of candy bars of different types that a particular group of people ate.

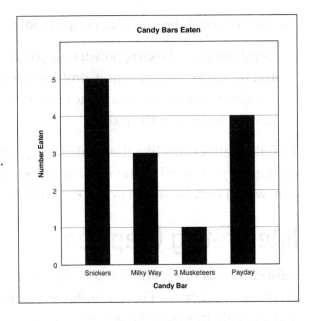

Pie Chart

A pie chart is useful for representing all of something— in this case, the whole group of people surveyed about their favorite kind of pie. Larger wedges mean larger percentages of people liked a particular kind of pie. Percentage values may be written directly on the chart or in a key to the side.

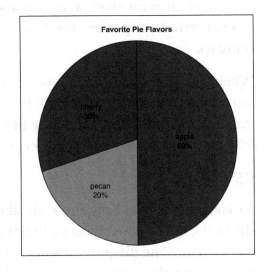

Let's Review!

- A summary restates the main ideas of a text in different words.
- A summary should objectively restate ideas in the present tense and give credit to the original author.
- Effective readers need to mentally reconstruct the basic sequence of events authors present out of order.
- Effective readers need to approach complex instructions by grouping steps into categories or considering how best to approach the steps.
- Information may be presented graphically in the form of diagrams, flowcharts, graphs, or charts.

Understanding Primary Sources, Making Inferences, and Drawing Conclusions

Effective readers must understand the difference between types of sources and choose credible sources of information to support research. Readers must also consider the content of their reading materials and draw their own conclusions.

Primary Sources

When we read and research information, we must differentiate between different types of sources. Sources are often classified depending on how close they are to the original creation or discovery of the information they present.

Primary sources include firsthand witness accounts of events, research described by the people who conducted it, and any other original information. Contemporary researchers can often access mixed media versions of primary sources such as video and audio recordings, photographs of original work, and so on. Note that original content is still considered primary even if it is reproduced online or in a book.

> **Examples:** Diaries, scientific journal articles, witness testimony, academic conference presentations, business memos, speeches, letters, interviews, and original literature and artwork.

Secondary sources respond to, analyze, summarize, or comment on primary sources. They add value to a discussion of the topic by giving readers new ways to think about the content. However, they may also introduce errors or layers of bias. Secondary sources may be very good sources of information, but readers must evaluate them carefully.

> **Examples:** Biographies, books and articles that summarize research for wider audiences, analyses of original literature and artwork, histories, political commentary.

Tertiary sources compile information in a general, highly summarized, and sometimes simplified way. Their purpose is not to add anything to the information, but rather to present the information in an accessible manner, often for audiences who are only beginning to familiarize themselves with a topic.

> **Examples:** Encyclopedias, guidebooks, literature study guides.

Source Materials in Action

Primary sources are often considered most trustworthy because they are closest to the original material and least likely to contain errors. However, readers must take a common sense approach to evaluating trustworthiness. For example, a single letter written by one biased witness of a historical event may not provide as much insight into what really happened as a secondary account by a historian who has considered the points of view of a dozen firsthand witnesses.

Tertiary sources are useful for readers attempting to gain a quick overview of understanding about a subject. They are also a good starting point for readers looking for keywords and subtopics to use for further research of a subject. However, they are not sufficiently detailed or credible to support an article, academic paper, or other document intended to add valuable analysis and commentary on a subject.

Evaluating Credibility

Not everything you read is equally trustworthy. Many sources contain mistakes, faulty reasoning, or deliberate misinformation designed to manipulate you. Effective readers seek out information from **credible**, or trustworthy, sources.

There is no single formula for determining credibility. Readers must make judgment calls based on individual texts and their purpose.

FOR EXAMPLE

Most sources should attempt to be objective. But if you're reading an article that makes an argument, you do not need to demand perfect objectivity from the source. The purpose of a persuasive article is to defend a point of view. As long as the author does this openly and defends the point of view with facts, logic, and other good argumentative techniques, you may trust the source.

Other sources may seem highly objective but not be credible. For example, some scientific studies meet all the criteria for credibility below except the one about trustworthy publishers. If a study is funded or conducted by a company that stands to profit from it, you should treat the results with skepticism no matter how good the information looks otherwise.

Sources and References

Credible texts are primary sources or secondary sources that refer to other trustworthy sources. If the author consults experts, they should be named, and their credentials should be explained. Authors should not attempt to hide where they got their information. Vague statements like "studies show" are not as trustworthy as statements that identify who completed a study.

Objectivity

Credible texts usually make an effort to be objective. They use clear, logical reasoning. They back arguments up with facts, expert opinions, or clear explanations. The assumptions behind the arguments do not contain obvious stereotypes.

Emotional arguments are acceptable in some argumentative writing, but they should not be manipulative. For example, photos of starving children may be acceptable for raising awareness of a famine, but they need to be respectful of both the victims and the audience—not just there for shock value.

Date of Publication

Information changes quickly in some fields, especially the sciences and technology. When researching a fast-changing topic, look for sources published in the last ten years.

Author Information

If an author and/or a respected organization take public credit for information, it is more likely to be reliable. Information published anonymously on the Internet may be suspicious because nobody is clearly responsible for mistakes. Authors with strong credentials such as university professors in a given field are more trustworthy than authors with no clear resume.

Publisher Information

Information published by the government, a university, a major national news organization, or another respected organization is often more credible. On the Internet, addresses ending in .edu or .gov may be more trustworthy than .com addresses. Publishers who stand to profit or otherwise benefit from the content of a text are always questionable.

> **BE CAREFUL!**
> Strong credentials only make a source more trustworthy if the credentials are related to the topic. A Columbia University Professor of Archeology is a credible source on ancient history. But if she writes a parenting article, it's not necessarily more credible than a parenting article by someone without a flashy university title.

Professionalism

Credible sources usually look professional and present information free of grammatical errors or major factual errors.

Making Inferences and Drawing Conclusions

In reading—and in life—people regularly make educated guesses based on limited information. When we use the information we have to figure out something nobody has told us directly, we are making an **inference**. People make inferences every day.

> **Example:** You hear a loud thump. Then a pained voice says, "Honey, can you bring the first aid kit?"

From the information above, it is reasonable to infer that the speaker is hurt. The thumping noise, the pain in the speaker's voice, and the request for a first aid kit all suggest this conclusion.

When you make inferences from reading, you use clues presented in the text to help you draw logical conclusions about what the author means. Before you can make an inference, you must read the text carefully and understand the explicit, or overt, meaning. Next, you must look for clues to any implied, or suggested, meanings behind the text. Finally, consider the clues in light of your prior knowledge and the author's purpose, and draw a conclusion about the meaning.

> As soon as Raizel entered the party, someone handed her a plate. She stared down at the hot dog unhappily.
>
> "What?" asked an unfamiliar woman nearby with an edge to her voice. "You don't eat dead animal?"

From the passage above, it would be reasonable to infer that the unfamiliar woman has a poor opinion of vegetarians. Several pieces of information suggest this: her combative tone, the edge in her voice, and the mocking question at the end.

When you draw inferences from a text, make sure your conclusion is truly indicated by the clues provided.

> Author Glenda Davis had high hopes for her children's book *Basketball Days*. But when the novel was released with a picture of a girl on the cover, boys refused to pick it up. The author reported this to her publisher, and the paperback edition was released with a new cover—this time featuring a dog and a basketball hoop. After that, many boys read the book. And Davis never heard anyone complain that the main character was a girl.

The text above implies that boys are reluctant to read books with a girl on the cover. A hasty reader might stop reading early and conclude that boys are reluctant to read about girls—but this inference is not suggested by the full text.

BE CAREFUL!

Before you make a conclusion about a text, consider it in light of your prior knowledge and the clues presented.

After reading the paragraph above, you might suspect that Raizel is a vegetarian. But the text does not fully support that conclusion. There are many reasons why Raizel might not want to eat a hot dog.

Perhaps she is keeping kosher, or she has social anxiety that makes it difficult to eat at parties, or she simply isn't hungry. The above inference about the unfamiliar woman's dislike for vegetarians is strongly supported. But you'd need further evidence before you could safely conclude that Raizel is actually a vegetarian.

Let's Review!

- Effective readers must consider the credibility of their sources.
- Primary sources are usually considered the most trustworthy.
- Readers must often make inferences about ideas that are implied but not explicitly stated in a text.

Chapter 5 Key Ideas and Details Practice Quiz

1. Which type of graphic element would be most helpful for teaching the names of the parts of a bicycle?

   A. Diagram

   B. Pie chart

   C. Bar graph

   D. Flowchart

Read the following sentence and answer questions 2-4.

Numerous robotic missions to Mars have revealed tantalizing evidence of a planet that may once have been capable of supporting life.

2. Imagine this sentence is a *supporting detail* in a well-developed paragraph. Which of the following sentences would best function as a *topic sentence*?

   A. Venus is an intensely hot planet surrounded by clouds full of drops of sulfuric acid.

   B. Of all the destinations within human reach, Mars is the planet most similar to Earth.

   C. Liquid water—a necessary ingredient of life—may once have flowed on the planet's surface.

   D. Space research is a costly, frivolous exercise that brings no clear benefit to people on Earth.

3. Imagine this sentence is the *topic sentence* of a well-developed paragraph. Which of the following sentences would best function as a *supporting detail*?

   A. Of all the destinations within human reach, Mars is the planet most similar to Earth.

   B. Venus is an intensely hot planet surrounded by clouds full of drops of sulfuric acid.

   C. Space research is a costly, frivolous exercise that brings no clear benefit to people on Earth.

   D. Liquid water—a necessary ingredient of life—may once have flowed on the planet's surface.

4. How could this sentence function as a *supporting detail* in a persuasive text arguing that space research is worth the expense and effort because it teaches us more about Earth and ourselves?

   A. By using statistics to back up an argument that needs support to be believed

   B. By showing how a space discovery could earn money for investors here on Earth

   C. By providing an example of a space discovery that enhances our understanding of life

   D. By developing the main idea that no space discovery can reveal information about Earth

The bar graph below provides information about book sales for a book called *The Comings*, which is the first book in a trilogy. Study the image and answer questions 5-6.

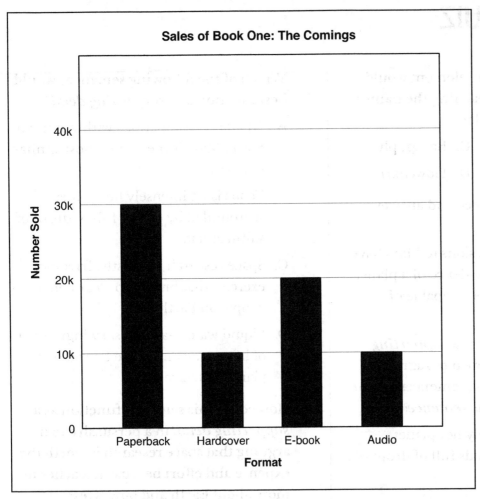

5. Which type of book has sold the most copies?

   A. E-book   C. Paperback

   B. Hardcover   D. Audio book

6. The marketing director for *The Comings* wants to use a different strategy for publishing book two in the series. Which argument does the bar graph *best* support?

   A. The first book in the trilogy has only sold 10,000 copies.

   B. The second book in the trilogy should not be released in hardcover.

   C. The second book in the trilogy should only be released as an e-book.

   D. The second and third books in the trilogy should be combined into one.

Study the infographic below and answer questions 7-9.

Credit: Center for Disease Control and Prevention. https://www.cdc.gov/nccdphp/dnpao/multimedia/infographics/getmoving.html

7. Which of the following is not a sign that the infographic is credible?

   A. The use of verifiable facts

   B. The list of source materials

   C. The professional appearance

   D. The inclusion of an author's name

8. Zetta is unsure of the credibility of this source and has never heard of the Centers for Disease Control (CDC). Which fact could help her decide to trust it?

   A. The CDC is located in Atlanta.

   B. The CDC has a .gov web address.

   C. The CDC creates many infographics.

   D. The CDC is also listed as a source consulted.

9. What could a skeptical reader do to verify the facts on the infographic?

   A. Interview one teenager to ask about his or her screen time.

   B. Follow the links for the sources and determine their credibility.

   C. Check a tertiary source like Wikipedia to verify the information.

   D. Find different values for screen time on someone's personal blog.

CHAPTER 5 KEY IDEAS AND DETAILS PRACTICE QUIZ – ANSWER KEY

1. A. A diagram illustrates complex visual ideas, so it could show which part of a bicycle is which and how they fit together. **See Lesson: Summarizing Text and Using Text Features.**

2. B. The sentence above conveys factual information about Mars in an excited tone that suggests a positive interest in the subject. This makes it most likely to fit into an informational paragraph sharing facts about Mars. **See Lesson: Main Ideas, Topic Sentences, and Supporting Details.**

3. D. If the above sentence were a topic sentence, its supporting details would likely share information to develop the idea that Mars may have supported life in the past. **See Lesson: Main Ideas, Topic Sentences, and Supporting Details.**

4. C. The sentence above could act as an example to show how space discoveries teach us about Earth and ourselves. **See Lesson: Main Ideas, Topic Sentences, and Supporting Details.**

5. C. Larger bars in a bar graph indicate higher numbers. This book has sold more paperback copies than any other. **See Lesson: Summarizing Text and Using Text Features.**

6. B. The bar graph shows fewer hardcover sales than any other kind. This could help support an argument that later books should only be released in electronic and paperback forms. **See Lesson: Summarizing Text and Using Text Features.**

7. D. It is usually a good sign if an author is clearly named in a source. Although this source is authored by an organization, the CDC, instead of a single author, there are many other signs it is credible. **See Lesson: Understanding Primary Sources Making Inferences and Drawing Conclusions.**

8. B. When presenting this type of information, a government organization with a .gov web address is typically considered a reputable source. **See Lesson: Understanding Primary Sources Making Inferences and Drawing Conclusions.**

9. B. One way to verify facts is to check the sources an author used. Verifying facts elsewhere may also be a good idea, but it is important to use reputable primary or secondary sources. **See Lesson: Understanding Primary Sources Making Inferences and Drawing Conclusions.**

CHAPTER 6 CRAFT AND STRUCTURE

FORMAL AND INFORMAL LANGUAGE

In English, there is formal language that is used most often in writing, and informal language that is most often used in speaking, but there are situations where one is more appropriate than the other. This lesson will cover differentiating contexts for (1) formal language and (2) informal language.

Formal Language

Formal language is often associated with writing for professional and academic purposes, but it is also used when giving a speech or a lecture. An essay written for a class will always use **formal language**. **Formal language** is used in situations where people are not extremely close and when one needs to show respect to another person. Certain qualities and contexts differentiate **formal language** from informal language.

Formal language does not use contractions.

- It doesn't have that - It does not have that.
- He's been offered a new job - He has been offered a new job.

Formal language also uses complete sentences.

- So much to tell you - I have so much to tell you.
- Left for the weekend - We left for the weekend.

Formal language includes more formal and polite vocabulary.

- The class starts at two - The class commences at two.
- I try to be the best person I can be - I endeavor to be the best person I can be.

Formal language is not personal and normally does not use the pronouns "I" and "We" as the subject of a sentence.

- I argue that the sky is blue - This essay argues that the sky is blue.
- We often associate green with grass - Green is often associated with grass.

Formal language also does not use slang.

- It's raining cats and dogs - It is raining heavily.
- Patients count on doctors to help them - Patients expect doctors to help them.

Informal Language

Informal language is associated with speaking, but is also used in text messages, emails, letters, and postcards. It is the language a person would use with their friends and family.

Informal language uses contractions.

- I can't go to the movie tomorrow.
- He doesn't have any manners.

Informal language can include sentence fragments.

- See you
- Talk to you later

Informal language uses less formal vocabulary such as slang.

- The dog drove me up the wall.
- I was so hungry I could eat a horse.
- I can always count on you.

Informal language is personal and uses pronouns such as "I" and "We" as the subject of a sentence.

- I am in high school.
- We enjoy going to the beach in the summer.

Let's Review!

- **Formal language** is used in professional and academic writing and talks. It does not have contractions, uses complete sentences, uses polite and formal vocabulary, not slang, and is not personal and generally does not use the pronouns "I" and "We" as the subject of a sentence.
- **Informal language** is used in daily life when communicating with friends and family through conversations, text messages, emails, letters, and postcards. It uses contractions, can be sentence fragments, uses less formal vocabulary and slang, and is personal and uses pronouns such as "I" and "We" as the subject of a sentence.

TONE, MOOD, AND TRANSITION WORDS

Authors use language to show their emotions and to make readers feel something too. They also use transition words to help guide the reader from one idea to the next.

Tone and Mood

The **tone** of a text is the author's or speaker's attitude toward the subject. The tone may reflect any feeling or attitude a person can express: happiness, excitement, anger, boredom, or arrogance.

Readers can identify tone primarily by analyzing word choice. The reader should be able to point to specific words and details that help to establish the tone.

Example: The train rolled past miles and miles of cornfields. The fields all looked the same. They swayed the same. They produced the same dull nausea in the pit of my stomach. I'd been sent out to see the world, and so I looked, obediently. What I saw was sameness.

Here, the author is expressing boredom and dissatisfaction. This is clear from the repetition of words like "same" and "sameness." There's also a sense of unpleasantness from phrases like "dull nausea" and passivity from words like "obediently."

Sometimes an author uses an ironic tone. Ironic texts often mean the opposite of what they actually say. To identify irony, you need to rely on your prior experience and common sense to help you identify texts with words and ideas that do not quite match.

Example: With that, the senator dismissed the petty little problem of mass shootings and returned to the really important issue: his approval ratings.

> **BE CAREFUL!**
>
> When you're asked to identify the tone of a text, be sure to keep track of *whose* tone you're supposed to identify, and which part of the text the question is referencing. The author's tone can be different from that of the characters in fiction or the people quoted in nonfiction.
>
> **Example:** The reporter walked quickly, panting to catch up to the senator's entourage. "Senator Biltong," she said. "Are you going to take action on mass shootings?"
>
> "Sure, sure. Soon," the senator said vaguely. Then he turned to greet a newcomer. "Ah ha! Here's the man who can fix my approval ratings!" And with that, he returned to the really important issue: his popularity.
>
> *
>
> In the example above, the author's tone is ironic and angry. But the tone of the senator's dialogue is different. The line beginning with the words "Sure, sure" has a distracted tone. The line beginning with "Ah ha!" has a pleased tone.

Here the author flips around the words most people would usually use to discuss mass murder and popularity. By calling a horrific issue "petty" and a trivial issue "important," the author highlights what she sees as a politician's backwards priorities. Except for the phrase "mass shootings," the words here are light and airy—but the tone is ironic and angry.

A concept related to tone is **mood**, or the feelings an author produces in the reader. To determine the mood of a text, a reader can consider setting and theme as well as word choice and tone. For example, a story set in a haunted house may produce an unsettled or frightened feeling in a reader.

Tone and mood are often confused. This is because they are sometimes the same. For instance, in an op-ed article that describes children starving while food aid lies rotting, the author may use an outraged tone and simultaneously arouse an outraged mood in the reader.

However, tone and mood can be different. When they are, it's useful to have different words to distinguish between the author's attitude and the reader's emotional reaction.

> **Example:** I had to fly out of town at 4 a.m. for my trip to the Bahamas, and my wife didn't even get out of bed to make me a cup of coffee. I told her to, but she refused just because she'd been up five times with our newborn. I'm only going on vacation for one week, and she's been off work for a month! She should show me a little consideration.

Here, the tone is indignant. The mood will vary depending on the reader, but it is likely to be unsympathetic.

Transitions

Authors use connecting words and phrases, or **transitions**, to link ideas and help readers follow the flow of their thoughts. The number of possible ways to transition between ideas is almost limitless.

Below are a few common transition words, categorized by the way they link ideas.

Transitions	Examples
Time and sequence transitions orient the reader within a text. They can also help show when events happened in time.	*First, second, next, now, then, at this point, after, afterward, before this, previously, formerly, thereafter, finally, in conclusion*
Addition or emphasis transitions let readers know the author is building on an established line of thought. Many place extra stress on an important idea.	*Moreover, also, likewise, furthermore, above all, indeed, in fact*
Example transitions introduce ideas that illustrate a point.	*For example, for instance, to illustrate, to demonstrate*
Causation transitions indicate a cause-and-effect relationship.	*As a result, consequently, thus*
Contrast transitions indicate a difference between ideas.	*Nevertheless, despite, in contrast, however*

Transitions may look different depending on their function within the text. Within a paragraph, writers often choose short words or expressions to provide transitions and smooth the flow. Between paragraphs or larger sections of text, transitions are usually longer. They may use some of the key words or ideas above, but the author often goes into detail restating larger concepts and explaining their relationships more thoroughly.

Between Sentences: Students who cheat do not learn what they need to know. *As a result,* they get farther behind and face greater temptation to cheat in the future.

Between Paragraphs: *As a result of the cheating behaviors described above,* students find themselves in a vicious cycle.

Longer transitions like the latter example may be useful for keeping the reader clued in to the author's focus in an extended text. But long transitions should have clear content and function. Some long transitions, such as the very wordy "due to the fact that" take up space without adding more meaning and are considered poor style.

Let's Review!

- Tone is the author's or speaker's attitude toward the subject.
- Mood is the feeling a text creates in the reader.
- Transitions are connecting words and phrases that help readers follow the flow of a writer's thoughts.

The Author's Purpose and Point of View

In order to understand, analyze, and evaluate a text, readers must know how to identify the author's purpose and point of view. Readers also need to attend to an author's language and rhetorical strategies.

Author's Purpose

When writers put words on paper, they do it for a reason. This reason is the author's **purpose**. Most writing exists for one of three purposes: to inform, to persuade, or to entertain.

> **TEST TIP**
>
> You may have learned about a fourth purpose for writing: conveying an emotional experience. Many poems as well as some works of fiction, personal essays, and memoirs are written to give the reader a sense of how an event or moment might feel. This type of text is rarely included on placement tests, and if it is, it tends to be lumped in with literature meant to entertain.

If a text is designed to share knowledge, its purpose is to **inform**. Informational texts include technical documents, cookbooks, expository essays, journalistic newspaper articles, and many nonfiction books. Informational texts are based on facts and logic, and they usually attempt an objective tone. The style may otherwise vary; some informational texts are quite dry, whereas others have an engaging style.

If a text argues a point, its purpose is to **persuade**. A persuasive text attempts to convince a reader to believe a certain point of view or take a certain action. Persuasive texts include op-ed newspaper articles, book and movie reviews, project proposals, and argumentative essays. Key signs of persuasive texts include judgments, words like *should,* and other signs that the author is sharing opinions.

If a text is primarily for fun, its purpose is to **entertain**. Entertaining texts usually tell stories or present descriptions. Entertaining texts include novels, short stories, memoirs, and some poems. Virtually all stories are lumped into this category, even if they describe unpleasant experiences.

> **CONNECTIONS**
>
> You may have read elsewhere that readers can break writing down into the following basic categories. These categories are often linked to the author's purpose.
>
> **Narrative** writing tells a story and is usually meant to entertain.
> **Expository** writing explains an idea and is usually meant to inform.
> **Technical** writing explains a mechanism or process and is usually meant to inform.
> **Persuasive** writing argues a point and, as the label suggests, is meant to persuade.

A text can have more than one purpose. For example, many traditional children's stories come with morals or lessons. These are meant both to entertain children and persuade them to behave in ways society considers appropriate. Also, commercial nonfiction texts like popular science books are often written in an engaging or humorous style. The purpose of such a text is to inform while also entertaining the reader.

Point of View

Every author has a general outlook or set of opinions about the subject. These make up the author's **point of view**.

To determine point of view, a reader must recognize implicit clues in the text and use them to develop educated guesses about the author's worldview. In persuasive texts, the biggest clue is the author's explicit argument. From considering this argument, a reader can usually make some inferences about point of view. For instance, if an author argues that parents should offer kids opportunities to exercise throughout the day, it would be reasonable to infer that the author has an overall interest in children's health, and that he or she is troubled by the idea of kids pursuing sedentary behaviors like TV watching.

It is more challenging to determine point of view in a text meant to inform. Because the writer does not present an explicit argument, readers must examine assumptions and word choice to determine the writer's point of view.

> **Example:** Models suggest that at the current rate of global warming, hurricanes in 2100 will move 9 percent slower and drop 24 percent more rain. Longer storm durations and rainfall rates will likely translate to increased economic damage and human suffering.

It is reasonable to infer that the writer of this passage has a general trust for science and scientists. This writer assumes that global warming is happening, so it is clear he or she is not a global warming denier. Although the writer does not suggest a plan to prevent future storm damage, the emphasis on negative effects and the use of negative words like "damage" and "suffering" suggest that the author is worried about global warming.

Texts meant to entertain also contain clues about the author's point of view. That point of view is usually evident from the themes and deeper meanings. For instance, a memoirist who writes an upbeat story about a troubled but loving family is likely to believe strongly in the power of love. Note, however, that in this type of work, it is not possible to determine point of view merely from one character's words or actions. For instance, if a character says, "Your mother's love doesn't matter much if she can't take care of you," the reader should *not* automatically assume the writer agrees with that statement. Narrative writers often present a wide range of characters with varying outlooks on life. A reader can only determine the author's point of view by considering the work as a whole. The attitudes that are most emphasized and the ones that win out in the end are likely to reflect the author's point of view.

Rhetorical Strategies

Rhetorical strategies are the techniques an author uses to support an argument or develop a main idea. Effective readers need to study the language of a text and determine how the author is supporting his or her points.

One strategy is to appeal to the reader's reason. This is the foundation of effective writing, and it simply means that the writer relies on factual information and the logical conclusions that follow from it. Even persuasive writing uses this strategy by presenting facts and reasons to back up the author's opinions.

Ineffective: Everyone knows *Sandra and the Lumps* is the best band of the new millennium.

Effective: The three most recent albums by *Sandra and the Lumps* are the first, second, and third most popular records released since the turn of the millennium.

Another strategy is to establish trust. A writer can do this by choosing credible sources and by presenting ideas in a clear and professional way. In persuasive writing, writers may show they are trustworthy by openly acknowledging that some people hold contradicting opinions and by responding fairly to those positions. Writers should never attack or misrepresent their opponents' position.

Ineffective: People who refuse to recycle are too lazy to protect their children's future.

Effective: According to the annual Throw It Out Questionnaire, many people dislike the onerous task of sorting garbage, and some doubt that their effort brings any real gain.

A final strategy is to appeal to the reader's emotions. For instance, a journalist reporting on the opioid epidemic could include a personal story about an addict's attempts to overcome substance abuse. Emotional content can add a human dimension to a story that would be missing if the writer only included statistics and expert opinions. But emotions are easily manipulated, so writers who use this strategy need to be careful. Emotions should never be used to distort the truth or scare readers into agreeing with the writer.

Ineffective: If you don't take action on gun control, you're basically killing children.

Effective: Julie was puzzling over the Pythagorean Theorem when she heard the first gunshot.

Let's Review!

- Every text has a purpose.
- Most texts are meant to inform, persuade, or entertain.
- Texts contain clues that imply an author's outlook or set of opinions about the subject.
- Authors use rhetorical strategies to appeal to reason, establish trust, or invoke emotions.

CHAPTER 6 CRAFT AND STRUCTURE PRACTICE QUIZ

1. **Which of the following sentences uses the MOST informal language?**

   A. The house creaked at night.

   B. I ate dinner with my friend.

   C. It's sort of a bad time.

   D. The water trickled slowly.

2. **In which of the following situations would it be best to use informal language?**

   A. In a seminar.

   B. Writing a postcard.

   C. Talking to your boss.

   D. Participating in a professional conference.

3. **Which of the following sentences uses the MOST formal language?**

   A. Thanks for letting me know.

   B. I want to thank you for telling me.

   C. Thank you for telling me about this issue.

   D. I appreciate you bringing this issue to my attention.

Read the passage below and answer questions 4-6.

The train was the most amazing thing ever even though it didn't go "choo choo." The toddler pounded on the railing of the bridge and supplied the sound herself. "Choo choo! Choo choooooo!" she shouted as the train cars whizzed along below.

In the excitement, she dropped her favorite binky.

Later, when she noticed the binky missing, all the joy went out of the world. The wailing could be heard three houses down. The toddler's usual favorite activities were garbage—even waving to Hank the garbage man, which she refused to do, so that Hank went away looking mildly hurt. It was clear the little girl would never, ever, ever recover from her loss.

Afterward, she played at the park.

4. **Which adjectives best describe the tone of the passage?**

   A. Ironic, angry

   B. Earnest, angry

   C. Ironic, humorous

   D. Earnest, humorous

5. **Which sentence from the passage is clearly ironic?**

   A. "Choo choo! Choo choooooo!" she shouted as the train cars whizzed along below.

   B. Later, when she noticed the binky missing, all the joy went out of the world.

   C. The wailing could be heard three houses down.

   D. Afterward, she played at the park.

6. The author of the passage first establishes the ironic tone by:

   A. describing the child's trip to play at the park.

   B. calling the train "the most amazing thing ever."

   C. pretending that the child can make the sounds "choo chooooo!"

   D. claiming inaccurately that the lost binky was the child's "favorite."

7. What is the most likely purpose of a popular science book describing recent advances in genetics?

   A. To decide   C. To persuade

   B. To inform   D. To entertain

8. Which phrase describes the set of techniques an author uses to support an argument or develop a main idea?

   A. Points of view

   B. Logical fallacies

   C. Statistical analyses

   D. Rhetorical strategies

9. What is the most likely purpose of an article that claims some genetic research is immoral?

   A. To decide   C. To persuade

   B. To inform   D. To entertain

CHAPTER 6 CRAFT AND STRUCTURE PRACTICE QUIZ – ANSWER KEY

1. C. *It's sort of a bad time.* The sentence has contractions and uses informal and slang words. **See Lesson: Formal and Informal Language.**

2. B. *Writing a postcard.* It is an informal mode of communication between close friends and relatives. **See Lesson: Formal and Informal Language.**

3. D. *I appreciate you bringing this issue to my attention.* The sentence uses the most formal and polite vocabulary. **See Lesson: Formal and Informal Language.**

4. C. This passage ironically is a humorous description of a toddler's emotions, written by an adult who has enough experience to know that a toddler's huge emotions will pass. **See Lesson: Tone and Mood, Transition Words.**

5. B. Authors use irony when their words do not literally mean what they say. The joy does not really go out of the world when a toddler loses her binky—but it may seem that way to the child. **See Lesson: Tone and Mood, Transition Words.**

6. B. This passage establishes irony in the opening sentence by applying the superlative phrase "the most amazing thing ever" to an ordinary occurrence. **See Lesson: Tone and Mood, Transition Words.**

7. B. If a book is describing information, its purpose is to inform. **See Lesson: Understanding the Author's Purpose, Point of View, and Rhetorical Strategies.**

8. D. The techniques an author uses to support an argument or develop a main idea are called rhetorical strategies. **See Lesson: Understanding the Author's Purpose, Point of View, and Rhetorical Strategies.**

9. C. An article that takes a moral position is meant to persuade. **See Lesson: Understanding the Author's Purpose, Point of View, and Rhetorical Strategies.**

CHAPTER 7 INTEGRATION OF KNOWLEDGE AND IDEAS

FACTS, OPINIONS, AND EVALUATING AN ARGUMENT

Nonfiction writing is based on facts and real events, but most nonfiction nevertheless expresses a point of view. Effective readers must evaluate the author's point of view and form their own conclusions about the points in the text.

Fact and Opinion

Many texts make an **argument.** In this context, the word *argument* has nothing to do with anger or fighting. It simply means the author is trying to convince readers of something.

Arguments are present in a wide variety of texts. Some relate to controversial issues, for instance by advocating support for a political candidate or change in laws. Others may defend a certain interpretation of facts or ideas. For example, a literature paper may argue that an author's story suggests a certain theme, or a science paper may argue for a certain interpretation of data. An argument may also present a plan of action such as a business strategy.

To evaluate an argument, readers must distinguish between **fact** and **opinion.** A fact is verifiably true. An opinion is someone's belief.

> **Fact:** Seattle gets an average of 37 inches of rain per year.

> **Opinion:** The dark, rainy, cloudy weather makes Seattle an unpleasant place to live in winter.

Meteorologists measure rainfall directly, so the above fact is verifiably true. The statement "it is unpleasant" clearly reflects a feeling, so the second sentence is an opinion.

The difference between fact and opinion is not always straightforward. For instance, a text may present a fact that contains an opinion within it:

> **Fact:** Nutritionist Fatima Antar questions the wisdom of extreme carbohydrate avoidance.

Assuming the writer can prove that this sentence genuinely reflects Fatima Antar's beliefs, it is a factual statement of her point of view. The reader may trust that Fatima Antar really holds this opinion, whether or not the reader is convinced by it.

If a text makes a judgment, it is not a fact:

Opinion: The patient's seizure drug regimen caused horrendous side effects.

This sentence uses language that different people would interpret in different ways. Because people have varying ideas about what they consider "horrendous," this sentence is an opinion as it is written, even though the actual side effects and the patient's opinion of them could both be verified.

COMPARE!

Small changes to the statement about seizure drugs could turn it into a factual statement:

Fact: The patient's seizure drug regiment caused side effects such as migraines, confusion, and dangerously high blood pressure.

The above statement can be verified because the patient and other witnesses could confirm the exact nature of her symptoms. This makes it a fact.

Fact: The patient reported that her seizure drug regimen caused horrendous side effects.

This statement can also be verified because the patient can verify that she considers the side effects horrendous. By framing the statement in this way, the writer leaves nothing up to interpretation and is clearly in the realm of fact.

The majority of all arguments contain both facts and opinions, and strong arguments may contain both fact and opinion elements. It is rare for an argument to be composed entirely of facts, but it can happen if the writer is attempting to convince readers to accept factual information that is little-known or widely questioned. Most arguments present an author's opinion and use facts, reasoning, and expert testimony to convince readers.

Evaluating an Argument

Effective readers must evaluate an argument and decide whether or not it is valid. To do this, readers must consider every claim the author presents, including both the main argument and any supporting statements. If an argument is based on poor reasoning or insufficient evidence, it is not valid—even if you agree with the main idea.

KEY POINT!

Most of us want to agree with arguments that reflect our own beliefs. But it is inadvisable to accept an argument that is not properly rooted in good reasoning. Consider the following statements about global climate change:

Poor Argument: It just snowed fifteen inches! How can anyone say the world is getting warmer?

Poor Argument: It's seventy degrees in the middle of February! How can anyone deny global warming?

Both of these arguments are based on insufficient evidence. Each relies on *one* weather event in *one* location to support an argument that the entire world's climate is or is not changing. There is not nearly enough information here to support an argument on either side.

Beware of any argument that presents opinion information as fact.

False Claim of Fact: I know vaccines cause autism because my niece began displaying autism symptoms after receiving her measles vaccine.

The statement above states a controversial idea as fact without adequate evidence to back it up. Specifically, it makes a false claim of cause and effect about an incident that has no clear causal relationship.

Any claim that is not supported by sufficient evidence is an example of **faulty reasoning**.

Type of Faulty Reasoning	Definition	Example	Explanation
Circular Reasoning	Restating the argument in different words instead of providing evidence	Baseball is the best game in the world because it is more fun than any other game.	Here, everything after the word *because* says approximately the same thing as everything before it. It looks like the author is providing a reason, but no evidence has actually been offered.
Either/Or Fallacy	Presenting an issue as if it involves only two choices when in fact it is not so simple	Women should focus on motherhood, not careers.	This statement assumes that women cannot do both. It also assumes that no woman needs a career in order to provide for her children.
Overgeneralizations	Making a broad claim based on too little evidence	All elderly people have negative stereotypes of teenagers.	This statement lumps a whole category of people into a group and claims the whole group shares the same belief—always an unlikely prospect.

Most texts about evaluating arguments focus on faulty reasoning and false statements of fact. But arguments that attempt to misrepresent facts as opinions are equally suspicious. A careful reader should be skeptical of any text that denies clear physical evidence or questions the truth of events that have been widely verified.

Assumptions and Biases

A well-reasoned argument should be supported by facts, logic, and clearly explained opinions. But most arguments are also based on **assumptions**, or unstated and unproven ideas about what is true. Consider the following argument:

Argument: To improve equality of opportunity for all children, schools in underprivileged areas should receive as much taxpayer funding as schools in wealthy districts.

This argument is based on several assumptions. First is the assumption that all children should have equal opportunities. Another is that taxpayer-funded public schools are the best way to provide these opportunities. Whether or not you disagree with either of these points, it is worth noting that the second idea in particular is not the only way to proceed. Readers who examine the assumptions behind an argument can sometimes find points of disagreement even if an author's claims and logic are otherwise sound.

Examining an author's assumptions can also reveal a writer's biases. A **bias** is a preconceived idea that makes a person more likely to show unfair favor for certain thoughts, people, or groups. Because every person has a different experience of the world, every person has a different set of biases. For example, a person who has traveled widely may feel differently about world political events than someone who has always lived in one place.

Virtually all writing is biased to some degree. However, effective writing attempts to avoid bias as much as possible. Writing that is highly biased may be based on poor assumptions that render the entire argument invalid.

Highly biased writing often includes overgeneralizations. Words like *all, always, never,* and so on may indicate that the writer is overstating a point. While these words can exist in true statements, unbiased writing is more likely to qualify ideas using words like *usually, often,* and *rarely.*

Another quality of biased writing is excessively emotional word choice. When writers insult people who disagree with them or engage the emotions in a way that feels manipulative, they are being biased.

> **Biased:** Power-hungry politicians don't care that their standardized testing requirements are producing a generation of overanxious, incurious, impractical kids.

> **Less biased:** Politicians need to recognize that current standardized testing requirements are causing severe anxiety and other negative effects in children.

Biased writing may also reflect stereotypical thinking. A **stereotype** is a particularly harmful type of bias that applies specifically to groups of people. Stereotypical thinking is behind racism, sexism, homophobia, and so on. Even people who do not consider themselves prejudiced can use language that reflects common stereotypes. For example, the negative use of the word *crazy* reflects a stereotype against people with mental illnesses.

Historically, writers in English have used male nouns and pronouns to indicate all people. Revising such language for more inclusivity is considered more effective in contemporary writing.

> **Biased:** The history of the human race proves that man is a violent creature.

> **Less biased:** The history of the human race proves that people are violent.

Let's Review!

- A text meant to convince someone of something is making an argument.
- Arguments may employ both facts and opinions.
- Effective arguments must use valid reasoning.
- Arguments are based on assumptions that may be reasonable or highly biased.
- Almost all writing is biased to some degree, but strong writing makes an effort to eliminate bias.

EVALUATING AND INTEGRATING DATA

Effective readers do more than absorb and analyze the content of sentences, paragraphs, and chapters. They recognize the importance of features that stand out in and around the text, and they understand and integrate knowledge from visual features like maps and charts.

Text Features

Elements that stand out from a text are called **text features**. Text features perform many vital functions.

- **Introducing the Topic and Organizing Information**

> **COMPARE!**
> The title on a fictional work does not always state the topic explicitly. While some titles do this, others are more concerned with hinting at a theme or setting up the tone.

- *Titles* – The title of a nonfiction text typically introduces the topic. Titles are guiding features of organization because they give clues about what is and is not covered. The title of this section, "Text Features," covers exactly that—not, for example, implicit ideas.
- *Headings and Subheadings* – Headings and subheadings provide subtopic information about supporting points and let readers scan to see how information is organized. The subheadings of this page organize text features according to the functions they perform.

- **Helping the Reader Find Information**

- *Table of Contents* – The table of contents of a long work lists chapter titles and other large-scale information so readers can predict the content. This helps readers to determine whether or not a text will be useful to them and to find sections relevant to their research.
- *Index* – In a book, the index is an alphabetical list of topics covered, complete with page numbers where the topics are discussed. Readers looking for information on one small subtopic can check the index to find out which pages to view.
- *Footnotes and Endnotes* – When footnotes and endnotes list sources, they allow the reader to find and evaluate the information an author is citing.

- **Emphasizing Concepts**

- *Formatting Features* – Authors may use formatting features such as *italics*, **boldfacing** or <u>underlining</u> to emphasize a word, phrase, or other important information in a text.
- *Bulleting and numbering* – Bullet points and numbered lists set off information and allow readers to scan for bits of information they do not know. It also helps to break down a list of steps.

- **Presenting Information and Illustrating Ideas**

  - *Graphic Elements* – Charts, graphs, diagrams, and other graphic elements present data succinctly, illustrate complex ideas, or otherwise convey information that would be difficult to glean from text alone.

- **Providing Peripheral Information**

  - *Sidebars* – Sidebars are text boxes that contain information related to the topic but not essential to the overall point.

  - *Footnotes and Endnotes* – Some footnotes and endnotes contain information that is not essential to the development of the main point but may nevertheless interest readers and researchers.[1]

FUN FACT!

Online, a sidebar is sometimes called a *doobly doo*.

P.S. This is an example of a sidebar.

Maps and Charts

To read maps and charts, you need to understand what the labels, symbols, and pictures mean. You also need to know how to make decisions using the information they contain.

Maps

Maps are stylized pictures of places as seen from above. A map may have a box labeled "Key" or "Legend" that provides information about the meanings of colors, lines, or symbols. On the map seen here, the key shows that a solid line is a road and a dotted line is a trail.

There may also be a line labeled "scale" that helps you figure out how far you need to travel to get from one point on the map to another. In the example, an inch is only 100 feet, so a trip from one end to the other is not far.

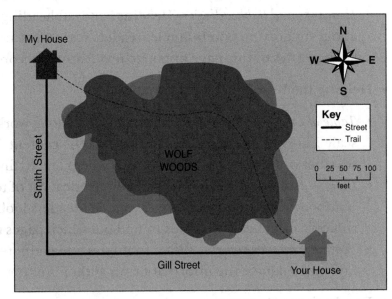

Some maps, including the example above, have compasses that show directions. If no compass is pictured, assume the top of the map is north.

---

[1] Anthony Grafton's book *The Footnote: A Curious History* is an in-depth history of the origins and development of the footnote. (Also, this is an example of a footnote.)

Charts

Nutrition Facts Labels

Nutrition facts labels are charts many people see daily, but not everyone knows how to read them. The top third of the label lists calorie counts, serving sizes, and amount of servings in a package. If a package contains more than one serving, a person who eats the entire contents of the package may be consuming many times the number of calories listed per serving.

The label below lists the content of nutrients such as fats and carbohydrates, and so on. According to the label, a person who eats one serving of the product in the package will ingest 30 mg of cholesterol, or 10% of the total cholesterol he or she should consume in a day.

KEEP IN MIND . . .

The percentages on a Nutrition Facts label do not (and are not meant to) add up to 100. Instead, they show how much of a particular nutrient is contained in a serving of the product, as a proportion of a single person's Daily Value for that nutrient. The Daily Value is the total amount of a nutrient a person is supposed to eat in a day, based on a 2000-calorie diet.

In general, a percentage of 5% or less is considered low, whereas a percentage of 20% or more is considered high. A higher percentage can be good or bad, depending on whether or not a person should be trying to get more of a particular ingredient. People need to get plenty of vitamins, minerals, and fiber. In contrast, most people need to limit their intake of fat, cholesterol, and sodium.

Tables

Tables organize information into vertical columns and horizontal rows. Below is a table that shows how much water falls on areas of various sizes when it rains one inch. It shows, for instance, that a 40' x 70' roof receives 1,743 gallons of rain during a one-inch rainfall event.

Area	Area (square miles)	Area (square kilometers)	Amount of Water (gallons)	Amount of Water (liters)
My roof 40 x 70 feet	.0001	.000257	1,743 gallons	6,601 liters
1 acre (1 square mile = 640 acres)	.00156	.004	27,154 gallons	102,789 liters
1 square mile	1	2.6	17.38 million gallons	65.78 million liters
Atlanta, Georgia	132.4	342.9	2.293 billion gallons	8.68 billion liters
United States	3,537,438	9,161,922	61,474 billion gallons	232,700 billion liters

Let's Review!

- Readers must understand how and why text features make certain information stand out from the text.
- Readers must understand and interpret the content of maps and charts.

Types of Passages, Text Structures, Genre and Theme

To read effectively, you must understand what kind of text you are reading and how it is structured. You must also be able to look behind the text to find its deeper meanings.

Types of Passages

There are many ways of breaking texts down into categories. To do this, you need to consider the author's **purpose**, or what the text exists to do. Most texts exist to inform, persuade, or entertain. You also need to consider what the text does—whether it tells a story, describes facts, or develops a point of view.

Type of Passage	Examples
Narrative writing tells a story. The story can be fictional, or it can describe real events. The primary purpose of narrative writing is to entertain.	• An autobiography • A memoir • A short story • A novel
Expository writing provides an explanation or a description. Many academic essays and informational nonfiction books are expository writing. Stylistically, expository writing is highly varied. Although the explanations can be dry and methodical, many writers use an artful or entertaining style. Expository writing is nonfiction. Its primary purpose is to inform.	• A book about a historical event • An essay describing the social impacts of a new technology • A description of changing gender roles in marriages • A philosophical document exploring the nature of truth. • Recipes
Technical writing explains a complex process or mechanism. Whereas expository writing is often academic, technical writing is used in practical settings such as businesses. The style of a technical document is almost always straightforward and impersonal. Technical writing is nonfiction, and its purpose is to inform.	• Instructions • User manuals • Process descriptions
Persuasive writing makes an argument. It asks readers to believe something or do something. Texts that make judgments, such as movie reviews, are persuasive because they are attempting to convince readers to accept a point of view. Texts that suggest a plan are also persuasive because they are trying to convince readers to take an action. As the name "persuasive writing" indicates, the author's primary purpose is to persuade.	• Op-ed newspaper articles • Book reviews • Project proposals • Advertisements • Persuasive essays

> **BE CAREFUL!**
>
> Many texts have more than one purpose.
>
> A text that tells a story is usually meant to entertain, but it can also be meant to persuade. For example, there is a well-known story called "Never Cry Wolf" about a boy who habitually lies. At the end, when he needs help, nobody believes him. This story is meant to entertain, but it is also trying to convince readers not to tell lies.
>
> Similarly, many explanatory texts are meant to inform readers in an entertaining way. For example, a nonfiction author may describe a scientific topic using humor and wacky examples to make it fun for popular audiences to read.
>
> Also, expository writing can look similar to persuasive writing, especially when it touches on topics that are controversial or emotional. For example, if an essay says social media is changing society, many readers assume it means social media is changing society *in a negative way*. If the writing makes this kind of value judgment or uses words like *should*, it is persuasive writing. But if the author is merely describing changes, the text is expository.

Text Structures

Authors rarely present ideas within a text in a random order. Instead, they organize their thoughts carefully. To read effectively, you must be able to recognize the **structure** of a text. That is, you need to identify the strategies authors use to organize their ideas. The five most common text structures are listed below.

Text Structure	Examples
In a **sequence** text, an author explains what happened first, second, third, and so on. In other words, a sequence text is arranged in **chronological order**, or time order. This type of text may describe events that have already happened or events that may happen in the future.	<ul><li>A story about a birthday party.</li><li>A historical paper about World War II.</li><li>A list of instructions for baking a cake.</li><li>A series of proposed steps in a plan for business expansion.</li></ul>
A **compare/contrast** text explains the similarities and differences between two or more subjects. Authors may compare and contrast people, places, ideas, events, cultures, and so on.	<ul><li>An essay describing the similarities and differences between women's experiences in medieval Europe and Asia.</li><li>A section in an op-ed newspaper article explaining the similarities and differences between two types of gun control.</li></ul>
A **cause/effect** text describes an event or action and its results. The causes and effects discussed can be actual or theoretical. That is, the author can describe the results of a historical event or predict the results of a possible future event.	<ul><li>An explanation of ocean acidification and the coral bleaching that results.</li><li>A paper describing a proposed new law and its likely effects on the economy.</li></ul>
A **problem-solution** text presents a problem and outlines a solution. Sometimes it also predicts or analyzes the results of the solution. The solution can be something that already happened or a plan the author is proposing. Note that a problem can sometimes be expressed in terms of a wish or desire that the solution fulfills.	<ul><li>An explanation of the problems smallpox caused and the strategies scientists used to eradicate it.</li><li>A business plan outlining a group of potential customers and the strategy a company should use to get their business.</li></ul>

Text Structure	Examples
A **description** text creates a mental picture for the reader by presenting concrete details in a coherent order. Description texts are usually arranged spatially. For instance, authors may describe the subject from top to bottom, or they may describe the inside first and then the outside, etc.	• An explanation of the appearance of a character in a story. • A paragraph in a field guide detailing the features of a bird. • A section on an instruction sheet describing how the final product should look.

CONNECTIONS

Different types of texts can use the same structures.

1. A story about a birthday party is a narrative, and its purpose is to entertain.
2. A historical paper about a war is an expository text meant to inform.
3. A list of instructions for baking a cake is a technical text meant to inform.
4. A series of proposed steps in a plan for business expansion is a persuasive text meant to persuade.

If all of these texts list ideas in chronological order, explaining what happened (or what may happen in the future) first, second, third, and so on, they are all using a sequence structure.

Genre and Theme

Literature can be organized into categories called **genres**. The two major genres of literature are fiction and nonfiction.

Fiction is made up. It can be broken down into many sub-genres, or sub-categories. The following are some of the common ones:

- Short story – Short work of fiction.
- Novel – Book-length work of fiction.
- Science fiction – A story set in the future
- Romance – A love story
- Mystery – A story that answers a concrete question, often about who committed a crime
- Mythology – A traditional story that reflects cultural traditions and beliefs but does not usually teach an explicit lesson
- Legends – Traditional stories that are presented as histories, even though they often contain fantastical or magical elements
- Fables – Traditional stories meant to teach an explicit lesson

> **COMPARE!**
>
> The differences between myths and fables are sometimes hard to discern.
>
> Myths are often somewhat religious in nature. For instance, stories about Ancient Greek gods and goddesses are myths. These stories reflect cultural beliefs, for example by showing characters being punished for failing to please their gods. But the lesson is implicit. These stories do not usually end with a moral lesson that says to readers, "Do not displease the gods!"
>
> Fables are often for children, and they usually end with a sentence stating an explicit moral. For example, there's a story called "The Tortoise and the Hare," in which a tortoise and a hare agree to have a race. The hare, being a fast animal, gets cocky and takes a lot of breaks while the tortoise plods slowly toward the finish line without stopping. Because the tortoise keeps going, it eventually wins. The story usually ends with the moral, "Slow and steady win the race."

Nonfiction is true. Like fiction, it can be broken down into many sub-genres. The following are some of the common ones:

- Autobiography and memoir – The author's own life story
- Biography – Someone else's life story (not the author's)
- Histories – True stories about real events from the past
- Criticism and reviews – A response or judgment on another piece of writing or art
- Essay – A short piece describing the author's outlook or point of view.

> **CONNECTIONS**
>
> Everything under "Fiction" and several items under "Nonfiction" above are examples of narrative writing. We use labels like "narrative" and "persuasive" largely when we discuss writing tasks or the author's purpose. We could use these labels here too, but at the moment we're more concerned with the words that are most commonly used in discussions about literature's deeper meanings.

Literature reflects the human experience. Texts from different genres often share similar **themes**, or deeper meanings. Texts from different cultures do too. For example, a biography of a famous civil rights activist may highlight the same qualities of heroism and interconnectedness that appear in a work of mythology from Ancient India. Other common themes in literature may relate to war, love, survival, justice, suffering, growing up, and other experiences that are accessible to virtually all human beings.

Many students confuse the term *theme* with the term *moral*. A **moral** is an explicit message contained in the text, like "Don't lie" or "Crime doesn't pay." Morals are a common feature of fables and other traditional stories meant to teach lessons to children. Themes, in contrast, are implicit. Readers must consider the clues in the story and figure out themes for themselves. Because of this, themes are debatable. For testing purposes, questions focus on themes that are clearly and consistently indicated by clues within the text.

Let's Review!

- Written texts can be organized into the following categories: narrative, expository, technical, and persuasive.
- Texts of all categories may use the following organizational schemes or structures: sequence, compare/contrast, cause/effect, problem-solution, description.
- Literature can be organized into genres including fiction, nonfiction, and many sub-genres.
- Literature across genres and cultures often reflects the same deeper meanings, or themes.

KEEP IN MIND . . .

The text structures above do not always work in isolation. Authors often combine two or more structures within one text. For example, a business plan could be arranged in a problem-solution structure as the author describes what the business wants to achieve and how she proposes to achieve it. The "how" portion could also use a sequence structure as the author lists the steps to follow first, second, third, and so on.

CHAPTER 7 INTEGRATION OF KNOWLEDGE AND IDEAS
PRACTICE QUIZ

1. Which of the following is *not* a function of text features?

   A. Introducing the topic

   B. Emphasizing a concept

   C. Making the theme explicit

   D. Providing peripheral information

2. If a map does not have a compass, north is:

   A. up.

   B. down.

   C. right.

   D. left.

3. The purpose of an index is to tell readers:

   A. how to find sources that back up key ideas in the text.

   B. who wrote the text and what his or her credentials are.

   C. where to find information on a given subject within a book.

   D. why the author believes the main idea of a text is important.

Read the following passage and answer questions 4-5.

Overworked public school teachers are required by law to spend extra time implementing

Individual Educational Plans for students with learning and attention challenges. This shortchanges children who are actually engaged in their education by depriving them of an equal amount of individualized attention.

4. What assumption behind this passage reflects negative stereotypical thinking?

   A. Public school teachers are generally overworked and underpaid.

   B. Students with learning disabilities are not engaged in their education.

   C. Laws require teachers to provide accommodations to certain students.

   D. Teachers have a finite amount of attention to divide between students.

5. The above argument is invalid because the author:

   A. suggests that some students do not need as much attention because they learn the material more quickly.

   B. uses derogatory and disrespectful word choice to describe people who think, learn, and process information differently.

   C. describes public school teachers in a negative way that makes it seem as though they have no interest in helping students.

   D. professes an interest in equality for all students while simultaneously suggesting some students are more worthy than others.

6. **Which statement, if true, is a fact?**

   A. The 1918 flu pandemic killed more people than World War I.

   B. The 1918 flu pandemic was more devastating than World War I.

   C. The 1918 flu pandemic was a terrifying display of nature's power.

   D. The 1918 flu pandemic caused greater social instability than the plague.

Read the following passage and answer questions 7-9.

There is inherent risk associated with the use of Rip Gym facilities. Although all Rip Gym customers sign a Risk Acknowledgment and Consent Form before gaining access to our grounds and equipment, litigation remains a possibility if customers suffer injuries due to negligence. Negligence complaints may include either staff mistakes or avoidable problems with equipment and facilities. It is therefore imperative that all Rip Gym employees follow the Safety Protocol in the event of a customer complaint.

Reports of Unsafe Equipment and Environs

Rip Gym employees must always respond promptly and seriously to any customer report of a hazard in our equipment or facilities, even if the employee judges the complaint frivolous. **Customers may not use rooms or equipment that have been reported unsafe until the following steps have been taken, in order, to confirm and/or resolve the problem.**

1. Place "Warning," "Out of Order," or "Off Limits" signs in the affected area or on the affected equipment, as appropriate. **Always follow this step first, before handling paperwork or attempting to resolve the reported problem.**

2. Fill out a Hazard Complaint Form. Include the name of the customer making the complaint and the exact wording of the problems being reported.

3. Visually check the area or equipment in question to verify the problem.

   a) If the report appears to be **accurate** and a resolution is necessary, proceed to step 4.

   b) If the report appears to be **inaccurate**, consult the manager on duty.

4. Determine whether you are qualified to correct the problem. Problems **all** employees are qualified to correct are listed on page 12 of the Employee Handbook.

   a) Employees who have **not** undergone training for equipment repair and maintenance must....

7. **This passage is best described as a(n):**

   A. narrative text.

   B. technical text.

   C. expository text.

   D. persuasive text.

8. Which term best describes the structure of the opening paragraph?

    A. Sequence

    B. Description

    C. Problem-solution

    D. Compare/Contrast

9. Which term best describes the structure of the section under the subheading "Reports of Unsafe Equipment and Environs"?

    A. Sequence

    B. Description

    C. Cause/effect

    D. Compare/contrast

Chapter 7 Integration of Knowledge and Ideas
Practice Quiz – Answer Key

1. C. Although the title of a fictional work may hint at a theme, a theme is a message that is, by definition, not stated explicitly. **See Lesson: Evaluating and Integrating Data.**

2. A. By convention, north on a map is up. Mapmakers include a compass if they break this convention for some reason. **See Lesson: Evaluating and Integrating Data.**

3. C. An index lists subtopics of a book along with page numbers where those topics will be covered. **See Lesson: Evaluating and Integrating Data.**

4. B. The writer of this passage suggests implicitly that only students without learning and attention challenges are engaged in their education. This assumption reflects a negative stereotype that renders the entire argument faulty. **See Lesson: Facts, Opinions, and Evaluating an Argument.**

5. B. The author of the passage uses the phrase "students with learning and attention challenges" to refer to students who think and learn differently. This is not derogatory, but even so, the passage implies that people who experience these differences are less engaged in their education. **See Lesson: Facts, Opinions, and Evaluating an Argument.**

6. A. All of these statements contain beliefs or feelings that are subject to interpretation except the statement about the number of people killed in the 1918 flu pandemic compared to World War I. This is a verifiable piece of information, or a fact. **See Lesson: Facts, Opinions, and Evaluating an Argument.**

7. B. This is a technical text written to inform the reader about a complex process. **See Lesson: Types of Passages, Text Structures, Genre and Theme.**

8. C. The opening paragraph has a problem-solution structure. The problem it describes involves risks of injury and litigation, and the solution is that employees follow a process designed to minimize those risks. **See Lesson: Types of Passages, Text Structures, Genre and Theme.**

9. A. The step-by-step instructions under the subheading follow a sequential structure. Note key words and phrases such as "first" and "in order." **See Lesson: Types of Passages, Text Structures, Genre and Theme.**

SECTION III. THE ESSAY

CHAPTER 8 ESSAY WRITING

THE WRITING PROCESS

Effective writers break the writing task down into steps to tackle one at a time. They allow a certain amount of room for messiness and mistakes in the early stages of writing but attempt to create a polished finished product in the end.

KEEP IN MIND . . .

If your writing process varies from the steps outlined below, that's okay—as long as you can produce a polished, organized text in the end. Some writers like to write part or all of the first draft before they go back to outline and organize. Others make a plan in the prewriting phase, only to change the plan when they're drafting. It is not uncommon for writers to compose the body of an essay before the introduction, or to change the thesis statement at the end to make it fit the essay they wrote rather than the one they intended to write.

The point of teaching the writing process is not to force you to follow all the steps in order every time. The point is to give you a sense of the mental tasks involved in creating a well-written text. If you are drafting and something is not working, you will know you can bounce back to the prewriting stage and change your plan. If you are outlining and you end up fleshing out one of your points in complete sentences, you will realize you still need to go back to finish the rest of the plan before you continue drafting.

In other words, it is fine to change the order of steps from the writing process,* or to jump around between them. Published writers do it all the time, and you can too.

*But almost everyone really does benefit from saving the editing until the end.

The Writing Process

A writer goes through several discrete steps to transform an idea into a polished text. This series of steps is called the **writing process**. Individual writers' processes may vary somewhat, but most writers roughly follow the steps below.

Prewriting is making a plan for writing. Prewriting may include brainstorming, free writing, outlining, or mind mapping. The prewriting process can be messy and include errors. Note that if a writing task requires research, the prewriting process is longer because you need to find, read, and organize source materials.

Drafting is getting the bulk of the text down on the page in complete sentences. Although most writers find drafting difficult, two things can make it easier: 1) prewriting to make a clear plan, and 2) avoiding perfectionism. Drafting is about moving ideas from the mind to the page, even if they do not sound right or the writer is not sure how to spell a word. For writing tasks that involve research, drafting also involves making notes about where the information came from.

Revising is making improvements to the content and structure of a draft. Revising may involve moving ideas around, adding information to flesh out a point, removing chunks of text that are redundant or off-topic, and strengthening the thesis statement. Revising may also mean improving readability by altering sentence structure, smoothing transitions, and improving word choice.

Editing is fixing errors in spelling, grammar, and punctuation. Many writers feel the urge to do this throughout the writing process, but it saves time to wait until the end. There is no point perfecting the grammar and spelling in a sentence that is going to get cut later.

For research projects, you also need to craft **citations,** or notes that tell readers where you got your information. If you noted this information while working on your prewriting and first draft, all you need to do now is format it correctly. (If you did not make notes as you worked, you will have to search laboriously through all your research materials again.) If you are using MLA or APA styles, citations are included in parentheses at the ends of sentences. If you are using Chicago style, citations appear in footnotes or endnotes.

Prewriting Techniques

Prewriting encompasses a wide variety of tasks that happen before you start writing. Many new writers skip or skimp on this step, perhaps because a writer's prewriting efforts are not clearly visible in the final product. But writers who spend time gathering and organizing information tend to produce more polished work.

Thinking silently is a valid form of prewriting. So is telling someone about what you are planning to write. For very short pieces based on your prior knowledge, it may be enough to use these—but most long writing tasks go better if you also use some or all of the strategies below.

Gathering Information

- **Conducting research** involves looking for information in books, articles, websites, and other sources. Internet research is almost always necessary, but do not overlook the benefits of a trip to a library, where you can find in-depth printed sources and also get help from research librarians.
- **Brainstorming** is making a list of short phrases or sentences related to the topic. Brainstorming works best if you literally write down every idea that comes to mind, whether or not you think you can use it. This frees up your mind to find unconscious associations and insights.
- **Free writing** is writing whatever comes to mind about your topic in sentences and paragraphs. Free writing goes fast and works best if you avoid judging your ideas as you go.

Organizing information

- **Mind mapping** arranges ideas into an associative structure. Write your topic, main idea, or argument in a circle in the middle of the page. Then draw lines and make additional circles for supporting points and details. You can combine this step with brainstorming to make a big mess of ideas, some of which you later cross out if you decide not to use them. Or you can do this after brainstorming, using the ideas from your brainstormed list to fill in the bubbles.

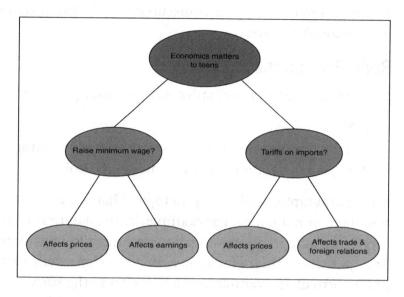

- **Outlining** arranges ideas into a linear structure. It starts with an introduction, includes supporting points and details to back them up, and ends with a conclusion. Traditionally, an outline uses Roman numerals for main ideas and letters for minor ideas.

Example:

I. Introduction - Economics should be a required subject in high school because it affects political and social issues that matter to students.

II. Domestic Issues - Minimum wage
   a. How do people decide if the minimum wage should be raised?
   b. They need to know how changes to the minimum wage affect workers, businesses, and prices.

III. Foreign Issues - Tariffs
   a. How do people decide if they favor taxes on imports?
   b. They need to know how tariffs affect prices and trade.

IV. Conclusion – These issues affect how much money high school graduates can earn and what they can afford to buy.

Paragraph Organization

Paragraphs need to have a clear, coherent organization. Whether you are providing information, arguing a point, or entertaining the reader, the ultimate goal is to make it easy for people to follow your thoughts.

Introductions

The opening of a text must hook the reader's interest, provide necessary background information on the topic, and state the main point. In an academic essay, all of this typically happens in a single paragraph. For instance, an analytical paper on the theme of unrequited love in a novel might start with a stark statement about love, a few sentences identifying the title and author of the work under discussion, and a thesis statement about the author's apparently bleak outlook on love.

Body Paragraphs

In informational and persuasive writing, body paragraphs should typically do three things:

1. Make a point.
2. Illustrate the point with facts, quotations, or examples.
3. Explain how this evidence relates to the point.

Body paragraphs need to stay on topic. That is, the point needs to relate clearly to the thesis statement or main idea. For example, in an analytical paper about unrequited love in a novel, each body paragraph should say something different about the author's bleak outlook on love. Each paragraph might focus on a different character's struggles with love, presenting evidence in the form of an example or quotation from the story and explaining what it suggests about the author's outlook. When you present evidence like this, you must introduce it clearly, stating where it came from in the book. Don't assume readers understand exactly what it has to do with your main point; spell it out for them with a clear explanation.

The structure above is useful in most academic writing situations, but sometimes you need to use other structures:

Chronological – Describe how events happen in order.
Sequential – Present a series of steps.
Descriptive – Describe a topic in a coherent spatial order, e.g. from top to bottom.
Cause/Effect – Present an action and its results.
Compare/Contrast – Describe the similarities and differences between two or more topics.

Conclusions

Like introductions, conclusions have a unique structure. A conclusion restates the thesis and main points in different words and, ideally, adds a bit more. For instance, it may take a broader outlook on the topic, giving readers a sense of why it matters or how the main point affects the world. A text should end with a sentence or two that brings the ideas together and makes the piece feel finished. This can be a question, a quotation, a philosophical statement, an intense image, or a request that readers take action.

Let's Review!

- The writing process includes prewriting, drafting, revision, and editing.
- For projects that involve research, writers must include the creation of citations within the writing process.
- Effective writers spend time gathering and organizing information during the prewriting stage.
- Writers must organize paragraphs coherently so that readers can follow their thoughts.

Essay Revisions and Transitions

A well-written essay should be easy to follow and convincing. The words should be well-chosen, and the transitions should be smooth.

Content, Organization, and Coherence

To revise an essay effectively, you must read through your own work with a critical eye. As you read, consider the content, organization, and flow of ideas.

Content

Every time you write, you are setting out to communicate something. Check to make sure you have clearly and succinctly stated an argument or main point, usually in a one-sentence thesis statement at the end of the first paragraph. Does your essay follow through on this point? By the end, you should have defended or developed it completely without leaving any holes or veering off onto other subjects. If you have not done this, add or delete information.

Organization

The ideas in your essay need to appear in an order that makes sense and avoids repetition. As you revise, check to make sure your ideas flow in a logical order, and move sentences around if they do not. Some topics lend themselves naturally to a particular type of organization. For instance, sometimes you will use chronological order, or you will outline causes first and effects second.

However, many analytical and persuasive papers do not fall into one natural organization. In this case, just choose an order that makes sense to you. In an argumentative paper, for instance, you could place your strongest arguments first and last, with the less impactful ones in the middle. No matter what, be sure each paragraph makes a point that is clearly distinguishable from the points in the other paragraphs. Do not just repeat the same idea in different words.

Coherence

When the ideas in an essay flow in a logical and consistent way that readers can easily follow, we say the writing has **coherence**. A well-written essay makes it possible for readers to follow the writer's thoughts. Make sure you have clear topic sentences in each paragraph to link back to the main idea. Do not bounce off onto new subtopics without explaining how they relate. Within paragraphs, explain your points and evidence explicitly. Do not leave gaps or make readers guess how one point relates to another.

Rhetorical Effectiveness and Use of Evidence

When you revise a persuasive essay, you must evaluate your work for **rhetorical effectiveness**. In other words, you need to make sure it is convincing. The cornerstones of rhetorically effective writing are reason, trust, and emotions.

Every good argument is grounded in logic and reasoning. When you offer opinions, you should present facts and logic to back them up. For example, if you are arguing that young children should not be required to do hours of homework every night, you could cite a study showing that kids under twelve did not learn more when they spent additional time doing homework outside of class.

Good arguments must also inspire trust. One of the primary ways to do this is to use credible sources and identify them clearly. The evidence above would generally be considered trustworthy if the study was conducted by a Harvard professor with a doctorate in education. It is a good idea to share information like this in an essay. It is not a good idea to use evidence if it comes from a source that is not credible.

It is also appropriate to engage the emotions in persuasive writing. In an essay opposing homework, you could call on readers' nostalgia and sense of fun by briefly describing the enjoyable activities kids could do instead of homework. But be careful. Good writing never uses personal attacks or scare tactics. In other words, it would be inappropriate to call people who believe in homework "fun killers" or to make an exaggerated suggestion that kids forced to do too much homework will suffer deep psychological damage.

Using Evidence

There are several rules of thumb for using evidence to back up your ideas.

- It must genuinely back up your thesis. Imagine you are arguing that kids under 12 should not do homework at all, and you find a study that says elementary school kids who did three hours of homework per night did not learn any more than kids who did only one hour. The study supports limited homework; it does not clearly support your thesis.
- If evidence comes from an outside source, it must be introduced and cited correctly. In general, you should name and share the credentials of your source the first time you introduce it. Afterward, you may refer to the same source by last name only.
- You need to explain how the evidence fits the argument. Readers may not understand what you are thinking about the evidence you present unless you spell it out for them.
- You need the right amount of evidence—not too much, not too little. Back up every opinion. One to three pieces of evidence per point should suffice. Do not continue piling on additional evidence to support a point you have already defended.

Word Choice

After you have revised for major issues like content, organization, and evidence, it is time to consider your word choice. This means you should attempt to use the right word at the right time. Below are several thoughts to consider as you hone your word choice.

Simplicity

The first goal of writing is to be understood. Many students try to use the biggest words they can, but it is usually a better style choice to choose an ordinary word. Do not use fancy vocabulary unless you have a good reason.

Precision

Sometimes the need for precision is a good reason for choosing a fancier word. There are times when it is best to say you hurt your knee, and there are times when it is best to say you injured your anterior cruciate ligament. Consider what your readers need to know and why. An audience of doctors might need or appreciate the medical terminology, whereas a general audience would likely be better served by the simpler language.

Tone

You can establish a clear tone by considering and manipulating the connotations of the words you use. Many words have a positive or negative connotation, whereas others are more neutral. *Cheap* has a negative tone, whereas *economical* is positive and *inexpensive* is neutral. If you are writing about making a purchase, choosing one or another of these words can subtly convey your attitude about what you bought.

Formality

Our language contains many levels of formality. Academic writing usually calls for slightly more formal language than daily speech. In academic writing, you should avoid slang, contractions, and abbreviations like *idk* or *tfw* that are commonly used in text messages and on the Internet. Depending on the writing task, you may also choose more formal words like *purchase* rather than less formal words like *buy*.

Inclusivity

Aim to use language that includes everyone, not language that plays into stereotypes and gender biases. Avoid referring to the entire human race as *man* or *mankind*. Use gender-neutral words like *firefighter* over gender-specific words like *fireman*. Do not assume people are male or female just because they belong to a certain profession. For example, do not automatically refer to a doctor as *he* or a preschool teacher as *she*. Note that using plurals can make it possible to write around gendered pronouns entirely. That is, if you refer to doctors or preschool teachers in the plural, you can refer back to them neutrally as *they*.

Transitions

At the very end of your revision process, read your work and make sure that your ideas flow smoothly from one to the next. Use connecting words and phrases, or **transitions**, to link ideas and help readers follow the flow of your thoughts. The number of possible ways to transition between ideas is almost limitless. Below are a few common transition words, categorized by the way they link ideas.

Type of Transition	Example
Time and sequence transitions help show when events happened in time.	first, second, next, now, then, at this point, after, afterward, before this, previously, formerly, thereafter, finally, in conclusion
Addition or emphasis transitions let readers know when you are building on an established line of thought or stressing an important idea.	moreover, also, likewise, furthermore, above all, indeed, in fact
Example transitions introduce ideas that illustrate a point.	for example, for instance, to illustrate, to demonstrate
Causation transitions indicate a cause-and-effect relationship.	as a result, consequently, thus, therefore
Contrast transitions indicate a difference between ideas.	nevertheless, despite, in contrast, however

Different types of transitions are necessary in different parts of an essay. Within a paragraph, you should use short transitions of one or two words to show how the information in one sentence is linked to the information preceding it. But when you are starting a new paragraph or making another major shift in thought, you may take time to explain relationships more thoroughly.

Between Sentences: Clara was in a minor car accident last week. *Afterward*, she experienced headaches and dizziness that worsened over time.

Between Paragraphs: *Because of her worsening headaches and dizziness*, Clara has found it increasingly difficult to work at her computer.

Note that longer transitions are long because they have content to explain how ideas relate. Some long transitions, such as the very wordy "due to the fact that" take up space without adding more meaning than simpler words like "because." Very long-winded transitions are considered poor style.

Let's Review!

- When you revise an essay, consider content, organization, and coherence first.
- Rhetorically effective writing appeals to the reader's reason and inspires trust and emotions appropriately.
- Use clear evidence to back up every opinion in your writing.
- Aim to use exactly the right words for the writing task at hand.
- Use appropriate transitions to create a smooth flow of ideas.

ACTIVE AND PASSIVE VOICE

Active and passive voice are two different styles of writing that are used to create a certain effect. This lesson will cover how to recognize, form, and use (1) active voice and (2) passive voice in writing.

Active Voice

Active voice is most often used in non-scientific academic writing. In active voice, the subject of the sentence performs the action of the verb.

Active voice sentences are more concise. Using the active voice prevents wordy and convoluted sentences and makes the meaning clear. The subject is acting on something and not being acted on.

- The dog bit the boy.
- Half of the class failed the exam.
- The actress joined the cast of the play.
- He turned on the window fan.

Passive Voice

Passive voice is used in scientific writing. In passive voice, the subject is being acted upon as the subject receives the action of the verb.

The words "by the" indicate the subject in a passive voice sentence. Passive voice will always include a form of the verb "to be."

Passive voice in academic writing can make the essay seem uninteresting, but sometimes passive voice can be a stylistic choice. Scientific writing uses passive voice to remain objective.

- The boy was bitten by the dog.
- The exam was failed by half of the class.
- The cast of the play was joined by the actress.
- The window fan was turned on by him.

Let's Review!

- In **active voice**, the subject performs the action of the verb. These sentences are clearer and more concise.
- In **passive voice**, the subject is acted upon. The subject receives the action of the verb. The use of the verb "to be" and the words "by the" indicate passive voice.

THE WRITING SECTION

The Writing Section of the TASC exam consists of a 45-minute "Extended Response" essay that assesses your writing skills. This test builds on the skills required in the English and reading tests by allowing you to demonstrate practical knowledge of the conventions of standard written English. You will be asked to read a pair of passages and write an argumentative essay that develops your perspective about the issue.

You will be assessed on your ability to clearly state a main idea, provide specific examples and details to back up your main idea, and follow the conventions of standard English. You will not be allowed to outside resources, such as a dictionary, but you may use plain scratch paper (provided at the testing center) to plan your essay and write your rough draft(s).

How to Write an Argumentative Essay

The purpose of the TASC extended response essay is to analyze the arguments that are presented in the stimulus text and explain why one of these arguments is better. It is not an opinion essay; therefore, your own opinion about the subject matter is not relevant.

A successful argumentative essay should:

- Clearly state the issue and your position on it in the introduction
- Use language appropriate to the audience you are addressing
- Support your position with facts, statistics, and reasons from the stimulus texts
- Show clear reasoning
- Conclude with a summary of your main points and state your claim

An argumentative essay follows the traditional paragraph structure that includes an introductory paragraph, body paragraphs, and a concluding paragraph. Your essay should be between 4 to 7 paragraphs long. Aim for 3 to 7 sentences in each paragraph, with 300-500 words in total.

The Introductory Paragraph:

The goal of your **introductory paragraph** is to introduce your topic. The introduction should contain a strong opening sentence that states your claim or thesis statement. In this exercise, you will be analyzing two stimulus texts that contain opposing viewpoints about a topic and determining which argument is stronger. Your position statement should be clear and direct so the reader understands what you are trying to accomplish with your essay.

The Body Paragraphs:

The **body paragraphs** are where you will develop your position about your subject. This is where you present reasoning and evidence to support your claim. You can state facts, examples, and explanations from the stimulus text to support your main ideas. Each body paragraph should contain one well-developed example.

Your goals for each body paragraph are to: introduce an example, describe the example, explain how the example fully supports your thesis. Use evidence from the stimulus prompt and NOT your own opinions to support your position. Be sure to use transition words at the beginning of each body paragraph to introduce your next example.

The Conclusion:

The ultimate goal of your conclusion is to summarize your main points and restate your claim. In your **concluding paragraph**, you might introduce the opposing side to your argument. Then refute their position by reinforcing the validity of your thesis. Use a strong ending sentence to emphasize the main point of your essay.

Sample Essay Prompts

Before you sit for your exam, practice writing a sample essay to become familiar with the process and comfortable with the format. Below is an essay prompt.

Try to follow the paragraph organization as outlined in this lesson. Then, once you have written your draft, review the rules of grammar and conventions of English (spelling, punctuation, capitalization) in the Reasoning Through Language Arts section of this study guide to help you fine-tune your writing. If the opportunity permits, ask a teacher, relative, or friend read your essay and offer feedback on your work.

Essay Prompt:
Is Curling a Sport?

Curling has been around for centuries. The first recorded curling match took place in 16th century Scotland, as evidenced by paintings of peasants playing the game. When people immigrated to North America, they brought curling with them. In 1807, the first Canadian curling club was established in Montreal, followed by the first American club in 1828, located in Michigan. Even with its lengthy history, the debate over whether or not curling is a sport wages on the Internet, in bars, amongst sportswriters, and even in ice arenas.

Proponents say that curling meets the definition of "sport" found in the dictionary. Curling requires physical exertion, coordination, and skill; it adheres to a specific set of rules, and is recognized as a sport by athletic associations, fans, the media, and more. They point to curling's inclusion in the Olympics, starting with the 1924 Winter Olympics in Chamonix, France, as further evidence of its qualification as a sport.

Opponents say that curling should be considered a "game" and not a "sport." They argue that curling does not require rigorous physical activity and can be played professionally by people who are generally non-athletic or overweight. They argue that curling is a game or leisure activity.

Pro Arguments

According to fitness tracking programs, participating in curling burns 272 calories. This is approximately the same amount of calories per hour as bowling or practicing yoga. While this is not as much as gymnasts, who burn 345 calories per hour, the standard curling competition includes eight 15-minute long matches that are completed in about two hours.

Curling matches adhere to a set of rules that is governed by the World Curling Federation. There are specific guidelines for equipment, such as the stones, brooms, and specialized footwear. Each of the four players on a curling team has a specific role to play. The "lead" player sets up the match by throwing the first two stones. The "second" playing throws the next two stones. The third player is called the "vice skip." This is the player who holds the broom. And lastly, the "skip" is the captain and chief strategist of the team.

Con Arguments

Unlike a sport, curling does not require rigorous physical activity. Burning 272 calories per hour while curling is much less than the number of calories burned per hour in competitive sports. Soccer players burn 900/hour while football, basketball players burn 727 calories/hour. Professional curlers are sometimes overweight, old, or out of shape. There is no running, jumping, or cardiovascular activity in curling.

Sports experts agree that curling lacks the athletic rigor needed to be a real sport. Curling was ranked 56 out of 60 activities by a panel of sports scientists, athletes, and journalists assembled by ESPN. They ranked the athletic difficulty of 60 activities based on ten categories such as endurance, agility, and strength.

Prompt

In your response, analyze both positions presented in the article to determine which one is best supported. Use relevant and specific evidence from the article to support your response.

You should expect to spend up to 45 minutes for planning, drafting, and editing your response.

SECTION IV. SOCIAL STUDIES

CHAPTER 9 CIVICS AND GOVERNMENT

TYPES OF GOVERNMENTS

Introduction

Countries around the world have different types of government. Some countries change their type of government over time.

All types of governments determine who holds power and usually have one of three approaches: one person, a few people, or many people hold the power.

Section 1: The American Constitutional Democracy

A government chosen by the people is called a democracy. A **direct democracy** is a type of government in which citizens vote directly, not through representatives, on government decisions. New England town meetings are current examples of direct democracy in the United States. In this type of gathering, all members of a community come together to make decisions for the group. In contrast, in a representative democracy, citizens vote for representatives who then vote on proposed laws and policies. A **representative democracy** is a type of government in which citizens elect representatives to make decisions about laws. The U.S. Congress is the legislative branch of the United States, which is a representative democracy. In addition, the United States is a **constitutional democracy**. In a constitutional democracy, a document called a **constitution** establishes the organization of government and describes powers of each of the branches.

The U.S. Constitution is the basis of U.S. law and government and is considered the supreme law of the United States. The Constitution is made up of seven articles that describe how the power of the government is distributed:

- Article I describes the power of the legislative branch, made up of Congress (the Senate and the House of Representatives).
- Article II describes the power of the executive branch, made up of the president and advisers.
- Article III describes the power of the judicial branch, made up of the Supreme Court and lower federal courts.
- Article IV describes the responsibilities of each state along with what each state can expect from the federal government.
- Article V describes how the Constitution can be amended, or changed.
- Article VI says that the country must respect its debts and also states that the Constitution is the highest law of the land.
- Article VII describes the process for **ratifying** the Constitution.

The Constitution both gives power to the government and efficiently limits that power to protect the basic rights of American citizens. To accomplish this, concepts such as separation of powers, checks and balances, and federalism are written in the Constitution.

Separation of powers is the idea of splitting the power of the federal government into separate branches—legislative, executive, and judicial—so that no one branch can abuse its power.

Checks and balances is the idea that each branch monitors the actions of the others. The Supreme Court interprets the law. The president can veto a law, but if Congress has enough votes, it can override a presidential veto. Rules like these keep government officials in check.

Federalism is the idea that the power of a country should be divided between the central federal government and smaller units, for example, states.

Section 2: Origins of America's Constitutional Democracy

In the 1600s, British people moved to North America to build new lives. These people, called colonists, settled parts of North America for England and remained under the rule of King George III, the king of England.

The colonists eventually thought they should be able to govern themselves. One of the colonists' grievances was that Great Britain would send troops to the colonies, and colonists were responsible for paying to house and feed them. Another thing that angered colonists was a series of taxes they felt were unfair. They also believed they had no voice in the government. The colonists first resisted these taxes with boycotts and protests. Colonists told members of the British government and King George III their grievances, but the British government ignored them.

The **Articles of Confederation** was the United States' first constitution. It was a written document that described the powers of the central government as the colonists fought for their independence from Britain. The Articles called for a confederation of sovereign states that were loosely connected by a weak central government. The federal government was made up delegates from each state. There was no president. The states were hesitant to give a lot of power to a central government because they were rebelling against a government that they felt had abused its power. The Articles of Confederation outlined how states would vote and how they would pay taxes. Some people, such as Benjamin Franklin, suggested the Framers would need to revisit the document in the future.

Several years after the adoption of the Articles of Confederation, representatives from all states except Rhode Island met in Philadelphia to revise the Articles. The meeting became known as the Constitutional Convention. Instead of revising the document, the Founders replaced it with the U.S. Constitution.

One aim of the new document was to give the federal government enough power to operate without infringing on any rights of the people. The Constitution included a structure for the three branches of government, including the responsibilities of the branches. This new document added a chief executive, known as the president. Thus, America became a **presidential democracy**, a type of government in which citizens elect a president to serve as head of state and chief executive.

Section 3: Other Types of Governments

Not all countries are democracies. Other types of governments include the following:

- Monarchy

  - Absolute monarchy
  - Constitutional monarchy
- Parliamentary democracy
- Oligarchy
- Dictatorship

Great Britain's government is a constitutional **monarchy**. In a monarchy, leadership is passed down through family lines. Many countries, such as Monaco, Qatar, and Spain, have monarchies. In an **absolute monarchy**, like Saudi Arabia, the monarchy holds all the power of government. Great Britain, like most modern monarchies, is a constitutional monarchy. In a **constitutional monarchy**, the monarch's power is limited according to the rules of the country's constitution.

In a constitutional monarchy, the monarch serves as a head of state, or the chief public representative of a country, but much of the governing is done by **parliament**. A parliament is a type of legislature, similar to Congress in the United States. In a **parliamentary democracy**, people vote for the legislative body that, in turn, selects the chief leader of parliament. The leader of parliament also holds executive power of the government. The chief executive is often called a **prime minister**. The political party that holds the majority in parliament elects the prime minister. The prime minister is the head of the government and the leader of the political party that has the most seats in parliament. A presidential democracy is different from a parliamentary democracy because the president does not necessarily belong to the majority party in Congress.

An **oligarchy** is a political system in which power is held by a small group of people, usually the nobility, military, or wealthy citizens. Examples of oligarchies are Russia and China.

In a **dictatorship**, a single person takes authority and shares power with no one. Leaders are not elected. North Korea is ruled by a dictator. Benito Mussolini in Italy and Adolf Hitler in Germany were dictators before and during World War II.

Let's Review!

- The United States is a constitutional democracy and a representative democracy.
- The U.S. Constitution is the basis of American government and law and incorporates many of the country's founding principles, such as separation of powers, checks and balances, and federalism.
- Colonists in what is now the United States revolted against British rule because they felt they were not represented in the government.
- Delegates from the newly formed United States first wrote the Articles of Confederation as their constitution and later replaced it with the U.S. Constitution.
- Democracy is not the only type of government. Other types include oligarchies, monarchies, and dictatorships.

PRINCIPLES OF AMERICAN CONSTITUTIONAL DEMOCRACY

Introduction

The Founders who shaped the U.S. government drew many of their ideas from popular European philosophers of the 1600s and 1700s. The Founders used the newest ideas about successful governments when they wrote the U.S. Constitution. This lesson introduces the most important ideas in the U.S. Constitution.

Section 1: The Founding Principles

One of the central ideas of the American constitutional democracy is **natural rights**. A philosopher named John Locke introduced the idea that human beings had certain rights, such as the rights to life, liberty, and property, that could not be violated by any other person or law. According to Locke, the job of government is to protect citizens' natural rights.

The idea of natural rights was so important to the Founders that they made reference to the principle in the **Declaration of Independence**. In the Declaration of Independence, Thomas Jefferson wrote that all people "are endowed by their Creator with certain unalienable Rights, that among these are Life, Liberty and the pursuit of Happiness." These rights are protected by the first 10 amendments to the Constitution, known as the Bill of Rights.

Another philosophy that is foundational to the American government is the **rule of law**—it is the concept on which the American legal system was founded. Under the rule of law, in the United States a the government can only punish a person if that person is proven to have broken a law. The rule of law applies to both citizens and government officials.

Much like natural rights, the Founders alluded to the concept of rule of law in the Declaration of Independence in several of the entries on a list of grievances aimed toward Great Britain. They accused King George III of "depriving us in many cases, of the benefit of trial by jury" and of protecting armed troops "from punishment for any murders which they should commit on the Inhabitants of these States."

The principle of rule of law states that all persons, institutions, and entities are accountable to laws that are

- publicly promoted;
- equally enforced;
- independently adjudicated; and
- consistent with international human rights principles.

John Adams said of the rule of law that America would "be a government of laws, not men." In other words, all people are subject to the laws written in the Constitution, not the whims of people in charge. The Founders ensured the sanctity of the rule of law in Article VI of the Constitution, which states that the Constitution is the "supreme law of the land." All laws and enforcers of the law are subject to the rules in the Constitution.

Courts are largely responsible for enforcing the rule of law by interpreting the Constitution. Sometimes, the job of judges is to protect the rights of people who hold minority beliefs from being violated by those in the majority. Preserving those minority rights through the rule of law is a fundamental part of the American system.

Another founding principle of the American Constitution is **consent of the governed**. During the birth of the United States, many philosophers wrote about what qualified as good government. One idea was that the power of the government comes from people's willingness to give up some of their natural freedom to enjoy the benefits and protections of living under a government.

The American Revolution took place because American colonists grew tired of being ruled by a government in which they felt they had no voice. The Declaration of Independence alludes to the concept of "consent of the governed" when it states that "to secure these [natural] rights, Governments are instituted among Men, deriving their just powers from the consent of the governed."

Popular sovereignty, the belief that government is created by and subject to the will of the people, is another central principle of the U.S. Constitution. This means that a government has power because the citizens allow it to have power, and the people hold the ultimate power. Government answers to the people. If the people want to change their government, they can vote to change laws or elect new leaders.

This concept is stated in the Declaration of Independence: "Whenever any Form of Government becomes destructive of these ends, it is the Right of the People to alter or to abolish it, and to institute new Government." Popular sovereignty also guides the Constitution. Article V states that the people can change the constitution by amending it. The Ninth Amendment states that any power not specifically given to government belongs to the people. Even the Preamble to the Constitution notes who is putting forth the ideas it expresses: "We the People of the United States . . ."

Section 2: Constitutionalism, Separation of Powers, and Checks and Balances

The Founders crafted the Constitution to serve as an instructional manual for the organization of the new country's government. The people who served in the government would be limited by the powers outlined in the Constitution. The idea that government officials' power over citizens should be limited as outlined in an official document is known as **constitutionalism**.

The U.S. Constitution gives power to the government but also limits that power so that it cannot be abused. Power must be limited because the most important thing that must be protected is people's natural rights. Limited government protects government officials from violating citizens' natural rights.

The American government is structured to limit the power of each branch of government. The **separation of powers** refers to the provision in the Constitution that power is separated into three branches of government:

- The legislative branch makes laws.
- The executive branch enforces the laws.
- The judicial branch interprets the laws.

The purpose of separating the powers of the three branches is to ensure no one branch of the government assumes powers different from those set forth in the Constitution. **Check and balances** is the process by which this takes place. An example of checks and balances is how the Supreme Court (the judicial branch) has authority to declare legislation by Congress (the legislative branch) or acts by the president (the executive branch) unconstitutional. Another example is how Congress can impeach a president or a presidentially appointed judge. Finally, the president can veto legislation from Congress and nominate judges to the Supreme Court.

Section 3: Other Principles of Limited Government

Majority rule is the idea that when a decision needs to be made, the result will be the one with which more than half of voters agree. If there are more than two options and a majority vote is not necessary, the U.S. government sides with the plurality, or the option that gets the most votes. The purpose of majority rule is to ensure that the citizens of the United States, who hold the ultimate power, are consulted on issues that affect them.

This principle applies when Americans elect the candidate in an election who earned the most votes or, in the case of a presidential election, the greatest number of Electoral College votes. On the basis of majority rule, all citizens accept election results.

However, the Founders also took into consideration **minority rights**, the idea that people with views that go against the majority may express those ideas without fear. The Bill of Rights was created to protect certain minority rights. A majority cannot interfere with someone's religious beliefs because every citizen has freedom of religion. A person with beliefs different from those of the majority cannot be silenced because every citizen has freedom of speech. The balance of majority rule and minority rights allows citizens the freedom to discuss ideas without punishment. A majority could abuse the rights of a minority, but the principle of minority rights prevents this.

Individual rights are spelled out in the first 10 amendments to the Constitution, known as the Bill of Rights. These rights allow Americans certain freedoms with which the government may not interfere, such as freedom of speech and freedom of religion.

Another important principle of limited government is **federalism**. The principle of federalism states that the power of a country should be divided between the central federal government and smaller units, for example, states. The American divides power between the federal government and the state governments. This was a matter of contention when drafting the Constitution. Federalists argued for a stronger central government, while Anti-Federalists argued for a weaker federal government. Their compromises resulted in the U.S. Constitution. The federal government is in control of issues that affect the entire nation, such as foreign trade and international wars. State governments are responsible for local issues and any responsibilities not explicitly given to the federal government in the Constitution.

The Framers also crafted the **necessary and proper clause**, sometimes called the **elastic clause**, in Article I, Section 8, giving Congress the power to "make all laws which shall be necessary" to running the federal government. This means that Congress can suggest new federal laws that may be in addition to the enumerated powers, and the Supreme Court can decide if the laws are Constitutional.

Let's Review!

- The United States was founded on principles that are embedded in the U.S. Constitution, such as natural rights, rule of law, consent of the governed, and popular sovereignty.
- The U.S. Constitution incorporates the ideas of its founding principles, such as separation of powers, checks and balances, and constitutionalism.
- The principles on which America was founded protect the rights of all people, even those who hold views that are different from those of the majority. In America, all citizens get to voice their opinion.

THE STRUCTURE OF THE UNITED STATES GOVERNMENT

Section 1: Structure and Authority of the Federal Government

The concept of **separation of powers**, or splitting the federal government into three distinct branches that monitor one another, is the foundation of U.S. government. The Framers included this structure in the Constitution to limit the power of each branch. Distributing power among three branches prevents any one branch from abusing it.

The U.S. Constitution creates three branches of federal government, each with distinct powers:

- The legislative branch makes the laws.
- The executive branch enforces the laws.
- The judicial branch interprets the laws.

Limiting the powers of each branch creates a system of **checks and balances**. Each branch checks the others, and powers are balanced among the branches. The three-branch government structure was introduced by the French philosopher Montesquieu in the 1700s. He believed this system of government would promote freedom and prevent people who had power from abusing it.

Section 2: Powers of the Federal Government, Government Positions

The following charts show the composition and explain the responsibilities of each branch of the federal government.

Legislative Branch	
The legislative branch (Congress) is made up of two houses: • The U.S. Senate • The House of Representatives	
The House of Representatives is often called the Lower House.	The U.S. Senate is often called the Upper House.
Representatives in the House serve two-year terms.	Senators serve six-year terms
Representatives are elected by districts in their state, each of which includes an equal number of voters. Every 10 years, the United States holds a census and the districts are redrawn.	Senators serve six-year terms. Every two years, one-third of the senators are elected. They are elected by all voters throughout the state.

The number of representatives is based on the population of each state. States with larger populations have more representatives in the House than states with smaller populations.	Each state elects two senators regardless of its population.
Positions in the Legislative Branch	
Speaker of the House	The presiding officer of the House of Representatives. The Speaker of the House has always been a member of the party that holds a majority of seats in the House of Representatives.
President of the Senate	The vice president of the United States presides over the Senate.
Representative	An elected member of the House of Representatives
Senator	An elected member of the U.S. Senate

Powers of the Legislative Branch

Article I of the Constitution outlines the powers of Congress. Each power that is listed is referred to as an **enumerated power**. Most powers are assigned to both houses, but some are given to the House of Representatives or Senate only.

The following are powers of the legislative branch:

- Veto other house's bills
- Approve presidential nominations (Senate only)
- Control the budget
- Impeach the president (House only)
- Impeach judges (House only)
- Make laws
- Tax citizens
- Regulate commerce and currency
- Introduce bills
- Declare war
- Maintain the army and navy
- Admit new states into the Union
- Approve treaties (Senate only)

The **elastic clause** in the Constitution allows Congress to make laws that are necessary for the country. This clause gives Congress more power than that listed in the enumerated powers.

Judicial Branch
The judicial branch has several levels:
• Supreme Court • Appeal courts • District courts • Other special courts

The Supreme Court, the highest court in the land, is made up judges called justices who are appointed by the president and confirmed by the Senate. They serve during good behavior, which is usually for life. Their job is to decide whether laws adhere to the rules laid out in the Constitution. Decisions are made when a majority of justices agree. When the Supreme Court interprets a law, lower courts must follow the interpretation.	
District courts are the trial courts in the federal system.	
Courts of appeals review appeals from the trial courts.	

Positions in the Judicial Branch	
Chief Justice	Leader and spokesperson of the Supreme Court justices
	Administers the Oath of Office at inaugurations
	Presides over Impeachment hearings
Associate Justices	Supreme Court justices who are not the Chief Justice

Powers of the Judicial Branch

The Supreme Court has the following powers:

- Ruling on cases involving laws that may violate the Constitution
- Declaring a president's actions unconstitutional
- Declaring laws that Congressed has passed unconstitutional
- Determining whether laws are constitutional through judicial review

Executive Branch
The following are positions in the executive branch: - President - Vice president - Cabinet - Government agencies
The president is the chief executive of the federal government, and there are several people whose role is to brief, or advise, the president on a variety of subjects. These people are known as the president's cabinet.
The vice president and the heads of the 15 executive departments are members of the cabinet.

Positions in the Executive Branch	
President of the United States	Chief executive of the federal government
	Elected for a four-year term and can serve no more than two terms.
	Must be at least 35 years old
	Must be a natural-born U.S. citizen
	Must have lived in the United States for at least 14 years

Vice President of the United States	Assumes presidency if president cannot fulfill the duties of office
	Must be prepared to take over the presidency at a moment's notice
	Serves as president of the U.S. Senate
	Votes in the U.S. Senate in the event of a tie
Executive Department Heads	Appointed by the president, confirmed by the Senate Title is usually Secretary, except for the Attorney General who runs the Justice Department
	Departments include agriculture, commerce, defense, education, energy, health and human services, homeland security, housing and urban development, interior, labor, state, transportation, treasury, and veterans affairs Department heads run agencies and advise the president in their areas of expertise.
White House Staff	People who work closely with the president and other officials in the White House are considered part of the executive branch.

Powers of the Executive Branch

The following are powers and responsibilities of the president:

- Nominates judges to courts in judicial branch
- Serves as commander in chief of armed forces
- Nominates executive officers and secretaries
- Enforces Congress's laws
- Can veto bills sent by Congress
- Signs treaties with other countries (treaties must be ratified by two-thirds of Senate).
- Gives an address to a joint session of Congress in January regarding the state of the union

Section 3: The Powers and Responsibilities of State Governments

The U.S. Constitution outlines the separation of powers between the state and federal governments. This division of power is called **federalism**. The Tenth Amendment states that the powers not delegated to the federal government by the U.S. Constitution belong to the states. In other words, any power that is not explicitly given to the federal government belongs to the states. Both federal and state governments constantly strive to adapt to new challenges and preserve the balance of power.

Some responsibilities belong only to the federal government or only to state governments. **Exclusive powers** are those that belong to *either* state *or* federal government. **Concurrent powers**, also called **shared powers**, are shared by the state and federal governments. An exclusive federal power is creating U.S. currency. An exclusive state power is conducting local elections. A concurrent power is the power to tax citizens.

In a federal republic, citizens have multiple layers of government. Each citizen must follow town, city, state, and national laws. Most Americans interact with state and local government more than with federal government. The Framers of the constitution imagined the state governments doing most of the work of governing, with federal government officials intervening only when necessary. Early in the nation's history, the distribution of powers between the U.S. federal government and the states was less complicated than it is now.

At times, state governments need help from the federal government. During national crises, the federal government provides aid to states. This help comes with a promise from the state to follow certain federal regulations. The federal government has tax money to give out to states, but only if the states agree to spend the money in a way the federal government approves.

Each state has its own constitution. State governments are split into three branches because they are modeled after the federal government. The executive branch is headed by the governor. The legislative branch is made up of elected officials who manage the state budget and create state laws. The judicial system hears all of the court cases that do not require a federal court. Each state's judicial system makes and interprets its own state laws. This is why laws can vary from state to state.

The following are some of the exclusive responsibilities of states:

- Licensing drivers
- Educating state citizens
- Providing aid benefits such as welfare
- Establishing local governments
- Conducting local and state elections
- Building and maintaining roads and other local infrastructure
- Amending the state constitution

Powers shared between federal and state governments include the following:

- Making laws
- Enforcing laws
- Taxing citizens
- Establishing courts

The following are some exclusive powers of the federal government:

- Declaring war
- Creating money

- Maintaining the U.S. Postal System
- Dealing with foreign entities
- Establishing naturalization rules

Section 4: Governmental Departments and Agencies

There are several small government agencies tasked with oversight and improvement in specific areas. Some examples are the Occupational Safety and Health Administration (OSHA) and the Bureau of Land Management.

There are 15 executive departments led by secretaries appointed by the president and approved by the Senate. Each has a responsibility for overseeing how an aspect of the country functions.

Executive Department	Responsibility
Department of Agriculture	Provides direction of food, agriculture, farming, and natural resources
Department of Commerce	Works with businesses and workers on job creation, economic growth, development, and improving standards of living
Department of Defense	Provides military forces needed to deter war and protect the safety of the United States
Department of Education	Ensures equal access to education for all citizens
Department of Energy	Manages the country's nuclear infrastructure, energy policies, and scientific research
Department of Health and Human Services	Protects the health of Americans by providing education and services
Department of Homeland Security	Protects the security of the United States, including borders, customs, and immigration, disasters, antiterrorism, and cybersecurity
Department of Housing and Urban Development	Maintains programs that provide housing and community development, works to ensure fair and equal housing opportunities for all citizens
Department of Justice	Enforces federal laws, oversees punishment for the guilty, ensures impartial administration of justice
Department of Labor	Makes federal labor laws to ensure workers' rights
Department of State	Advises the president and takes care of foreign policy issues, negotiates with foreign entities, represents the United States at the United Nations
Department of the Interior	Manages public lands and upholds the nation's responsibilities to Native Americans and Native Alaskans, also responsible for environmental conservation

Executive Department	Responsibility
Department of the Treasury	Manages federal finances by collecting taxes, paying bills, managing currency, enforces finance and tax laws
Department of Transportation	Plans and coordinates federal transportation, sets safety regulations for modes of transportation
Department of Veterans Affairs	Runs programs that benefit veterans and their families

Let's Review!

- The structure of the U.S. government relies on the concept of separation of powers.
- Each branch of the government has authority and powers outlined in the U.S. Constitution.
- State governments have powers and responsibilities distinct from those of federal government. State governments also share some powers with federal government.
- The cabinet includes the leaders of each of 15 executive departments that provide government services to citizens.
- There are several other organizations, called agencies, working to improve the lives of American citizens.

Individual Rights and Civic Responsibilities

Section 1: Amendment Process

Article IV of the Constitution states that the Constitution can be changed. The Founders knew that the government would need to adapt and change the Constitution as time went on. A change made to the U.S. Constitution is called an **amendment**. Each amendment is given a number. There are currently 27 amendments to the U.S. Constitution.

The Constitution outlines an **amendment process** for ratifying an amendment. Either Congress or a group of state legislatures can propose an amendment if it meets certain requirements (agreement by two-thirds of representatives in both the House and Senate or two-thirds of state legislatures).

Next, the amendment is presented to the states as a joint resolution, an agreement passed by both the Senate and the House of Representatives. The proposal needs to go through each state's legislature for approval. When three-fourths of state legislatures approve an amendment, it is ratified, or becomes law. To **ratify** means to officially approve.

Section 2: The Bill of Rights

The **Bill of Rights** is another name for the first 10 amendments to the U.S. Constitution. James Madison wrote the amendments because several states argued that the U.S. Constitution should include stronger protection for citizens' individual rights. **Individual rights** are the freedoms granted to every individual.

One of the main disagreements between the Federalists, those who wanted a strong central government, and the Anti-Federalists, those who favored a weaker central government, was that the Anti-Federalists wanted a Bill of Rights added to the Constitution to protect people's individual rights. Federalists believed that the Constitution provided sufficient protection for individual liberties, but Anti-Federalists insisted that the Bill of Rights was necessary.

The Bill of Rights was based on several similar documents written at the time of its creation. The rights protected by the Bill of Rights are collectively known as **civil liberties**.

- The First Amendment protects the following rights:
    - Freedom of religion
    - Freedom of speech
    - Freedom of the press
    - Freedom of assembly
    - Right to petition the government regarding grievances
- The Second Amendment gives citizens the right to bear arms.

- The Third Amendment prohibits the government from quartering troops in private homes.

  - One of the biggest complaints of colonists prior to the Revolutionary War was that colonists had to bear the cost of quartering, or housing, British troops. If the British government ran out of room to house soldiers, the troops stayed in the homes of the colonists. The Third Amendment forbids this practice.
- The Fourth Amendment protects citizens from unreasonable searches and seizures.
- The Fifth Amendment protects citizens from criminal prosecution and punishment without due process of law. Due process means that all legal proceedings must follow the rule of law. The rule of law ensures fairness: laws must be well defined and established, and the people who enforce the laws must follow them strictly.
- The Sixth Amendment assures the right to a speedy trial by a jury of peers and the right to an attorney for criminal defendants who are **indigent**. *Indigent* means that a person does not have the funds to pay an attorney.
- The Seventh Amendment provides for trial by jury in civil cases.
- The Eighth Amendment protects citizens from cruel and unusual punishment.
- The Ninth Amendment ensures that all rights not enumerated, or explicitly mentioned, in the Constitution belong to the people.
- The Tenth Amendment assigns all powers not delegated to the federal or state government to either the states or the people.

Section 4: Civil Liberties and Civic Responsibilities

The rights that the Constitution and the Bill of Rights grant U.S. citizens are known as **civil liberties** or **personal freedoms**. Civil liberties are protections against government actions. For example, people can practice their religion without government interference.

There are certain expectations of U.S. citizens known as **civic responsibilities**. The word *responsibility* can also mean **duty**. When every person keeps up with each of these responsibilities, the democratic system functions well. Civic responsibilities/duties include the following:

- Supporting and defending the Constitution
- Voting
- Staying educated on current issues
- Respecting the rights, beliefs, and opinions of others
- Paying taxes
- Serving as a witness in court
- Performing jury duty
- Obeying laws
- Serving on government boards and committees

Let's Review!

- The Constitution includes a process for implementing changes to it called the amendment process.
- The first 10 amendments to the Constitution are known as the Bill of Rights, and they describe citizens' personal freedoms that the government cannot violate.
- U.S. citizens have civic responsibilities to participate in the democratic process.

Political Parties, Campaigns, and Elections in American Politics

Section 1: Political Parties and Interest Groups

Political parties are groups of people with aligned beliefs who seek power in the government. The function of a political party is to organize people who have similar ideologies to elect like-minded candidates to influence the government's choices. Political parties stand behind candidates who are running for office.

Political parties were not part of the original U.S. government. During the American Revolution, colonists resisted the formation of political parties. There were no political parties when George Washington, the first American president, took office. Washington strongly opposed political parties. In his farewell address as president, he warned against "the baneful effect of the spirit of the party." He cautioned that political parties would attempt to change the government for their own gain, not for the good of the people.

The first political parties in the United States were based on ideas about how much power the federal government should have. As the Framers crafted the U.S. Constitution and discussed how the powers of the government should be separated, citizens who felt strongly about this issue formed factions.

In 1787, the Federalist Party formed, led by Alexander Hamilton, the Secretary of the Treasury at the time. The Federalists argued for a strong central government and supported the U.S. Constitution. The people in this group tended to favor business and industry. Years later, Thomas Jefferson, Secretary of State, led a group of Anti-Federalists, who argued for states holding more power than the central government. They wanted the federal government to have as little power as possible. They called themselves Democratic-Republicans. The people in this group tended to earn money through agriculture.

Today, the two most powerful political parties are the Republicans (also known as the GOP) and the Democrats. The core beliefs of each party are important to their identities. Democrats are generally more liberal, or progressive, and support an active government. Democrats argue for laws that protect the middle class and minorities and the federal programs that help them. Two of the most well-known presidents from the modern Democratic Party are Franklin D. Roosevelt and John F. Kennedy. Republicans are generally considered more conservative and seek a limited federal government. They favor laws that protect business owners and tend to support the idea that the government should not be responsible for solving social problems. Two of the most well-known presidents from the modern Republican Party are Dwight D. Eisenhower and Ronald Reagan.

There are smaller minor parties, but it is difficult for their candidates to win national elections. For that reason, they are sometimes called third parties. The Libertarian Party is a third party that argues for very little government intervention in citizens' lives. The Green Party promotes environmentalism and social justice. There have been many third parties in America's history. President Theodore Roosevelt formed the Progressive Party, also known as the Bull Moose Party, because he was considered "strong as a bull moose" at the time.

Interest groups are groups that attempt to change public policy because of a shared concern on a particular issue. This may be a problem they want fixed or a cause they think does not get enough attention. They seek to change government policy to solve the problem. Interest groups usually do not have their own political candidates. Instead, they spread their message through the media and by working with candidates and elected officials.

Lobbyists are people who aim to persuade public officials, usually legislators in Congress, to vote a certain way. Often, lobbyists are paid to push the agendas of businesses, industries, and interest groups so that laws can be changed to work in their favor. Some citizens and policymakers believe that lobbyists have too much power over government because they can draw more attention to their causes than individual citizens. Both individuals and lobbyists can appeal to the government in various ways—by writing letters, protesting, and speaking to politicians about their wants.

Section 2: Campaigns, Elections, and the Electoral Process

An **election** is an organized process of choosing a person to lead others. National elections take place every two years, on the first Tuesday after the first Monday in November in even-numbered years. In **national elections**, Americans vote for the people who will serve in the federal government, including legislators and the president. Presidential elections are held every four years. Each state runs its own **state elections**, and some states require that people reside in a state for a certain amount of time before they can vote there. Within states, there are **local elections** for cities and towns for positions such as mayor.

On voting day, eligible voters go to their polling place where they cast a ballot. If people are unable to get to a **polling place**, they may vote by absentee ballot. In some elections, voters may cast their votes early at polling places. All of the votes are counted, and the results are announced. Voting is private. No one has to tell whom he or she voted for.

American citizens must meet certain qualifications to vote. Voters must be citizens of the United States and be at least 18 years of age. Citizens are not required to pay a tax to vote; however, they do need to register. To register, people fill out a form with their address and other basic information.

Leading up to the presidential election, parties hold **primary elections** to determine who will run for their party. In a primary election, candidates from a party run against one another to become the party's candidate in a **general election**, the election where voters determine which party's candidate will take office. When candidates seek election, they run a **political campaign**.

For a period of time leading up to the election, the candidates explain their principles and try to win people's votes.

In political campaigns, candidates tend to explain what problems they see and offer their ideas for solutions. Candidates try to reach voters in several ways. They pay for advertisements on radio, television, billboards, direct mail, and the Internet. They call people's homes, email voters, and participate in social media feeds. Candidates for office may debate each other on their ideas or attend **town hall meetings**, where they speak directly to voters about their ideas. People who believe strongly in a candidate can join the campaign, spreading the candidate's message to other voters.

The **electoral process** is the method by which the president is elected. Voters are called the **electorate**. Every American citizen can cast a ballot for a candidate for president, but the voters do not elect the president. The **popular vote** is the term for the people's voting choice—that is, the candidate who receives the most votes wins the popular vote. However, the president is elected by the Electoral College, which is made up of representatives from each state who are selected to vote for the candidate who won the popular vote in that state. The **electoral vote** is the choice made by the **electors**, the members of the Electoral College.

The Electoral College is described in Article II, Section 1 of the U.S. Constitution. Some of the Framers of the Constitution feared that some political parties and groups could become so powerful that they could become tyrannical in their ability to dominate elections. Their intention in creating the Electoral College was to allow the American electorate to vote for the president but allowing knowledgeable electors to cast the final decision.

In the **Electoral College**, each state has a certain number of electors that is equal to the state's number of senators and representatives in Congress. To become president of the United States, a candidate must earn at least half of the electoral votes. Because of the Electoral College, the person who receives the majority of the popular votes for president is not always elected president. This has happened several times.

Year	Popular Vote Winner	Electoral College Winner
1876	Samuel J. Tilden	Rutherford B. Hayes
1888	Grover Cleveland	Benjamin Harrison
2000	Al Gore	George W. Bush
2016	Hillary Clinton	Donald Trump

Section 3: Contemporary Public Policy

Choices a government makes regarding current issues are known as its **contemporary public policy**.

Government officials enact public policy by passing new laws, creating new agencies, and allocating more funds to address issues that are important to them. Politicians create policy to respond to problems that need attention.

The following are some of the most significant areas of public policy:

- Health – how to take care of the health and medical needs of citizens
- Criminal justice – how to deliver justice to those charged with crimes
- Education – how to educate people of various ages
- Environment – how to preserve natural resources and take care of air and water
- Foreign affairs – how to interact with other countries

The executive branch of government is responsible for implementing the public policy that the legislative branch enacts and funds. An example of public policy is gun control.

Let's Review!

- Political parties and interest groups are groups of citizens who seek to effect change in the government.
- Candidates for government offices run campaigns, hoping to be chosen through the electoral process.
- Contemporary public policy consists of all the actions the government takes to solve current problems.

Chapter 9 Civics and Government Practice Quiz

1. Which BEST describes the government of the United States?

   A. Direct democracy

   B. Monarch democracy

   C. Parliamentary democracy

   D. Constitutional democracy

2. What is often called the supreme law of the United States?

   A. The U.S. Constitution

   B. Separation of Powers

   C. Checks and Balances

   D. The U.S. Supreme Court

3. From whom did the Founders get ideas for the U.S. Constitution?

   A. Citizens of Europe

   B. The monarchy of Great Britain

   C. The president of the United States

   D. Philosophers of the 1600s and 1700s

4. Which of the following principles does the following quote address?

   "We hold these truths to be self-evident, that all men are created equal, that they are endowed by their Creator with certain unalienable Rights, that among these are Life, Liberty and the pursuit of Happiness."

   A. Rule of law

   B. Federalism

   C. Natural rights

   D. Popular sovereignty

5. Which of the following BEST defines separation of powers?

   A. Giving all government officials the same powers

   B. Having one person in government distribute powers

   C. Splitting the federal government into three branches

   D. Dividing government between state and local governments

6. Why did the Framers of the Constitution want separation of powers explained in the Constitution?

   A. To show the Constitution was necessary

   B. To limit the power of each of the branches

   C. To protect citizens who have been accused of crimes

   D. To prove they had invented the concept of separation of powers

7. A change made to the Constitution is called a(n) _____.

   A. bill

   B. amendment

   C. individual right

   D. personal freedom

8. The steps for making a change to the Constitution are known as the _____.

   A. Bill of Rights

   B. civil liberties

   C. civic responsibilities

   D. amendment process

9. Which BEST defines political parties?

   A. Citizens who work during elections

   B. Politicians who help one another run for office

   C. People with similar beliefs who support political candidates

   D. that have a common interest but do not support candidates

10. Which issue led to the formation of the first political parties?

    A. How the states should be divided

    B. How the country should write the Constitution

    C. How much power should stay with Great Britain

    D. How much power should be given to the federal government

CHAPTER 9 CIVICS AND GOVERNMENT PRACTICE QUIZ – ANSWER KEY

1. D. The United States is a constitutional democracy. People agree to allow the government to have power as long as the government officials abide by the rules laid out in the Constitution. **See Lesson: Types of Governments.**

2. A. The U.S. Constitution is the basis of the law and government and is often called the supreme law of the United States. **See Lesson: Types of Governments.**

3. D. The Founders were thinkers and readers. They followed ideas about government put forth by the philosophers of their time. **See Lesson: Principles of American Constitutional Democracy.**

4. C. This quote from the Declaration of Independence refers to natural rights, the concept that by nature of being human, people have certain rights that cannot be violated. **See Lesson: Principles of American Constitutional Democracy.**

5. C. The concept of separation of powers, or splitting the federal government into three distinct branches that monitor one another, is the foundation of U.S. government. **See Lesson: The Structure of the United States Government.**

6. B. The Framers included the separation of powers in the Constitution to limit the power of each of the branches. **See Lesson: The Structure of the United States Government.**

7. B. An amendment is a change made to the U.S. Constitution. **See Lesson: Individual Rights and Civic Responsibilities.**

8. D. The Constitution outlines an amendment process for ratifying an amendment. **See Lesson: Individual Rights and Civic Responsibilities.**

9. C. Political parties are groups of people with aligned beliefs who support political candidates. **See Lesson: Political Parties, Campaigns, and Elections in American Politics.**

10. D. The first political parties in America argued over how much power should be given to the federal government. **See Lesson: Political Parties, Campaigns, and Elections in American Politics.**

CHAPTER 10 U.S. HISTORY

THE EARLIEST AMERICANS AND THE AGE OF EXPLORATION

Introduction

In this lesson, you will learn about the early history of North America, beginning with Native Americans, continuing through the Age of European Exploration, and finishing with an overview of the 13 English colonies.

Section 1: Native Americans

Archaeologists believe that the first generations of Native Americans crossed over the Bering land bridge from Asia around 12,000 BCE. As the various groups spread across the continent, they developed distinct customs, languages, and ways of life. Prior to European arrival in 1492, the population of North America was anywhere from 2 million to 18 million people.

The map shows the different cultural groups that existed in North America prior to European arrival. Some of those groups depended heavily on hunting for food. For example, the Sioux and Cheyenne tribes in the Great Plains group relied on the buffalo for subsistence. The Arctic peoples, which include the Inuit, relied on a combination of hunting and fishing to survive in an area with little plant life. Other groups relied on agriculture for food. Tribes from the Woodlands regions such as the Iroquois and the Cherokee grew maize for food, as did the Hopi and Navajo tribes in the Southwest. Despite the distances between the regions, tribes traded with one another.

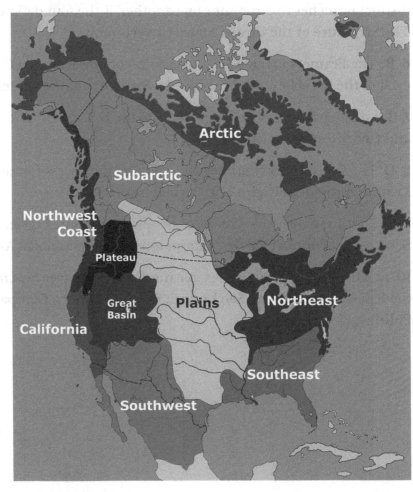

Although some Europeans claimed that Native Americans were not builders or that they were all nomadic, this is not true. As early as 3500 BCE, groups known as the Mound Builders built large earthworks with cities on top, often in elaborate shapes. The largest, Cahokia, was home to between 20,000 and 30,000 people. In the Southwest, the Anasazi built settlements into the cliff walls.

Native American tribes could be very different from one another. Some of the tribes were patriarchal, meaning that men held most of the power, but in others women had more power and influence. Some of the tribes developed complicated power systems. By the time of European arrival in North America, the Iroquois Confederacy consisted of six different tribes that managed their own affairs but came together to make decisions that would affect the whole group. Internally, many tribes were democratic and made decisions based on the will of the majority.

Did You Know?

There are 175 Native American languages still spoken in the United States today, though many of them have only a few speakers left.

Example

How did humans first enter North America?

A. Crossing over from Greenland	B. Migrating north from South America	C. Walking across the Bering land bridge	D. Traveling in boats across the Pacific Ocean

A. The first people to arrive in North America crossed over the Bering land bridge into what is now Alaska.

Section 2: The Age of Exploration

The Age of Exploration was a period between the fifteenth and seventeenth centuries when Europeans traveled all over the world. Explorers from Spain, Portugal, France, and Great Britain led expeditions down the coast of Africa, to Asia, and to the Americas.

Several reasons pushed Europeans to travel abroad. One was the pursuit of wealth—in particular, valuable or rare goods like spices, silk, and gold. India and China produced valuable goods, and explorers like Christopher Columbus traveled in part to find a shorter route to Asia. Others went to spread Christianity to non-Christians or to escape religious persecution at home. Europe was undergoing a period known as the wars of religion as Catholics and Protestants went to war against each other. Finally, competition among different countries encouraged exploration. After Spain claimed land in the Americas, England and other nations hurried to do the same.

Acting as an agent of Spain, Christopher Columbus arrived in the Caribbean in 1492 and claimed the region for Spain. Expeditions to Mexico led by Hernán Cortés conquered the Aztec

Empire and brought it under Spanish control by 1521, and the Inca Empire in Peru was taken over by Francisco Pizarro in 1532. The Spanish also launched expeditions into North America, though their only permanent settlement was in Florida, and they took centuries to expand into what is now Arizona and Colorado.

> **DID YOU KNOW?**
> Although Christopher Columbus is given credit for "discovering" North America, he wasn't even the first European to travel there. The Vikings established a small base at L'Anse aux Meadows in Newfoundland around 1000 CE.

In North America, the British founded their first permanent settlement in Virginia at Jamestown in 1607, in the hopes of finding gold. In 1620, a sect of English Christians called the Puritans settled in what is now Massachusetts at Plymouth Rock. Other colonies were established by investment companies or the English monarchy for trade and investment. France launched several expeditions to explore North America, founding Quebec City in 1608 in what is now Canada. The Dutch established a small trading post in what they called New Amsterdam, which is modern-day New York. England seized control of the city in 1664.

[Illustrative Simple: A map showing the division of North America circa 1750 or slightly before. This should reflect the British, Spanish, and French territories.]

Example

Christopher Columbus explored on behalf of which European power?

   A. England   B. France   C. Spain   D. Portugal

   C. Christopher Columbus was working on behalf of the Kingdom of Spain.

Section 3: The English Colonies

In North America, the English had the most populous colonies, though they were confined to the Atlantic coast. Neighboring New France, in what is now Canada, had just 25,000 settlers in 1720, while the English colonies had an estimated 466,000 people that same year.

The colonies did not all develop at the same time or in the same way. Many began as the creation of private companies and were later brought under the control of the British monarchy. Individuals came to the colonies for the prospect of land, to find religious freedom, or to escape poverty back in England.

While each colony was unique, they can be classified into three groups: New England, Middle, and Southern.

New England: These colonies were Massachusetts, New Hampshire, Rhode Island, and Connecticut. Settlement in New England began because of the Puritans, whose rules were very strict but who also encouraged education for all of the colonists. Although the land in this region could be difficult to farm, the fisheries nearby were rich, and the dense forests provided for good lumber that could be sold back to England. Boston became the major city of the region, and the region soon depended on trade and industry, particularly shipbuilding. Although slavery existed in the New England colonies, it became less important by the mid-eighteenth century.

Middle: These colonies were New York, New Jersey, Pennsylvania, and Delaware. Because the land was well suited to agriculture, it attracted settlers who grew foodstuffs. The Dutch influence in New York and elsewhere guaranteed religious toleration, which meant that settlers in this region came from all over Europe. The two largest cities were New York and Philadelphia.

Southern: The Southern colonies consisted of Virginia, Maryland, Georgia, and Carolina, which was later split into North and South Carolina. These regions were the most rural and underpopulated, which was part of the reason that English planters encouraged the African slave trade as a way to keep a steady labor pool. The economy in these colonies was based on the cultivation of tobacco, indigo, and rice, which were labor-intensive crops that increased demand for enslaved Africans.

Let's Review!

- The first people to come to North America arrived in approximately 12,000 BCE.
- They spread across North America and can be classified into a variety of different groups with different lifestyles.

> **KEEP IN MIND . . .**
> The early development of these colonies affected the later history of the United States. Think about how the early circumstances of these colonies shaped their later history.

- The Age of Exploration is the period between the fifteenth and seventeenth centuries during which European explorers traveled the world.
- The Age of Exploration was primarily led by Spain, Portugal, France, and Britain.
- The Age of Exploration was driven by a combination of desire for wealth, territory, and religious conversion.
- England eventually became the dominant power in North America.
- The 13 English colonies developed differently depending on the economic and social factors.

THE AMERICAN REVOLUTION AND THE GROWTH OF A NATION

Introduction

This lesson offers a short overview of U.S. history from the time of the American Revolution to just before the Civil War.

Section 1: The American Revolution

Over time, the 13 colonies began to distance themselves from Great Britain. One of the major precipitating factors was the French and Indian War. Britain was able to conquer Canada, but it left the empire heavily in debt. To pay its debts, Britain imposed taxes on the colonists, beginning with the Stamp Act in 1765. Although the amounts of money were small, the colonists objected strongly because they had no representation in Parliament. When taxes on tea were passed in 1773, Americans in Boston dumped tea into the harbor in what became known as the Boston Tea Party, and Parliament passed a number of laws restricting the freedom of colonial assemblies. When British troops tried to seize militia weapons at Lexington and Concord in 1775, war broke out.

The American colonists declared themselves independent with the Declaration of Independence in 1776 and selected George Washington to be the commander of the Continental Army. Though the colonists experienced several early defeats and were often short of soldiers and money,

> **KEEP IN MIND . . .**
> The American colonists were not necessarily angry because they had to pay, but because they were not given any voice in the decision.

Washington was able to hold the army together. In addition, the colonists won support from France following a victory at Saratoga. With French support, Washington forced the British army to surrender at Yorktown in 1781. In 1783, the Treaty of Paris formally established the independence of the United States.

The aftermath of the war was difficult for the United States. Unable to trade with the British, the American economy suffered. The new government was based on the Articles of Confederation, and it was unable to fix the problems the new country faced. It had little control over the state governments, and it could rarely take action because implementing a decision required unanimous approval. States printed their own money, which became worthless, and there was little gold for hard currency. The low point came when a group of farmers, angered by taxes they could not pay, led a rebellion to seize weapons in Massachusetts in what was called Shays' Rebellion. Washington came out of retirement to lead the army to crush the rebellion, which had exposed the weakness of the American government.

Example

In which of the following cities did protesting American colonists dump tea into the harbor?

   A. Boston   B. New York   C. Charleston   D. Philadelphia

   B. Boston was the site of the Boston Tea Party, a protest during which colonists dumped tea into Boston Harbor.

Section 2: Important Ideas in Early American History

In 1776, the Declaration of Independence stated a number of principles that became important in American political life. Written by Thomas Jefferson, the document is perhaps most famous today for its second line, "We hold these truths to be self-evident that all men are created equal," but it laid forth a number of important principles. Jefferson invoked natural law and claimed that governments existed to serve their citizens. If governments stopped doing that, citizens were free to form a new government. The declaration also listed a number of grievances with the king that would be revisited during the debate about a new constitution.

Because the Articles of Confederation proved inadequate, in 1787 representatives from all the states met in Philadelphia to draft a new constitution in meetings that lasted from May to September. Different states wanted different things. New Jersey, reflecting the interests of the smaller states, put forth the New Jersey Plan, which would give each state one vote. Virginia, reflecting the interests of the larger states, submitted the Virginia Plan, which allotted seats in the legislature based on population.

The resulting compromise became known as the Connecticut Compromise. It combined aspects of both plans to balance power between larger and smaller states by creating the Senate and the House of Representatives. The other stumbling block was over slavery. New England had largely eliminated slavery, but it existed in all other states, most predominantly in the South. The Southern delegates refused any changes that could threaten the status of slavery. The compromise they accepted was banning the international slave trade in 1808 and counting each enslaved person as three-fifths of a person for determining representation.

The last hurdle was a bill of rights. Some representatives, such as Alexander Hamilton, felt it was unnecessary, but others, such as James Madison, felt it was critical to Americans who were worried about the central government being too strong.

CONNECTIONS

When you study government and civics, think about how the early history you've learned shaped the Constitution. For example, how did the Bill of Rights address problems the Americans faced when they were still in the British Empire?

Early Americans were also interested in westward expansion. One of their quarrels with the British had been the restrictions placed on settlements in Ohio and Kentucky, and with independence, Americans seeking land began pushing the boundaries of the country. This would later become an idea known as Manifest Destiny, which was the belief that the United States should expand across the entire continent.

Example

Why did Americans want to replace the Articles of Confederation?

A. The states were on the verge of civil war.

B. The central government was too powerful.

C. It was a condition of independence from Britain.

D. The central government was too weak to solve problems.

D. Under the Articles of Confederation, the central government could not raise taxes or manage state governments.

Section 3: The Early Republic

George Washington was elected president after the Constitution was ratified, and he served two four-year terms, from 1789 to 1797. Washington set a precedent of not using too much power while in office to find a balance between two factions: the Federalists, who favored a strong central government, and the Democratic-Republicans (also known as the Republicans), led by Thomas Jefferson, who wanted small government and focused on farmers. Washington's successor, John Adams, was president for a single term, from 1797 to 1801. Both presidents worked to create a national bank and to repair the economic damage of the 1780s.

> **BE CAREFUL!**
> The Republican Party to which Jefferson belonged is not the same as the Republican Party today. The parties have the same name, but they have different ideas.

Thomas Jefferson was elected president in 1801. His most significant act was the Louisiana Purchase in 1803. Under Napoleon, France needed money for its various wars, so Napoleon sought to sell the remaining territory France had in North America. Although he was concerned that he did not have the

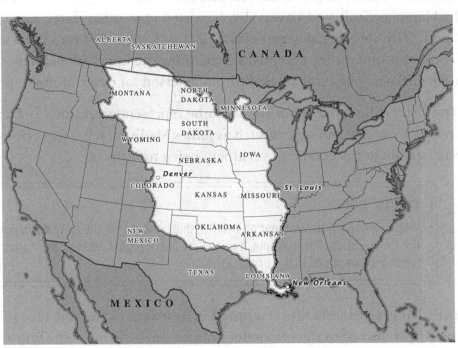

authority to make this decision, Jefferson accepted the offer, doubling the size of the United States.

Napoleon's war in Europe was with Britain and other powers, and that war had a powerful effect on Jefferson's second term as president. Great Britain launched a blockade of Europe to prevent trade from reaching France, and to ensure it had sufficient sailors, the Royal Navy would impress, or seize, British citizens from merchant ships. Some Americans were caught this way, and Jefferson launched a widely criticized embargo of Britain that hurt the economy and failed to stop impressment.

These issues continued under Jefferson's successor, James Madison. Combined with British refusal to abandon forts in the west and its tacit support for Native American raids, Congress voted to declare war against Britain on June 18, 1812. The war proved to be a difficult stalemate for the United States. Most of the country soon came under a British blockade, devastating the economy. Attempts to invade Canada stalled, and the Americans suffered a humiliating defeat when the British burned Washington, DC, in August 1814. However, the Americans were able to prevent a land invasion of the United States and hold their own against the British. The Treaty of Ghent in 1814 ended the fighting, as well as British support for the Native American tribes, effectively opening the west to the United States.

Did You Know?

Fighting continued after the Treaty of Ghent because of the time it took for news to cross the Atlantic. A future president, Andrew Jackson, led an American force to victory against the British outside New Orleans in early 1815.

Example

Against which country did the United States go to war in 1812?

A. Spain   B. France   C. Mexico   D. Great Britain

D. The United States fought Great Britain in the War of 1812. See Lesson: The American Revolution and the Growth of a Nation.

Section 4: Industrial Revolution

The nineteenth century was a period of enormous change around the world, particularly from an economic perspective. Beginning in Britain in about 1760, economies began to shift toward manufacturing. Textiles were one of the first areas to industrialize, with the invention of devices like the spinning jenny, which allowed weavers to work far faster than before. It spread to a variety of different areas, including transportation, chemicals, and even energy.

While this process occured more slowly in the United States than it did in Britain, by the beginning of the nineteenth century the United States was beginning to industrialize. New England was the first region to industrialize, initially relying on river systems to provide power for mills and factories. British immigrants to the United States brought technical expertise from factories in Britain. In 1793, the first textile mill opened in Pawtucket, Rhode Island; soon, similar mills opened throughout the Northeast.

Another major innovation that came from the United States was the concept of interchangeable parts, first proposed by Eli Whitney and perfected over the next two decades. Creating interchangeable parts simplified manufacturing. In the United States, Simeon North proposed a division of labor among workers to allow them to concentrate exclusively on one task. Following the British example, New York led the way in developing a canal system to transport goods, which other states emulated.

Even in the rural South, the Industrial Revolution had important effects. The cotton gin, invented by Eli Whitney in 1807, was designed to remove cotton seeds from the fiber. The explosive growth of textile mills fueled demand for cotton, and the cotton gin made it dozens of times faster to produce cotton for textile production. This increased its value and also increased the demand for enslaved workers in the southern states.

Example

In which country did the Industrial Revolution begin?

A. France   B. Germany   C. Great Britain   D. United States

A. The Industrial Revolution began in Great Britain. See Lesson: The American Revolution and the Growth of a Nation.

Let's Review!

- Ties between Britain and the United States weakened because the colonists wanted control over their own affairs.
- Victory in the Revolutionary War was made possible through help from other European powers, especially the French.
- The Declaration of Independence established a number of important principles, including the principle of equality among citizens (although, at the time, "citizens" only included white male landowners).
- The Constitution was established to create a stronger government after the Articles of Confederation.
- Americans were motivated to expand westward to claim more land.
- The Louisiana Purchase doubled the size of the United States and made westward expansion possible.
- The War of 1812 won the United States respect from Britain and other European powers.
- The Industrial Revolution transformed parts of the Northeast into manufacturing-heavy areas.
- Even the South, which remained rural, was shaped by the Industrial Revolution.

CIVIL WAR TIMES

Introduction

This lesson will focus on the lead-up to the Civil War, Reconstruction, and the settling of the far West.

Section 1: Abolition and Women's Rights

Criticism of slavery did not begin in the nineteenth century. Quakers, a Christian sect, refused to own enslaved people or engage in the slave trade because they believed it was inhumane and against Christian teachings. Beginning in 1777, states in the North, starting with Vermont, abolished slavery. The hope of many of the Founders, George Washington included, was that slavery would die out over time.

As the nation developed, slavery remained important to the economy, particularly in the South. Abolitionism—that is, opposition to slavery and activism to end it—evolved in two directions. One branch argued against slavery on moral grounds because of its inhumane treatment. Many of these activists became known as radical abolitionists because they both categorically opposed slavery and, in some cases, supported civil rights for freed enslaved people. The antislavery novel *Uncle Tom's Cabin*, written by Harriet Beecher Stowe in 1853, supported the radical abolitionists' views.

The other branch of antislavery sentiment was more pragmatic. Its adherents believed that to protect slavery, the South was seeking more power in Congress by trying to expand slavery into new states. Many white Americans weren't concerned about the rights or lives of enslaved people, but they felt that slavery was unfair competition economically. These feelings were widespread in the new states of the West.

Abolitionism also provided a point of entry for reformers seeking to expand rights for women. A few male abolitionists such as William Lloyd Garrison encouraged women to participate in the antislavery movement. At a time when women's husbands or fathers controlled their financial and work lives, women reformers began writing in the 1830s and 1840s, first about the evils of slavery and then about the need for women to take control of their own lives. This culminated in a series of small legal victories protecting women's property when they married.

> **KEEP IN MIND . . .**
> The resentment of slavery and what was called the "Slave Power" was an important factor in the lead-up to the Civil War. As Southerners strengthened their congressional advantages, some Westerners saw this as a conspiracy to seize power in the United States.

The Seneca Falls Convention, held in 1848, was the first women's rights convention. Organized by Elizabeth Cady Stanton with a group of Quaker women, it gave Stanton an opportunity to write the Declaration of Sentiments that, among other things, took the radical step of suggesting that women should be allowed to vote.

Example

Abolition is opposition to _____.

    A. slavery   B. feminism   C. socialism   D. capitalism

    A. Abolition is support for freeing enslaved people. See **Lesson: Civil War Times.**

Section 2: The Civil War

Compromises over slavery failed to solve the growing conflict between North and South. The Missouri Compromise of 1820 prohibited the spread of slavery north of the 36°30' parallel. The Compromise of 1850 allowed Utah and New Mexico to vote on whether to adopt slavery, but it also included a Fugitive Slave Act that included punishment for anyone who helped enslaved people escape. This angered many Northerners, who could now be imprisoned for aiding enslaved people. The South tried to stop the addition of new "free states." The Kansas-Nebraska Act overturned the Missouri Compromise, allowing states to vote on slavery. To many, this was unacceptable and furthered the rise of the second Republican Party. The *Dred Scott* Supreme Court decision held that even enslaved people who had been freed could not become citizens.

In 1860, the Republican Party selected Abraham Lincoln as its candidate. Lincoln maintained that he did not want to eliminate slavery; he only wanted to prevent its further expansion. Southerners refused to accept this, and when Lincoln won the presidential election, Southern states seceded. Ultimately, 11 states left the United States to form the Confederate States of America; several slave states remained in the Union. Lincoln waited until the Confederate States attempted to seize federal property—Fort Sumter in South Carolina—in 1861 before mobilizing troops to end the rebellion.

The South was ill-matched against the North: it had a smaller population, a less-industrialized economy, and little international support. Nevertheless, it had the advantages of fighting a defensive war and of strong generalship, and the war remains the bloodiest in U.S. history to this day. Ultimately, the South was ground down by force of arms and a lack of supplies.

By 1862, Lincoln believed that making the end of slavery a goal for the war would unite the North and rally Europe firmly to the Union cause. Following the Battle of Antietam, Lincoln issued the Emancipation Proclamation. Although it only applied to areas that had rebelled against the Union, it ended toleration for slavery in the United States. Lincoln drove home this point in his famous Gettysburg Address, claiming that the sacrifice of who died meant that the survivors needed to create a government based on equality.

> **DID YOU KNOW . . .**
> Lincoln's views on slavery evolved substantially during his lifetime. He was initially a supporter of "colonization": sponsoring freed enslaved people to return to Africa. He began the war saying that his sole goal was the preservation of the Union, but during the course of the war he came to support total abolition.

Example

Which of the following acts banned slavery north of the 36°30' parallel?

A. The Fugitive Slave Act

C. The Kansas-Nebraska Act

B. The Compromise of 1850

D. The Missouri Compromise

A. The Missouri Compromise banned slavery north of the 36°30' parallel. See **Lesson: Civil War Times.**

Section 3: Reconstruction

Rebuilding the South after the devastation of the war while reintegrating it back into the Union was a monumental task. Before he was assassinated in April 1865, Lincoln had developed plans for a "soft" Reconstruction that would allow states back into the Union easily as long as they ended slavery. Lincoln's successor, Andrew Johnson, was even more determined to speedily reunite the country.

However, members of the Republican Party didn't only seek to end slavery—they also wanted to resolve the status of the newly freed enslaved people. Some members also desired to punish the South for the war's devasation, but Johnson was opposed to both of these ideas. However, with no Southerners able to sit in Congress, Republicans were able to bypass Johnson by overriding all of his vetoes.

Republicans in Congress known as Radical Republicans passed a much more difficult plan for Reconstruction that involved division of the South into military districts that could rejoin as states once they approved state constitutions in line with Republican principles. They passed the Thirteenth Amendment banning slavery, the Fourteenth Amendment providing citizenship to anyone born in the United States, and the Fifteenth Amendment prohibiting states from denying voting rights on the basis of skin color. In the South, Republicans tried to set up an ambitious program of education for millions of formerly enslaved people who had not learned to read. The program provided medical care and some land reform to give them livelihoods.

This program of Reconstruction was detested in the South, and white Southern militias resisted it violently, giving birth to the Ku Klux Klan, a terrorist group. For a while, the North kept troops in the South to prevent violence, but a number of factors brought Reconstruction's end. An economic crash in 1873 eroded the credibility of Republicans around the country, while the continued violence in the South created a sense of war weariness in the North. In 1877, the last Northern troops left the South. At the time, many saw Reconstruction as a failure. Subsequent generations have appraised it more favorably for protecting African American rights.

Example

Reconstruction occurred in which region of the United States?

A. The West   B. The North   C. The South   D. The Midwest

B. Reconstruction occurred in the South. See **Lesson: Civil War Times.**

Section 4: The Gilded Age

Mark Twain called the period after Reconstruction the Gilded Age because it was an era during which great wealth and great poverty existing side by side: superficially, it looked like gold, but it was ugly underneath. It was the largest period of sustained economic growth in the country's history. It was a period of political corruption as well, the most famous example being Boss Tweed of New York. By skimming money from construction contracts, he stole millions of dollars.

This era coincided with the Second Industrial Revolution, which was concentrated in steel, heavy manufacturing and, above all, railroads. This growth was matched in agriculture, where devices like Cyrus McCormick's industrial reaper made it possible to harvest substantially more wheat. Economic growth led to the rise of large businesses called corporations. Some corporations became so large that in certain sectors of the economy one company effectively dominated the market, creating monopolies or oligopolies. They were also referred to as trusts.

FOR EXAMPLE . . .
Standard Oil is one of the most well-known trusts. Founded by John D. Rockefeller in 1870, Standard Oil aggressively took over its competitors. It bought up and down the supply chain so that it controlled every step of oil production. By 1904, the company controlled 91 percent of refining and 85 percent of sales.

Railroads had existed since the 1830s, but between 1865 and 1898, the miles of track increased by 567 percent. During the war, President Lincoln signed a law authorizing a transcontinental railroad that would make it possible to travel across the United States. Finished in 1869, the railroad was followed by several other coast-to-coast railroads.

The construction of these railroads enabled settlement in places such as Wyoming, Montana, the Dakotas, and other parts of the Great Plains. The Homestead Act of 1862 gave 160 acres of land to anyone willing to live on a plot of land for five years and make improvements to it. This land was difficult to farm because the Great Plains usually receives relatively little rainfall, but railroad companies that depended on having goods to ship to and from locations advertised the plains as excellent farmland. This settlement provoked the last wave of wars with

Native Americans in the Plains whose land had been left untouched. By the 1880s, the Native Americans had been either starved into surrender or beaten on the battlefield.

Example

Who coined the term "The Gilded Age"?

A. Mark Twain

B. Abraham Lincoln

C. Cyrus McCormick

D. John D. Rockefeller

C. Mark Twain coined the term. See **Lesson: Civil War Times.**

Let's Review!

- Abolition was a social movement that grew in the first half of the nineteenth century, for both moral and economic reasons.
- Women's rights advocates focused on gaining equal legal rights for women, such as the right to control their own finances.
- The Seneca Falls Convention in 1848 called for the right to vote for women.
- A series of political compromises postponed but did not resolve the dispute over slavery.
- The Civil War broke out because the Southern states feared that their right to own slaves was under assault.
- The North embraced emancipation during the war.
- Reconstruction attempted to give the freed enslaved people a new place in American society, with varying degrees of success.
- After the Civil War, the Gilded Age was a period of economic growth.
- Railroad expansion made it possible to travel across the country far more quickly and settle previously unsettled areas.

Becoming a World Power

Introduction

This section will cover the events leading to World War I, the interwar period, and World War II.

Section 1: The Buildup to World War I

In his farewell address, George Washington had cautioned his fellow Americans against becoming involved in European affairs. As the country grew in size and power, however, this proved impossible.

Europe was the center of world power in the late nineteenth and early twentieth centuries. European empires controlled almost all of Africa and Asia, and they held powerful influence over the territories that they did not control directly. Great Britain was the largest power among these, with an empire that covered one-quarter of the globe, followed by France with the second-largest empire. Germany had a smaller overseas empire but a dynamic and expanding economy that, by 1900, had overtaken Great Britain and was second only to the United States. Austria-Hungary was expanding at the expense of the neighboring Ottoman Empire in Turkey, taking land in the Balkans as the Turks withdrew. During this period, the Russian Empire was attempting expansion at the expense of Austria-Hungary.

These six powers coalesced into an alliance system. On one side, France, Russia, and eventually Great Britain became known as the **Triple Entente**. Each of the members was interested in blocking German or Austrian expansionism. On the other side, Germany and Austria-Hungary made up the **Central Powers**, with the Ottoman Empire joining in 1914. Germany was interested in both overseas expansion and protecting Austria-Hungary, its most reliable ally in Europe.

[Illustration Sample: A map of Europe pre-1914 showing the Triple Entente and the Central Powers, preferably color-coded, and listing each member.]

> **KEEP IN MIND . . .**
> There was a great deal of history between these powers that contributed to the outbreak of war. France had lost to Germany in a war in 1870, and its people and government were still angry over the territory it had lost to Germany.

A number of events contributed to the slide toward war. Germany embarked on a long period of battleship construction to improve its navy, which threatened Britain's position as the greatest maritime power and led to a shipbuilding race between the countries. This pushed Britain into an alliance with France and Russia. Austria-Hungary annexed the territories of Bosnia and Herzegovina in 1908, threatening the neighbor country of Serbia and angering its ally, Russia. The defeat of the Ottoman Empire in 1912 and

1913 created new territories for expansionist states and left Turkey looking for allies to protect its remaining territory.

Example

Which country had the largest empire in the world in 1900?

A. France   B. Russia   C. Great Britain   D. Austria-Hungary

C. Great Britain had the largest empire in the world by total territory and population in 1900.

Section 2: World War I

The event that sparked World War I after years of increasing international tensions was the assassination of Austrian Archduke Franz Ferdinand in Sarajevo on June 28, 1914. Austria blamed Serbia for the killing and mobilized troops to attack Serbia. Serbia's alliance with Russia meant that Russia was bound to protect Serbia, so all of the Triple Entente and Central Powers mobilized to defend one another. By August 4, all of the major countries in Europe were at war.

The war soon became an intractable stalemate that was more violent than any previous war in European history. Part of this was due to the technology, which gave the advantage to the defenders and allowed them to inflict many casualties on the attacking forces. It was also because the two sides were relatively evenly matched in terms of strength, though in the long run Britain and its allies were in a better position because they controlled the seas and could starve Germany through naval blockades.

[Illustration Sample: A map of the western front. Different colored lines should show how the front changed, with a key linking each color to a specific year.]

At the beginning of the war, the United States supplied goods and weapons to the Triple Entente. While neutral, the Entente was able to ship arms and supplies across the ocean, and American bankers offered enormous loans to the governments of the Entente. At the same time, Russia underwent two revolutions, the first of which removed the royal family from power in March 1917, and the second of which in **November 1917 (November Revolution)** brought the communists to power, who reformed the country into the Soviet Union.

Facing eventual defeat through starvation, Germany embarked on a campaign of unrestricted submarine warfare to attack enemy shipping, which put American lives at risk. This led President Woodrow Wilson to ask for a declaration of war, and in April 1917 the United States entered the war. It took time for the American army to be

KEEP IN MIND . . .
Many Americans didn't have strong feelings about either side in the war. Irish-Americans and German-Americans didn't necessarily like the British Empire, but few of them wanted to fight for Germany.

built up, but once troops began entering Europe in 1918, defeat was inevitable for Germany, and an armistice was signed on November 11, 1918. Wilson issued a document called the **Fourteen Points** that called for specific peace terms that would reduce militaries, lower trade barriers, and work to prevent future wars.

Example

The United States fought against which of the following countries in World War I?

   A. France   B. Russia   C. Germany   D. Great Britain

   D. Germany was one of the countries the United States fought during World War I.

Section 3: Interwar Period

In an attempt to prevent another war, the European powers and the United States sponsored a peace conference at Versailles in France to resolve outstanding issues. Woodrow Wilson proposed a **League of Nations** that would prevent future wars, but opposition at home stopped the United States from joining. The **Treaty of Versailles** imposed a harsh peace on Germany, including huge debts to the victorious nations and blame for the war. Austria-Hungary and the Ottoman Empire were broken up into smaller states. Germany also lost some parts of its territory to other countries.

Many Germans were angered by the terms of the peace, though after an economic crisis ended in 1924, Germany experienced several years of stability made possible by regular loans from the United States. However, in 1929 the **Great Depression** began in the United States and affected the entire world. In this economic climate, the loans ended, and the German economy failed. A right-wing leader named Adolf Hitler was able to negotiate his way to power, bringing Germany under the control of the Nazi Party in 1933.

Hitler was a committed **anti-Semite** who believed that Jews were seeking to control the world and weaken other races. He wanted to take land in Eastern Europe for German use, but he knew that doing so would provoke a war, so he began a program of rearmament. Because of the Great Depression and the difficulties facing France, Great Britain, and the United States, they failed to act as

> **KEEP IN MIND . . .**
> In the United States, the Great Depression was a catastrophe. By 1933, unemployment was at 25 percent. Although the New Deal under Franklin Roosevelt improved things somewhat, the economy remained poor until 1941.

Germany built a new army and annexed surrounding territories. Americans, in particular, felt they had been forced into World War I and didn't want to go war again.

Simultaneously, Japan embarked on a period of expansionism. Japan had been a rising power in Asia since the mid-nineteenth century, and by the 1920s Japan's military felt blocked from global power. In 1931, Japan invaded Manchuria on the Chinese border, and in 1937 it invaded China. These invasions angered the U.S. government under Franklin Roosevelt.

Example

Which of the following countries did not join the League of Nations?

A. Russia B. France C. Austria-Hungary D. The United States

B. The United States did not join the League of Nations.

Section 4: World War II

Hitler invaded Poland on September 1, 1939, leading to counter-declarations of war from France and Great Britain. Poland quickly fell, and in April 1940 Hitler launched an invasion of France that led to the swift capitulation of that country in June. Great Britain stayed in the war, partly through aid from the United States, and partly because of its own navy. With Britain stalemated, Hitler turned his attention to the Soviet Union, which he attacked on June 22, 1941. While he inflicted terrible casualties on the Russians, he was unable to defeat them. Germany, Japan, and Italy also formed an alliance known as the **Axis Pact**.

The United States made large aid commitments through **Lend-Lease** to countries fighting Germany. Roosevelt also tried to stop Japan's expansion by halting sales of rubber and oil, which led Japan to attack the United States at **Pearl Harbor** on December 7, 1941. Hitler declared war on the United States three days later, bringing the United States into the war. In many senses, this represented the beginning of the end of the war because the sheer economic power and population Russia, Britain, and the United States together was able to overwhelm Germany and Japan.

Both Japan and Nazi Germany were determined to continue the fight, even as the tide turned against them, and the war lasted until 1945. Approximately 60 million people died as a result of the fighting, including millions of civilians and noncombatants. Hitler was responsible for millions of these casualties because he targeted Jews, Roma, homosexuals, communists, and other groups he deemed to be inferior. Death squads, concentration camps, and extermination camps ultimately took the lives of at least six million Jews and smaller numbers of other groups in what is known as the **Holocaust**.

World War II left the United States and the Soviet Union as the two largest and strongest powers in the world. It ended Europe's status as the center of the world and set the stage for a new conflict between the two new powers.

COMPARE...

How similar were the United States' reasons for going to war in 1917 and in 1941? Were they the same reasons? If not, what made them different?

Let's Review!

- World War I began because of a tangled network of alliances and rivalries among European powers.
- World War I began in 1914 and turned into a stalemate between the Triple Entente and the Central Powers.
- The entry of the United States into the war forced Germany and Austria-Hungary to surrender.
- The Treaty of Versailles failed to resolve many of the European issues.
- The Great Depression pushed Japan and Germany to embrace militarism and prepare for new wars.
- Nazi Germany began World War II by invading Poland, followed by France and other European countries.
- Japan attacked the United States, bringing the country into the war. The United States, Russia, and Britain defeated Germany and Japan.
- Both wars were extraordinarily violent, with tens of millions left dead, and the balance of power shifted toward the United States and the Soviet Union.

THE TWENTIETH CENTURY AND BEYOND

Section 1: Civil Rights Movement

African Americans' fight for equal rights began immediately after the Civil War, and the Civil Rights Movement of the 1950s and 1960s was a continuation of that struggle. After African Americans were freed, they had to fight for better treatment from society. After Reconstruction ended, lawmakers in the South limited the rights of African Americans until they had lost the right to vote, had separate public accommodations, and were kept in a deliberate second-class economic status. Southerners murdered thousands of African Americans in lynchings. The migration of many African Americans north and west in the **Great Migration** was part of an attempt to escape persecution.

After World War II, the Civil Rights Movement gained strength as African Americans fought for their rights. The most visible leader in time was **Martin Luther King, Jr.**, a Southern Baptist preacher who advocated nonviolent resistance to racist laws. Other groups and individuals also played prominent roles. The **National Association for the Advancement of Colored People (NAACP)** fought racist laws in court, overturning school segregation in 1954 with the Supreme Court decision Brown v. Board of Education. The Congress of Racial Equality led sit-ins and boycotts of businesses with racist practices, and the Student Nonviolent Coordinating Committee carried out voter registration in Alabama and Mississippi.

Much of the Civil Rights Movement focused on drawing attention to and disobeying racist laws in the South, which were collectively termed "**Jim Crow**" laws. While usually nonviolent, this often provoked violent responses from Southerners. By the early 1960s, Americans from all over the country watched as law enforcement in the South attacked peaceful protesters with fire hoses and dogs. This created momentum for civil rights legislation. African Americans around the country put pressure on their representatives to pass federal laws to end Jim Crow practices. The bad press this created for the United States also pressured representatives—the U.S. government found that the negative press over racism was embarrassing internationally. In 1964 and 1965, President Lyndon Johnson signed the Civil Rights Act and Voting Rights Act, respectively, ending many of the Jim Crow laws.

Example

The Civil Rights Movement was about winning equality for each group?

A. Women

B. Chicanos

C. Jewish Americans

D. African Americans

BE CAREFUL!

The Civil Rights Movement was not confined to the South. African Americans across the country protested against racism, ranging from workplace discrimination to police violence.

D. The Civil Rights Movement focused on African Americans, though there were other groups striving for civil rights in this period.

Section 2: The Cold War, Part 1

The end of World War II did not resolve all international tensions. After the war, the United States and the Soviet Union struggled to dominate world affairs in a fight called the **Cold War**. The Soviet Union's communist ideology threatened many in the United States, and Soviet leaders in turn were afraid of the United States. Both countries began jockeying for power in Europe and around the world, beginning with the division between a capitalist Western Europe and a communist Eastern Europe.

[Simple Illustration: The division of Europe into eastern and western blocs.]

The United States embraced a policy of **containment**, hoping that confining communism to countries in which it already existed would lead to its reform or collapse. In Europe, this meant supporting reconstruction financially through the **Marshall Plan** in 1947 and committing to a regional defense pact called the **North Atlantic Treaty Organization (NATO)** in 1949. It became U.S. policy to send aid to countries that were resisting communist aggression in some way, first articulated through the **Truman Doctrine**.

KEY POINT!
Containment became the basis for U.S. foreign policy for the next 40 years, with minor revisions.

In Korea, which had been divided into a communist north and a U.S.-aligned south, war broke out in 1950, and the United States fought in the **Korean War** from 1950 to 1953. This war ended in a stalemate. Both the Soviet Union and the United States offered both evelopment aid and military aid to countries that were gaining independence, a practice that fueled conflict around the world. After creating and supporting an independent South Vietnam for some time, the United States became engaged in a protracted war called the **Vietnam War** that ended with South Vietnam's defeat in 1975.

Both the United States and the Soviet Union researched and developed nuclear weapons as a deterrent against the other. The United States had used the first atomic bomb against Japan to force its surrender in 1945, but the weapon took on a new significance during the Cold War. The Soviet Union tested its first atomic bomb in 1949, and both the United States and the Soviet Union tested hydrogen bombs in the 1950s. Soon, their arsenals grew to include thousands of these weapons, enough to destroy each other several times over, and the strategy of **Mutually Assured Destruction** ensured that both sides, if they attacked, would be annihilated.

Example

Which coutry was the rival of the United States during the Cold War?

A. France   B. Germany   C. Great Britain   D. The Soviet
                                                                Union

D. The United States fought the Cold War against the Soviet Union.

Section 3: The Cold War, Part 2

By the 1970s, the two superpowers were trying to find a way to lessen tensions between them to prevent a possible world-ending war. This period, during which both sides passed arms control agreements to limit their number of nuclear weapons, was known as **détente**. But détente failed to solve the issue of competition between them, and the Cold War grew worse after 1975 as the two powers competed in countires like Angola, Nicaragua, and Afghanistan.

Until the 1970s, the Soviet economy had grown steadily, but it weakened after 1970 as it came to increasingly rely on the sale of oil. For a time, this worked because oil prices were high in the 1970s, but those prices crashed in the 1980s and hurt the Soviet economy. The United States had been hurt by high oil prices in the 1970s, but when those prices decreased, the U.S. economy was in a position to perform better.

Ronald Reagan became president of the United States in 1981, and he oversaw the end of the Cold War. In his first term, Reagan promised to fight the Cold War more vigorously and to abandon détente. To do this, he raised military spending and committed to fighting communists or communist sympathizers around the world.

However, Reagan grew progressively concerned about nuclear war, recognizing that even an accident could spark a conflict that might end all life on the planet. He began making overtures to Soviet leadership, and by 1985, a younger Soviet leader named **Mikhail Gorbachev** expressed interest in working to eliminate certain nuclear weapons. Reagan developed a strong relationship with Gorbachev, and by 1988, as he prepared to leave office, Reagan felt confident in saying that the Soviet Union was no longer evil. In 1989, the communist countries of Eastern Europe transitioned from communism to democracy, and by 1991, the Soviet Union had dissolved, ending the Cold War.

Example

Ronald Reagan was president of which country?

A. Germany   B. Great Britain   C. The United   D. The Soviet
                                            States   Union

D. Ronald Reagan was president of the United States.

Section 4: 9/11 and After

In the decade after the end of the Cold War, U.S. foreign policy lost some of the focus it had during the Cold War. Although global terrorism remained a concern, the United States had no rivals, and the country's chief focus internationally was on trade deals and security. This changed with the terrorist attacks on **September 11**, orchestrated by a fundamentalist Islamic terrorist group called Al-Qaeda and an individual named Osama Bin Laden. Hijackers flew airplanes into the World Trade Center in New York City and the Pentagon in Washington, DC. Bin Laden viewed the United States as an imperial power. This marked the beginning of the **War on Terror**, which aimed to punish organizations that supported the attack, and grew to encompass any state that harbored or supported terrorists.

Afghanistan had been the base of operations for Al-Qaeda, and it was run by a totalitarian Islamic regime known as the **Taliban**. Cooperating with local resistance movements, U.S. troops invaded in October 2001 and removed the Taliban from power. This set off an insurgent movement as members of the Taliban and those opposed to U.S. occupation fought against the new government and U.S. troops. This war has been ongoing, with varying levels of intensity, since 2001.

Members of the George W. Bush administration set their sights on Iraq, which the United States had fought in 1991. Members of the administration erroneously believed that the Iraqi government under Saddam Hussein was supporting members of Al-Qaeda and stockpiling weapons of mass destruction. After Hussein ignored ultimatums to surrender power, the United States invaded in March 2003. The occupation of the country proved more difficult than predicted as foreign fighters and Iraqis fought the United States, leading to a protracted war.

Elsewhere, U.S. troops, special forces, and advisers became involved around the world fighting or assisting against terrorist cells. In some places, this has meant using drone strikes to kill suspected terrorists without deploying troops, which has resulted in the deaths of innocent civilians and bystanders. Countries that have an American presence in the War on Terror include Pakistan, Yemen, Somalia, and the Philippines.

COMPARE!

Is the War on Terror similar to or different from containment during the Cold War? How so?

Example

The September 11 attacks occurred in what year?

A. 2000 B. 2001 C. 2002 D. 2003

B. The September 11 attacks occurred in 2001.

Let's Review!

- The Civil Rights Movement sought to win equal rights for African Americans.

- Civil rights activists used a combination of boycotts, nonviolent resistance, court challenges, and lobbying for federal laws to end racist laws.
- The Cold War took place between the United States and the Soviet Union.
- The United States and the Soviet Union competed around the world for influence, sometimes directly fighting wars and other times supplying aid to other countries.
- The Cold War ended as the Soviet Union reformed, ultimately dissolving in 1991.
- The September 11 attacks pushed the United States into the War on Terror.
- The War on Terror led the United States to invade Afghanistan and Iraq.

CHAPTER 10 U.S. HISTORY PRACTICE QUIZ

1. The Bering land bridge allowed people to cross over into North America from _____.

   A. Asia

   B. Africa

   C. Europe

   D. Greenland

2. What part of the world were European explorers most interested in reaching?

   A. Asia

   B. Africa

   C. Mexico

   D. Canada

3. Why were American colonists angry about having to pay additional taxes after 1763?

   A. The amounts were greater than those paid in Britain.

   B. The colonists felt they had no say in making the decision.

   C. They felt the British needed to repay their debt themselves.

   D. The colonists had never wanted to go to war against France.

4. Support from which power was critical in the U.S. victory in the Revolutionary War?

   A. Spain

   B. France

   C. Prussia

   D. The Netherlands

5. Which state was the first in the United States to abolish slavery?

   A. Virginia

   B. Vermont

   C. New Jersey

   D. Massachusetts

6. How did the Homestead Act help populate unsettled parts of the United States?

   A. It offered free land to those willing to farm it.

   B. It provided know-how and tools for would-be farmers.

   C. It built railroads to remote regions to make settlement easier.

   D. It removed Native Americans from the land and gave it to settlers.

7. Which of the following countries was a member of the Triple Entente?

   A. Turkey

   B. France

   C. Germany

   D. Austria-Hungary

8. Which of the following answers BEST explains how the alliance system contributed to the outbreak of war in 1914?

   A. The alliances didn't include smaller powers.

   B. The alliances forced countries into going to war.

   C. The alliances tricked each country into thinking it was safe.

   D. The alliances encouraged the major powers to take risky actions.

9. **What did the Supreme Court decision *Brown v. Board of Education* change?**

   A. School segregation

   B. Segregation in public places

   C. African Americans' right to vote

   D. Employers' ability to discriminate based on race

10. **The Taliban was the government of which country?**

   A. Iraq

   C. Afghanistan

   B. Nicaragua

   D. The Soviet Union

CHAPTER 10 U.S. HISTORY
PRACTICE QUIZ – ANSWER KEY

1. **A.** The Bering land bridge formed in the Bering Sea between Asia and North America **See Lesson: The Earliest Americans and the Age of Exploration.**

2. **A.** European explorers were chiefly interested in Asia because of the value of the spices and other goods produced there. **See Lesson: The Earliest Americans and the Age of Exploration.**

3. **B.** The colonists protested their lack of representation in Parliament. **See Lesson: The American Revolution and the Growth of a Nation.**

4. **B.** Financial support and troops sent by the French government enabled the American victory in the war. **See Lesson: The American Revolution and the Growth of a Nation.**

5. **B.** Vermont was the first state to abolish slavery. **See Lesson: Civil War Times.**

6. **A.** The Homestead Act offered land to those willing to farm it for a number of years. **See Lesson: Civil War Times.**

7. **B.** France was a member of the Triple Entente. **See Lesson: Becoming a World Power.**

8. **B.** Once one ally was attacked, other countries with which the country had alliances were bound to defend it. **See Lesson: Becoming a World Power.**

9. **A.** *Brown v. Board of Education* banned racial segregation in schools. **See Lesson: The Twentieth Century and Beyond.**

10. **C.** The Taliban was the government in Afghanistan. **See Lesson: The Twentieth Century and Beyond.**

CHAPTER 11 ECONOMICS

THE FUNDAMENTALS OF ECONOMICS

This lesson discusses fundamentals of economics, including the five major economic assumptions.

Section 1: What Is Economics?

Economics is the study of how individuals, businesses, and societies (run by a governing body) handle **scarcity**. The principles of economics provide a foundation for good decision making for all three groups.

There are two branches of economics: **macroeconomics** and **microeconomics**. Microeconomics is the study of how individuals or individual businesses allocate resources. Macroeconomics looks at how the economy as a whole works.

Individuals, businesses, and societies have

- unlimited wants; and
- limited resources (land, money, labor, time, and so on).

Because wants are unlimited and resources are limited, decisions need to be made about how to use the available resources. Something must be given up to get or achieve something else.

- **Trade-offs** are ALL the alternatives that are given up when a choice is made about how to use resources.
- **Opportunity cost** is the most desirable alternative that is given up when a choice is made.

Any decision that involves a choice between two or more options has an opportunity cost. Going to a restaurant involves time and money. That time can't be used to study for a test, and that money can't be spent on going to a concert. Every choice has a value. The final choice has more value than another choice that was available.

People go to work or to school because they are self-interested. They seek personal gain. The reward, or **incentive**, for going to work is a paycheck. The reward for going to school may be a better job with a bigger paycheck.

- Decisions are influenced by incentives, which can be rewards or punishments.
- Self-interest is the prime motivator in decision making.
- In general, people take action when the benefit is greater than the cost.

Adam Smith, the father of modern economics, reasoned that the best economic benefit for all can usually be accomplished when individuals act in their own self-interest.

To summarize, there are five major economic assumptions:

- Individuals, businesses, and societies have unlimited wants and limited resources (scarcity).
- Choices must be made due to scarcity. Every choice has a cost, or something that was given up to get it (trade-off).
- Everyone reacts to incentives and their own self-interest.
- Everyone makes decisions by weighing the benefits and costs of every choice.
- Real-life situations can be explained and analyzed through models and graphs.

Section 2: Economic Systems

Every society must answer three questions:

- What goods and services should be produced?
- How should these goods and services be produced?
- Who consumes these goods and services?

The economic system that a society uses is determined by the way it answers these three questions. Therefore, an economic system is the method a society uses to produce and distribute goods and services.

There are two major types of economic systems:

- Centrally planned (**command economy**): China has a primarily centrally planned economy.
- Free market (**capitalist economy**): The United States has a primarily free market economy.

The government owns all the resources in a centrally planned economy. The government tells workers where they should work and what jobs they should perform. The government decides what to produce, how to produce it, and for whom to produce it.

Individuals decide what to produce and how to produce it in a free market economy. The market (consumers) dictates what products are available. If consumers don't buy a product, there is no market for it, and no company will make it.

The **invisible hand**, the most important concept of capitalism, recognizes that a society will meet its goals as individuals take self-interested actions. In other words, there are social benefits when individuals in a society better themselves.

Competition and self-interest act as an invisible hand that regulates the free market. For example, if consumers want gas-efficient cars:

- companies produce more gas-efficient cars;
- competition among companies results in high quality, greater efficiency, and low prices; and
- the needs of society are met.

Almost all countries, including the United States, have **mixed economies**. Each country has a free market and some government involvement. The amount and type of involvement varies from country to country.

Markets are usually the best way to organize economic activity. In a market economy, resources are allocated through the decentralized decisions of many companies and individuals as they interact in markets for goods and services.

Market economies are more effective than centralized economies. Market price usually reflects the value to consumers and the cost to producers. Centrally planned economies fail because they do not allow the market to function. In centrally planned economies, individuals and businesses have little incentive to succeed.

Section 3: Production Possibilities Curve

A **production possibilities curve** (frontier) is a model that shows alternative ways that an entity can use its scarce resources. The model displays trade-offs, opportunity costs, scarcity, and efficiency.

In the example below, a production possibilities curve (PPC) is used to chart the quantity of hamburgers and chicken dinners that can be made. If five hamburgers are made, zero chicken dinners are made, and so on.

	A	B	C	D	E	F
Hamburgers	5	4	3	2	1	0
Chicken Dinners	0	1	2	3	4	5

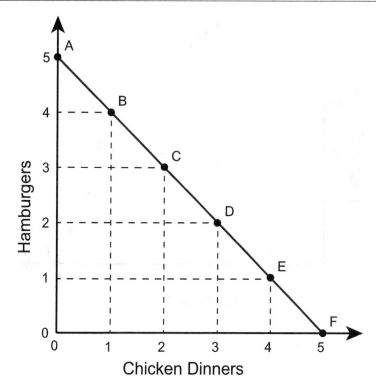

Points on a PPC can fall into three areas:

- Inside the curve – represents inefficiency/unemployment
- Outside the curve – are not possible with the given resources
- On the curve – represents efficiency

When points fall on the curve, all resources, like restaurant equipment and workers, are being used to produce the two items. There is a constant opportunity cost in this example, resulting in a straight line PPC. This means that the same adaptable resources are used for making both items. This is uncommon.

In contrast, the **law of increasing opportunity cost** states that as more of any item is produced, the opportunity cost (production of another item that was given up) increases. In other words, when two goods are produced, an increasing amount of the second good is given up. The reason is that resources are not easily adaptable between the production of the two items. In these cases, the PPC has a concave (inward) curve.

The information below can be charted with a concave curve. As more windows are made, fewer kitchen cabinets are made (opportunity cost increases).

	A	B	C	D	E	F
Kitchen Cabinets	25	24	21	15	5	0
Windows	0	1	2	3	4	5

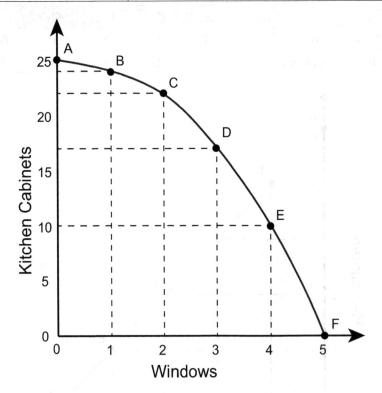

Four key assumptions are made when analyzing production possibilities:

- Resources are used to produce one or both of only two goods.
- The amount of available resources does not change.
- Technology and production techniques do not change.
- Resources are used in a technically efficient way.

Section 4: Specialization and Trade

Trade allows for specialization. Specialization enables countries (and people) to spend their time doing what they do best. The United States is capable of flooding the marketplace with clothing. However, the vast majority of clothing is made in other countries. The United States chooses to specialize in other areas, such as making movies.

- **Absolute advantage** – the producer requires the least amount of resources or can produce the most output.
- **Comparative advantage** – the producer has the lowest opportunity cost.

A country should specialize in trade when it has comparative advantage. The United States has an absolute advantage in clothing and a comparative advantage in movies.

There is a significant benefit to trade between countries. Given the available resources, a country can consume more of a particular item than if it produces that item on its own. For example, the United States doesn't have the resources to produce the amount of clothing that consumers currently buy.

Two countries can benefit from trade if they each have relatively lower opportunity costs. There are never trade benefits in every term. Each country negotiates conditions of trade until the countries make a deal that benefits both of them. The **terms of trade** measure the rate of exchange of one product for another.

To figure out comparative advantage, per unit opportunity cost is calculated. There are two types of questions: output and input.

Output is the number of units produced. The United States has an absolute advantage in the production of airplanes and vehicles in the example below. In this instance, Canada should trade airplanes for vehicles from the United States since the most units (1,500) are produced with this trade. (50 x 30). Canada has comparative advantage in airplane production, and the United States has comparative advantage in vehicle production.

(in thousands)	Airplanes	Vehicles
United States	60	30
Canada	50	20

Key Terms

- **Investment** is the money businesses spend to improve their production.
- **Consumer goods** are created for direct consumption (apple pie).
- **Capital goods** are created for indirect consumption (ovens). They are used to make consumer goods.
- **Human capital** is any knowledge or skill a worker gains through education and experience.

Let's Review!

- Economics is the study of the choices that society makes to satisfy wants and needs.
- Economics is based on the concept of scarcity, or limited resources, to meet unlimited wants.
- The concept of the invisible hand of the market states that if individuals do what is best for themselves, they do what's best for society at the same time.
- With a trade-off, something is given up to get something else. For example, there is no such thing as a free lunch because a resource (time) is given up to take advantage of the offer.
- Decisions are made by weighing the benefits and cost of every choice.
- The cost of something is what is given up to get it.
- Adam Smith, author of *The Wealth of Nations*, is considered the father of modern economics.
- Opportunity cost is the next-best possible alternative that is given up when a decision is made.
- Firms and individuals act in their own best interest in a market economy.
- Command and capitalist economies are the two major types of economic systems.
- Market (capitalist) economies are more effective than centralized (command) economies.
- Trade allows a country to consume more of a particular item than it can produce.

MICROECONOMICS

This lesson discusses fundamentals of microeconomics.

Section 1: Circular Flow Model

The **circular flow model** displays how firms, households, and governments interact with one another in a capitalist society. The model illustrates the flow of goods and services through the economy. Money makes the circular flow function. Money is the medium of exchange in a market economy.

Firms are entities established by **entrepreneurs**, or individuals from households who want to start a business to earn money. Funds flow from households to firms every time individuals invest in firms through bonds, stocks, or other types of investment.

In a market economy, there is a product market and a resource market. Firms sell products and buy resources. Households buy products and sell resources. Specifically, households sell four resources: labor, **capital**, land, and entrepreneurial activity. These resources are called the **factors of production**.

A **market** is a place where buyers and sellers meet to engage in mutually beneficial exchanges with one another.

In **product markets**

- firms supply and sell goods and services; and
- households demand and buy goods and services.

In **resource markets**

- households supply and sell labor, capital, land, and entrepreneurial activity in exchange for income: wages, rent, and interest; and
- firms demand and buy labor, capital, land, and entrepreneurial activity.

In its simplest form, the circular flow model shows that goods and services flow through the economy in one direction while money flows in the opposite direction.

(insert circular flow model)

The goal of firms is to maximize profits. To do this, firms must sell their goods and services for more than they spent on resources to produce these goods and services. The goal of households is to maximize utility, or happiness. Happiness is achieved through consumption of goods and services.

Circular flow is ongoing between firms and households. The circular flow of income is important within an economy because it

- measures the national income;
- explains the nonstop nature of economic activities;
- provides understanding of **economic interdependence**; and
- shows **injections** (investment, government spending, and exports) and **leakages** (households and firms save part of their incomes).

A **monopoly** and an **oligopoly** are economic market structures. In a monopoly, there is one firm in the market. Therefore, that firm has no competition. In an oligopoly, fewer than 10 large producers work together to set pricing that is beneficial to all of them.

Section 2: Supply and Demand

The **law of supply and demand** describes the interaction between the supply of and demand for a resource and the effect on its price. This concept is the backbone of a market (capitalist) economy. Resources are allocated in the most efficient way possible in a market economy.

- Demand is how much of a product or service consumers want.
- Supply is how much of a product the market can offer.

The **law of demand** states that when the price of a good goes up, consumers buy less of that good. When the price of an item goes down, consumers buy more. The **law of supply** states that when the price goes up, more is produced. When the price goes down, less is produced.

- The price of an item will rise when that item is scarce but many people want it.
- The price of an item will fall when there is a large amount of that item but little consumer demand.

There are two different effects, the substitution effect and the income effect, if the price of a good increases. The **substitution effect** explains how a change in the price of a good affects demand compared to other goods.

A good is more expensive than alternative goods when its price increases; therefore, consumers may switch to a cheaper, sometimes inferior, good. For example, if steak increases in price, consumers may switch to hamburger.

The **income effect** explains how a change in demand for a good is affected by a change in disposable income. An increase in price reduces disposable income, and this lower income reduces demand. Consumers spend less in general, and they may buy goods of higher or lower value.

As an example, if the price of college tuition rises, this increase reduces disposable income. Therefore, demand will fall. A consumer may still purchase lobster take-out meals but do it once a month instead of once a week.

Marginal utility is the benefit gained from consuming one additional unit of a good or service. The **law of diminishing marginal utility** states that the first unit of consumption of a good or service has more use than the following units of consumption. For example, a second candy bar, in general, is less satisfying than the first candy bar.

Section 3: Quantity and Price

As previously stated, there is interaction between the supply of and demand for a resource, and this interaction affects the resource's price. **Elasticity** shows how quantity changes when there is a change in price.

Elastic Demand:

- If the price increases, quantity demanded decreases a lot.
- If the price decreases, quantity demanded increases a lot.

Elastic goods have some or all of the following characteristics:

- Have many substitutes
- Are luxuries
- Have competitive markets
- Are bought frequently

Inelastic Demand (insensitive to a change of price):

- If the price increases, quantity demanded decreases a little.
- If the price decreases, quantity demanded increases a little.

Inelastic goods have some or all of the following characteristics:

- Have few substitutes
- Are necessities
- Have little competition
- Are bought infrequently
- Require a small percent of income
- Are used in the short run

Demand increases for **normal goods** when income increases. Demand for organic vegetables is an example. Demand for inferior goods, such as canned vegetables, increases when income decreases. This is called the **income elasticity of demand**.

There is **equilibrium** when market supply and demand balance each other and, as a result, prices become stable. The government sets **price controls**, or price floors and ceilings, when there is no market equilibrium.

- **Price ceiling** is the maximum legal price a seller can charge for a product.
- **Price floor** is the minimum legal price a seller can charge for a product.

The goal of a price ceiling is to make the product affordable by keeping the price from reaching equilibrium. Price ceilings are maximum prices set for particular goods and services that the government believes are being sold at too high a price. Therefore, consumers need some help purchasing them.

The goal of a price floor is to keep the price from falling to the market equilibrium. Price floors are minimum prices set for certain commodities and services that the government believes are being sold at too low a price. Therefore, their producers deserve some assistance in an unfair market.

The **utility maximization** rule addresses consumer choice. *Utility* refers to the usefulness, or satisfaction, that a consumer obtains from any good. The rule states that a consumer attempts to get the greatest value possible from spending the least amount of money when purchasing a good. The consumer's objective is to maximize the total value obtained from the money that is available.

Section 4: Consumer Economics

People keep their money in banks and receive a small amount of interest. The bank takes this money and lends it out at much higher interest rates. This system is necessary in a free market economic system because it provides resources for people to buy things like homes or for industries to expand their businesses.

In short, banks take unused funds from savers and turn them into funds that society can use for various activities. In addition to accepting savings deposits, banks get income from the credit card business, buying and selling currencies, **custodian business** such as stocks and bonds, and **cash management services** like money market funds. There are three types of banks:

- **Consumer banks**, also known as retail banks, are typical mass-market banking institutions that provide local branches for customers' convenience.
- **Investment banks** specialize in large, complex financial transactions. Individuals, corporations, and governments are charged a yearly fee for services, and there are no commissions on sales.
- **Merchant banks** deal in commercial loans and investments and are experts in international trade. Instead of loans, banks provide capital to companies in the form of share ownership.

Credit unions provide the same financial services as banks but focus on shared value rather than profit maximization. Their goal is to help members create opportunities like starting small businesses or building family homes. Credit unions are controlled by their members, who elect a board of directors.

Consumers can also use a credit card or debit card to purchase goods and services. Credit cards have higher **annual percentage rates** (APRs) than other lines of credit and forms of consumer loans. The APR is the annual cost of taking out a loan. There is no interest on purchases if the balance is paid in full each month by the due date. Debit cards may be free to use, or there may be processing fees.

- **Debit cards** take money from a checking account when a purchase is made.
- **Credit cards** charge the cost of a purchase to a line of credit.

Let's Review!

- The circular flow model illustrates the flow of goods and services through the economy.
- Money is the medium of exchange in a market economy.
- A market is a place where buyers and sellers meet to engage in exchanges with one another.
- There is a product market and a resource market in a market economy.
- The goal of firms is to maximize profits, and the goal of households is to maximize utility.
- As long as leakages are equal to injections, the circular flow of income continues indefinitely.
- The concept of supply and demand controls a market economy.
- There are two possible effects if the price of a good increases.
- Marginal utility deals with consumption of a good or service.
- Demand is elastic if it changes a lot when the price changes. Soda is an example.
- Demand is inelastic if it does not respond much to price changes. Gas is an example.
- Price controls change the market equilibrium in a free market.
- The most common price floor is the minimum wage, the minimum amount that can be paid for labor.
- Financial institutions include three types of banks as well as credit unions.

MACROECONOMICS

This lesson introduces the fundamentals of macroeconomics.

Section 1: GDP

Every economy, regardless of economic system, has three major goals:

- Promote economic growth (produce more)
- Limit unemployment
- Keep prices stable (limit **inflation**)

Gross domestic product (GDP) is a measurement used to determine the size of the economy at a given point in time and growth of the economy over time. GDP measures final goods and services, or goods and services sold to an end user. As an example, tires are sold to companies that produce cars. These tires are not counted in GDP. They are an intermediate good used in the production of a final good. When a consumer buys tires to replace worn-out tires, they are counted in GDP.

- **GDP** is the dollar value (total market value) of all final goods and services produced within a country's borders in a year.
- **GDP per capita** (per person) is the GDP divided by the population. It identifies, on average, how many goods and services a person produces.

Final goods and services do not need to be produced by U.S. companies to be included in the U.S. GDP. As long as the companies are within the United States' borders, production is counted in GDP. If U.S. companies produce final goods and services in another country, production is not counted in the U.S. GDP.

Real GDP is the best measure of economic growth.

- **Nominal GDP** is measured in current prices. It does not account for inflation from year to year. Nominal GDP increases with inflation and decreases with deflation.
- **Real GDP** is measured in constant, or unchanging, dollars. It adjusts for inflation.
- A change in GDP could mean that
- the country has produced more goods and services;
- the country has produced the same goods and services, but prices have increased; or
- the country has some combination of more goods and services produced and higher prices.

GDP can be estimated by using the expenditure approach:

- $Y = C + I + G + (X - M)$ **OR**
- GDP = consumption + investment + government purchases + (exports - imports)

The following are NOT included in GDP:

- Financial transactions like stocks, bonds, and real estate (non-production transactions)
- Used goods like old cars (non-production transactions)
- Household products made at home (non-market)
- Illegal activities like unpaid work or drugs
- Intermediate goods

Section 2: Unemployment

Usually, real GDP is used to analyze an economy. An economy goes up and down over time. Likewise, a **business cycle** is the natural rise and fall of economic growth. It is a pattern of expansion, contraction, and recovery in an economy. The business cycle is usually measured and followed in terms of GDP and **unemployment**.

- GDP rises and unemployment falls during business cycle expansion phases.
- GDP falls and unemployment rises during business cycle recession phases.

Workers who are considered to be unemployed are not working, but they are actively looking for a job. The unemployment rate is the percent of people in the labor force who want a job but are not working.

- Unemployment rate = number of employed/number in the labor force × 100

The **labor force** is the number of people age 16 and over who are willing and able to work. Jobless people who are not looking for work (such as stay-at-home parents and students) are not included in the labor force. The **labor force participation rate** is the percent of the population in the labor force.

There are three types of unemployment. Frictional unemployment is the first type. In this type, workers have transferable skills. Unemployment is temporary, or workers are between jobs. Seasonal unemployment is a type of frictional unemployment caused by the time of year and nature of the job.

The second type of unemployment is structural unemployment. In this type, workers' skills are obsolete because of changes in the labor market. Workers had jobs that will never come back. They do not have transferable skills, and they must learn new skills to get a job. Technological unemployment is a type of structural unemployment in which workers are replaced by automation and machinery.

Cyclical unemployment is the third type of unemployment, and it occurs during periods of recession. Demand for goods and services falls as economic growth falls. Because consumers are purchasing fewer goods and services, demand for labor falls and workers are laid off.

The goal is not to have zero unemployment in a good economy. There will always be frictional and structural unemployment, regardless of the health of the economy. This is referred to as the natural rate of unemployment (NRU).

Section 3: Inflation

The economy can be in one of three phases at any one time:

- Recession with falling GDP and employment
- Expansion with increasing GDP and full employment
- Inflationary gap with an increase in real GDP, which increases consumption, causing prices to rise in the long term

When there is **inflation**, each dollar of income buys fewer goods and services. Therefore, it takes more money to buy items in the marketplace. **Disinflation** is a decrease in the rate of inflation. In this situation, inflation has been occurring for some time, but it has slowed down. **Deflation** is a decrease in the price of goods and services.

There are two types of wages:

- **Nominal wage** is measured by dollars rather than by **purchasing power**.
- **Real wage** is adjusted for inflation.

If a worker gets a 6 percent raise but there is 12 percent inflation, the worker has not gotten a raise. The worker's nominal wage increased by 6 percent, but the real wage declined by 6 percent.

The **nominal interest rate** is the stated interest rate and the actual monetary price that borrowers pay to lenders. If a loan has a 3 percent interest rate, borrowers will pay $3 of interest for every $100 loaned to them.

The **real interest rate** is calculated by subtracting the inflation rate from the nominal interest rate (Nominal interest rate – Inflation = Real interest rate). If a loan has a 10 percent interest rate and the inflation rate is 8 percent, then the real interest rate is 2 percent.

- The nominal interest rate is the percentage increase in money that a borrower pays, not adjusting for inflation.
- The real interest rate is the percentage increase in purchasing power that a borrower pays. If inflation goes up, the real interest rate decreases. Unexpected inflation hurts lenders and helps borrowers.

The **Consumer Price Index** (CPI) is one of the principal ways to measure price changes and inflation over a period of time. A conceptual market basket is analyzed. The base year is given an index of 100. To compare, each year is also given an index number.

- CPI = Price of Market Basket/Price of Market Basket in Base Year × 100

There are three causes of inflation:

- The government prints too much money.
- Demand pulls up prices.
- Higher production costs increase prices.

KEEP IN MIND . . .
The CPI is not a dollar value like GDP. The CPI is an index number or a percentage change from the base year.

Section 4: Fiscal and Monetary Policy

The Federal Reserve (the Fed) is the central bank of the United States. The Fed regulates and oversees the nation's commercial banks by ensuring that banks have enough money in reserve to avoid bank runs. A **bank run** happens when many people withdraw their money from a bank at the same time because they think the bank will fail. The bank cannot provide the amount of money that is requested.

The Fed also conducts **monetary policy**. It increases or decreases the money supply to speed up or slow down the economy. The Fed manipulates interest rates by changing the money supply. When interest rates are low, it is easier to pay back loans, so consumers borrow more and spend more. Consumers borrow less and spend less when interest rates are high.

The Fed loans money to banks with interest that is set at a discount rate. The lower the rate, the more banks will borrow and the more money will go into circulation. Consumer banks set the interest rates they charge slightly higher than the Fed's rate. Therefore, the Fed determines interest rates in the economy.

The Fed can also increase or decrease the total supply of money through **open market operations** (OMO). This tool, applied to bonds of all maturities, allows the Fed to buy and sell Treasury bonds in the **open market**. Because an OMO changes the total supply of money, interest rates are affected.

If the Fed buys bonds from consumers, it increases the money supply in the economy by removing bonds in exchange for cash. Prices are pushed higher, and interest rates decrease.

If the Fed sells bonds to consumers, it decreases the money supply in the economy by removing cash in exchange for bonds. Prices are pushed down, and interest rates increase.

The Federal Reserve

- is an independent entity;
- is subject to little government regulation;
- has a board of governors and chairperson that are not elected; and
- is organized to remain independent and insulated from politics.

Government and central banks put a **stabilization policy** into place to keep price levels, unemployment, and economic growth stable. Monetary and **fiscal policy** can **stabilize** demand and, therefore, production and employment. A fiscal policy can lower disposable income—and thus demand—with a tax increase. A tax decrease boosts demand by increasing disposable income.

Let's Review!

- Healthy economies promote economic growth, limit unemployment, and keep prices stable.
- GDP measures the value of economic activity within a country.

- These items are not included in GDP: intermediate goods, non-production transactions, non-market transactions, and illegal activities.
- GDP per capita identifies how many goods or services each person produces.
- Real GDP adjusts for inflation; nominal GDP does not.
- The expenditure approach to estimating GDP is represented by the equation: $Y = C + I + G + (X - M)$.
- When there is inflation in an economy, there is an increase in prices and a fall in the purchasing value of money.
- Inflation is limited when prices are stable; average prices are constant over time or rising at a predictable and very low rate.
- The amount of unemployment that exists regardless of the health of the economy is called the natural rate of unemployment.
- Cyclical unemployment occurs during periods of recession.
- Business cycles are measured and followed in terms of GDP and unemployment.
- The Fed regulates and oversees the nation's commercial banks and conducts monetary policy.
- Monetary policies determine interest rates and the supply of money in circulation.
- Fiscal policies determine whether taxes are increased or decreased and how much money is spent on projects to stimulate the economy and increase employment.

ECONOMICS THROUGH HISTORY

This lesson presents economics through history.

Section 1: Economic Drivers of Exploration and Colonization

During the **Age of Exploration**, also known as the Age of Discovery, overseas exploration was a big part of European culture. The period began in the early fifteenth century and lasted through the end of the seventeenth century. Although the primary motives of European countries were economic, desire to spread religious beliefs also played a role in their decision to travel the seas.

Three motivations, known as the **3 Gs**, fostered the Age of Exploration:

- **Glory** is national pride and prestige. More land meant more power for a monarch.
- **Gold** is wealth. Gold, silver, and other raw resources meant more riches.
- **God** was central to European life during this period. Newly discovered populations meant more opportunity to spread religious beliefs.

The capitalist economy of a European country improved with successful exploration. European ships traveled around the world in search of new trading routes and partners willing to be part of the thriving free market in Europe. This was the beginning of **economic globalization**. In addition, monarchs could directly increase their wealth if explorers from their country found an area that had gold, silver, or other natural resources.

Spanish, French, and English explorers wanted to find a faster way to bring back goods from Asia than existing overland routes. The explorers believed that the Northwest Passage, an open waterway through northern North America, could be a direct and efficient route to East Asia. Asian countries had goods like spices and silks to trade.

Columbus was one of the explorers who looked for a quicker route to Asia. Instead, he found North and South America. After realizing how rich the New World was in resources, Spain, France, and England began setting up colonies.

King James I of England established 13 colonies along the coast of North America that would come together to form the United States. For the most part, the colonies were business ventures. Economic policy of the time advanced the main goal of exploration: making the mother country, and its monarch, rich.

Mercantilist laws created a trade system whereby the 13 colonies provided raw goods to England. England used these raw goods to produce manufactured goods that were sold back to the colonies and in European markets. England and other European countries wanted to export as much as possible and import as little as possible.

Section 2: Relationships between Political and Economic Freedoms

England's mercantilist economic policy led to the American Revolution. Under mercantilist policy, colonists were banned from competing with manufacturers in the mother country. In addition, the policy included taxes and tariffs on imports. One of the goals of a **tariff** is to entice consumers to buy more goods and services produced in their own country by making imported products more expensive.

The Navigation Acts, enforced from the 1650s to the 1760s, regulated and taxed trade with the colonies. These laws required colonists to trade only with English ships and only from a list of approved goods. The laws also forbade the colonies from exporting goods directly to other countries. The Sugar Act (1764), the Stamp Act (1765), and the Townshend Acts (1767) were new taxes and tariffs imposed on the colonies that were designed to help England pay its debts.

Colonists were vehemently opposed to this new taxation. Their slogan was "No taxation without representation." They argued that these dictates violated their natural commercial rights. The Boston Tea Party was a political and mercantile protest that occurred in 1773. This protest against taxation of tea escalated into the American Revolution.

Scotland's Adam Smith wrote *Wealth of Nations* in 1776, the same year that the Declaration of Independence was written. Smith promoted free trade and attacked mercantilism. He condemned trade guided by government regulation and policy. He said that an "invisible hand" of supply and demand should guide markets. He championed a new economic system of capitalism.

These two documents supported the creation of a **republic** with both economic and political freedom. Restrictions on trade and industry ended after the 13 colonies declared independence as the United States of America. However, after the war, debt was enormous, and Continental currency had a huge inflation rate, with purchasing power that had depreciated dramatically.

The first federal government had to deal with a bad economy throughout the 1780s. Motivation to create a robust central government under the new Constitution was strong because of the difficult economic times. Alexander Hamilton was chosen to direct federal economic policy as the Treasury secretary. His economic philosophies became standards of the current American capitalist economy.

Section 3: Scientific and Industrial Revolutions

Europeans' medieval beliefs and institutions led to profound political and economic changes that began in the 13 colonies and continued when the colonies united. Changes included capitalism and industrialization. Many ideas that took hold in the colonies could be traced back to the **Scientific Revolution**, an era that lasted from about 1550 to 1700. It began with Nicholas Copernicus, who proposed a sun-centered cosmos.

Copernicus was one of many people who used experiments and mathematics to explain natural phenomena. These explorations led to new beliefs and disproved many existing beliefs. The emergence of modern science was marked by developments in mathematics, astronomy, physics, chemistry, and biology. In addition, the Scientific Revolution fostered the creation of a new intellectual movement.

The **Enlightenment**, also called the **Age of Reason**, was part of culture in the late seventeenth and early eighteenth centuries. The movement focused primarily on freedom of speech, equality, freedom of the press, and religious tolerance. Reason and facts were considered more important than church ideology. Many of the ideas of the American Revolution formed during the Enlightenment.

In the eighteenth century, the **Agricultural Revolution** paved the way for the **Industrial Revolution**. Improvements in agriculture included better farming techniques like crop rotation and new technology like the seed drill that allowed seeds to be planted at an exact depth and space.

With improvements in agriculture, more crops were produced so more food was available; therefore, prices were lower. In addition, breeding large animals led to the production of higher-quality meat. People could afford to eat better, so they were healthier. This led to population growth.

Because of advances in technology, fewer workers were needed to work on farms. This left a large number of people in the labor force unemployed. The Industrial Revolution resulted in an increase in production made possible by the use of machines and often by the use of new energy sources such as steam and coal. Unemployed workers could find work in cities, where most factories were located.

Section 4: Key Economic Events That Have Shaped American Government and Policies

> **KEEP IN MIND . . .**
> Without the factors of production, land, labor, capital, and entrepreneurship, there could be no industrialization.

The United States was dealing with economic problems caused by the American Revolutionary War when George Washington was inaugurated as the first president in 1789. A series of import taxes passed by Congress that year provided a steady stream of revenue and protected domestic goods from foreign competition.

Secretary of the Treasury Alexander Hamilton wanted to use federal government power to expand a trade and manufacturing economy. Politicians like Thomas Jefferson and James Madison thought that a manufacturing economy would lead to corruption. Jefferson believed that decentralized agriculture, headed by land-owning farmers, was the best economic model.

Hamilton was in favor of creating a National Bank. He thought the economy should be protected by high tariffs and helped with infrastructure improvements. In his *Report on Manufactures*, Hamilton stated that the United States could only be independent when it was self-sufficient in all required economic products.

The War of 1812 encouraged the growth of domestic manufacturing. Factories were needed to replace foreign goods that were unavailable. By that time, the country's market economy, based on both farming and commerce, had been growing for 25 years. But following the war, there were more than 20 recessions and a few periods of economic growth in the remaining years of the nineteenth century.

The industrial transformation of the American workforce occurred in the **age of mass immigration**. A flood of European immigrants came to America from 1880 to 1920 when immigration laws were lenient. Only certain classes of people, such as beggars and anarchists, were barred from entering the United States. Immigrants were the mainstay of the industrial workforce.

In the twentieth century, innovations improved the standard of living for American consumers and increased business opportunities for firms. Many firms grew by taking advantage of **economies of scale**, or lowered costs of manufactured goods per unit, and better communication and transportation to run nationwide operations.

Kentucky Senator Henry Clay's **American System** was implemented in the early nineteenth century. This economic policy was built on doctrine advocated by Alexander Hamilton. Ideas found in this policy are still used today. The American System had the following three goals:

- Target government investments toward improvements in infrastructure.
- Protect industry through selective high tariffs and through **subsidies**.
- Maintain a national bank.

Section 5: Economic Causes and Impacts of Wars

The United States has fought in 12 major wars, beginning with the American Revolution. The country has been left with a staggering amount of debt after each war. The United States had a poor economy during its first years as a republic because of war debt. An examination of the economic causes of the Civil War offers insight into the multifactor justification for war.

Although slavery was the dominant issue that divided the North and the South, other issues like the federal tariff and internal improvements fueled animosity between the two regions.

- A tariff is a list of taxes on specified imported goods. Tariffs are used to raise revenue.
- Internal improvements are major domestic transportation projects paid for by Congress. These projects include canals, roads, and ports.

In theory, the tariff would raise the money needed to pay for the internal improvements. Therefore, the tariff would finance the infrastructure in a nationally linked market, making it easy to transport goods. The U.S. economy would prosper independent of foreign trade.

Most Northern businesses supported the American System, while most Southern businesses did not. The North thought the federal tariff would allow young American industry to grow, protected from mature English competition. The South believed the federal tariff was an unconstitutional system that enhanced the power of the North.

KEEP IN MIND . . .

Tariffs + National Bank + Infrastructure development = American System

The South was not exempt from the tariff. But eventually, tariff rates were lowered for buyers from the South, and tensions between the two regions eased. However, the South was economically dependent on slavery, while abolitionists in the North were trying to end slavery. This conflict led to the Civil War.

Economic reasoning can be used to make sense of any war. It is important to remember that peace and free trade reinforce each other. The more specialized people in different regions become, the more they grow to depend upon each other. This makes them more vulnerable to interruptions in market activities. Therefore, people in different regions have reason to cooperate with each other peacefully. Regardless of the reasons for a war, there is almost always an economic motive underlying the conflict.

Let's Review!

- The Age of Exploration, lasting from the fifteenth to the seventeenth century, was characterized by overseas exploration by countries like Spain, France, and England.
- Economic globalization began during the Age of Exploration.
- After the New World was discovered, England established 13 colonies along the coast of North America.
- Mercantilism helped European countries amass wealth through trade.
- The Navigation Acts were some of the mercantilist policies that favored England, the mother country. Colonists could trade only with English ships and only from a list of approved goods.
- Protests against taxation led to the American Revolution.
- The Declaration of Independence and Adam's Smith's *Wealth of Nations* were written in 1776.
- The Scientific Revolution, the Agricultural Revolution, and the Industrial Revolution improved living standards.
- The Enlightenment was a movement that emphasized individualism, reason, and skepticism. The movement challenged traditional religious views.
- During the Enlightenment, philosophers used the ideas and reason of the Scientific Revolution to solve problems in government and society.

- The American System united regions in the United States economically while encouraging a self-sufficient economy.
- During the age of mass immigration, from about 1880 to 1920, there was massive emigration out of Southern and Eastern Europe and into the United States.
- Economies of scale are the decrease in the per unit cost of production as the amount of production increases.
- Industrialization allowed industries to prosper and grow by taking advantage of economies of scale and a huge immigrant workforce.
- The American Civil War began for economic reasons, including a tariff and a Southern economy that depended on enslaved workers.
- Wars usually have an underlying economic reason.

Chapter 11 Economics Practice Quiz

1. Those who study economics understand _____

   A. why entrepreneurs fail.

   B. how scarcity is handled.

   C. decisions governments make.

   D. the best ways to spend money.

2. Which of the following is considered a basic assumption in economics?

   A. Individuals respond in predictable ways to incentives.

   B. Society is hurt when individuals do what is best for them.

   C. The value of a good is equal to the amount it costs to produce it.

   D. Trade between two countries always produces goods that cost less.

3. What does the expression "There's no such thing as a free lunch" imply?

   A. The production possibilities curve is concave.

   B. Free lunches are impossible in a capitalist economy.

   C. There are unintended social benefits when free lunches are offered.

   D. Opportunity costs are incurred when resources are used to produce goods/services.

4. What is the goal of households in a market economy?

   A. Maximize utility

   B. Buy goods and services

   C. Exchange resources with firms

   D. Get income through interest, wages, and rent

5. Resources are allocated most efficiently in a _____

   A. trade market.

   B. market economy.

   C. command economy.

   D. centrally planned society.

6. The U.S. GDP is the dollar value of all final goods and services _____

   A. produced by U.S. companies in a year.

   B. produced in the United States in a year.

   C. produced by U.S. companies and gained in trade in a year.

   D. minus intermediate goods made in the United States in a year.

7. What happens when a country limits inflation?

A. GDP goes down.

B. GDP per capita falls.

C. Prices remain stable.

D. Unemployment rises.

8. To whom did the 13 colonies provide raw materials?

A. Asia

B. Mother country

C. Native Americans

D. Spain and France

9. What are the 3Gs?

A. Three types of trade

B. Capitalist economic policy

C. Mercantilist economic policy

D. Motivations that fostered the Age of Exploration

10. What does a tariff do?

A. Lower prices

B. Restrict trade

C. Stop mercantilist economic policies

D. Make it easier to import goods into a country

CHAPTER 11 ECONOMICS
PRACTICE QUIZ – ANSWER KEY

1. B. Economics is the study of how individuals, businesses, and societies handle scarcity. **See Lesson: The Fundamentals of Economics.**

2. A. Decisions are influenced by incentives. Generally, people take action when the benefit is greater than the cost. **See Lesson: The Fundamentals of Economics.**

3. D. Opportunity cost is the most desirable alternative that is given up when a choice is made. Lunch is free, but a resource, time, is given up to eat the lunch. Therefore, the lunch is not really free. **See Lesson: The Fundamentals of Economics.**

4. A. The goal of households is to maximize utility, or happiness. Happiness is achieved through consumption of goods and services. **See Lesson: Microeconomics.**

5. B. In a market economy, society determines what products are produced; how, when and where products are made; to whom they are offered; and at what price they are offered—all based on supply and demand. **See Lesson: Microeconomics.**

6. B. GDP is the total market value of all final goods and services produced within a country's borders in a year. **See Lesson: Macroeconomics.**

7. C. Low inflation is beneficial for an economy. Consumers are encouraged to buy goods and services when prices remain stable. **See Lesson: Macroeconomics.**

8. B. Mercantilist laws created a trade system whereby the 13 colonies provided raw goods to England, the colonies' mother country. **See Lesson: Economics Through History.**

9. D. Glory, Gold, and God are the reasons that Europeans explored the world. **See Lesson: Economics Through History.**

10. B. Tariffs make imported goods more expensive than goods created by domestic workers. This encourages consumers to buy the cheaper domestic goods. **See Lesson: Economics Through History.**

CHAPTER 12 GEOGRAPHY AND THE WORLD

WORLD GEOGRAPHY: HUMAN/ENVIRONMENT INTERACTION

Introduction

This lesson describes how geography has affected the development of civilizations. It also examines the relationships between the environment and the development of societies.

Section 1: Nationhood and Statehood

Geography is the study of where people, places, and things are located and how each of these relates to the others.

A **nation** is a culturally defined group that has a shared past and desires a shared future. Nationhood relates to territory and political goals. Nations can be formed based on the following characteristics:

- Ethnicity
- Language
- Religion
- Physical geography

For example, Kosovo is a nation that was created out of the former Yugoslavia by ethnic Albanians who are Muslims and compose a majority of the population.

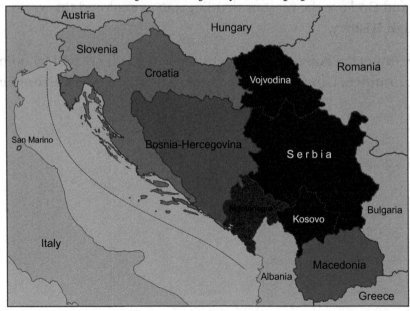

Name	Location	Bordering Nations	Population
Republic of Kosovo	Balkan area of Europe	Serbia, Macedonia, Albania, Montenegro	Muslim majority / Serbian minority

Language affects the formations of nations. Two examples are South Africa and Russia.

Country	Location	Official Language
Russia	Europe and Asia	35 languages; Russian, based on the Cyrillic alphabet, is the official language.
South Africa	Africa	11 languages including Swahili, African dialects, and Dutch Afrikaner; Swahili is the official language.

Religion can divide a nation and lead to the creation of a new nation. For example, Northern Ireland, a Protestant nation, shares the island of Ireland with the Republic of Ireland, a Catholic country.

<Insert map of Ireland, showing both Northern Ireland and the Republic of Ireland.>

Physical geography affects how nations are formed and how civilizations develop. River valleys and oceans are two examples of physical geography that have affected how nations form.

Body of Water or Waters	Country
Nile River valley	Egypt
Indus River valley	India
Yellow River and Yangtze River valley	China
Amazon River	Brazil
Atlantic and Pacific Oceans	United States

Physical geography affected the development of classical civilizations. Examples include the Maya, Rome, Greece, China, and India.

Group	Empire or Name	Location	Contributions
Maya	Mayan Empire	Central America and Mexico; modern-day Yucatan peninsula in Mexico, Guatemala, Belize	Hieroglyphic writing system; concept of zero; calendar
Greeks	Classical Greece	Mediterranean area of Europe	Philosophers; epics; poetry; drama and comedy (theater); Ionic, Doric, and Corinthian architecture; democracy

Group	Empire or Name	Location	Contributions
Romans	Classical Rome and Roman Empire	Mediterranean area of Europe	Roads, aqueducts, arches; legal system
Guptas	Gupta Dynasty	India	Advances in math, astronomy, arts, and technology
Hans	Han Dynasty	China	Historiography; silk trade; centralized government.
Qin	Qin Dynasty (first in China)	China	Standardized alphabetic script; Great Wall; terra cotta warriors

Statehood means being recognized as an independent state or country. Elements of statehood are

- territory;
- population;
- government; and
- political goals.

Examples of states are Germany and Poland in Europe, Argentina and Bolivia in South America, and Michigan and Texas in the United States.

Example

Which civilization developed because of a fertile river valley?

A. Polish

C. Egyptian

B. Peruvian

D. Canadian

KEEP IN MIND . . .
Nations can be formed because of language, geography, religion, ethnicity or a combination of these factors.

C. Egyptian. The Nile River valley provided fishing and a fertile soil for the development of agriculture. See **Lesson: World Geography: Human/Environment Interaction.**

Section 2: Sustainability

To *sustain* means "to give strength to" or "to support." In terms of geography, sustainability means to make good use of resources to meet current needs while protecting the needs of future generations.

Sustainability includes practices in which people should and should not participate, such as the following:

- Don't harm the environment.
- Don't deplete natural resources.
- Do use energy wisely.
- Do develop products to help the environment.
- Do practice ways of life to save resources.
- Do try to "go green."

"**Going green**" means making decisions that help the environment and sustain resources.

Examples	Results - Benefits
Recycling	Reduces pollution
Buying glass rather than plastic bottles	Reduces litter
Using less water	Saves resources for future generations
Turning off lights when leaving a room	Saves energy and money
Saving emails on the computer rather than printing them on paper	Saves paper, trees, and money
Carpooling	Saves fuel, decreases air pollution
Landscaping	Prevents or decreases erosion of soil

Sustainability can be affected by climate change. **Climate change** is the shift in weather patterns that can be global or regional. Climate change is caused by human activities that put more carbon dioxide into the air. Examples of human activities that cause climate change include the following:

- Burning fossil fuels such as coal and gas
- Deforestation

Putting increased pollution and gases in the atmosphere causes a **greenhouse effect**. A greenhouse effect occurs when gases trap the sun's heat and gradually increase the temperature of the atmosphere. This effect is similar to the temperature increases in the glass houses, called greenhouses, where flowers and plants are grown. These greenhouses are warm to help the flowers and plants grow. The gases from the warm air do not escape the building. When pollution and gases are placed in the atmosphere, the atmosphere traps them and the gases trap the sun's heat, increasing Earth's temperature.

Global warming affects sustainability. **Global warming** is increasing global temperatures as a result of the greenhouse effect. Glaciers are melting and temperatures are rising because of global warming.

Example

Which is an example of global warming?

A. Reforestation   C. Colder winters

B. "Green living"   D. Melting of glaciers

KEEP IN MIND . . .

Maintaining sustainability for future generations includes protecting current resources.

D. When Earth's atmosphere becomes warmer because of greenhouses gases, Earth's surface warms. See **Lesson: World Geography: Human/Environment Interaction.**

Section 3: Technology

Technology uses tools to create, describe, and analyze information. Information technology is used in the field of geography to describe and explain the spatial structure of people and their world. Examples of information technology include the following:

- Mapping
- Global/Geographic Information Systems (GIS)
- Global Positioning Systems (GPS)

Computerized mapping is the process of making maps with computers instead of cartographers (map makers) drawing the maps by hand.

Geographic Information Systems (GIS) are computer databases that individuals, businesses, and governments use to study sustainability and the spatial structure of society. The databases

- collect data;
- manage data;
- analyze data; and
- provide data results.

This table describes examples of possible uses of GIS databases.

Field	Application
Industry	Transportation routes
	Manufacturing processes
	Marketing demographics
	Population density
	Production efficiency
	Sales
Health	Disease control – tracking location and spread of diseases
	Location of healthcare centers
	Population densities for insurance rates
	Access to medical supplies
	Death rates from various causes, such as cancer
Safety and Emergency Services	Tracking location of law enforcement, ambulance, and fire services
	Tracking and improving response time
Weather	Causes and effects of climate change and global warming
	Tracking storms
	Probabilities of disasters, such as earthquakes, hurricanes, and floods
	Glacial melting
	Locations and effects of droughts

Field	Application
Conservation	Destruction of forests and wildlife habitats
Government Aid	Locations
	Types needed
	Amounts of aid
	Resources for aid
	Personnel needed
	Similarity of past conditions in other areas

A **Global Positioning System (GPS)** can be useful for businesses to track shipments and for transportation providers to determine directions to destinations. In the past, drivers used hard copies of road maps for directions to a destination. Today, they likely use GPS. Government agencies and departments use a GPS system in various situations, depending on the project. For example, a local government may use GPS to track vehicles, such as snowplows, to provide better services and to conserve funds.

Example

Which of the following is a difference between GIS and GPS?

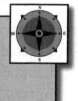

KEEP IN MIND . . .
Technology can help individuals access and analyze data to become better informed.

   A. They are positioning devices.

   B. They are information databases.

   C. Individuals use GIS, but governments and businesses use GPS.

   D. GIS is a computer-based information system, but GPS obtains its information from satellites.

   D. GIS and GPS are different technology tools that serve different purposes.

Section 4: Natural Resources

Natural resources are substances that appear in nature and are not made by humans. They include both renewable and nonrenewable sources of energy. Fossil fuels such as coal, oil, and natural gas are nonrenewable natural resources. Trees are an example of a renewable resource.

Resources are found in all countries. Examples are shown in this table.

Resource	Location
Water	Oceans and lakes
Air	Atmosphere
Oil	Middle East, Russia, United States, China
Natural gas	Russia, Middle East, United States, Venezuela, Algeria, Nigeria

Resource	Location
Forests	All continents except Antarctica. However, fossilized woods have been found there, indicating forests once existed on the continent.
Salt	Mines: China, United States, Pakistan, Bolivia, Canada; Sea Salt
Tin	Bolivia, Nigeria, Southeast Asia
Gold	South Africa, Canada, United States, Russia, China, Peru, Australia
Coal	United States, China, Russia, Canada
Iron ore	China, United States, Australia, Brazil, South Africa, Ukraine, India
Wetlands	All continents except Antarctica; inland and on coasts.

Natural resources are important. Some are critical to human existence. Water and air are examples. Others are used in everyday life to heat homes, build structures, feed the population, and power vehicles.

Natural resources can be depleted. To **deplete** means "to use up." Fish and seafood can be depleted by overfishing. Overuse can deplete forests, coal, and other metals. When consumer demand increases, supplies of resources may decrease. As population increases, the demand for resources becomes greater. Natural resources can be preserved, for example, by using fewer fossil fuels and preserving clean water supplies. Reforestation and protecting wetlands can also help preserve natural resources.

Example

Which of the following natural resources is necessary for human existence?

A. Air   B. Coal   C. Iron ore   D. Wetlands

A. The only listed natural resource that is necessary for existence is air. The others are used in everyday life but are important, not necessary.

Section 5: Human Changes to the Environment

Humans can positively and negatively affect the environment. When you have an effect, or leave your mark, on the environment, you are said to leave your "footprint."

Negative changes affecting the environment include the following:

- Overpopulation
- Polluted air and water
- Deforestation
- Depleting the atmosphere's ozone level

Results of negative changes are given in this table.

Overpopulation	Using too many natural resources, making more living space while reducing greenspaces, damaging ecosystems, depleting forests, using too many fossil fuels, increasing levels of gases in the air to cause global warming and climate change
Polluted air and water	Smog, coral reefs die, garbage in waters causes impure waters, marine life starves and dies from plastics in waters, acid rain due to too much carbon dioxide in air
Deforestation	More greenhouse gases, removal of animals' habitats, depleted soil, loss of building materials
Ozone depletion	Atmosphere unable to absorb ultraviolet light, more gases in atmosphere, eye damage, skin cancers

Humans also affect the environment in positive ways, such as the following:

- Protecting endangered species
- Recycling
- Establishing parks and wildlife preserves
- Developing greenspaces
- Establishing government agencies such as the Environmental Protection Agency
- Avoiding littering
- Reforesting

Example

When Earth's ozone level in the atmosphere is decreased, _____.

> **BE CAREFUL!**
> The footprint you leave on Earth depends on the way you interact with the environment. It may be positive or negative!

    A. acid rain occurs

    B. soils become more acidic

    C. greenspaces are difficult to establish

    D. people may be at higher risk of skin cancer

    D. Ultraviolet rays cannot be properly absorbed when the ozone layer is depleted. Ultraviolet rays can cause skin cancer. See **Lesson: World Geography: Human/ Environment Interaction.**

Let's Review!

- Geography affects the development of civilizations
- Geography describes the relationship between the environment of the development of societies.
- Nationhood and statehood are affected by geography.
- Sustainability means to make good use of current resources to protect future needs.
- Technology is used in geography to describe and explain the spatial structure of the world and human populations.
- Natural resources are sources of energy that are renewable but can be depleted
- Human changes to the environment can have a negative or positive "footprint" on the environment

Global Connections: Cultures & Society

Introduction:

This lesson describes the concept of borders between peoples and nations and the forms of human migration.

Section 1: Borders between Peoples and Nations

A **border** is an edge or line that separates or defines the characteristics of something, such as countries, geographic areas, transportation areas, or soil types. Borders may be fixed or fluid, changing as circumstances and conditions change. In the field of geography, borders are important in studying the concept of regions and places. A **region** is an area. It may have a fixed border, or the border may be moveable or flexible. A region can be defined in various ways for different purposes. Three types of regions are important to consider in the study of geography:

- Formal
- Functional
- Perceptual, vernacular, or uniform

A **formal region** has characteristics that cannot be changed. It may be an area of a specific type of landform, such as mountains. A formal region shares common traits and has boundaries. If the U.S. government has set aside a national forest for protection, the boundaries for the forest will include all lands set aside by the government. A region may have a specific location, such as Central Asia, the Midwest (in the United States), Latin America, or the Balkans (in Europe). Politicians refer to "Red" and "Blue" states to show strength of the Republican and Democratic parties in the United States during election years.

A **functional region** focuses on an activity. It may be a common trait, such as a school district, or the area of a large city, called the metropolis. It may also be the suburban area of a city or a region of the world that encompasses an area of poverty or wealth. One example is industrial areas such as the steel-making areas of Birmingham, England, and the Saar Industrial Region of Germany.

A **perceptual**, **vernacular**, or **uniform** region is an area where people have shared values, shared history, or shared culture. The region may be based on religion or common ancestry.

A **place** is a location. In geography, there are two types of locations:

- Absolute location
- Relative location

An absolute location can be described by lines of latitude and longitude, which pinpoint it exactly on Earth's surface. A street address is another example of an absolute location. A **relative location** explains where something is in relation to something else. For example, the statement that "the Seine River in France begins in northeast France, runs through Paris, and empties into the English Channel near LaHavre" tells the listener the general location of where the river flows but does not provide an exact (absolute) location.

Example

2211 Lower Avenue is an example of a(n) _____.

   A. border   B. boundary   C. relative location   D. absolute location

   D. It is an absolute location because it is described exactly. See **Lesson: Global Connections: Cultures & Society.**

Natural and cultural diversity are important aspects relating to the concept of borders between peoples and nations. **Natural diversity** refers to the plants and animals that are in ecosystems. Another name for natural diversity is biodiversity. Diversity applies to differences within species, among species, and among ecosystems. Diversity within species results from genetics. Does a person have blue eyes or brown? Blond hair or black? Genes determine such traits. When there is diversity among species, a region contains a variety of different plants and animals. For example, several species of squirrels, a species of deer, and a few species of rabbits may life in a forest region. Diversity also applies to differences among ecosystems. An **ecosystem** is a community of organisms connected to their environment. A rainforest ecosystem, for example, is located in a warm, tropical climate and has a variety of animals living in a forest that has an abundance of rain and a dense plant growth. El Yunque, a rainforest in Puerto Rico that has a variety of plants and animals, is the only rainforest in the U.S. forest system. The plants and animals living in an ecosystem depend on one another for food, water, and shelter.

Cultural diversity means there are a variety of groups within a society. The variety is based on culture and ethnicity. Culture includes shared values, beliefs, behaviors, language, and religion. Boston, Massachusetts, is a city in which many cultural groups live. Many Irish immigrants came to the city during the early and mid-1840s. They shared a common language, religion, values, and beliefs. They settled in the North End of the city near the waterfront. The Italians also settled the North End of Boston in the early 1800s. Today, they have carried on their culinary traditions by establishing restaurants featuring foods and recipes brought from their country and ancestors. The contributions of these two groups and others show the multiculturalism of the United States.

Cultural and natural diversity are connected because they are both important to the variety of the environment. Both need to be preserved, and both contribute to society.

Example

Which of the following regions includes desert ecosystems?

   A. Canada   B. England   C. New York   D. North Africa

D. North Africa has dry areas where there is little vegetation and little rain. The environment is harsh and hostile to both plants and animals.

Geographic tools are used to obtain and analyze information to better society. Geographic tools include the following:

- Maps
- Charts
- Globes
- Graphs
- Diagrams
- Photographs
- Remote images from space

Geographic tools help explain ideas that can be difficult to explain in words. Maps, whether on paper or on GPS systems, can help locate landmarks, set transportation routes, and assist in fighting disease. Maps can show population densities, locations of religious and cultural groups, transportation centers, areas of rainfall, and weather areas. Keys and legends on a map help people interpret what information the map shows. When maps are drawn to scale, the scale is uniform.

Graphs and charts are particularly good for showing percentages and large numbers. Circle graphs may show percentages of ethnic groups in a populated area; a bar graph may show the rise or fall of unemployment over a four-decade period. A diagram is a drawing that shows how something works. As a geographic tool, a diagram may show how a transport system should work to efficiently move agricultural goods from farm to market.

A photograph or image from space can show Earth's surface in detail. Photographs can show precise areas of forest that need to be replanted. They can also show the benefits of cultural diversity, issues with ecosystems, and weather patterns.

Example

Which geographical tool would be BEST to explain a historical event, such as the linking of the railroads that formed the first transcontinental railroad?

A. Map   B. Chart   C. Globe   D. Photograph

D. A photograph can show workers driving the "golden spike" to join the railroads.

Section 2: Forms of Human Migration

There are four main forms of human migration:

- Immigration, emigration, and diaspora
- Culture, cultural diffusion, and assimilation
- Population trends and issues

- Rural and urban settlement

Immigration is coming into a foreign country to live there permanently. People who entered the United States from a foreign country during the Industrial Revolution of the 1880s and 1890s to live in the United States permanently were immigrants. They mainly emigrated from southeastern Europe. To **emigrate** means to leave a country of one's residence and move to another country permanently to make a home. The people who move are referred to as **migrants**.

Diaspora refers to people living outside their homeland. These groups spread their cultures in the places where they are living but remain loyal to their homelands. Diaspora from India, for example, have come to the United States in great numbers. Albanian Kosovars moved from Kosovo during the Kosovo War in the 1990s and found homes in Switzerland, Germany, and Turkey. They continue to support their families remaining in Kosovo in several ways, including sending money to relative. They also maintain a connection with family and return for visits.

Culture is the beliefs, values, and ways of life associated with a specific group of people. It may include religious beliefs, the ways holidays are celebrated, and how children are educated. Certain types of food are associated with different cultures. For example, sushi is associated with Japanese cultures, and pierogies are associated with Polish culture (and other cultures from Eastern Europe).

To diffuse means to spread over a large area. Cultural diffusion is the spreading of a culture over an area.

Cinco de Mayo is a Mexican holiday that has spread to the United States and other countries with large Mexican populations. Adding a different kind of main course for a Christmas Day or Christmas Eve meal is a Slovakian tradition that has become popular with some people in the United States who like fish. Carp, a special fish

> **KEEP IN MIND . . .**
> Foods you enjoy from other countries—curries from Thailand, crepes from France, and stollen from Germany—are part of the cultural diffusion from those countries!

for the Slovak people, is traditional to serve on Christmas Eve. Some children have a piñata at a birthday celebration. A piñata is a container that is made of pottery or paper mâché and holds candy or little toys. Celebrating in this way is a Mexican tradition that has been culturally diffused to other cultures and geographic areas.

While the word *diffusion* means "spreading," the term *assimilate* means "absorbing." Cultural assimilation occurs when cultural groups absorb, or adopt, some of the practices and language of their new country. People who come to the United States become assimilated when they learn English. They may also become assimilated by eating foods that are considered "American." People who move to Poland, for example, become assimilated in the Polish culture by learning the Polish language, joining in celebrations significant to Poles, and learning to enjoy the foods of the country.

Population trends and issues have global connections. A *trend* is something that is current at a certain time. Trends change. What is popular in clothing styles one year may change the next. Population trends, such as the size of a population or the area in which a population lives, also change. There were more than 7 million people in the world in 2018, and the numbers of people are expected to increase over the next few years. Reasons for this increase include the following:

- People live longer.
- Birth rate is greater than death rate.
- There are more multigenerational households.

As the number of people on the globe increases, issues can arise:

- Urban areas can become overcrowded. People move to or live in areas where they believe they can have a good life for themselves and their families. A good life means a job, shelter, and education. Urban infrastructures are not always able to meet the needs of increasing populations. An **infrastructure** consists of the services and facilities needed to make a city or area function. It may include water and sanitation services and a transportation system. It also includes schools, healthcare facilities, and sources of food. If these services and facilities are inadequate, then the infrastructure cannot support the increase in population.
- The number of immigrants can increase. For example, in the 2010s, European countries have experienced a swell of immigrants from war-torn countries in Africa and the Middle East. Many do not speak the language of the country to which they move, and it can take time for them to adapt to the culture of their new home.

Migration also affects rural and urban settlement. There is a trend of young people moving away from small towns and rural areas where they grew up. Fewer young family members want to take over the farming responsibilities of their parents who have produced agricultural products for the nation. There is not enough work in many rural areas throughout the world, resulting in people moving to urban areas. In some areas of the world, droughts and famine have caused people to move to urban areas from rural areas. In other areas, people are unable to survive on subsistence farming. **Subsistence farming** is a type of farming that provides enough for the family but does not provide enough for sale. The following distribution map shows the population centers in various locations.

(Please insert a map, chart, etc. to show urban/rural population centers. It should be similar to the one shown in this link:https://www.groasis.com/en/planting/migration-from-the-countryside-to-urban-areas)

Example

A multigenerational family is one that _____.

A. has a single adult

B. has a single person

C. has a mother and father

D. has parents, children, and grandparents

D. A multigenerational family includes several generations. See **Lesson: Global Connections: Cultures & Society.**

Let's Review!

- Regions are areas of the world that may have fixed borders.
- Regions can be defined in various ways for different purposes.
- Locations can be absolute or relative.
- Natural diversity refers to plants and animals in ecosystems.
- Cultural diversity refers to the variety of cultures in a society.
- Geographic tools can be used to obtain, analyze, and utilize information.
- Migrants are people who move.
- Cultural diffusion and assimilation can take place in the same country or region.
- Population trends change over time.

CHAPTER 12 GEOGRAPHY AND THE WORLD PRACTICE QUIZ

1. Kosovo's nationhood resulted primarily from which element of geography?

   A. Religion

   B. Ethnicity

   C. Language

   D. Physical geography

2. Modern-day India was the home of which dynasty?

   A. Qin

   B. Han

   C. Maya

   D. Gupta

3. The Great Wall, which was built to keep invaders out of the country, was built by which dynasty?

   A. Qin

   B. Han

   C. Gupta

   D. Mayan

4. The line that separates Thailand from Cambodia is a(n) _____.

   A. area

   B. region

   C. border

   D. boundary

5. Southeast Asia is a(n) _____.

   A. area

   B. region

   C. country

   D. boundary

6. A region that has characteristics that cannot be changed is a _____ region.

   A. fixed

   B. formal

   C. uniform

   D. functional

Chapter 12 Geography and the World Practice Quiz – Answer Key

1. **B.** The nation was formed by the Albanian majority. Although most people in Kosovo speak Albanian, ethnicity was the primary basis for the formation of the nation. **See Lesson: World Geography: Human/Environment Interaction.**

2. **D.** The Gupta Dynasty, which advanced mathematics and the arts, was located in present-day India. **See Lesson: World Geography: Human/Environment Interaction.**

3. **A.** While the Hans developed the silk trade, the Qin were builders and protectors of China. They built the Great Wall to protect their country from the Mongols. **See Lesson: World Geography: Human/Environment Interaction.**

4. **C.** A border is a line that separates countries. **See Lesson: Global Connections: Cultures & Society.**

5. **B.** Southeast Asia is made up of several countries and is a region. **See Lesson: Global Connections: Cultures & Society.**

6. **B.** A formal region has characteristics that cannot be changed. **See Lesson: Global Connections: Cultures & Society.**

SECTION V. SCIENCE

CHAPTER 13 SCIENTIFIC REASONING

DESIGNING AN EXPERIMENT

This lesson introduces the idea of experimental design and the factors one must consider to build a successful experiment.

Scientific Reasoning

When conducting scientific research, two types of scientific reasoning can be used to address scientific problems: inductive reasoning and deductive reasoning. Both forms of reasoning are also used to generate a hypothesis. **Inductive reasoning** involves drawing a general conclusion from specific observations. This form of reasoning is referred to as the "from the bottom up" approach. Information gathered from specific observations can be used to make a general conclusion about the topic under investigation. In other words, conclusions are based on observed patterns in data.

FOR EXAMPLE

Use your inductive reasoning to determine the next item in the sequence of events:

1. fall, winter, spring . . .
2. 4, 8, 12 . . .

Deductive reasoning is the logical approach of making a prediction about a general principle to draw a specific conclusion. It is recognized as the "from the top down" approach. For example, deductive reasoning is used to test a theory by collecting data that challenges the theory.

DID YOU KNOW?

While Francis Bacon was developing the scientific method, he advocated for the use of inductive reasoning. This is why inductive reasoning is considered to be at the heart of the scientific method.

Example

Which is an example of deductive reasoning?

    A. A scientist concludes that a plant species is drought resistant after watching it survive a hot summer.

    B. After a boy observes where the sun rises, he tells his mom that the sun will rise in the east in the morning.

    C. Since it is well established that noble gases are stable, scientists can safely say that the noble gas neon is stable.

    D. A state transportation department decides to use sodium road salt after studies show that calcium road salt is ineffective.

The correct answer is **C**. The statement that noble gases are stable is a general principle or well-accepted theory. Thus, the specific conclusion that the noble gas neon is stable can be drawn from this general principle.

Designing an Experiment

According to the scientific method, the following steps are followed after making an observation or asking a question: (1) conduct background research on the topic, (2) formulate a hypothesis, (3) test the hypothesis with an experiment, (5) analyze results, and (6) report conclusions that explain whether the results support the hypothesis. This means after using logical reasoning to formulate a hypothesis, it is time to design a way to test this hypothesis. This is where **experimental design** becomes a factor.

Experimental design is the process of creating a reliable experiment to test a hypothesis. It involves organizing an experiment that produces the amount of data and right type of data to answer the question. A study's validity is directly affected by the construction and design of an experiment. This is why it is important to carefully consider the following components that are used to build an experiment:

- **Independent variable:** This factor does not depend on what happens in the experiment. The independent variable has values that can be changed or manipulated in an experiment. Data from the independent variable is graphed on the x-axis.
- **Dependent variable:** This factor depends on the independent variable. Recognized as the outcome of interest, its value cannot change. It can only be observed during an experiment. Data from the dependent variable is graphed on the y-axis.
- **Treatment group:** This is the group that receives treatment in an experiment. It is the item or subject in an experiment that the researcher manipulates. During an experiment, treatment is directly imposed on a group and the response is observed.
- **Control group:** This is a baseline measure that remains constant. Used for comparison purposes, it is the group that neither receives treatment nor is experimentally manipulated. One type of control is a **placebo**. This false treatment is administered to a

control group to account for the placebo effect. This is a psychological effect where the brain convinces the body that a fake treatment is the real thing. Often, experimental drug studies use placebos.

> **TEST TIP**
>
> It can be hard to remember the differences between an independent and a dependent variable. Use the following mnemonic to help keep those differences clear:
>
> **D** = dependent　　　　**M** = manipulated variable　**Y** = y-axis
> **R** = responding variable　**I** = independent variable　**X** = x-axis

Example

A control group

A. modifies the desired outcome of an experiment.

B. fluctuates in value if an experimental factor is manipulated.

C. establishes a baseline measure to compare dependent variables to.

D. depends on the type of independent variable chosen for an experiment.

The correct answer is **C.** A control group functions as a baseline measure or constant that is not influenced by experimental manipulations. It does not receive treatment in a study.

Data Analysis and Interpretation

When researchers test their hypotheses, the next step in the scientific method is to analyze the data and collect empirical evidence. **Empirical evidence** is acquired from observations and through experiments. It is a repeatable form of evidence that other researchers, including the researcher overseeing the study, can verify. Thus, when analyzing data, empirical evidence must be used to make valid conclusions.

While analyzing data, scientists tend to observe cause-and-effect relationships. These relationships can be quantified using correlations. **Correlations** measure the amount of linear association between two variables. There are three types of correlations:

- **Positive correlation:** As one variable increases, the other variable also increases. This is also known as a direct correlation.

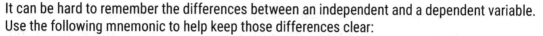

> **FOR EXAMPLE**
>
> Studies have shown there is a positive correlation between smoking and lung cancer development. The more you smoke, the greater your risk of developing lung cancer. An example of a negative correlation is the relationship between speed and time when distance is kept constant. The faster a car travels, the amount of time to reach the destination decreases.

- **Negative correlation:** As one variable increases, the other decreases. The opposite is true if one variable decreases. A negative correlation is also known as an inverse correlation or an indirect correlation.
- **No correlation:** There is no connection or relationship between two variables.

From graphs to tables, there are many ways to visually display data. Typically, graphs are a powerful way to visually demonstrate the relationships between two or more variables. This is the case for correlations. A positive correlation is indicated as a positive slope in a graph, as shown below. Negative correlations are indicated as a negative slope in a graph. If there is no correlation between two variables, data points will not show a pattern.

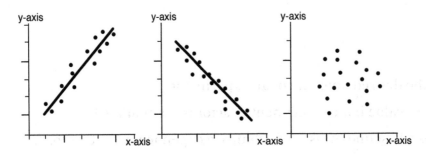

Examples

1. **What is another term used to describe a direct correlation?**

    A. Positive slope   B. Negative slope   C. Inverse correlation   D. Indirect correlation

    The correct answer is **A**. A direct correlation occurs when one variable increases as another increases. Graphically, this is shown as a positive slope.

2. **If a researcher notices a negative slope while analyzing his data, what can he conclude?**

    A. The variables exhibit no correlation.

    B. A different control group should be used.

    C. The variables exhibit a direct correlation.

    D. The variables exhibit an indirect correlation.

    The correct answer is **D**. A negative slope is indicative of an indirect, negative, or inverse correlation.

Scientific Tools and Measurement

Researchers use a wide variety of tools to collect data. The most common types of measuring tools are outlined below:

Barometer	Used to determines the air pressure in a space.
Clock or stopwatch	Used to record time.
Graduated cylinder	Used to measure the volume of liquid.
Ruler	Used to measure the length of an object.
Thermometer	Used to measure temperature. Measurement values may be expressed in degrees Celsius or Fahrenheit.
Triple beam balance	Used to measure the mass of an object or to determine the unit of mass. Electronic balances are used to measure very small masses.

Measured values are often associated with scientific units. Typically, the metric system is preferred when reporting scientific results. This is because nearly all countries use the metric system. Additionally, there is a single base unit of measurement for each type of measured quantity. For example, the base unit for length cannot be the same as the base unit for mass. The following base units are used:

Unit of Measurement	Base Unit Name	Abbreviation
Length	Meter	m
Mass	Gram	g
Volume	Liter	L

Another benefit of the metric system is that units are expressed in multiples of 10. This allows a researcher to express reported values that may be very large or small. This expression is facilitated by using the following metric prefixes, which are added to the base unit name:

Prefix	Abbreviation	Value	Description
kilo	k	1,000	thousand
hecto	h	100	hundred
deka	da	10	ten
BASE	N/A	1	one
deci	d	0.1	tenth
centi	c	0.01	hundredth
milli	m	0.001	thousandth

Example

What base measurement unit is associated with reported values measured by a graduated cylinder?

A. Celsius   B. Gram   C. Liter   D. Meter

The correct answer is **C**. Liter is a base unit for volume. Volume is measured using a graduated cylinder.

Let's Review!

- Formulating a hypothesis requires using either inductive or deductive reasoning.
- A good experimental design properly defines all variables and considers how data will be analyzed.
- Correlations illustrate the cause-and-effect relationships between two variables.
- Positive and negative correlations can be displayed graphically by analyzing the slope of a line.
- Different devices are used to measure objects in an experimental study.
- The metric system is usually used when expressing the units of measured values.

SCIENTIFIC NOTATION

This lesson begins by explaining how to convert measurements with very large or very small values into more manageable numbers using scientific notation. It then explores the structure of the atom and describes how to determine the number of protons, neutrons, and electrons in an atom of a specific element. Finally, it describes the relationship between isotopes of the same element and the effects that these isotopes have on the average atomic mass of an element.

Scientific Notation

Scientists often work with very large and very small numbers. For example, the radius of Earth's orbit around the sun is very large: 15,000,000,000,000 centimeters. On the other extreme, the radius of a hydrogen atom is very small: 0.00000000529 centimeters. To make these numbers more manageable, scientists write them using **scientific notation**. Scientific notation is a way to represent numbers and contains three components, which are shown in the diagram below.

Understanding how these components relate to one another makes it possible to convert between standard notation and scientific notation. The coefficient is a number that has a value of at least 1 but less than 10 and includes all significant digits in the given value. Another way to think about this is that there should always be one non-zero digit before the decimal point.

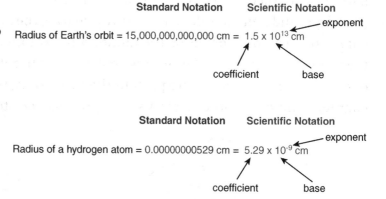

In scientific notation, the base is always 10.

The exponent indicates the number of places the decimal point needs to move. Notice that when the exponent is positive, the decimal place moves to the right; this is how larger numbers are represented. When the exponent is negative, the decimal place moves to the left; this is how smaller numbers are represented. When the decimal must move beyond the digits that are in the measurement, the "empty" spaces are filled in with zeros.

> **KEY POINT**
> When converting from scientific notation to standard notation, a negative exponent requires the decimal point to move to the left, and a positive exponent requires the decimal point to move to the right.

Example

The length of a year is 31,560,000 seconds. What is this value in scientific notation?

A. 0.3156×10^{-6} s   B. 3.156×10^{-7} s   C. 3.156×10^{7} s   D. 31.56×10^{6} s

The correct answer is **C**. The coefficient is a value between 1 and 10 and includes all digits, which is 3.156. Starting with that coefficient, the decimal must be moved seven places to the right to get the value in standard notation, which means that the exponent is a positive seven.

The Atom

All matter is made of atoms. Every atom contains a dense core in the center called a **nucleus**. The nucleus is composed of subatomic particles called **protons** and **neutrons**. Surrounding this core is an area known as the **electron cloud**, in which smaller subatomic particles known as **electrons** are moving.

The Bohr model below shows these components of the atom. In the model, each subatomic particle is marked with a charge. Protons have a positive (+) charge, electrons have a negative (–) charge, and neutrons do not carry any charge; they are neutral. Therefore, the overall charge of an atom depends on the numbers of protons and electrons and is not influenced by the number of neutrons. An atom is neutral if the number of protons is equal to the number of electrons. If there are more protons than electrons, the atom will have an overall positive charge; if there are more electrons than protons, the atom will have an overall negative charge.

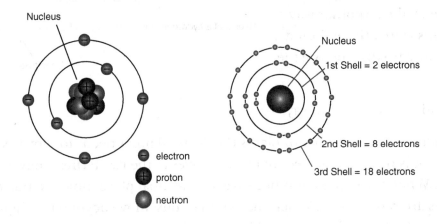

COMPARE THE BOHR MODEL TO A REAL ATOM.

Note that this model is not to scale. The nucleus should be much smaller because it is about 10,000 times smaller than the electron cloud in a real atom. Also, the space between the electrons a real atom is much greater than in the model. In a real atom, the electron cloud is mostly empty space.

To further compare these three subatomic particles, their locations, charges, and masses are shown in the table below. The unit used for mass is the **atomic mass unit (amu)**. The masses of a proton or neutron are considerably larger than the mass of an electron. This difference in mass has important implications. First, because the nucleus is so small relative to the overall size of the atom and contains the more massive protons and neutrons, it is extremely dense. Second, because the electrons are almost 2,000 times less massive than the other subatomic particles, they do not significantly influence the atom's mass.

Subatomic Particle	Symbol	Location	Charge	Mass (amu)
Proton	$p+$	Nucleus	+1	1.0
Neutron	$n0$	Nucleus	0	1.0
Electron	$e-$	Electron cloud	–1	0.00054

One final note about the Bohr model of the atom is that the electrons lie on rings. These rings represent energy levels, sometimes referred to as electron "shells." Electrons that occupy energy levels that are closest to the nucleus have the least energy. Electrons found farther from the nucleus have more energy. A limited number of electrons can occupy each energy level. The first energy level can fit up to 2 electrons. The second energy level can fit up to 8 electrons. The third energy level can fit up to 18 electrons. An atom in its normal state will have electrons lying in the lowest possible energy levels.

While the Bohr model provides a good way to visualize the atom, its representation of the electron cloud is not completely accurate. Electrons move around the nucleus in different energy levels, but this movement is not restricted to specific circular orbits as the Bohr model indicates. The **quantum mechanical model** (also known as the electron cloud model) describes the probable locations of electrons because their exact pathways, locations, and speeds cannot be determined simultaneously.

Example

Which subatomic particles affect the overall charge of the atom?

A. Only protons

B. Protons and neutrons

C. Protons and electrons

D. Protons, neutrons, and electrons

The correct answer is **C**. Because protons are positively charged and electrons are negatively charged, they affect the overall charge of the atom. Neutrons do not affect the charge because they are uncharged.

The Periodic Table of the Elements

The atom is not only the basic building block of matter, but also the smallest unit of an element that can be defined as that element. All known elements are listed in the periodic table.

Periodic Table of Elements

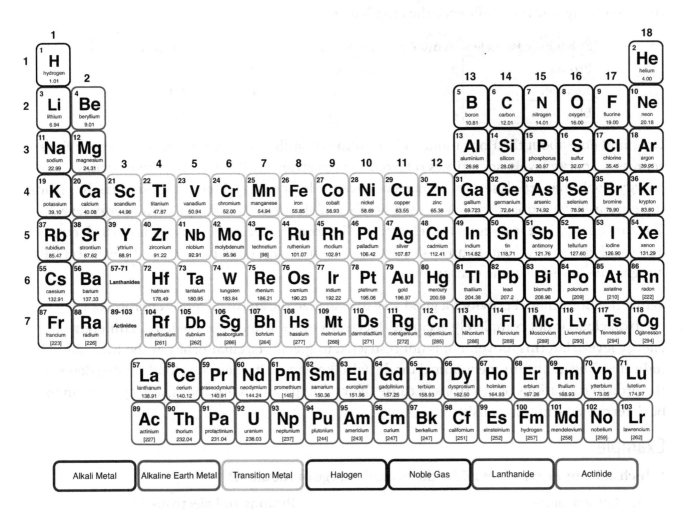

In the periodic table, elements are arranged in rows, also known as **periods**, and columns, also known as **groups**. Both the periods and the groups can be referred to by number. For example, argon is in period 3 and group 18.

Elements with similar properties are put into families that are outlined in different colors in the periodic table above. Note that these families generally correspond to the groups in the periodic table. For example, the elements in group 18 are in a family called the noble gases, while the elements in group 2 are all alkaline earth metals.

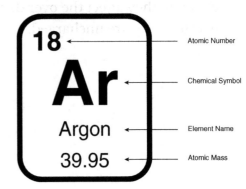

Periodic tables differ in the information they provide, and an example of a block is shown above. This block shows the name of the element and its **chemical symbol**, which is an abbreviation for the name. The chemical symbol is one, two, or three letters with the first letter capitalized and all subsequent letters letter lowercase. The symbol for the element argon is Ar.

DID YOU KNOW?

While many elements have chemical symbols that resemble their names, like argon (Ar), some elements have chemical symbols that are different from their names. This is because the symbols are derived from either the Latin or the Greek names for the elements rather than the English names. The symbol for sodium is Na because the Latin name for the element is natrium.

Each element is assigned an **atomic number**. The atomic number is equal to the number of protons in a single atom of that element and is how an element is identified. Argon, for example, has an atomic number of 18. Therefore, every atom of argon has 18 protons, regardless of how many neutrons or electrons it has.

Example

Which of the following statements is true?

A. A tin atom has 22 protons.

B. An iron atom has 26 protons.

C. A sodium atom has 16 protons.

D. A potassium atom has 15 protons.

The correct answer is **B**. In the periodic table, iron has an atomic number of 26, which means it has 26 protons.

Average Atomic Mass and Mass Number

Some periodic tables also provide the **average atomic mass** of an element in atomic mass units (amu). Because not all atoms of argon have the same mass, the periodic table shows the average mass of all argon atoms. These forms of argon are differentiated based on their **mass numbers**, which are determined by adding the number of protons and neutrons. Argon has three stable forms, called isotopes, which are shown in the table below.

Name	Abundance	Mass (amu)	Mass Number	Number of protons	Number of neutrons
Argon-36	0.337%	35.97	36	18	18
Argon-38	0.063%	37.96	38	18	20
Argon-40	99.6%	39.96	40	18	22

The mass number can be used to determine the number of neutrons, as shown by the equation below. Argon-40 is the most abundant and has a mass number of 40. Its 18 protons contribute 18 to the mass number of the atom. The remaining mass is from the neutrons.

mass number = number of protons + number of neutrons

40 = 18 + number of neutrons

number of neutrons = 40 − 18 = 22 neutrons

To determine the number of electrons, the charge of the atom must be considered. If a charge is not indicated, it can be assumed that the atom in question is neutral. A neutral atom has an equal number of positively charged protons and negatively charged electrons. Therefore, a neutral atom of argon has 18 electrons that balance the charge of its 18 protons, given by the atomic number.

Example

CHECKLIST

Here are reminders for how to determine the numbers of subatomic particles using information found in the periodic table:

Number of protons = atomic number
Number of neutrons = mass number − number of protons (atomic number)
Number of electrons = number of protons (atomic number) in a neutral atom

---

Using the periodic table, determine how many protons and electrons a neutral atom of potassium has.

A. 19 protons, 19 electrons

B. 19 protons, 20 electrons

C. 19 protons, 39 electrons

D. 39 protons, 39 electrons

The correct answer is **A.** The atomic number of potassium is 19, which means it has 19 protons. Because the atom is neutral, the number of electrons must equal the number of protons.

Isotopes

All atoms of an element have the same number of protons, but the number of neutrons may be different. Atoms that have the same number of protons but different numbers of neutrons are called **isotopes**. Because they have the same number of protons, they are the same element. However, because they contain different numbers of neutrons, their masses and mass numbers are different. The Bohr models for three isotopes of carbon are shown below.

All three isotopes have 6 protons because they are all different forms of carbon. They all have 6 electrons because these are neutral atoms of carbon, which means that the positive and negative charges balance each other. The different numbers of neutrons and the different masses differentiate these isotopes.

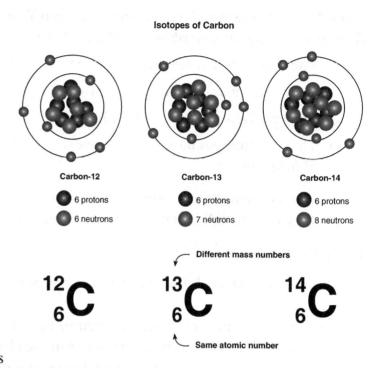

The isotopes can be named according to their masses. Carbon-12 has a mass number of 12, with 6 protons and 6 neutrons. Carbon-13 has a mass number of 13, with 6 protons and 7 neutrons. Carbon-14 has a mass number of 14, with 6 protons and 8 neutrons. The figure above shows how isotopes can be represented using the element symbols.

Isotopes are present in varying amounts. Carbon-12 makes up 98.93% of all carbon on Earth, and carbon-13 makes up 1.07%. Although carbon-14 exists, its amount is negligible. When calculating the average atomic mass, all isotopes are taken into account. In the periodic table, carbon has an atomic mass of 12.01 amu, which is extremely close to the mass of the most abundant isotope, carbon-12. Though not always true, the average atomic mass of an element is often closest to the mass of the most common isotope.

Example

Atom X has 7 protons and 8 neutrons, and Atom Y has 7 protons and 7 neutrons. Which of the following statements describes the relationship between Atom X and Atom Y?

A. They are different elements because they have different masses.

B. They are different elements because they have different numbers of neutrons.

C. They are isotopes because they have different atomic numbers but the same masses.

D. They are isotopes because they have the same number of protons but different numbers of neutrons.

The correct answer is **D**. Atom X and Y are different isotopes of nitrogen. They both have 7 protons, but the different numbers of neutrons give them different masses.

Let's Review!

- Scientific notation is used to make very large numbers and very small numbers easier to use.
- An atom is composed of protons, neutrons, and electrons. Protons and neutrons are found in the nucleus, and electrons are found in the electron cloud that surrounds the nucleus.
- The number of protons in an atom determines its identity (which element it is).
- The mass number of an atom is determined by adding the number of protons and the number of neutrons.
- The charge of an atom is determined by the numbers of protons and electrons.
- Isotopes are atoms of the same element that have different numbers of neutrons and, therefore, different masses.

TEMPERATURE AND THE METRIC SYSTEM

This lesson introduces the metric system, including how to do metric conversions and use prefixes. It also explores the three different types of temperature systems.

The English and Metric System

A universal language is used in science and research. This scientific language is called the **metric system**. Also known as the International System of Units (SI), the metric system is easy to use, and its design is simple. Prior to the metric system, several different units were used in scientific measurement, which led to confusion. The metric system was created to standardize units and simplify how they are used. By using a universally accepted measurement standard, scientists around the world can easily communicate with one another.

There are two principles of the metric system to keep in mind:

- Only one unit is assigned to a given quantity that is measured. This unit is called the **SI base unit**. The three most common base units are gram (for mass), meter (for length), and liter (for volume).
- The base unit can be expressed in multiples of 10 to account for measured objects that are very large or very small. This means when performing a metric conversion, the base units can either be multiplied or be divided by 10.

FOR EXAMPLE
A large container that holds 250,000 grams of sand can be said to hold 250 kilograms of sand.

When performing metric conversions, it is important to understand the **metric prefixes**. These are used to distinguish among the base units according to size. The following table provides a list of the most commonly used metric prefixes, including the multiplying factor. Metric prefixes are attached to the beginning of a base unit term. The prefixes can be added to any of the base units.

Metric Prefix	Symbol	Multiplying Factor	Equivalent Value
tera	T	10^{12}	1,000,000,000,000
giga	G	10^{9}	1,000,000,000
mega	M	10^{6}	1,000,000
kilo	k	10^{3}	1,000
hecto	h	10^{2}	100
deca	da	10^{1}	10
deci	d	10^{-1}	0.1
centi	c	10^{-2}	0.01
milli	m	10^{-3}	0.001

Metric Prefix	Symbol	Multiplying Factor	Equivalent Value
micro	μ	10^{-6}	0.000001
nano	n	10^{-9}	0.000000001
pico	p	10^{-12}	0.000000000001
femto	f	10^{-15}	0.000000000000001

The **English system** is another recognized system of measurement. It is not universally accepted, and it consists of several units of measurements that are not functionally related to one another. This means the multiple of 10 cannot be used to convert one English unit to another. The following list provides the equivalent values of commonly used English measurements for length, weight, and volume. These values can be used when performing conversions from one English unit to another.

Length

- 12 inches = 1 foot (ft)
- 3 feet = 1 yard (yd)
- 5,280 feet = 1 mile (mi)

Weight

- 16 ounces (oz) = 1 pound (lb)
- 1 ton = 2,000 pounds

Volume

- 8 ounces = 1 cup (c)
- 2 cups = 1 pint (pt)
- 2 pints = 1 quart (qt)
- 4 quarts = 1 gallon (gal)

DID YOU KNOW?

The English system was created because people needed a way to describe measurements. Many of the measurements were based on the size of body parts and familiar objects. Eventually, this system was standardized into the system used today.

Example

Thalia wants to measure the distance a solar-powered toy car travels over time. What SI base unit should she use?

A. Feet   B. Inches   C. Liter   D. Meter

The correct answer is **D**. Meter is an SI base unit that is used to measure length or distance. When recording the distance the car travels, Thalia would use meters as the unit.

Metric Conversions

Recall that the metric system involves the use of prefixes and base units. The prefixes help a person identify how big or small the measured object is. What happens if one base unit needs to be converted to a different base unit? This is where the concept of using multiples of 10 is important.

When making metric conversions, it is helpful to create a metric staircase, as shown below.

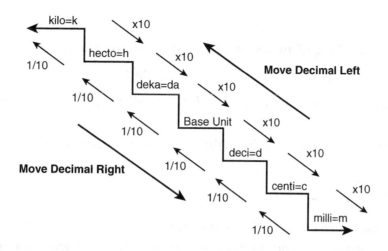

Look at each step on the staircase. It represents a ten-fold change in the metric system. In other words, each step indicates that the decimal place of the measured unit value moves to the left or to the right. Moving to the right (or down the staircase) requires multiplication, which involves using multiples of 10 to convert the larger unit to a smaller unit. When moving to the left (or up the staircase), a smaller unit is converted to a larger unit by dividing using a multiple of 10.

Sometimes, it is necessary to do conversions between the metric and English systems. The following list provides commonly used English measurements and their respective (approximate) metric equivalent values.

Length
- 1 inch = 2.54 centimeters
- 1 yard = 0.91 meters

Weight
- 1 ounce = 28.3 grams
- 2.20 pounds = 1 kilogram

Volume
- 1.06 quart = 1 liter
- 3.79 liters = 1 gallon

KEEP IN MIND

It is helpful to use the following mnemonic to remember the order of the metric prefixes to ensure proper movement of the decimal between units from largest to smallest.

King Henry Doesn't [Usually] Drink Chocolate Milk

Where *king* means "kilo," *Henry* means "hecto," *doesn't* means "deca," *usually* represents the base unit, *drink* means "deci," *chocolate* means "centi," and *milk* means "milli."

FOR EXAMPLE

How many grams are in 2.52 kilograms?

The metric staircase indicates that kilogram is a larger unit than gram. Going down the staircase means the decimal must move to the right to give a value of 2,520 grams. If 2.52 is multiplied by the multiplying factor of 10^3, this will give the same value.

Example

A patient needs a dose of 0.3 g of medicine. How much medicine is this in milligrams?

A. 3   B. 30   C. 300   D. 3,000

The correct answer is **C**. Gram is a larger unit than milligram. Thus, this value must be divided by a factor of 0.001 to get 300 milligrams. If using the metric staircase, the decimal in 0.3 g would move three units to the right to give 300 milligrams.

Temperature Systems

Three temperature scales are commonly used in science: Fahrenheit (F), Celsius (C), and Kelvin (K). **Temperature** measures the amount of kinetic energy that particles of matter have in a substance. Imagine that someone wants to boil a pot of water. Initially, the water molecules move very little. As the temperature rises to water's boiling point, these molecules move faster, bouncing off each other and generating kinetic energy. Movement slows down as the temperature lowers to water's freezing point.

The Fahrenheit temperature scale is part of the English system of measurement. It is not commonly used for scientific purposes like the Celsius (or centigrade) scale is. However, it is important to recognize and know how to use the conversion formulas between Celsius and Fahrenheit. The formulas are shown below:

$$F = \left(\frac{9}{5}\right)C + 32 \text{ and } C = \frac{5}{9}(F - 32).$$

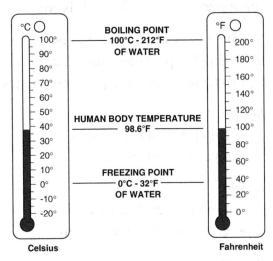

The Fahrenheit scale is based on 32°F for the freezing point of water and 212°F for the boiling point of water. This corresponds to 0°C and 100°C, respectively, on the Celsius scale. The Celsius scale is part of the metric system, which means it is universally accepted when reporting temperature measurements. A thermometer is used to measure temperature. The following thermometers show common temperature values.

Kelvin is another temperature scale that is used. Its degrees are similar in size to degrees Celsius, but its zero is set to an absolute zero, or 0 K. This is the point where all molecular motion ends. On the Kelvin scale, the freezing point of water is 273.15 K. The boiling point is 373.15 K. The following equation is used to convert a Celsius reading to Kelvin:

BE CAREFUL!
A degree sign is not used in the temperature designation for Kelvin. This symbol is only used with Fahrenheit and Celsius measurements.

$$K = °C + 273$$

Example

On which molecule's boiling and freezing points are the Celsius and Fahrenheit scales based?

A. Alcohol   B. Chloride   C. Glucose   D. Water

The correct answer is **D**. Both the Fahrenheit and Celsius scales are based on the boiling and freezing point of water. The boiling point of water is 212°F (100°C), and the freezing point is 32°F (0°C).

Let's Review!

- The metric system is a universally accepted standard method that is used to determine the units of a given measurement.
- The English system is not universally accepted but provides a collection of measurements whose units are functionally unrelated.
- Meter (length), gram (weight), and liter (volume) are the most common types of SI base units.
- Metric prefixes are added to base units to describe the measurement of an object according to size.
- The metric staircase can be used for metric-metric conversions, and specific equivalent values are used for English-metric conversions.
- Three temperature scales, Celsius, Fahrenheit, and Kelvin, are used in science.
- Formulas are used to convert Celsius values to Fahrenheit or to Kelvin.

CHAPTER 13 SCIENTIFIC REASONING PRACTICE QUIZ

1. Why must researchers consider the placebo effect?

   A. Monitor the outcome of the experiment

   B. Ensure a proper independent variable is chosen

   C. Account for the body's response to fake treatments

   D. Create a baseline measure for experimental analysis

2. As a variable increases, another variable increases. This describes a(n)

   A. positive variation.

   B. negative variation.

   C. inverse correlation.

   D. indirect correlation.

3. An electric balance measures an object's

   A. mass.   C. temperature.

   B. length.   D. volume.

4. Which of the following statements describes the mass of an electron?

   A. The mass of an electron is less than the mass of a proton or neutron.

   B. The mass of an electron is about the same as the mass of a proton or neutron.

   C. The mass of an electron is greater than that of a neutron but less than that of a proton.

   D. The mass of an electron is greater than that of a proton but less than that of a neutron.

5. Which of the following describes one difference between the two most abundant isotopes of iron, iron-54 and iron-56?

   A. Iron-56 has more protons than iron-54.

   B. Iron-56 has more neutrons than iron-54.

   C. Iron-54 and iron-56 have different atomic numbers.

   D. Iron-54 and iron-56 contain different numbers of electrons.

6. Which of the following parts of an atom takes up the most space in terms of area?

   A. Neutrons

   B. Electron cloud

   C. Individual electrons

   D. Protons and neutrons

7. Four cups of water are poured into a flask. What is this volume in pints?

   A. 1

   C. 3

   B. 2

   D. 4

8. How many ounces are in 3 cups?

   A. 5

   C. 11

   B. 8

   D. 24

9. It is advantageous to use the English system when

   A. converting units using multiples of 10.

   B. describing a reported value using tons.

   C. working with functionally related base units.

   D. communicating information around the world.

CHAPTER 13 SCIENTIFIC REASONING PRACTICE QUIZ – ANSWER KEY

1. C. The placebo is a false treatment given to a group to account for the body's psychological response to this type of treatment in a study. **See Lesson: Designing an Experiment.**

2. A. When a variable increases as another variable increases, this relationship is described as a positive correlation, direct correlation, or positive variation. **See Lesson: Designing an Experiment.**

3. A. The mass of an object is determined by using a balance. Electric balances are used to measure a very small mass. **See Lesson: Designing an Experiment.**

4. A. The mass of a proton or neutron is 1.0 amu, and the mass of an electron is much less, 0.00054 amu. **See Lesson: Scientific Notation.**

5. B. Because iron-54 and iron-56 are isotopes of the same element, they have the same number of protons and the same atomic number, but the numbers of neutrons and mass numbers are different. **See Lesson: Scientific Notation.**

6. B. The protons and neutrons are in the nucleus, which is very small and dense. The electron cloud makes up most of the atom in terms of area. **See Lesson: Scientific Notation.**

7. B. Two cups is equivalent to one pint of a solution, so four cups is two pints. **See Lesson: Temperature and the Metric System.**

8. D. There are 8 ounces in 1 cup. Multiplying 3 cups by 8 yields a total of 24 ounces. **See Lesson: Temperature and the Metric System.**

9. B. The English system is not universally accepted and consists of a collection of functionally unrelated units. However, it is useful when reporting values of weight in tons. **See Lesson: Temperature and the Metric System.**

CHAPTER 14 LIFE AND PHYSICAL SCIENCES

FOUNDATIONS OF BIOLOGY

This lesson introduces the basics of biology, including the process researchers use to study science. It also examines the classes of biomolecules and how substances are broken down for energy.

Biology and Taxonomy

The study or science of living things is called **biology**. Some characteristics, or traits, are common to all living things. These enable researchers to differentiate living things from nonliving things. Traits include reproduction, growth and development, **homeostasis**, and energy processing. Homeostasis is the body's ability to maintain a constant internal environment despite changes that occur in the external environment. With so many living things in the world, researchers developed a **taxonomy** system, which is used for classification, description, and naming. As shown below, there are seven classification levels in the classical Linnaean system.

KINGDOM Animalia

PHYLUM Chordata

CLASS Mammalia

ORDER Carnivora

FAMILY Ursidae

GENUS Ursus

SPECIES Ursus arctos

Specificity increases as the levels move from kingdom to species. For example, in the image the genus level contains two types of bears, but the species level shows one type. Additionally, organisms in each level are found in the level above it. For example, organisms in the order level are part of the class level. This classification system is based on physical similarities across living things. It does not account for molecular or genetic similarities.

DID YOU KNOW?
Carl Linnaeus only used physical similarities across organisms when he created the Linnaean system because technology was not advanced enough to observe similarities at the molecular level.

Example

A researcher classifies a newly discovered organism in the class taxonomy level. What other taxonomic level is this new organism classified in?

A. Order   B. Family   C. Species   D. Kingdom

The correct answer is **D**. Each level is found in the level above it. The levels above class are phylum and kingdom.

Scientific Method

To develop the taxonomic system, researchers had to ask questions. Researchers use seven steps to answer science questions or solve problems. Recall that these make up the **scientific method**, described below:

1. Problem: The question created because of an observation. *Example: Does the size of a plastic object affect how fast it naturally degrades in a lake?*
2. Research: Reliable information available about what is observed. *Example: Learn how plastics are made and understand the properties of a lake.*
3. Hypothesis: A predicted solution to the question or problem. *Example: If the plastic material is small, then it will degrade faster than a large particle.*
4. Experiment: A series of tests used to evaluate the hypothesis. Experiments consist of an **independent variable** that the researcher modifies and a **dependent variable** that changes due to the independent variable. They also include a **control group** used as a standard to make comparisons. *Example: Collect plastic particles both onshore and offshore of the lake over time. Determine the size of the particles and describe the lake conditions during this time period.*
5. Observe: Analyze data collected during an experiment to observe patterns. *Example: Analyze the differences between the numbers of particles collected in terms of size.*
6. Conclusion: State whether the hypothesis is rejected or accepted and summarize all results.
7. Communicate: Report findings so others can replicate and verify the results.

Sometimes, just a few steps of the scientific method are necessary to research a question. At other times, several steps may be repeated as needed. The goal of this method is to find a reliable answer to the scientific question.

TEST TIP

Using the first letter in each of the steps, you can create a mnemonic device to remember the steps. For example: "**P**eople **R**eally **H**ave **E**lephants **O**n **C**ompact **C**ars." Try creating your own mnemonic device!

Over the course of many years during which scientists are able to collect sufficient and reliable data, the scientific method can be used to create a law or theory. A **law** is a rule that describes patterns observed in nature. A **scientific theory** explains the how and why of things that happens in nature through observations and experiments. Scientists widely accept both laws and theories, but they can be modified over time.

Example

In a study, a researcher describes what happens to a plant following exposure to a dry and hot environment. What step of the scientific method does this most likely describe?

A. Forming a hypothesis

B. Making an observation

C. Communicating findings

D. Characterizing the problem

The correct answer is **B**. The researcher is collecting qualitative data by describing what happens to the plant under specific conditions. This data collection corresponds to the observation step of the scientific method.

Water and Biomolecule Basics

From oceans and streams to a bottle, water is fundamental for life. Without water, life would not exist. Because of water's unique properties, it plays a specific role in living things. The molecular structure of water consists of an oxygen atom bonded to two hydrogen atoms. The structure of water explains some of its properties. For example, water is polar. The oxygen atom is slightly negatively charged, while both hydrogen atoms are slightly positively charged.

As shown below, a single water molecule forms **hydrogen bonds** with nearby water molecules. This type of bonding creates a weak attraction between the water molecules. Hydrogen bonding contributes to water's high boiling point. Water is necessary for biochemical processes like photosynthesis and cellular respiration. It is also a universal solvent, which means water dissolves many different substances.

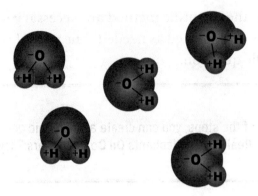

Only two water molecules are needed to show bonding. Remove the partial negative/positive signs and put a – sign next to the oxygen atom and a + sign next to each hydrogen (H) atom. Remove the solid lines between the H and O but keep the dashed line connecting one water molecule to the next.

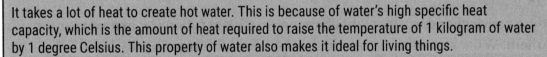

KEEP IN MIND

It takes a lot of heat to create hot water. This is because of water's high specific heat capacity, which is the amount of heat required to raise the temperature of 1 kilogram of water by 1 degree Celsius. This property of water also makes it ideal for living things.

Biomolecules, or biological molecules, are found in living things. These organic molecules vary in structure and size and perform different functions. Researchers group the wide variety of molecules found in living things into four major classes for organizational purposes: proteins, carbohydrates, lipids, and nucleic acids. Each class of biomolecules has unique **monomers** and **polymers**. Monomers are molecules that covalently bond to form larger molecules or polymers.

Phospholipids, a class of lipids, are a structure with a phosphate "head" and a fatty acid "tail". The phosphate head is a molecule structure consisting of a phosphate atom and four oxygen atoms, making the head carry a polar charge to be soluble in water; hydrophilic. This is opposite the two fatty acid chains in the tail, which are nonpolar and water insoluble, or hydrophobic. This structure is important in creating the permeable, or semi-permeable membranes of cells, which help the flow of specific ions through designated channels of a cell.

The following table lists characteristics of each class of biomolecule.

Biomolecule	Monomer(s)	Function	Example
Protein	Amino acid	A substance that provides the overall basic structure and function for a cell	Enzymes
Carbohydrate	Monosaccharides	A form of storage for energy	Glucose Cellulose Starch Disaccharides
Lipid	Glycerol and fatty acids	A type of fat that provides a long-term storage for energy	Fats Steroids Oils Hormones
Nucleic acid	Nucleotides	A substance that aids in protein synthesis and transmission of genetic information	DNA RNA

Example

During protein synthesis in a cell, the primary structure of the protein consists of a linear chain of monomers. What is another way to describe this structure?

A. A linear chain of fatty acids that are hydrogen-bonded together

B. A linear chain of nucleotides that are hydrogen-bonded together

C. A linear chain of amino acids that are covalently bonded together

D. A linear chain of monosaccharides that are covalently bonded together

The correct answer is **C**. The monomers of proteins include amino acids, which are covalently bonded together to form a protein.

The Metabolic Process

Just like water, energy is essential to life. Food and sunlight are major energy sources. Metabolism is the process of converting food into usable energy. This refers to all biochemical processes or reactions that take place in a living thing to keep it alive.

CONNECTIONS

Energy flows through living things. Energy from the sun is converted to chemical energy via photosynthesis. When living things feed on plants, they obtain this energy for survival.

A metabolic pathway is a series of several chemical reactions that take place cyclically to either build or break down molecules. An **anabolic pathway** involves the synthesis of new molecules. These pathways require an input of energy. **Catabolic pathways** involve the breakdown of molecules. Energy is released from a catabolic pathway.

Living things use several metabolic pathways. The most well-studied pathways include glycolysis, the citric acid cycle, and the electron transport chain. These metabolic pathways either release or add energy during a reaction. They also provide a continual flow of energy to living things.

1. **Glycolysis:** This is a catabolic pathway that uses several steps to break down glucose sugar for energy, carbon dioxide, and water. Energy that is released from this reaction is stored in the form of adenosine triphosphate (ATP). Two ATP molecules, two pyruvate molecules, and two NADH molecules are formed during this metabolic pathway.

> **BE CAREFUL!**
> Some of these metabolic pathways produce energy in different parts of the cell. Glycolysis takes place in the cytoplasm of the cell. But the citric acid cycle and oxidative phosphorylation occur in the mitochondria.

2. **Citric acid cycle:** The pyruvate molecules made from glycolysis are transported inside the cell's mitochondria. In this catabolic pathway, pyruvate is used to make two ATP molecules, six carbon dioxide molecules, and six NADH molecules.

3. **Electron transport chain and oxidative phosphorylation:** This also takes place in the cell's mitochondria. Many electrons are transferred from one molecule to another in this chain. At the end of the chain, oxygen picks up the electrons to produce roughly 34 molecules of ATP.

The following image provides an overview of **cellular respiration**. Glycolysis, the citric acid cycle, the electron transport chain, and oxidative phosphorylation collectively make up this process. Cellular respiration takes place in a cell and is used to convert energy from nutrients into ATP.

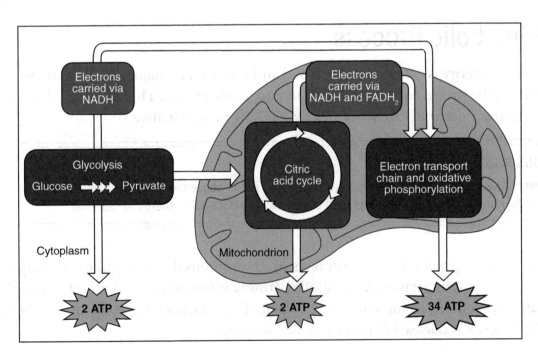

Example

Why are metabolic pathways cyclic?

    A. Metabolic reactions generally take place one at a time.

    B. All of the products created in metabolic reactions are used up.

    C. The reactions are continuous as long as reactants are available.

    D. Energy in the form of ATP is sent to different cells for various uses.

The correct answer is **C**. Metabolic reactions are cyclic, which means they keep occurring as long as enough starting materials are available to allow the reaction to proceed.

Let's Review!

- This lesson explored how living things are organized, what the scientific method is, and how biomolecules are classified. It also discussed how living things obtain energy via metabolism.
- Biology is the study of living things. Several characteristics distinguish living things from nonliving things.
- All living things are described, classified, and named using a taxonomic system.
- The scientific method uses seven steps to answer a question or solve a problem.
- Biomolecules are organic molecules that are organized into four classes: proteins, carbohydrates, lipids, and nucleic acids
- Living things rely on various metabolic pathways to produce energy and store it in the form of ATP.

CELL STRUCTURE, FUNCTION, AND TYPE

This lesson describes the cell structure and two different types of cells. The lesson also explores the functions of various cell parts.

Cell Theory and Types

All living things are made of cells. **Cells** are the smallest structural units and basic building blocks of living things. Cells contain everything necessary to keep living things alive. Varying in size and shape, cells carry out specialized functions. Robert Hooke discovered the first cells in the mid-eighteenth century. Many years later, after advancements in microscopy, the cell theory was formed. This theory, or in-depth explanation, about cells consists of three parts:

1. All living things are composed of one or more cells.
2. Cells are alive and represent the basic unit of life.
3. All cells are produced from preexisting cells.

DID YOU KNOW?

More than a trillion cells and at least 200 different types of cells exist in the human body!

Many different types of cells exist. Because of this, cells are classified into two general types: prokaryotic cells and eukaryotic cells. The following comparison table lists key differences between prokaryotes and eukaryotes:

Characteristic	Prokaryote	Eukaryote
Cell size	Around 0.2–2.0 mm in diameter	Around 10–100 mm in diameter
Nucleus	Absent	True nucleus
Organelles	Absent	Several present, ranging from ribosomes to the endoplasmic reticulum
Flagella	Simple in structure	Complex in structure

As shown in the image, prokaryotic cells lack nuclei. Their DNA floats in the **cytoplasm**, which is surrounded by a **plasma membrane**. Very simplistic in structure, these cells lack organelles but do have cell walls. **Organelles** are specialized structures with a specific cellular function. They also may have **ribosomes** that aid in protein synthesis. Also, these cells have a **flagellum** that looks like a tail attached to the cell. Flagella aid in locomotion. The **pili**, or hair-like structures surrounding the cells, aid in cellular adhesion. Bacteria and Archaea are the most common prokaryotes. Most prokaryotes are **unicellular**, or made of a single cell, but there are a few **multicellular organisms**.

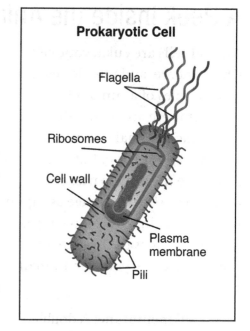

Eukaryotic cells contain a membrane-bound nucleus where DNA is stored. Membrane-bound organelles also exist in eukaryotic cells. Similar to prokaryotic cells, eukaryotic cells have cytoplasm, ribosomes, and a plasma membrane. Eukaryotic organisms can be either unicellular or multicellular. Much larger than prokaryotes, examples of eukaryotic organisms include fungi and even people.

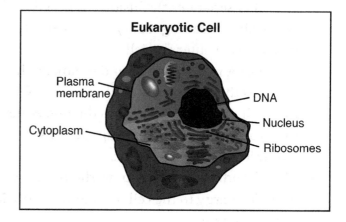

Example

What is an organelle?

   A. The building block of all living things

   B. A substance that is able diffuse inside a cell

   C. The specific receptor found on a cell's surface

   D. A membrane-bound structure with a special function

The correct answer is **D**. Organelles such as ribosomes and the nucleus are membrane-bound structures that have specific functions in a cell.

A Peek Inside the Animal Cell

Animal cells are eukaryotic cells. Cheek, nerve, and muscle cells are all examples of animal cells. Because there are many different types, each animal cell has a specialized function. But all animal cells have the same parts, or organelles. Use this image as a guide while going through following list, which describes the organelles found in a eukaryotic (or animal) cell.

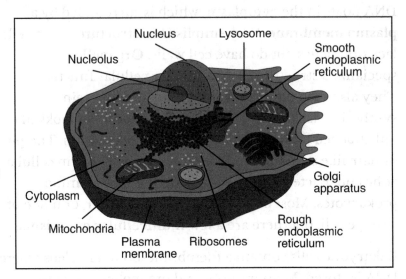

- **Cell membrane:** A double layer that separates the inside of the cell from the outside environment. It is semi-permeable, meaning it only allows certain molecules to enter the cell.
- **Nucleus:** A membrane-bound organelle that contains the genetic material, such as DNA, for a cell. Inside the nucleus is the **nucleolus** that plays a role in assembling subunits required to make ribosomes.

> **KEEP IN MIND!**
> Some of the organelles in animal cells are also present in plant cells. In addition, all organelles are found in the cytoplasm of the cell. The only exception is the nucleus, which it is separated from the cytoplasm because it has its own membrane.

- **Mitochondria:** The cell's powerhouses that provide energy to the cell for it to function. Much of the energy in the form of ATP is produced here.
- **Ribosomes:** The cell's protein factories that can be found floating in the cytoplasm or attached to the endoplasmic reticulum.
- **Vacuoles:** Small sacs in a cell that store water and food for survival. This organelle also stores waste material that is mostly in the form of water.
- **Endoplasmic reticulum:** A network of membranes that functions as a cell's transportation system, shuttling proteins and other materials around the cell. The **smooth endoplasmic reticulum** lacks ribosomes, and the **rough endoplasmic reticulum** has ribosomes.
- **Lysosomes:** Sac-like structures that contain digestive enzymes that are used to break down food and old organelles.
- **Golgi apparatus:** A stack of flattened pouches that plays a role in processing proteins received from the endoplasmic reticulum. It modifies proteins from the endoplasmic reticulum and then packages them into a vesicle that can be sent to other places in the cell.

Example

Which two organelles work together to facilitate protein synthesis?

    A. Cytoplasm and lysosome

    B. Vacuole and mitochondria

    C. Nucleus and cell membrane

    D. Ribosome and endoplasmic reticulum

The correct answer is **D**. After a protein is synthesized by ribosomes, it is shuttled to the endoplasmic reticulum, where it is further modified and prepared to be transported by vesicles to other places in the cell.

Plant Cells

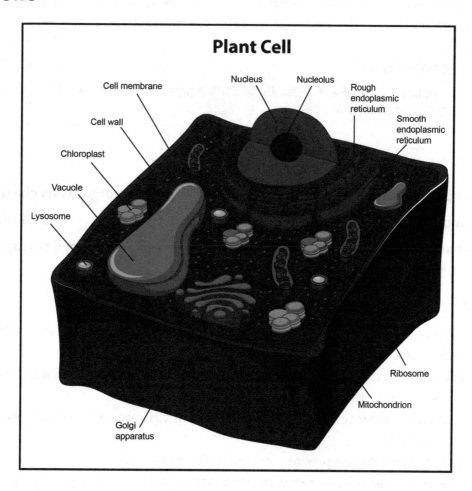

Recall that plant cells are also eukaryotic cells. Structurally, these cells are similar to animal cells because some of the parts in a plant cell are also found in an animal cell. However, there are some notable differences. The following image shows the structure of a plant cell.

First, only plant cells have a **cell wall**. The purpose of this structure is to provide protection and support to plant cells. The cell wall also enforces the overall structural integrity of the plant cell, and it is found outside the cell membrane. The next organelle is a chloroplast. It is found in the cytoplasm of only plant cells. **Chloroplasts** are photosynthetic compounds used to make food for plant cells by harnessing energy from the sun. These organelles play a role in photosynthesis.

Chloroplasts and mitochondria are both designed to collect, process, and store energy for the cell. Thus, organisms are divided into autotrophs or heterotrophs based on how they obtain energy. **Autotrophs** are organisms that make energy-rich biomolecules from raw material in nature. They do this by using basic energy sources such the sun. This explains why most autotrophs rely on photosynthesis to transform sunlight into usable food that can produce energy necessary for life. Plants and certain species of bacteria are autotrophs.

Animals are **heterotrophs** because they are unable to make their own food. Heterotrophs have to consume and metabolize their food sources to absorb the stored energy. Examples of heterotrophs include all animals and fungi, as well as certain species of bacteria.

DID YOU KNOW?
More than 99% of all energy for life on Earth is provided through the process of photosynthesis.

Example

Kelp use chlorophyll to capture sunlight for food. What are these organisms classified as?

A. Autotrophs   B. Chemotrophs   C. Heterotrophs   D. Lithotrophs

The correct answer is **A**. Kelp is an autotroph because it uses chlorophyll to trap energy from the sun to make food.

Let's Review!

- This lesson focused on the cell theory, different cell types, and the various cell parts found in plant and animal cells.
- The cell theory is an in-depth explanation, supported with scientific data, to prove a cell is a living thing and has unique characteristics.
- Cells are the basic building blocks of life. Coming in various sizes and shapes, cells have specialized functions.
- Two broad types of cells are prokaryotic and eukaryotic cells.
- Prokaryotes are single-celled organisms that lack a nucleus, while eukaryotes are multicellular organisms that contain a nucleus.
- Chloroplasts and cell walls are only found in plant cells.
- Both animal and plant cells have similar organelles such as ribosomes, mitochondria, and an endoplasmic reticulum.
- Living things can be classified as autotrophs or heterotrophs based on how they obtain energy.

CELLULAR REPRODUCTION, CELLULAR RESPIRATION, AND PHOTOSYNTHESIS

This lesson introduces basic processes including cellular reproduction and division, cellular respiration, and photosynthesis. These processes provide ways for cells to make new cells and to convert energy to and from food sources.

Cell Reproduction

Cells divide primarily for growth, repair, and reproduction. When an organism grows, it normally needs more cells. If damage occurs, more cells must appear to repair the damage and replace any dead cells. During reproduction, this process allows all living things to produce offspring. There are two ways that living things reproduce: asexually and sexually.

Asexual reproduction is a process in which only one organism is needed to reproduce itself. A single parent is involved in this type of reproduction, which means all offspring are genetically identical to one another and to the parent. All prokaryotes reproduce this way. Some eukaryotes also reproduce asexually. There are several methods of asexual reproduction.

Binary fission is one method. During this process, a prokaryotic cell, such as a bacterium, copies its DNA and splits in half. Binary fission is simple because only one parent cell divides into two daughter cells (or offspring) that are the same size.

Sexual reproduction is a process in which two organisms produce offspring that have genetic characteristics from both parents. It provides greater genetic diversity within a population than asexual reproduction. Sexual reproduction results in the production of **gametes**. These are reproductive cells. Gametes unite to create offspring.

Example

Binary fission is a method

A. where one daughter cell is produced.

B. required to produce reproductive cells.

C. that represents a form of asexual reproduction.

D. where two parent cells interact with each other.

The correct answer is **C**. Binary fission is a method organisms use to reproduce asexually. It involves a single parent cell that splits to create two identical daughter cells.

When the Cell Cycle Begins

For a cell to divide into more cells, it must grow, copy its DNA, and produce new daughter cells. The **cell cycle** regulates cellular division. This process can either prevent a cell from dividing or trigger it to start dividing.

> **KEEP IN MIND**
>
> The cell cycle is a circular process. This means after two daughter cells are made, they can participate in the cell cycle process, starting it over from the beginning.

The cell cycle is an organized process divided into two phases: **interphase** and the **M (mitotic) phase**. During interphase, the cell grows and copies its DNA. After the cell reaches the M phase, division and of the two new cells can occur. The G_1, S, and G_2 phases make up interphase.

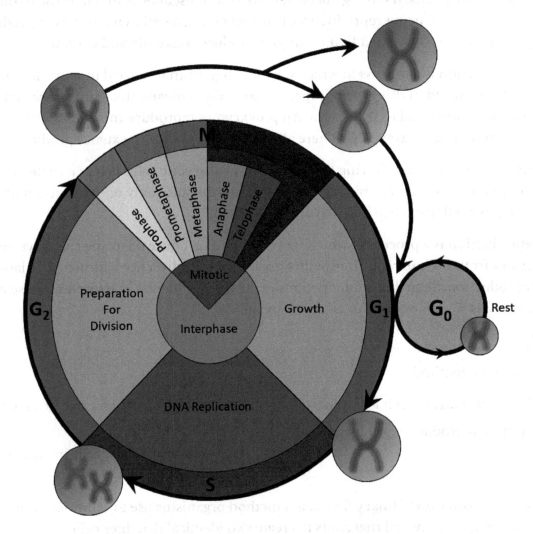

- G_1: The first gap phase, during which the cell prepares to copy its DNA
- **S**: The synthesis phase, during which DNA is copied
- G_2: The second gap phase, during which the cell prepares for cell division

It may appear that little is happening in the cell during the gap phases. Most of the activity occurs at the level of enzymes and macromolecules. The cell produces things like nucleotides for synthesizing new DNA strands, enzymes for copying the DNA, and tubulin proteins for building the mitotic spindle. During the S phase, the DNA in the cell doubles, but few other signs are obvious under the microscope. All the dramatic events that can be seen under a microscope occur during the M phase: the chromosomes move, and the cell splits into two new cells with identical nuclei.

Example

For an organism, the cell cycle is needed for

A. competition.   B. dispersal.   C. growth.   D. parasitism.

The correct answer is **C**. The cell cycle is the process during which a cell grows, copies its own DNA, and physically separates into new cells. With help from the cell cycle, more cells can be provided to help an organism grow.

Mitosis

Mitosis is a form of cell division where two identical nuclei are produced from one nucleus. DNA contains the genetic information of the cell. It is stored in the nucleus. During mitosis, DNA in the nucleus must be copied, or replicated. Recall that this happens during the S phase of the cell cycle. During the M phase, this copied DNA is divided into two complete sets, one of which goes to a daughter cell.

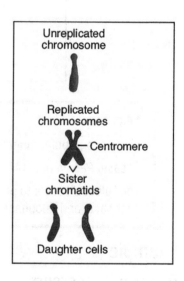

When DNA replicates, it condenses to form **chromosomes** that resemble an X. The DNA forms chromosomes by wrapping around proteins called histones. As shown below, it takes two identical sister chromatids to form a chromosome. A **centromere** holds the sister chromatids together.

Four phases take place during mitosis to form two identical daughter cells:

1. **Prophase:** The nuclear membrane disappears, and other organelles move out of the way. The spindle, made of microtubules, begins to form. During **prometaphase**, the microtubules begin to attach to the centromeres at the center of the chromosome.
2. **Metaphase:** Spindle fibers line the chromosomes at the center of the cell. This is because they are pulled equally by the spindle fibers, which are attached to the opposite poles of the cell.
3. **Anaphase:** The chromosomes are pulled to the opposite poles of the cell.
4. **Telophase:** The chromosomes de-condense, the nuclear membrane reappears, and other parts of the cell return to their usual places in the cell.

The cell divides into two daughter cells by way of **cytokinesis**. The illustration below demonstrates the process of mitosis.

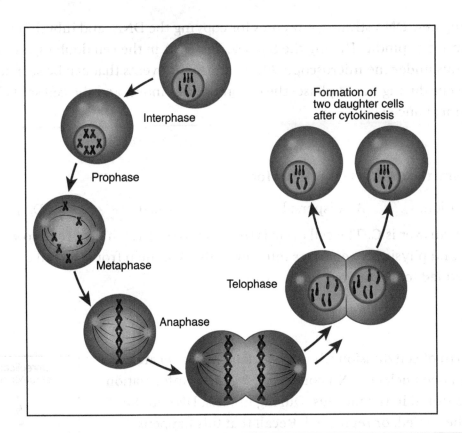

TEST TIP

There is a popular mnemonic to help remember the order of the phases for mitosis:

[Please] Pee on the MAT.

The "please" refers to prophase, while "pee" refers to prometaphase. MAT stands for metaphase, anaphase, and telophase, respectively.

Example

Before mitosis occurs

A. the spindle fibers must elongate.

B. DNA must wrap around histones.

C. chromosomes must split into chromatids.

D. the cell cycle process must be suspended.

The correct answer is **B**. After DNA replicates, it wraps around proteins called histones to form a chromosome. The chromosome must be formed for mitosis to occur.

Meiosis

Meiosis, sexual cell division in eukaryotes, involves two phases of mitosis that take place one after the other but without a second replication of DNA. This provides the reduction in chromosome number from $2n$ to n needed for fertilization to restore the normal $2n$ state.

Diploid multicellular organisms use meiosis, which reduces the number of chromosomes by half. Then, when two haploid (*n*) sex cells (sperm, egg) unite, the normal number of chromosomes is restored. Diploid organisms, such as humans and oak trees, have two copies of every chromosome per cell (2*n*), as opposed to *n*, when one copy of every chromosome is present per cell.

DID YOU KNOW?

During prophase I of meiosis, **crossing over** occurs to increase genetic diversity. Corresponding chromosomes from the mother and the father of the organism undergoing meiosis are physically bound, and *X*-shaped structures called **chiasmata** form. These are where corresponding DNA from the different parental chromosomes are exchanged, resulting in increased diversity.

(PATERNAL)   (MATERNAL)

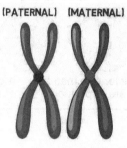

| NON-SISTER CHROMATIDS | HOMOLOGOUS CHROMOSOMES | TETRAD (4 CHROMATIDS) | GENETIC CROSSOVER |

The process of meiosis is divided into two rounds of cell division: meiosis I and meiosis II. The phases that occur in mitosis (prophase, metaphase, anaphase, and telophase) also occur during each round of meiosis. Also, cytokinesis occurs after telophase during each round of cell division. However, DNA replication does not happen when meiosis I proceeds to meiosis II. The result of meiosis is one diploid cell that divides into four haploid cells, as shown in the following image.

Cytokinesis looks different in plant and animal cells. Plant cells build a new wall, or cell plate, between the two cells, while animal cells split by slowly pinching the membrane toward the center of the cell as the cell divides. Microtubules are more important for cytokinesis in plant cells, while the actin cytoskeleton performs the pinching-off operation during animal cytokinesis.

Example

How many rounds of cell division occur during meiosis?

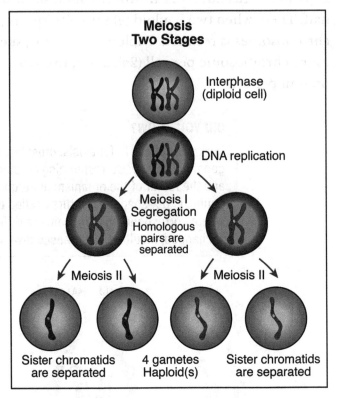

A. 1	C. 3
B. 2	D. 4

The correct answer is **B**. A difference between mitosis and meiosis is that meiosis requires two rounds of cell division. At the end of both rounds, four haploid daughter cells have been produced.

KEY POINT

Meiosis and mitosis both require cytokinesis to physically separate a cell into daughter cells. Also, the sequence of events that occur in mitosis are the same in meiosis. However, there are two primary differences between the types of cell division: (1) meiosis has two rounds of cell division, and (2) daughter cells are genetically identical to the parent cell in mitosis but are not genetically identical in meiosis.

Cell Respiration

Once cells have been made, they need to be powered. Plants and some other cells can capture the energy of light and convert it into stored energy in ATP. However, most prokaryotic cells and all eukaryotic cells can perform a metabolic process called **cellular respiration**. Cellular respiration is the process by which the mitochondria of a cell break down glucose to produce energy in the form of ATP. The following is the general equation for cellular respiration:

$$O_2 + C_6H_{12}O_6 \rightarrow CO_2 + H_2O + ATP$$

Reactions during cellular respiration occur in the following sequence:

1. **Glycolysis:** One molecule of glucose breaks down into two smaller sugar molecules called **pyruvate**. This is an anaerobic process, which means it does not need oxygen to be present.

Glycolysis takes place in the cell's cytoplasm. End product yield from this reaction per one glucose molecule is

- two molecules of ATP
- two molecules of pyruvate
- two molecules of NADH

2. **Oxidation of pyruvate:** Pyruvate is converted into **acetyl coA** in the mitochondrial matrix. This transition reaction must happen for pyruvate to enter the next phase of cellular respiration. Pyruvate is **oxidized**, which means it loses two electrons and a hydrogen molecule. This results in the formation of NADH and loss of CO_2.

DID YOU KNOW?
The citric acid cycle is not identical for all organisms. Plants have some differences in terms of the enzymes used and energy carriers produced.

3. **Citric acid cycle:** Also called the **Krebs cycle**, during this cycle an acetyl group detaches from the coenzyme A in the acetyl coA molecule. This process is **aerobic**, which means it must occur in the presence of oxygen. The net yield per one glucose molecule is

- two molecules of ATP
- six molecules of NADH
- two molecules of $FADH_2$
- four molecules of CO_2

KEEP IN MIND
Cellular respiration requires oxygen, but there are forms of **fermentation** that extract energy from food without using oxygen. Fermentation can be either alcoholic (makes ethanol as an end product, like yeast in the brewing of beer) or lactic acid type. Lactic acid is produced in a person's muscles during strenuous activity when the body cannot move enough oxygen to the cells.

4. **Electron transport chain:** This process happens in the inner mitochondrial membrane. It consists of a series of enzymatic reactions. Both NADH and $FADH_2$ molecules are passed through a series of enzymes so that electrons and protons can be released from them. During this process, energy is released and used to fuel **chemiosmosis**. During chemiosmosis, protons are transported across the inner mitochondrial membrane to the outer mitochondrial compartment. This flow of protons drives the process of ATP synthesis. This step of cellular respiration creates an approximate net yield of 34 ATP per glucose molecule. Six molecules of water are also formed at the end of the electron transport chain.

GENETICS AND DNA

The lesson introduces genetics, which is the study of heredity. Heredity is the characteristics offspring inherit from their parents. This lesson also examines Gregor Mendel's theories of heredity and how they have affected the field of genetics.

Gregor Mendel and Garden Peas

From experiments with garden peas, Mendel developed a simple set of rules that accurately predicted patterns of heredity. He discovered that plants either **self-pollinate** or **cross-pollinate**, when the pollen from one plant fertilizes the pistil of another plant. He also discovered that traits are either **dominant** or **recessive**. Dominant traits are expressed, and recessive traits are hidden.

Mendel's Theory of Heredity

To explain his results, Mendel proposed a theory that has become the foundation of the science of genetics. The theory has five elements:

1. Parents do not transmit traits directly to their offspring. Rather, they pass on units of information called **genes**.
2. For each trait, an individual has two factors: one from each parent. If the two factors have the same information, the individual is **homozygous** for that trait. If the two factors are different, the individual is **heterozygous** for that trait. Each copy of a factor, or **gene**, is called an **allele**.
3. The alleles determine the physical appearance, or **phenotype**. The set of alleles an individual has is its **genotype**.
4. An individual receives one allele from each parent.
5. The presence of an allele does not guarantee that the trait will be expressed.

Punnett Squares

Biologists can predict the probable outcomes of a cross by using a diagram called a **Punnett square**. In the Punnett square illustrated at the right, the yellow pea pods are dominant, as designated by a capital Y, and the green pea pods are recessive, as designated with a lowercase y. In a cross between one homozygous recessive (yy) parent and a heterozygous dominant parent (Yy), the outcome is two heterozygous dominant offspring (Yy) and two homozygous recessive offspring (yy), which gives a ratio of 2:2.

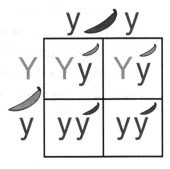

Example

In the Punnett square below, homozygous green pea pods are crossed with dominant yellow pea pods. What is the probability of a homozygous green pea pod?

A. 25%   C. 75%

B. 50%   D. 100%

The correct answer is **B**. There is a 2 out of 4, or 50%, chance of a homozygous green pea pod.

Chromosomes

A **gene** is a segment of DNA, deoxyribonucleic acid, which transmits information from parent to offspring. A single molecule of DNA has thousands of genes. A **chromosome** is a rod-shaped structure that forms when a single DNA molecule and its associated proteins coil tightly before cell division.

Chromosomes have two components:

- **Chromatids:** two copies of each chromosome
- **Centromeres:** protein discs that attach the chromatids together

Human cells have 23 sets of different chromosomes. The two copies of each chromosome are called **homologous** chromosomes, or homologues. An offspring receives one homologue from each parent. When a cell contains two homologues of each chromosome, it is termed **diploid (2n)**. A **haploid (n)** cell contains only one homologue of each chromosome. The only haploid cells humans have are the sperm and eggs cells known as **gametes.**

Example

What is the difference between a diploid cell and a haploid cell?

A. A haploid cell is only found in skin cells.

B. A diploid cell is only found in heart cells.

C. A diploid cell has a full number of chromosomes, and a haploid cell does not.

D. A haploid cell has a full number of chromosomes, and a diploid cell does not.

The correct answer is **C**. Diploid cells have a full number of chromosomes, and haploid cells have half the number of chromosomes.

Deoxyribonucleic Acid

The **DNA molecule** is a long, thin molecule made of subunits called **nucleotides** that are linked together in a **nucleic acid** chain. Each nucleotide is constructed of three parts: a **phosphate group**, **five-carbon sugar**, and **nitrogen base**.

The four nitrogenous bases are

- adenine (A);
- guanine (G);
- thymine (T); and
- cytosine (C).

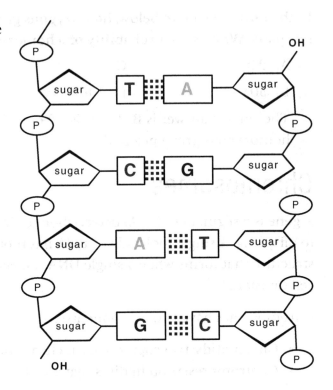

Adenine and guanine belong to a class of large, organic molecules called **purines**. Thymine and cytosine are **pyrimidines**, which have a single ring of carbon and nitrogen atoms. Base pairs are formed as adenine pairs with thymine and guanine pairs with cytosine. These are the only possible combinations.

DNA Replication

The process of synthesizing a new strand of DNA is called **replication**. A DNA molecule replicates by separating into two strands, building a complementary strand, and twisting to form a double helix.

Transcription

The first step in using DNA to direct the making of a protein is **transcription**, the process that "rewrites" the information in a gene in DNA into a molecule of messenger RNA. Transcription manufactures three types of RNA:

- Messenger RNA (mRNA)
- Transfer RNA (tRNA)
- Ribosomal RNA (rRNA)

Messenger RNA is an RNA copy of a gene used as a blueprint for a protein. In eukaryotes, transcription does not produce mRNA directly; it produces a pre-mRNA molecule. **Transfer RNA** translates mRNA sequences into amino acid sequences. **Ribosomal RNA** plays a structural role in ribosomes.

Transcription proceeds at a rate of about 60 nucleotides per second until the **RNA polymerase** (an enzyme) reaches a **stop codon** on the DNA called a **terminator** and releases the RNA molecule.

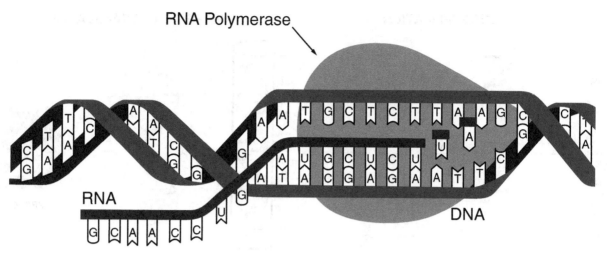

Translation

The components necessary for **translation** are located in the cytoplasm. Translation is the making of proteins by mRNA binding to a ribosome with the start codon that initiates the production of amino acids. A **peptide bond** forms and connects the amino acids together. The sequence of amino acids determines the protein's structure, which determines its function.

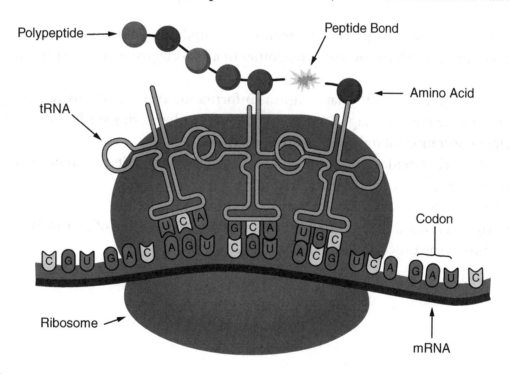

Example

Which type of RNA acts as an interpreter molecule?

A. mRNA   B. pre-mRNA   C. rRNA   D. tRNA

The correct answer is **D**. Transfer RNA (tRNA) acts as an interpreter molecule, translating mRNA sequences into amino acid sequences.

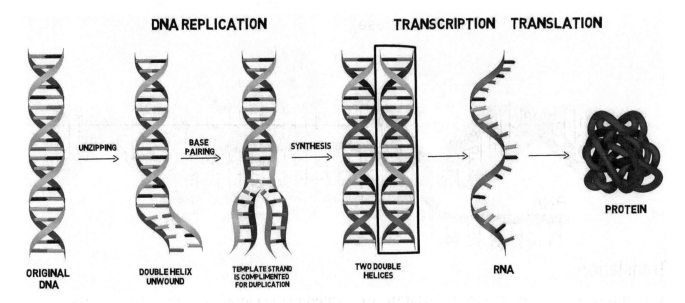

Let's Review!

- Gregor Mendel developed a simple set of rules that accurately predicts patterns of heredity.
- Mendel proposed a theory that has become the foundation of the science of genetics.
- Biologists can predict the probable outcomes of a cross by using a diagram called a Punnett square.
- A gene is a segment of DNA that transmits information from parent to offspring
- A chromosome is a rod-shaped structure that forms when a single DNA molecule and its associated proteins coil tightly before cell division.
- Deoxyribonucleic acid is a long, thin molecule made of subunits called nucleotides that are linked together in a nucleic acid chain.
- Replication is the process of synthesizing a new strand of DNA.
- Transcription is the first step in using DNA to direct the making of a protein.
- Translation is the process of making proteins.

Chapter 14 Life and Physical Sciences Practice Quiz

1. Which of the following helps differentiate a non-living thing from a living thing?

   A. Energy processing

   B. Behavior in nature

   C. Occurrence in nature

   D. Description of habitat

2. What standard is used to make comparisons in experiments?

   A. Sample size

   B. Control group

   C. Dependent variable

   D. Independent variable

3. What is the most basic unit of structure in living things?

   A. Cell

   B. Organelle

   C. Oxygen

   D. Pigment

4. A researcher discovers a cell that is less than 0.5 millimeters in diameter. This cell has pili surrounding its cell wall. What does the researcher classify this cell as?

   A. Autotroph

   B. Eukaryote

   C. Heterotroph

   D. Prokaryote

5. A chemist decides to study reactions occurring in a cell's cytoplasm. Which of the following reactions does she observe?

   A. Mitosis

   B. Cell cycle

   C. Glycolysis

   D. Carbon cycle

6. Which process involves crossing over?

   A. Mitosis

   B. Meiosis

   C. Calvin cycle

   D. Cell respiration

7. If an organism has a total of 12 chromosomes, 12 is the _____ number of chromosomes.

   A. diploid

   B. equivalent

   C. haploid

   D. neutral

8. The sequence of amino acids in a gene determines

   A. the primary structure of a codon.

   B. the primary structure of a protein.

   C. the primary structure of a nucleotide.

   D. the primary structure of a nucleic acid.

CHAPTER 14 LIFE AND PHYSICAL SCIENCES PRACTICE QUIZ – ANSWER KEY

1. A. There are several features that scientists use to identify living things. These features include: how living things process energy, growth and development, reproduction, and homeostasis. **See Lesson: An Introduction to Biology.**

2. B. A control group is a factor that does not change during an experiment. Due to this, it is used as a standard for comparison with variables that do change such as a dependent variable. **See Lesson: An Introduction to Biology.**

3. A. The most basic unit and building block of all living things is the cell. **See Lesson: Cell Structure, Function, and Type.**

4. D. Common characteristics of prokaryotic cells are that they are small and have hair-like structures called pili that surround their cell wall. **See Lesson: Cell Structure, Function, and Type.**

5. C. The first step of cellular respiration is glycolysis. This process happens in the cell's cytoplasm, where glucose is broken down to pyruvate, yielding two molecules of ATP. **See Lesson: Cellular Reproduction, Cellular Respiration, and Photosynthesis.**

6. B. Meiosis is a form of cell division that occurs when DNA from homologous chromosomes is exchanged. This exchange, or crossing over, increases genetic diversity in a population. **See Lesson: Cellular Reproduction, Cellular Respiration, and Photosynthesis.**

7. A. Diploid refers to the full number of chromosomes. **See Lesson: Genetics and DNA.**

8. B. The sequence of amino acids in a gene determines the primary structure of a protein. **See Lesson: Genetics and DNA.**

CHAPTER 15 CHEMISTRY

STATES OF MATTER

This lesson explains the differences between solids, liquids, gases, and plasmas. It also describes how a sample can change from one state of matter to another.

States of Matter

On Earth, substances are found in four states of matter: solid, liquid, gas, and plasma. Many properties of these states of matter are familiar. For example, solids are rigid and hard, liquids can flow inside their containers, and gases can spread throughout an entire room. But what happens at the molecular level may not be as familiar. The differences among them can be explained by the amount of energy that the particles have and the strength of the cohesive forces that hold the particles together. **Cohesion** is the tendency of particles of the same kind to stick to each other and is an important property to consider when looking at states of matter. The motion and density of particles in a substance and the tendency of a substance to take the shape and volume of its container differentiate states of matter.

Solids have the lowest energy. The particles are packed close together, and their structure is relatively rigid. Strong cohesive forces prevent particles from moving very far or very fast. Therefore, both the shape and volume of a solid are fixed.

> **DID YOU KNOW?**
> While particles are generally more tightly packed in solids than in other states, water is an exception. When liquid water freezes, it expands. The molecules are pushed apart as strong intermolecular forces, known as hydrogen bonds, allow the particles to form crystals. This property of water is important in many processes on Earth.

In **liquids**, particles have more energy than in solids and can overcome the cohesive forces to some degree. Since particles can move more freely, they flow and take the shape of their container. However, cohesive forces are strong enough to somewhat restrict the movement of particles. While the shape of the liquid is not fixed, the volume is.

Gases have more energy than solids or liquids. In a gas, the cohesive forces are very weak because the particles move very quickly. Gas particles move more freely than liquids, which means that gas particles can not only take the shape of the container, but also spread to occupy the entire volume of the container.

CONNECTIONS

Gases and liquids are considered fluids because of their ability to "flow" and take the shape of their containers.

In **plasma**, the particles have so much energy that the electrons separate from their nuclei. The result is a substance composed of moving positively and negatively charged particles. Although plasmas are less common in everyday life than the other states of matter, there are a few familiar examples. First, the hottest parts of the sun are made of plasma because of the high temperature (up to 15,000,000 K). Also, neon signs glow when plasma is produced by passing an electric current through a gas.

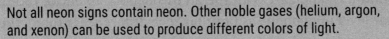

DID YOU KNOW?

Not all neon signs contain neon. Other noble gases (helium, argon, and xenon) can be used to produce different colors of light.

Example

In which state of matter are particles moving slowest?

A. Solid   B. Liquid   C. Gas   D. Plasma

The correct answer is **A**. Because solid particles have less energy than particles in other states of matter, they have the most restricted movement.

Phase Changes

Whenever a substance transforms from one state of matter to another, it undergoes a phase change. These processes are physical changes because the chemical composition of the substance remains the same; only its appearance is different. The six most common phase changes are summarized in the diagram and chart below. Note that the states of matter are arranged in order of increasing energy from left to right.

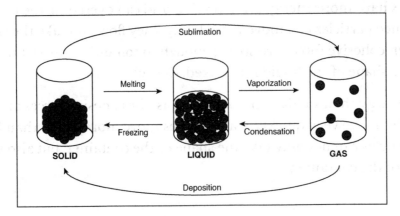

Phase Change	Name	Absorb or Release Energy
solid to liquid	melting	absorb
liquid to gas	vaporization	absorb
solid to gas	sublimation	absorb
liquid to solid	freezing	release
gas to liquid	condensation	release
gas to solid	deposition	release

All phase changes require the system to either absorb or release energy. Any phase change that moves to the right in the diagram above requires energy to be added to the system because the substance has more energy at the end of the phase change. The phase changes are **melting**, **vaporization (boiling)**, and **sublimation**. When energy is added, particles move faster and can break away from each other more easily as they move to a state of matter with a higher amount of energy. This is most commonly done by heating the substance.

Any phase change that moves to the left in the diagram requires energy to be removed from the system because the substance has less energy at the end of the phase change. These phase changes are **freezing, condensation**, and **deposition**. When the particles release energy, they move more slowly. The cohesive forces bring these particles closer together as they move to a state of matter with a lower amount of energy. This is most commonly done by cooling the substance.

The temperatures at which phase changes occur depends the strength of the cohesive forces between particles. For substances like metals that have high melting and boiling points, it takes a relatively large amount of energy to overcome the intermolecular forces enough to change states of matter. Similarly, substances with low melting and boiling points, like the gases that make up Earth's atmosphere, do not require as much energy to overcome their intermolecular forces.

Example

Which of the following phase changes requires a substance to release energy?

A. Boiling   B. Condensation   C. Melting   D. Sublimation

The correct answer is **B**. During condensation, a gas turns to a liquid. For this to occur, high-energy particles in the gas must release some energy for the cohesive forces to bring the particles closer together.

Heating and Cooling Curves

When studying phase changes, one can examine the heating or cooling curve of a substance. Heating and cooling curves are plots of temperature versus time that occur as energy is added to or removed from the system at a constant rate.

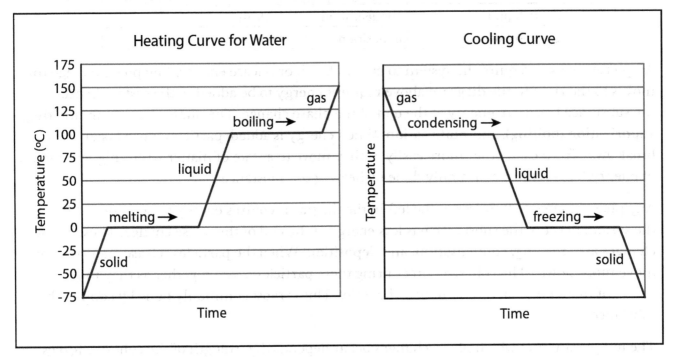

The heating curve for water is shown above. Notice that at the beginning of the experiment, the substance is a solid. As heat is added, the temperature of the solid increases until it reaches its melting point, 0°C. The temperature remains constant at the melting point until the entire sample has changed to a liquid. Note that even though heat is still being added, the temperature is not increasing. This is because the added energy is used to disrupt the cohesive forces in the solid, allowing the particles to move more freely as the substance changes to a liquid.

Once the sample is completely melted, the temperature increases again. It increases until the boiling point, 100°C, is reached. Heat is still being added, but the temperature remains constant as the substance boils. This time, the added energy is being used to break the intermolecular bonds in the liquid as the particles transform into a gas and move farther away from each other. It is not until the phase change is complete and the sample is entirely gas that the temperature starts increasing again.

KEEP IN MIND

The temperature of a substance is a measure of the kinetic energy of the particles that make up a substance. In other words, temperature is related to how fast the particles are moving.

A cooling curve has the opposite shape of a heating curve, as seen in the graph above. In these experiments, the sample starts as a high-temperature gas. As heat is removed, the temperature of the gas decreases to its boiling point. At this point, the temperature remains constant until the entire sample is liquid. The liquid then cools to a lower temperature until it reaches the freezing point. The temperature remains constant as the substance freezes, and once it is completely solid, the temperature decreases again.

> **KEY POINT!**
>
> As a substance undergoes a phase change, its temperature remains constant. The only time a substance experiences an increase or decrease in temperature is when it is entirely in one state of matter.

Example

If a sample of water is losing energy but its temperature is not changing, what may be happening?

A. Freezing   B. Melting   C. Sublimation   D. Vaporization

The correct answer is **A.** When a substance is freezing, the liquid particles lose enough energy to become a solid. The temperature will not change until the phase change is complete.

Let's Review!

- Solids, liquids, gases, and plasmas differ from one another in the amount of energy that the particles have and the strength of the cohesive forces that hold the particles together.
- A substance can undergo a phase change if it either absorbs or releases enough energy.
- Heating and cooling curves show the temperature of a substance as heat is consistently added or removed.
- As a substance changes states, its temperature remains constant. Any energy that is absorbed or released is used to change the way in which the particles interact with one another.

PROPERTIES OF MATTER

This lesson introduces the properties of matter, which are fundamental to the understanding of chemistry.

Matter and Its Properties

Aluminum, clothing, water, air, and glass are all different kinds of matter. **Matter** is anything that takes up space and has mass. A golf ball contains more matter than a table-tennis ball. The golf ball has more mass. The amount of matter that an object contains is its **mass**.

Table sugar is 100 percent sugar. Table sugar (sucrose) is an example of a substance. A **substance** is matter that has a uniform and definite composition. Lemonade is not a substance because not all pitchers of lemonade are identical. Different pitchers of lemonade may have different amounts of sugar, lemon juice, or water and may taste different.

All crystals of sucrose taste sweet and dissolve completely in water. All samples of a substance have identical physical properties. A **physical property** is a quality or condition of a substance that can be observed or measured without changing the substance's composition. Some physical properties of matter are color, solubility, mass, odor, hardness, density, and boiling point.

Just as every substance has physical properties, every substance has chemical properties. For example, when iron is exposed to water and oxygen, it corrodes and produces a new substance called iron (III) oxide (rust). The chemical properties of a substance are its ability to undergo chemical reactions and to form new substances. Rusting is a chemical property of iron. **Chemical properties** are observed only when a substance undergoes a change in composition, which is a chemical change.

Physical vs. Chemical Properties

Physical Properties	Chemical Properties
Color	Flammability
Shape	Rusting
Size	Burning
Density	Corrosion
Amount	Reactivity
Volume	

Intensive and Extensive Properties

Intensive properties do not depend on the amount of matter that is present. Intensive properties do not change according to the conditions. They are used to identify samples because their characteristics do not depend on the size of the sample. In contrast, **extensive** properties do depend on the amount of a sample that is present. A good example of the difference between the two types of properties is that mass and volume are extensive properties, but their ratio (density) is an intensive property. Notice that mass and volume deal with amounts, whereas density is a physical property.

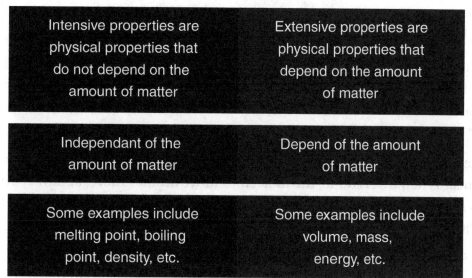

Intensive Properties
versus
Extensive Properties

Intensive properties are physical properties that do not depend on the amount of matter	Extensive properties are physical properties that depend on the amount of matter
Independant of the amount of matter	Depend of the amount of matter
Some examples include melting point, boiling point, density, etc.	Some examples include volume, mass, energy, etc.

Example

Which of the following explains the difference between chemical and physical properties?

   A. Physical properties can easily change, while chemical properties are constant.

   B. Chemical properties always involve a source of heat, and physical properties always involve light.

   C. Chemical properties involve a change in the chemical composition of a substance, while physical properties can easily be observed.

   D. Physical properties involve a change in the chemical composition of a substance, while chemical properties can easily be observed.

The correct answer is **C.** A physical property is a quality or condition of a substance that can be observed or measured without changing the substance's composition, while a chemical property is one where a change in chemical composition has occurred.

Phase Changes

There are six phase changes: condensation, evaporation, freezing, melting, sublimation, and deposition.

Condensation is the change of a gas or vapor to a liquid. A change in the pressure and the temperature of a substance causes this change. The condensation point is the same as the boiling point of a substance. It is most noticeable when there is a large temperature difference between an object and the atmosphere. Condensation is also the opposite of evaporation.

Evaporation is the change of a liquid to a gas on the surface of a substance. This is not to be confused with boiling, which is a phase transition of an entire substance from a liquid to a gas. The evaporation point is the same as the freezing point of a substance. As the temperature increases, the rate of evaporation also increases. Evaporation depends not only on the temperature, but also on the amount of substance available.

Freezing is the change of a liquid to a solid. It occurs when the temperature drops below the freezing point. The amount of heat that has been removed from the substance allows the particles of the substance to draw closer together, and the material changes from a liquid to a solid. It is the opposite of melting.

Melting is the change of a solid into a liquid. For melting to occur, enough heat must be added to the substance. When this is done, the molecules move around more, and the particles are unable to hold together as tightly as they can in a solid. They break apart, and the solid becomes a liquid.

Sublimation is a solid changing into a gas. As a material sublimates, it does not pass through the liquid state. An example of sublimation is carbon dioxide, a gas, changing into dry ice, a solid. It is the reverse of deposition.

Deposition is a gas changing into a solid without going through the liquid phase. It is an uncommon phase change. An example is when it is extremely cold outside and the cold air comes in contact with a window. Ice will form on the window without going through the liquid state.

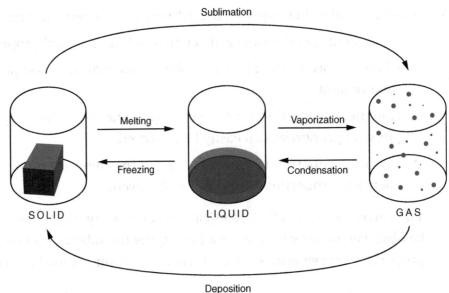

Example

Which of the six types of phase changes is the opposite of sublimation?

A. Condensation   B. Deposition   C. Evaporation   D. Freezing

The correct answer is **B.** Sublimation is the changing of a solid to a gas, and deposition is the changing of a gas to a solid.

Adhesiveness and Cohesiveness

Because of polarity, water is attracted to water, a property called **cohesion**. The typical water molecule has a polar configuration, as seen below.

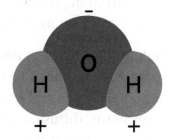

Notice that there is a negative end and a positive end. This means it is a polar molecule. In a **polar molecule**, one end of the molecule is slightly negative and one end is slightly positive.

Inside a plant, water has to travel up, against gravity, to reach all the leaves. Because the water molecules are attracted to each other, or demonstrate **cohesion**, they also adhere to the sides of the xylem vessels that transport water up to where it is needed in the plant. This is possible because of **adhesion**. Adhesion is water's ability to be attracted to other substances.

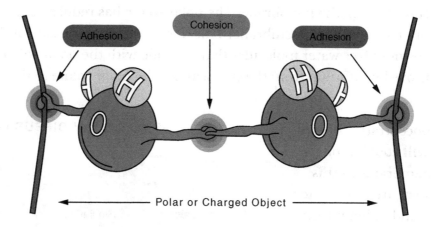

Example

What property allows water to flow against the force of gravity?

A. Adhesion   B. Cohesion   C. Polarity   D. Xylem

The correct answer is **A.** Adhesion is water's ability to be attracted to other substances. Because of adhesion, water is able to move upward.

Diffusion and Osmosis

When a bottle of perfume is opened, perfume molecules diffuse throughout a room. **Diffusion** is the tendency of molecules and ions to move toward areas of lower concentrations until the concentration is uniform throughout the room (that is, it reaches equilibrium). This random movement of individual particles has an important consequence. Because the movement is random, a particle is more likely to move from an area where there are a lot of molecules (area of high concentration) to an area where there are fewer molecules (an area of lower concentration). In the human lungs, oxygen diffuses into the bloodstream because there is a higher concentration of oxygen molecules in the lungs' air sacs than there is in the blood.

Solute and solvent particles tend to diffuse from areas where their concentration is high to areas where their concentration is lower. Imagine that a membrane separates two regions of liquid. As long as solute particles and solvent (water) molecules can pass freely through the membrane, diffusion will equalize the amount of solute and solvent on the two sides. The sides will reach equilibrium.

But what if a polar solute that cannot pass through the membrane is added to one side? This situation is common in cells. An amino acid cannot cross a lipid bilayer, and neither can an ion or a sugar molecule. Unable to cross the membrane, the polar solute particles form hydrogen bonds with the water molecules surrounding them. These "bound" water molecules are no longer free to diffuse through the membrane. The polar solute has reduced the number of free water molecules on that side of the membrane. This means the opposite side of the membrane (without solute) has more free water molecules than the side with the polar solute. As a result, water molecules move by diffusion from the side without the polar solute to the side with the polar solute.

Eventually, the concentration of free water molecules will equalize on the sides of the membrane. At this point, however, there are more water molecules (bound and unbound) on the side of the membrane with the polar solute. Net water movement through a membrane in response to the concentration of a solute is called **osmosis**. Stated another way, osmosis is the diffusion of water molecules through a membrane in the direction of higher solute concentration.

OSMOSIS and DIFFUSION

Osmosis

Molecules go through a semipermeable membrane. Just water

Similarities

Molecules move around to create equilibrium

Diffusion

Molecules spread out over a large area. Everything but water

Example

What is the goal of osmosis?

    A. The water will equalize on both side of the semipermeable membrane.

    B. The concentration of solutes will diffuse through the semipermeable membrane.

    C. The concentration of free water molecules will equalize on both sides of the membrane

    D. The solute particles will flow from an area of high concentration to an area of lower concentration.

The correct answer is **C**. As a result of osmosis, the concentration of free water molecules will equalize on both sides of the membrane.

Let's Review!

- Matter is anything that takes up space and has mass.
- The difference between physical and chemical properties is that chemical properties involve a change in a substance's chemical composition and physical properties do not.
- The difference between extensive and intensive properties is based on whether the properties depend on the amount of substance that is present.
- Cohesiveness is the attraction of water to itself, and adhesiveness is the attraction of water to other substances.
- Osmosis is the diffusion of water and the movement of molecules from an area of high concentration to an area of lower concentration.

CHEMICAL BONDS

This lesson introduces bonding and explains the three ways in which atoms can become stable. The rest of the lesson examines different types of bonds in more detail.

Introduction to Bonding

Chemical elements found in the periodic table have different levels of reactivity. The number of **valence electrons** in an atom is the most important factor in determining how an element will react. Valence electrons, which are found in an atom's outermost energy level, are involved in forming chemical bonds. The periodic table below shows the Bohr models of select elements. The valence electrons appear in red.

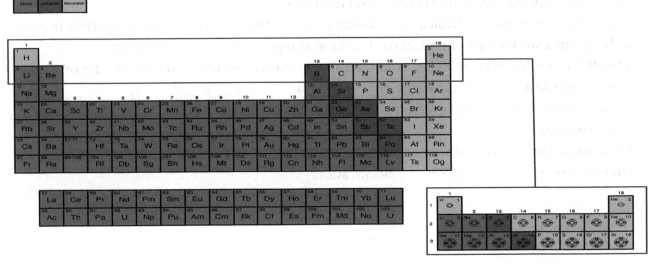

The **octet rule** states that atoms will lose, gain, or share electrons to obtain a stable electron configuration of eight valence electrons. In other words, if an atom needs to become stable, it will react with another atom, which can result in the formation of a chemical compound. Note that the elements in group 18, the noble gases, have eight valence electrons. Helium is an exception and is stable with two valence electrons. Because they have a stable electron configuration, the noble gases do not need to react with other elements to become stable. As a result, they are found in nature as single elements rather than in compounds.

KEY POINT!

The goal of forming chemical bonds is to become stable by having eight electrons in the outer shell. This is easy to remember because it is described in the *octet* rule. The prefix *octa-* means "eight," and it can be seen in other words, such as *octopus* and *octagon*.

Elements in other groups will react to become stable in predictable ways, depending on how many valence electrons they have. In the periodic table above, elements are classified as metals, nonmetals, or metalloids. Compared to other elements, metals have fewer valence electrons and tend to lose them to become stable. Notice that removing the red valence electrons from the outermost energy level exposes another energy level. This becomes the valence shell, and the atom is stable because it has eight valence electrons.

Nonmetals and metalloids have a relatively high number of valence electrons. Except for the noble gasses, these elements tend to gain or share electrons to become stable.

Ionic compounds are formed when electrons are transferred from a metal (which loses one or more electrons) to a nonmetal (which gains one or more electrons). **Covalent compounds** are formed when two nonmetals or metalloids share electrons.

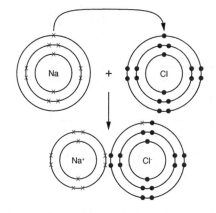

Ionic Bond

> **TEST TIP**
>
> A quick way to determine if atoms are held together by ionic or covalent bonds is to examine the types of elements involved. If a metal and a nonmetal bond, an ionic bond forms. If two nonmetals or metalloids bond, a covalent bond forms.

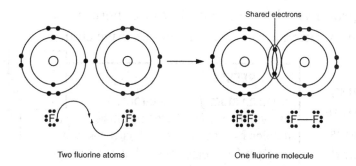

Shared electrons

Two fluorine atoms   One fluorine molecule

Covalent Bond

Example

In the compound sodium bromide (NaBr), electrons are _____. In the compound carbon tetrabromide (CBr_4), electrons are _____.

A. shared, shared   B. shared, transferred   C. transferred, shared   D. transferred, transferred

The correct answer is **C**. Electrons are transferred when an ionic compound like sodium bromide forms. Electrons are shared when a covalent compound like carbon tetrabromide forms.

Ion Formation

If an atom has an equal number of positively charged protons and negatively charged electrons, it is neutral and has no **net charge**. When electrons are transferred, atoms end up with either more protons than electrons or more electrons than protons. The atoms are considered **ions** because they have a net positive or negative charge.

KEEP IN MIND

Protons are positively charged subatomic particles and can be represented by the symbol $p+$. Electrons are negatively charged subatomic particles and can be represented by the symbol $e-$.

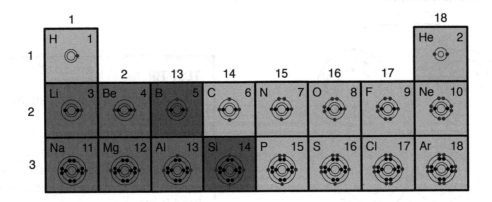

When a metal such as sodium reacts to become stable, it loses its valence electrons. At first, it is a neutral atom with 11 protons and 11 electrons. When it loses an electron, the number of protons does not change, and the atom has 11 protons and 10 electrons. Because there is one more positively charged proton, a **cation** forms. A cation is an ion with a net positive charge.

When a nonmetal such as chlorine reacts to become stable, it gains a valence electron. At first, it is a neutral atom with 17 protons and 17 electrons. When it gains an electron, the number of protons does not change, and the atom has 17 protons and 18 electrons. Because there is one more negatively charged electron, an **anion** forms. An anion is an ion with a net negative charge.

BE CAREFUL!

When an atom *gains* electrons, it has a net *negative* charge because it gains negatively charged particles. When an atom *loses* electrons, it has a net *positive* charge. After the loss, there are more protons than electrons, which means there are more positively charged particles.

The way in which an element reacts can be predicted based on that element's position in the periodic table. The table below summarizes the reactivity of elements according to their group number. Elements in each group have a specific number of valence electrons, which dictates what the atoms need to do to obtain a valence shell with eight electrons. Some will lose electrons, and others will gain electrons. This, along with the number of electrons that must be transferred, determines the charge of the stable ion that forms.

Group	1	2	13	14	15	16	17	18
Valence $e-$	1	2	3	4	5	6	7	8
Lose/Gain $e-$	Lose 1	Lose 2	Lose 3	Lose/Gain 4	Gain 3	Gain 2	Gain 1	N/A
Charge	+1	+2	+3	+/–4	–3	–2	–1	N/A

Example

What will strontium do to form a stable ion with a +2 charge?

A. Gain two protons

B. Lose two protons

C. Gain two electrons

D. Lose two electrons

The correct answer is **D**. Atoms gain or lose electrons, not protons, to form ions. Like other metals in group 2, strontium will lose its two valence electrons to become stable.

Ionic Bonding

An ionic compound is composed of a cation and an anion. An ionic bond is formed from the cation's attraction to the oppositely charged anion. The figure at the right shows how transferring an electron from sodium to chlorine results in the formation of an ionic bond.

Notice that the charges on sodium (Na$^+$) and chlorine (Cl$^-$) ions have the same magnitude (they both have a value of 1). Therefore, the charge of one sodium ion balances the charge of one chlorine ion. When an ionic compound is formed from ions that have equal but opposite charges, the elements will be present in a 1:1 ratio. Examples are shown in the table below.

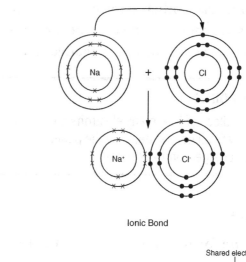

Ionic Bond

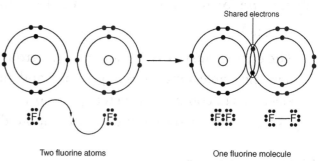

Two fluorine atoms   One fluorine molecule

Covalent Bond

Compound Name	Cation	Anion	Compound Formula
Potassium fluoride	K$^+$	F$^-$	KF
Magnesium oxide	Mg^{2+}	O^{2-}	MgO
Aluminum nitride	Al^{3+}	N^{3-}	AlN

In some cases, atoms need to lose or gain two, three, or, in rare cases, four electrons to become stable. For example, magnesium must give up two electrons to become stable. Because chlorine only needs one electron, magnesium can give an electron to two different chlorine atoms. Then, one magnesium cation with a +2 charge (Mg^{2+}) bonds with two chloride anions (Cl^-) to form magnesium chloride, ($MgCl_2$). The subscript 2 indicates that there are two chloride ions in this compound.

Compound Name	Cation	Anion	Compound Formula
Calcium bromide	Ca^{2+}	Br^-	$CaBr_2$
Aluminum fluoride	Al^{3+}	F^-	AlF_3
Rubidium oxide	Rb^+	O^{2-}	Rb_2O
Sodium phosphide	Na^+	P^{3-}	Na_3P
Aluminum oxide	Al^{3+}	O^{2-}	Al_2O_3
Calcium phosphide	Ca^{2+}	P^{3-}	Ca_3P_2

Similarly, when oxygen and lithium react, the oxygen atom receives an electron from each of two lithium atoms. This transfer results in two lithium cations (Li^+) and an oxygen anion (O^{2-}). They attract each other to form the compound lithium oxide with a formula of Li_2O. Other examples are shown in the table below. Notice that in all ionic compounds, the total positive charge balances out the total negative charge, resulting in a neutral compound.

KEY POINT!

Regardless of how many electrons are transferred, ionic compounds have net charges of zero. They are all neutral because the positive cations attract as many anions as they need to balance their charges, and vice versa.

Example

What is the formula for the compound formed between calcium and oxygen?

A. CaO   B. CaO_2 C. Ca_2O D. Ca_3O_2

The correct answer is **A**. Calcium is in group 2 and will lose its two valence electrons to become stable. Oxygen is in group 16 and, because it has six valence electrons, will gain two electrons to complete its octet. Therefore, one calcium ion requires one oxide ion to balance its charge to form a neutral ionic compound.

Covalent Bonding

When a nonmetal atom reacts with a nonmetal or metalloid, the atoms share electrons to obtain eight valence electrons each. An example can be seen in the model below. Both the Bohr models and the electron dot structures of the fluorine atoms show their seven valence electrons. After each atom shares an electron with the other, shown by the arrows, a covalent bond forms. In the newly formed fluorine molecule, both fluorine atoms have the stable electron configuration of eight valence electrons. The shared electrons can be represented by two dots or by a line in between the fluorine atoms.

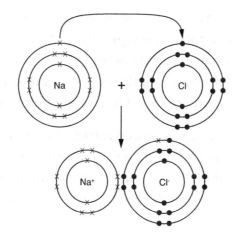

Ionic Bond

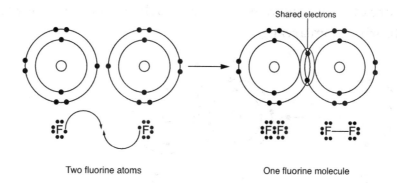

Two fluorine atoms   One fluorine molecule

Covalent Bond

Covalent compounds can be modeled in **Lewis structures**. Lewis structures for methane, ammonia, and water are shown below. In a Lewis structure, covalent bonds, also called shared electrons, are represented by lines between two atoms. Valence electrons that are not involved in bonding, also called **lone-pair electrons**, are represented by dots.

> **KEEP IN MIND**
>
> Each line (bond) in a Lewis structure represents two electrons, one from each atom involved in the bond.

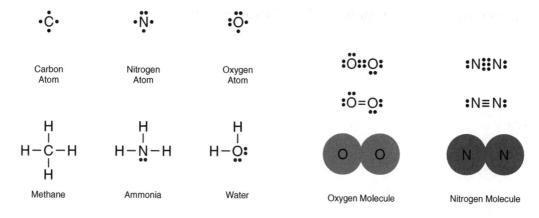

The number of bonds that an atom forms depends on the number of valence electrons that the atom has as a single atom. In a molecule of methane (CH_4), one carbon atom bonds to four hydrogen atoms. A single neutral carbon atom has four valence electrons and can share each one with a different hydrogen atom. In the end, it has four covalent bonds. Because each covalent bond involves two electrons, carbon has a total of eight valence electrons and is stable.

Similarly, in a molecule of ammonia (NH_3), one nitrogen atom bonds to three hydrogen atoms. Nitrogen shares six electrons total and has two remaining lone-pair electrons that are not involved in bonding for a total of eight. In a water molecule, an oxygen atom bonds to two hydrogen atoms. Oxygen has four shared electrons and four lone-pair electrons for a total of eight.

Example

In the Lewis structure of a fluorine molecule shown below, how are the eight valence electrons of each fluorine atom arranged?

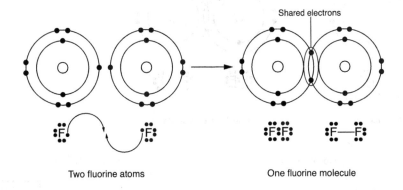

Two fluorine atoms   One fluorine molecule

Covalent Bond

A. 2 are shared, 6 are lone-pair.

B. 4 are shared, 4 are lone-pair.

C. 6 are shared, 2 are lone-pair.

D. 8 are shared, none are lone-pair.

The correct answer is **A**. A fluorine atom forms a single covalent bond with another fluorine atom, which means that two electrons are being shared. The other six valence electrons are lone-pair electrons and are represented by dots around the atom.

Types of Covalent Bonds

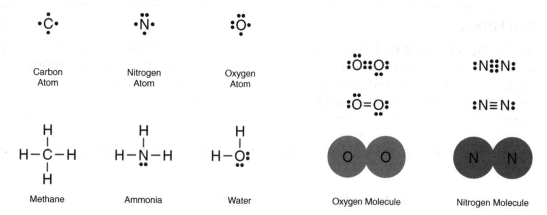

In methane, ammonia, and water, atoms are joined by **single covalent bonds** in which the atoms share two electrons. However, two atoms may need to share more than one pair of electrons to be stable. For example, two oxygen atoms form a **double bond**, in which two pairs of electrons (four electrons total) are shared. Similarly, two nitrogen atoms form a molecule with a **triple bond**, in which three pairs of electrons (six electrons total) are shared.

As more pairs of electrons are shared, the length of the bond decreases, and the bond strength increases. Single bonds are the longest and weakest bonds. They require the least energy to break because there is not as much energy stored in them.

CONNECTION

A pair of shared electrons between two atoms can be compared to a rubber band stretching between two objects. Having two or three rubber bands, rather than one, increases the strength of the "bond" that holds them together, making it harder to separate the objects.

Regardless of how many electrons are shared, the strength of a covalent bond comes from the positively charged nuclei of both atoms attracting the negatively charged electrons that are being shared. However, not all atoms attract shared electrons equally. This property is known as **electronegativity**, the tendency of an atom to attract shared electrons in a covalent bond. It is a measure of how hard an atom is pulling on shared electrons. Electronegativity increases going from left to right in the periodic table. Nonmetal atoms pull harder on electrons and do not tend to give them up. Therefore, the halogens in group 17 have the highest electronegativity of all elements.

If the two atoms share electrons equally, the bond is classified as **nonpolar covalent**. This occurs if the two atoms have similar electronegativities, which means that neither atom pulls significantly harder on the shared electrons than the other. If the two atoms share electrons unequally, the bond is **polar covalent**. This occurs if the electronegativity of one atom is significantly higher than the other, causing it to pull significantly harder on the shared electrons.

Example

> **CONNECTION**
>
> The sharing of electrons is like a game of tug-of-war in which two opposing teams are pulling on a rope in opposite directions. In a nonpolar bond, the opposing teams are pulling with the same force, and the rope is not moving toward one team or the other. In a polar bond, one team is winning by pulling the rope closer to its side.

An atom of which of the following elements has the strongest pull on shared electrons in a covalent bond?

A. Aluminum   B. Chlorine   C. Sodium   D. Sulfur

The correct answer is **B**. The element with the highest electronegativity will have the strongest pull on shared electrons in a covalent bond. Electronegativity increases moving from left to right across the periodic table, so the element farthest to the right in the period, chlorine, has the highest electronegativity.

Let's Review!

- As stated in the octet rule, any atom that does not have a stable electron configuration of eight valence electrons will lose, gain, or share electrons to become stable.
- Exceptions to the octet rule include hydrogen and helium, which are stable when they have two valence electrons.
- Ionic bonds are formed when electrons are transferred from a metal atom to a nonmetal atom.
- Covalent bonds are formed when two atoms share electrons. When two atoms need to share more than one pair of electrons, multiple bonds form. If two pairs are shared, a double bond forms. If three pairs are shared, a triple bond forms.
- The difference in the electronegativities of the two atoms determines if electrons are shared equally, forming a nonpolar covalent bond, or shared unequally, forming a polar covalent bond.

CHEMICAL SOLUTIONS

This lesson discusses the properties of different types of mixtures, focusing on solutions. Then, it examines aspects of chemical reactions, including the components of the reactions and the types of changes that occur.

Solutions

When elements and compounds are physically (not chemically) combined, they form a **mixture**. When the substances mix evenly and it is impossible to see the individual components, the mixture is described as **homogeneous**. When the substances mix unevenly and it is possible to see the individual components, the mixture is described as **heterogeneous**.

Solubility is the ability of a substance to dissolve in another substance. For example, salt and sugar are both substances that can dissolve in water. They are **soluble**. In contrast, sand does not dissolve in water. It is **insoluble**. Individual particles of sand can be seen in water, but individual particles of salt are completely mixed in.

When one substance dissolves in the other, a type of homogeneous mixture called a **solution** forms. The substance that is being dissolved is the **solute**. The substance in which the solute is dissolved is the **solvent**, which makes up a greater percentage of the mixture than the solute. When salt dissolves in water, salt is the solute, and water is the solvent. Saltwater is an example of an **aqueous solution**, which forms when any substance dissolves in water.

The **concentration** of a solution is the amount of solute in a given volume of solution and can be expressed in several ways:

- **Molarity** (number of moles of a substance in one liter of solution)
- **Molality** (number of moles of a substance per kilogram of solvent)
- **Percent composition by mass** (mass of a solute per unit mass of the solution)
- **Mole fraction** (moles of a solute divided by the total number of moles in the solution)

Solubility can also refer to the *amount* of a substance that can dissolve. Even for soluble substances, there is a limit to how much of it can dissolve. The lines in the

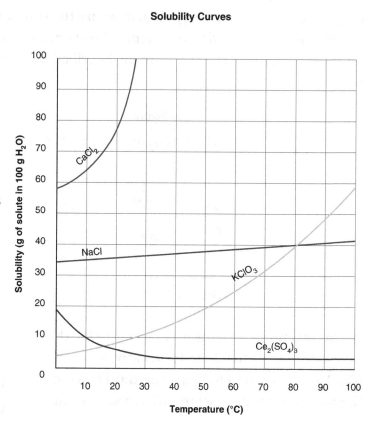

Solubility Curves

Solubility (g of solute in 100 g H_2O) vs. Temperature (°C)

$CaCl_2$, NaCl, $KClO_3$, $Ce_2(SO_4)_3$

graph below show these limits for different substances at different temperatures in 100 grams of water. The area below a line represents masses of solute that dissolve in 100 grams of water. This type of solution is **unsaturated** because more solute can be dissolved. At the line, the solution is **saturated** because the limit has been reached. Any solute added above that mass will remain undissolved.

Example

> **CONNECTION**
>
> The term *saturated* is also used in everyday life to describe things, such as sponges or clothing that have soaked up all the water that they can absorb.

A beaker contains 50 mL of oil and 50 mL of water. No matter how much the mixture is stirred, the oil and the water still separate into two layers. Which statement accurately describes this mixture?

A. Oil is insoluble in water.

B. It is an unsaturated solution.

C. It is a homogeneous mixture.

D. Water is a good solvent for oil.

The correct answer is **A**. Because the oil will not mix into the water, it is insoluble.

Chemical Reactions

A chemical reaction involves elements and compounds that combine, break apart, rearrange, or change form in some way. **Reactants** are the substances that are present at the beginning of the reaction and undergo a change. **Products** are the substances that are formed from the reactants. Chemical reactions can be described by chemical equations, an example of which is shown below.

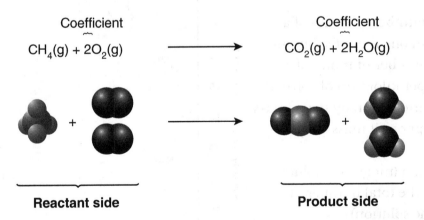

Coefficient

$CH_4(g) + 2O_2(g)$

Coefficient

$CO_2(g) + 2H_2O(g)$

Reactant side

Product side

In this reaction, methane (CH_4) is burned in the presence of oxygen (O_2) to form carbon dioxide (CO_2) and water (H_2O). In the chemical equation, the formulas of the reactants (CH_4 and O_2) and

KEEP IN MIND

Reactants will always be on the left side of the arrow, and products will always be on the right side.

products (CO_2 and H_2O) are used. If there is more than one reactant or more than one product, their formulas are separated by a plus sign (+). The reactants and products are separated by an arrow.

The state of matter may also be shown in the chemical equation in parentheses after the substance formula. Substances can be solid, liquid, or gas, indicated by (*s*), (*l*), or (*g*), respectively. If a substance is dissolved in water, forming an aqueous solution, that state is indicated by (*aq*) in a chemical equation.

Finally, coefficients may appear in chemical equations. These coefficients indicate how many particles (atoms or molecules) of each substance react or form. When there is no coefficient present, only one particle is involved. In the example above, one molecule of methane (CH_4) reacts with two molecules of oxygen (O_2). One molecule of carbon dioxide (CO_2) is produced, along with two molecules of water (H_2O).

Example

The equation describing the formation of ammonia (NH3) from nitrogen and hydrogen is shown below. Which of the following statements is true?

$$3H_2(g) + N_2(g)\ 2NH_3(g)$$

A. NH_3 is the reactant, and H_2 and N_2 are products.

B. H_2 and N_2 are the reactants, and NH_3 is the product.

C. N and H_3 are the reactants, and H_2 and N_2 are products.

D. H_2 and N_2 are the reactants, and N and H_3 are the products.

The correct answer is **B**. Two reactants, H_2 and N_2, are found on the left side of the arrow. One product, NH_3, is found on the right side of the arrow.

Types of Reactions

Chemical reactions can be classified according to the reactants and products involved. This lesson will cover five types of reactions: synthesis, decomposition, single-replacement, double-replacement, and combustion. The first four types are outlined in the table below.

Type of Reaction	Model	Example
Synthesis	A + B AB	$2H_2(g) + O_2(g)\ 2H_2O(g)$
Decomposition	AB A + B	$2H_2O_2(aq)\ 2H_2O(l) + O_2(g)$
Single-Replacement	AB + C AC + B	$2HCl(aq) + Zn(s)\ ZnCl_2(aq) + H_2(g)$
Double-Replacement	AB + CD AD + CB	$AgNO_3(aq) + NaCl(aq)\ AgCl(s) + NaNO_3(aq)$

Synthesis reactions involve two or more reactants (A and B) combining to form one product (AB). In the example provided, hydrogen (H_2) and oxygen (O_2) begin as separate elements. At the end of the reaction, the hydrogen and oxygen atoms are bonded in a molecule of water (H_2O).

Decomposition reactions have only one reactant (AB) that breaks apart into two or more products (A and B). In the example above, hydrogen peroxide (H_2O_2) breaks apart into two smaller molecules: water (H_2O) and oxygen (O_2).

Single-replacement reactions involve two reactants, one compound (AB) and one element (C). In this type of reaction, one element replaces another to form a new compound (AC), leaving one element by itself (B). In the example, zinc replaces hydrogen in hydrochloric acid (HCl). As a result, zinc forms a compound with chlorine, zinc chloride ($ZnCl_2$), and hydrogen (H_2) is left by itself.

Double-replacement reactions involve two reactants, both of which are compounds made of two components (AB and CD). In the example, silver nitrate, composed of silver (Ag^{1+}) and nitrate (NO_3^{1-}) ions, reacts with sodium chloride, composed of sodium (Na^{1+}) and chloride (Cl^{1-}) ions. The nitrate and chloride ions switch places to produce two compounds that are different from those in the reactants.

Combustion reactions occur when fuels burn, and they involve specific reactants and products, as seen in the examples below. Some form of fuel that contains carbon and hydrogen is required. Examples of such fuels are methane, propane in a gas grill, butane in a lighter, and octane in gasoline. Notice that these fuels all react with oxygen, which is necessary for anything to burn. In all combustion reactions, carbon dioxide, water, and energy are produced. When something burns, energy is released, which can be felt as heat and seen as light.

Fuel	Reaction
Methane (CH_4)	$CH_4 + 2O_2 \rightarrow CO_2 + 2H_2O$ + energy
Propane (C_3H_8)	$C_3H_8 + 5O_2 \rightarrow 3CO_2 + 4H_2O$ + energy
Butane (C_4H_{10})	$2C_4H_{10} + 13O_2 \rightarrow 8CO_2 + 10H_2O$ + energy
Octane (C_8H_{18})	$2C_8H_{18} + 25O_2 \rightarrow 16CO_2 + 18H_2O$ + energy

DID YOU KNOW?

The fuels used in combustion reactions belong to a class of compounds called *hydrocarbons* because they are composed of hydrogen and carbon atoms. Hydrocarbons can be found in crude oil and include fossil fuels such as coal and natural gas. They are referred to as *fossil fuels* because they formed from the decomposition of organisms that died millions of years ago.

Example

Which of the following equations shows a decomposition reaction?

A. $3H_2 + N_2 \rightarrow 2NH_3$

C. $2C_2H_2 + 5O_2 \rightarrow 4CO_2 + 2H_2O$

B. $2KClO_3 \rightarrow 2KCl + 3O_2$

D. $2Na + ZnCl_2 \rightarrow Zn + 2NaCl$

The correct answer is **B**. This reaction starts with a single compound as a reactant that breaks down into two smaller products.

Energy Diagrams

Energy diagrams can be used to show how the energy of the species in a reaction changes over time. The reactants have a certain amount of energy stored in their bonds, and the products usually have a different amount of energy. If energy is released, the products have less energy than the reactants, and the reaction is **exothermic**. If energy is absorbed, the products have more energy than the reactants, and the reaction is **endothermic**. The shapes of the energy diagrams are shown below.

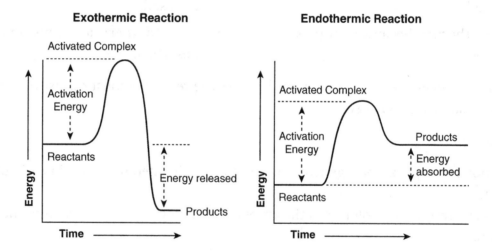

In every reaction, an **activated complex** must form between reactants. This complex can also be referred to as a transition state because it is required to convert, or provide a transition between, the reactants and products. In energy diagrams like the ones above, the activated complex has more energy than both the reactants and the products. The **activation energy** is the amount of energy required to transform the reactants into the activated complex, which then breaks apart to form the products.

CONNECTION

The difference between *endothermic* and *exothermic* reactions can be remembered by thinking about the meanings of the prefixes of these terms. In an *exo*thermic reaction, energy is released or "exits" the system. In an *endo*thermic reaction, energy "goes in."

The components of an energy diagram are as follows:

- Energy of reactants - energy of substances at the beginning of the reaction
- Energy of products - energy of substances at the end of the reaction
- Energy of the activated complex - energy of the substance represented by the maximum in the energy diagram
- Activation energy - difference in energy between the reactants and the activated complex
- Amount of energy released/absorbed - difference in energy between the reactants and products

Example

When iron reacts with oxygen, iron (III) oxide (Fe_2O_3), also known as rust, forms according to the equation below. The iron (III) oxide has less energy than the iron and oxygen. How is reaction classified, and why?

$4Fe(s) + 3O_2(g)\ 2Fe_2O_3(s)$

A. It is exothermic because energy is released.

B. It is exothermic because energy is absorbed.

C. It is endothermic because energy is released.

D. It is endothermic because energy is absorbed.

The correct answer is **A**. It is exothermic because the reactants must release energy to form a product that has less energy.

Let's Review!

- A solution is a type of homogeneous mixture that is formed when a solute dissolves in a solvent.
- The concentration of a solution is the amount of a substance in a given amount of solution.
- Chemical reactions occur when reactants combine, break apart, or rearrange to form products.
- Chemical equations represent chemical reactions using formulas and symbols.
- Chemical reactions can be classified as synthesis, decomposition, single-replacement, double-replacement, or combustion based on the reactants and products.
- Energy diagrams show how the energy of the species involved in the reaction changes as the reaction progresses.

ACIDS AND BASES

This lesson introduces the properties of acids and bases, including the various theories that define them. It also covers acid-base reactions and the pH scale.

Nature of Acids and Bases

Acids are compounds that contain at least one hydrogen atom or proton (H^+), which, when dissolved in water, can form a hydronium ion (H_3O^+). Acids dissolved in water generally have the following properties:

- Taste sour
- Turn litmus red
- Act corrosive

Acids are found in a variety of substances, from vinegar to apple juice. The following table provides a list of common acids and their sources or applications.

Name of Acid	Chemical Formula	Sources or Applications
Citric acid	$C_6H_8O_7$	Citrus fruits such as oranges and lemons
Lactic acid	$C_3H_6O_3$	Yogurt and buttermilk
Acetic acid	$C_2H_4O_2$ or CH_3COOH	Nail polish remover and vinegar
Hydrochloric acid	HCl	Stomach
Phosphoric acid	H_3PO_4	Detergents and soft drinks
Nitric acid	HNO_3	Fertilizers

Bases are compounds that form hydroxide ions (OH^-) in a water solution. They also accept hydronium ions from acids. Bases dissolved in water generally have the following properties:

- Slippery in solution
- Very corrosive
- Turn litmus blue
- Taste bitter

Like acids, bases have many applications. The following table provides examples of common bases and how they are used.

Name of Base	Chemical Formula	Applications
Sodium hydroxide	NaOH	Soap, oven cleaners, and textiles
Potassium hydroxide	KOH	Soap and textiles
Ammonia	NH_3	Cleaning agents and fertilizers
Magnesium hydroxide	$Mg(OH)_2$	Laxatives and antacids

Acidic solutions have more hydrogen ions than hydroxide ions, whereas basic solutions have more hydroxide ions than hydrogen ions. All water solutions have both ion types, but the relative numbers dictate whether an aqueous solution is acidic, basic, or neutral. Anything that is dissolved in water is an **aqueous solution**. Neutral solutions are neither acidic nor basic, meaning that an equal number of hydrogen and hydroxide ions are present. Pure water is an example of a neutral solution.

Water is the primary solvent used to create an aqueous solution. Thus, it is important to understand how pure water behaves in solution. A small fraction of water molecules breaks down to form hydronium and hydroxide ions. When two water molecules interact, one water molecule gives up a positively charged hydrogen ion to form a hydroxide ion. A hydronium ion forms when a water molecule accepts a hydrogen ion. The following equation illustrates this reaction:

> **KEEP IN MIND**
> Substances that form ions in aqueous solutions are called **electrolytes**. As electrolytes, acids and bases are conductors of electricity in solution. This is because they contain dissolved ions.

$$2H_2O \rightarrow H_3O^+ + OH^-$$

Examples

1. **Which of the following is an acid?**

    A. KNO_3 B. $BaCl_2$ C. $NaOH$ D. H_3PO_4

    The correct answer is **D**. Phosphoric acid (H_3PO_4) is a common acid that is capable of donating one of its hydrogen atoms to form a hydronium ion.

2. **Which is a characteristic of a basic solution?**

    A. Tastes sour   C. Turns litmus blue

    B. Accepts OH^- ions   D. Contains a lot of H_3O^+ ions

    The correct answer is **C**. A basic solution is made using water as a solvent. Basic solutions turn litmus paper from red to blue.

Acid and Base Classification

Recall that an acid produces hydrogen ions, and a base produces hydroxide ions. These compounds are defined as **Arrhenius** acids and bases. The Arrhenius theory explains how acids and bases form ions when dissolved in water. Take, for example, the acid HCl, shown in the equation below. When forming an aqueous solution of HCl, this acid dissociates, or splits, into hydrogen ions and chloride ions in water.

$$HCl\ (g) \rightarrow H^+\ (aq) + Cl^-\ (aq)$$

An Arrhenius base dissociates into hydroxide ions (OH^-) in an aqueous solution. This is the case for sodium hydroxide, NaOH, as shown in the following equation:

$$NaOH\ (s) \rightarrow Na^+\ (aq) + OH^-(aq)$$

One limitation of this theory is that it does not account for acids and bases that lack a hydrogen or hydroxide ion in their molecular structure. Another way to define acids and bases is by using the Brønsted-Lowry theory. A Brønsted-Lowry **acid** is a hydrogen ion donor that increases the concentration of hydronium ions in solution. A Brønsted-Lowry **base** is a hydrogen ion acceptor that increases hydroxide ion concentration in solution. The term *proton* is used interchangeably with the term *hydrogen ion*.

> **BE CAREFUL!**
>
> Free H+ ions do not float in an aqueous solution. Rather, they bind with water to form H_3O^+. However, it is not uncommon to see the two formulas, H+ and H_3O^+, used interchangeably in chemical reactions.

When a base accepts a hydrogen ion, it produces a conjugate acid. When an acid donates a hydrogen ion, it produces a conjugate base. In the following example, ammonia is the base, but its conjugate acid is ammonium ion. What is the conjugate base for the acid?

$$NH_3 + H_2O \longrightarrow NH_4^+ + OH^-$$

base   acid   conjugate acid   conjugate base

> **KEEP IN MIND**
>
> When substances such as pure water act as an acid or a base, they are **amphoteric**.

The last theory about acids and bases is called the Lewis theory. This theory is based on electron movement during an acid-base reaction. A **Lewis acid** accepts a pair of electrons, while a **Lewis base** donates an electron pair.

Example

What is the conjugate acid in the following equation?

$$CH_3COOH + H_2O \rightleftharpoons H_3O^+ + CH_3COO^-$$

A. H_3O^+ B. H_2O C. CH_3COO^- D. CH_3COOH

The correct answer is **A**. A conjugate acid is a substance that accepts a proton from a base. In this case, the base H_2O accepts a proton to form the conjugate acid, hydronium ion (H_3O^+).

Acid-Base Reactions

In an aqueous solution, a base increases the hydroxide concentration (OH^-), while an acid increases the hydrogen ion (H^+) concentration. Sometimes, **neutralization reactions** also occur. This type of reaction happens when an acid and a base react with each other to form water and salt. Salt is typically defined as an **ionic compound** that includes any cation except H^+ and any anion except OH^-. Consider the following example of a neutralization reaction between hydrobromic acid (HBr) and potassium hydroxide (KOH).

$$HBr + KOH \longrightarrow KBr + H_2O$$

> **BE CAREFUL!**
>
> Not all neutralization reactions proceed in the manner where all reactants are in the aqueous phase. In some chemical reactions, one reactant may be a solid. The neutralization reaction can still proceed to completion.

In the above equation, one molecule of water forms in addition to the salt potassium bromide (KBr). There are instances where acid-base reactions must be balanced because more than one molecule of an acid or a base react to form products. This is the case for the reaction between hydrochloric acid and magnesium hydroxide, as shown below.

$$2HCl + Mg(OH)_2 \longrightarrow MgCl_2 + 2H_2O$$

When two molecules of hydrochloric acid react with magnesium hydroxide, two water molecules and one molecule of salt, $MgCl_2$, form.

Example

Which is a product of a neutralization reaction?

   A. Acid   B. Base   C. Proton   D. Salt

   The correct answer is **D**. When an acid and a base react, they form a salt and water. This type of reaction is called a neutralization reaction.

Acid and Base Strength and pH

Acids and bases can be classified according to their strength. This strength refers to how readily an acid donates a hydrogen ion. The strength of a base is determined by how readily it removes a hydrogen ion from a molecule, or **deprotonates**. Strong acids are also known as strong electrolytes, which means that they completely ionize in solution. Weak acids are weak electrolytes because they partially ionize in solution. The following diagram shows what happens to a strong or weak acid in an aqueous solution.

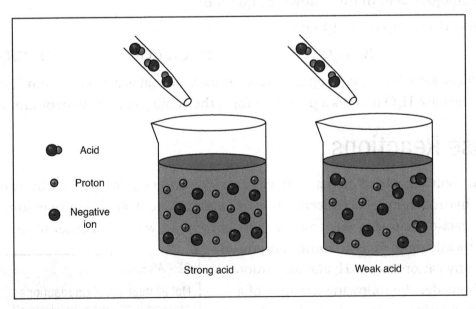

The maximum number of ions is produced when strong acids ionize. As shown in the following equations, the weak acid reaction is reversible (and incomplete) in aqueous solutions. This explains why weak acids produce fewer ions than strong acids.

Strong acid in solution

$$HNO_3 \longrightarrow H^+ + NO_3^-$$

Weak base in solution

$$NH_3 + H_2O \rightleftarrows NH_4^+ + OH^-$$

Like strong acids, strong bases fully dissociate in solution. They produce metal ions and hydroxide ions. Like weak acids, weak bases partially dissociate and participate in reversible reactions. The following table provides a list of common strong acids and bases and common weak acids and bases.

> **BE CAREFUL!**
>
> Ammonia is a weak base even though it does not have a hydroxide ion (OH^-) in its chemical formula. It will accept a proton and form hydroxide ions in aqueous solutions.

Strong Acid	Weak Acid	Strong Base	Weak Base
Hydrochloric acid (HCl)	Hydrofluoric acid (HF)	Sodium hydroxide (NaOH)	Ammonia (NH_3)
Nitric acid (HNO_3)	Carbonic acid (H_2CO_3)	Potassium hydroxide (KOH)	Methylamine (CH_3NH_2)
Perchloric acid ($HClO_4$)	Phosphoric acid (H_3PO_4)	Calcium hydroxide ($Ca(OH)_2$)	Hydrazine (N_2H_4)
Sulfuric acid (H_2SO_4)	Acetic acid ($C_2H_4O_2$ or CH_3COOH)	Lithium hydroxide (LiOH)	Pyridine (C_5H_5N)

Researchers can determine the strength of an acid or a base by measuring the **pH** of a solution. The pH value describes how acidic or basic a solution is. On pH scale, shown below, if the number is less than 7 the solution is acidic. A pH greater than 7 means the solution is basic. When the pH is exactly 7, the solution is neutral.

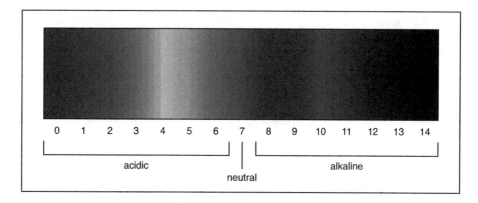

Example

Which of the following measured pH values means a solution is basic?

A. 2   B. 5   C. 7   D. 9

The correct answer is **D**. When the pH of an aqueous solution is greater than 7, which is the case for a solution that has a pH of 9, the solution is basic.

Let's Review!

- Acids and bases exhibit unique properties when dissolved in water.
- Arrhenius acids donate hydrogen ions, and Arrhenius bases accept hydrogen ions in solution.
- Brønsted-Lowry acids donate protons (or hydrogen ions), and Brønsted-Lowry bases accept protons (or hydrogen ions).
- Lewis acids are electron pair acceptors, and Lewis bases are electron pair donors.
- A neutralization reaction occurs when an acid and a base react to form a salt and water.
- Strong acids completely ionize in solution, and strong bases fully dissociate in solution.
- Weak acids and weak bases only partially dissociate in solution.
- The pH of a solution determines how acidic or basic it is.

CHAPTER 15 CHEMISTRY PRACTICE QUIZ

1. A stick of butter is melted in a dish in the microwave. After it melts, which of the following statements describes the butter?

   A. It has both the shape and volume of the dish.

   B. It has the shape but not the volume of the dish.

   C. It has the volume but not the shape of the dish.

   D. It has neither the shape nor the volume of the dish.

2. In the cooling curve for any substance, the freezing point is equal to the _____ in the heating curve of the same substance under the same conditions.

   A. boiling point

   B. melting point

   C. temperature at which the liquid changes to gas

   D. temperature at which the gas changes to liquid

3. What is the difference between evaporation and boiling?

   A. Evaporation occurs throughout a substance, and boiling occurs on the bottom of it.

   B. Evaporation occurs on the surface of a substance, and boiling occurs throughout it.

   C. Evaporation occurs on the bottom of a substance, and boiling occurs on the surface of it.

   D. Evaporation occurs on the surface of a substance, and boiling occurs on the bottom of it.

4. Which of the following represents a substance?

   A. Cup of water   C. Slice of pizza

   B. Bowl of stew   D. Bowl of salad

5. Which of the following elements will gain three electrons to become stable?

   A. Aluminum   C. Oxygen

   B. Boron   D. Phosphorus

6. What type of bond forms between calcium and iodine, and why?

    A. Ionic, because it involves two nonmetals

    B. Covalent, because it involves two nonmetals

    C. Ionic, because it involves a metal and a nonmetal

    D. Covalent, because it involves a metal and a nonmetal

7. A spoonful of sugar is added to a hot cup of tea. All the sugar dissolves. How can the resulting solution be described?

    A. Saturated and homogeneous

    B. Saturated and heterogeneous

    C. Unsaturated and homogeneous

    D. Unsaturated and heterogeneous

8. Sugar is dissolved in water. Which of the following statements best describes the components of this solution?

    A. Sugar and water are both solutes.

    B. Sugar and water are both solvents.

    C. Sugar is the solute, and water is the solvent.

    D. Sugar is the solvent, and water is the solute.

9. The strength of a base is determined by its ability to

    A. turn litmus paper blue.

    B. feel slippery to the touch.

    C. completely ionize in water.

    D. dissociate into hydroxide ions.

10. Which of the following determines the strength of an acidic solution?

    A. Litmus paper that turns red

    B. Litmus paper that turns blue

    C. Measured pH value equal to 7

    D. Measured pH value less than 7

CHAPTER 15 CHEMISTRY
PRACTICE QUIZ – ANSWER KEY

1. B. As the butter melts, it goes from a solid to a liquid, which takes the shape but not the volume of its container. **See Lesson: States of Matter.**

2. B. Any substance will melt and freeze at the same temperature, assuming these processes are carried out under the same conditions. This is the temperature at which the substance transitions between solid and liquid states. **See Lesson: States of Matter.**

3. B. Evaporation occurs on the surface of a substance, and boiling occurs throughout a substance. **See Lesson: Properties of Matter.**

4. A. A substance has is the same throughout and water is the only option that fits that definition. **See Lesson: Properties of Matter.**

5. D. Phosphorus is in group 15, which means it has five valence electrons. Gaining three would give it eight valence electrons, making the atom stable. **See Lesson: Chemical Bonds.**

6. C. Calcium is a metal, and iodine is a nonmetal. When these elements bond, valence electrons are transferred from calcium atoms to iodine atoms, creating an ionic bond. **See Lesson: Chemical Bonds.**

7. C. Because more solute could be added and dissolve, the solution has not yet reached its limit and is considered unsaturated. Because all the solute dissolves, the particles in the mixture are evenly distributed as a homogenous mixture. **See Lesson: Chemical Solutions.**

8. C. Generally, the solute dissolves in the solvent to form a solution. To make sugar water, the sugar dissolves in water. **See Lesson: Chemical Solutions.**

9. D. A weak base only partially dissociates in solution. A strong base fully dissociates, or contributes the maximum number of hydroxide ions, in solution. **See Lesson: Acids and Bases.**

10. D. Both litmus paper and a pH scale can be used to indicate whether a solution is acidic. However, a pH scale can also determine the strength of an acid. **See Lesson: Acids and Bases.**

CHAPTER 16 PHYSICS

THE NATURE OF MOTION

Introduction

This lesson introduces the basics of motion and the application of simple physical principles and basic vector math to problems involving moving bodies. It culminates with an introduction to projectile motion and a presentation of Newton's laws of motion, which summarize the classical view of physics.

Nature of Motion

The space that people perceive is filled with objects of various sizes and shapes, but these objects are not always in the same places. They change their distances and orientations relative to observers and to one another, although these changes do not take place all at once. Such changes are called **motion**, and they are measured as differences in position or orientation over time.

Systematically measuring motion requires standards of **distance** and **time**—two concepts that people use and understand in everyday situations but may have difficulty defining independently. Instead of tackling the philosophical problem of what time and distance are, most people take the pragmatic approach to using these concepts by employing a generally agreed-upon standard. For example, in the metric (SI) system, the **meter** (m) is the fundamental unit of length. Comparing the relative locations of objects to that standard enables an observer to measure the distance between them and report it in a way that others can understand.

Time is more esoteric. A standard for time requires reference to some periodic event (a concept that is itself based on some understanding of time). For example, the revolution of Earth around the sun (a year), the full rotation of Earth on its axis (a day), or even something as mundane as the drip of a faucet (a duration that depends on numerous factors) are periodic events that can be used as standards for time. In the metric (SI) system, the fundamental unit of time is the **second** (s). The critical point is that the event be periodic. Because it occurs at unchanging intervals, it provides a common standard of time to which everyone can refer.

> **DID YOU KNOW?**
> Time and distance are concepts that you use every day, but they are difficult to define because they are fundamental to human experience. Try thinking about how you would explain time or distance without referring to time or distance.

Simple Motion Measurement

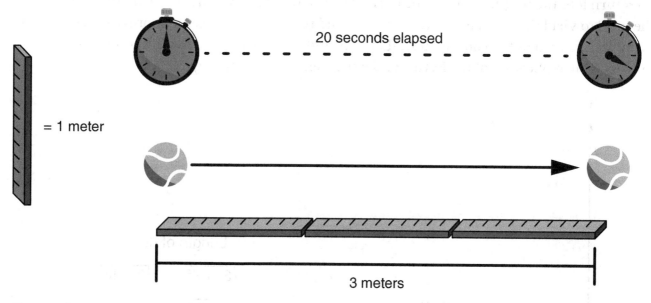

= 1 meter

20 seconds elapsed

3 meters

Example

Which approach would best serve as a common standard for measuring motion?

A. Comparing changes in distance using a peach and a sundial

B. Comparing changes in distance using a yardstick and a heartbeat

C. Comparing changes in distance using a quarter and a dripping faucet

D. Comparing changes in distance using an index card and a metronome

D. To measure motion in a way that is meaningful to others and consistent in different locations and on different days, the standards of time and distance must be consistent and reproducible. Although a quarter, a yardstick, and an index card all have consistent dimensions, peaches vary. A sundial and a metronome can provide consistent indications of time's passage, but heartbeats and dripping faucets vary. Thus, the best answer is an index card and a metronome.

Vectors and Scalars

Determining the change in the distance or orientation of an object with respect to some standard of time yields a measurement of the object's motion. Motion has two general characteristics: its direction and its quickness. Therefore, **vectors** are helpful in quantifying motion. A vector is a quantity that has a direction and a length (or magnitude) but no defined location. It is often depicted as an arrow that begins at one point (called the **tail**) and ends at another point (called the **head**). Because a vector has no location, it can move anywhere and remain the same vector. Variables representing vectors often appear in boldface (e.g., v) or with a small arrow above them (e.g., $\vec{v}$).

In a rectangular coordinate system, one representation of a vector is the coordinates of the head when the tail is at the origin. For example, a vector in two dimensions might be expressed as (3, −5). Because vectors have no location, however, the same vector can have its tail elsewhere. To return it to the origin, subtract the coordinates of the tail from the respective coordinates of the head to yield the standard vector form. To find the length of a vector expressed in standard form, square each of the coordinates, add them, and take the square root of the sum. This process is an application of the Pythagorean theorem for right triangles.

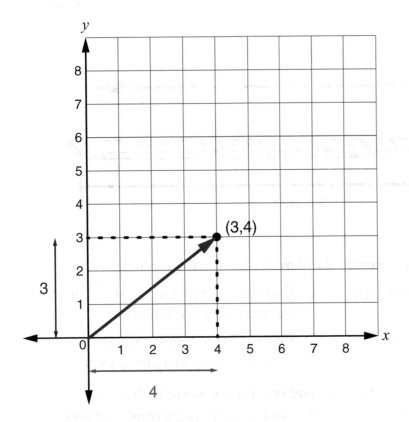

Length of (3,4) is

$$\sqrt{3^2 + 4^2} = \sqrt{9 + 16}$$

$$= \sqrt{25} = 5$$

In contrast with a vector is a **scalar,** which has a magnitude but no direction. A simple number such as 5 or 10.2 is a scalar. The length of a vector, for example, is a scalar.

Example

What is the length of a vector that has its head at (1, 3) and its tail at (−2, 7)?

A. 1   B. 5   C. 9   D. 25

B. First, convert the vector to standard form by subtracting the tail coordinates from the corresponding head coordinates: (1 − [−2], 3 − 7) = (3, −4). Then, calculate the length by squaring each coordinate, adding them, and taking the square root of the sum:

$$\sqrt{(3)^2 + (-4)^2} = \sqrt{9 + 16} = \sqrt{25} = 5$$

Basic Vector Operations

Adding two or more vectors yields a **resultant**. Graphically, adding two vectors involves placing the tail of one on the head of the other (and continuing this process when adding more vectors). The resultant is a new vector starting at the tail of the first and ending at the head of the second. Because the resultant vector is the same regardless of which way the vectors are added, vector addition is **commutative** (meaning $\vec{a} + \vec{b} = \vec{b} + \vec{a}$). Adding vectors in coordinate form just requires adding the respective coordinates of each. For example, $(7, 1) + (2, -3) = (7 + 2, 1 + [-3]) = (9, -2)$.

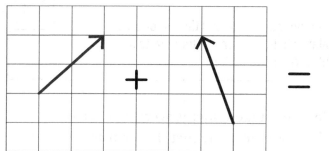 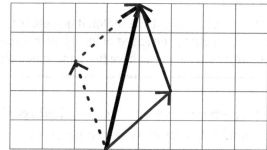

Subtracting vectors follows similar rules: for example, $(7, 1) - (2, -3) = (7 - 2, 1 - [-3]) = (5, 4)$.

> **KEY POINT!**
>
> Remember that because vectors have no location, they can be moved as necessary to aid in visualization, addition, or any number of purposes. As long as two vectors have the same direction and length (magnitude), they are the same vector.

To multiply a vector by a scalar, multiply each coordinate in the vector by that scalar. To divide a vector by a scalar, divide each coordinate by that scalar. Dividing a vector by its length (or, equivalently, multiplying by the reciprocal of its length) yields a new vector that has the same direction as the original but a length 1. Such a vector is called a **unit vector**. These rules also allow vector subtraction to be expressed as vector addition: $\vec{a} - \vec{b} = \vec{a} + ([-1] \times \vec{b}) = \vec{a} + (-\vec{b})$. They also enable easier graphical addition of vectors.

Example

If $\vec{u} = (2, 5)$ and $\vec{v} = (3, -1)$, what is $2\vec{u} - 3\vec{v}$?

    A. (−5, 13)   B. (−1, 6)   C. (1, −6)   D. (13, 7)

A. First, perform the multiplication of each vector by its respective scalar:

$$2\vec{u} - 3\vec{v} = 2(2, 5) - 3(3, -1) = (4, 10) - (9, -3)$$

Next, either convert to addition or simply subtract the respective coordinates:

$$(4, 10) - (9, -3) = (4 - 9, 10 - [-3]) = (-5, 13)$$

Velocity and Acceleration

Because motion has a direction and a magnitude of some type, vectors are a way to quantify it. One measurement of how quickly an object is moving is **speed**: the distance from one point to another divided by the travel time. For instance, if a plane moves 252 meters in 2.00 seconds, its speed is 252 meters ÷ 2.00 seconds = 126 meters per second (m/s). But for passengers on that plane, the direction of flight is just as important as the speed. Thus, multiplying the speed by a unit vector in the direction of travel yields a vector called **velocity**.

> **KEY POINT!**
>
> The *velocity* of an object is a vector: it quantifies both the magnitude and the direction of the object's motion. The *speed* of an object is a scalar: it is just the magnitude of its motion. Therefore, two objects can have the same speed but different velocities.

The rate at which velocity changes is called **acceleration**. Like velocity, acceleration has a magnitude and a direction, so it can be expressed as a vector. (Note that the term *acceleration* can also mean the magnitude of the acceleration vector, which is a scalar. The context of the problem will generally clarify whether the term refers to a vector or a scalar.) For instance, if a truck moving in a straight line is speeding up, its acceleration is in the same direction as its velocity; if the truck is slowing down, its acceleration is in the direction opposite to its velocity.

Quantitatively, the magnitude of the acceleration is the difference in speed divided by the elapsed time.

> **KEEP IN MIND:**
>
> These simple mathematical definitions of *velocity* and *acceleration* assume constant speed and acceleration scalars, respectively, over the time period in the calculation. If the speed or acceleration is changing, they yield *average* values for that time period.

Example

A runner finishes a 1,600-meter race in 5 minutes and 20 seconds. What was his average speed?

    A. 1 m/s   B. 5 m/s   C. 64 m/s   D. 320 m/s

B. The average speed of the runner is the distance divided by the running time. Before calculating the speed, convert the time to seconds: because 5 minutes is equal to 300 seconds, the total time is 320 seconds.

$$\frac{1{,}600\ m}{320\ s} = 5\ m/s$$

Projectile Motion

One special case of motion involves an object moving under the influence of gravity—for example, when a player hits a baseball or a cannon fires a cannonball. Ignoring any other forces (including air resistance), such an object moves in two dimensions, generally combining a horizontal component of motion and a vertical component. It experiences downward acceleration of 9.8 meters per square second (m/s²) but no horizontal acceleration.

Given a horizontal speed v_x and an initial horizontal position (coordinate) x_i, the object's horizontal position (assuming a starting time of $t = 0$) is $x(t) = x_i + v_x t$. However, the object's vertical distance from its starting point is complicated by the acceleration due to gravity. Some basic calculus shows that given an initial vertical speed v_y and an initial vertical position (coordinate) y_i, the object's vertical position (assuming a starting time of $t = 0$) is $y(t) = -\frac{1}{2}gt^2 + v_y t + y_i$. Note that g is the acceleration due to gravity (9.8 m/s²) and that the quadratic term is negative because gravity accelerates an object downward. Plotting the coordinates of the object at various times shows that it traces a parabola.

BE CAREFUL!

Make sure you know the height of the ground when analyzing projectile motion. Generally, an object won't be able to go any lower than ground level!

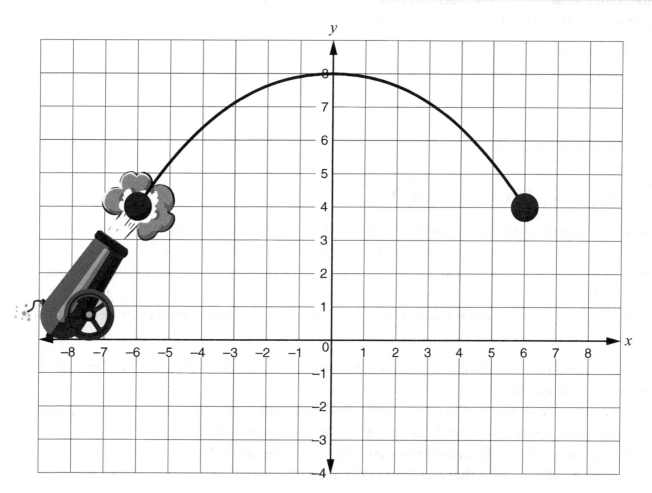

Example

A child throws a ball directly upward from the ground with an initial speed of 45 meters per second. How long will the ball take to return to the ground?

   A. 1.4 seconds   B. 2.0 seconds   C. 3.0 seconds   D. 9.2 seconds

D. Because the ball has no horizontal velocity, just use the equation for height with respect to time. The initial vertical velocity is 45 meters per second, and the initial height of the ball is 0. Also recall that the acceleration due to gravity is 9.8 m/s^2.

$$y(t) = -\frac{1}{2}gt^2 + v_y t + y_i = -\frac{1}{2}(9.8)t^2 + (45)t + 0 = -4.9t^2 + 45t$$

Next, set the height y equal to 0 and solve for t by factoring. $y(t) = 0 = -4.9t^2 + 45t$

$$0 = t(-4.9t + 45)$$

Note that the ball is at ground level at $t = 0$ (the factor t), but the solution to this problem is for t greater than 0 (the factor $-4.9t + 45$). Set the latter equal to 0 and solve for t.

$$-4.9t + 45 = 0$$

$$4.9t = 45$$

$$t = 9.2$$

The solution is 9.2 seconds.

Newton's Laws of Motion

Newton's laws of motion summarize the qualitative characteristics of moving objects. These laws refer to two important concepts in physics: **force** and **mass**. A force is a "push" or "pull" that an object experiences or exerts on another object; it is also a vector with a direction and magnitude. Mass is in some sense resistance to movement (or "displacement") by a force; it is a scalar. Thus, given a certain force, an object with less mass will move more than an object with more mass.

Newton's first law of motion, which deals with **inertia,** states that an object in motion will remain in motion unless a **net force** acts on it and that an object at rest will remain at rest unless a net force acts on it. Note that *net force* just means the object feels some force: it is the resultant of all forces acting on the object. If two people push with the same force against a cart but direct their efforts in precisely opposite directions, the cart will feel no net force. Another way understand this law is that an object's velocity will stay the same unless a force acts on the object.

Newton's second law of motion relates an object's mass, its acceleration, and the (net) force acting on it. This law says the force on an object (a vector $\vec{F}$) produces acceleration of the object ($\vec{a}$) that is proportional to the object's mass (m). Hence the well-known equation $\vec{F} = m\vec{a}$ (or $F = ma$ when dealing only in magnitudes—that is, scalars—not directions.) In SI units, the force is in newtons (N), the mass is in kilograms (kg), and the acceleration is in meters per square second (m/s²). Qualitatively, this law says that accelerating more-massive objects requires a greater force than accelerating less-massive objects.

Newton's third law of motion states that when an object exerts a force on another object, it experiences a force of equal magnitude but opposite direction from that other object. This law is sometimes expressed by saying that for every action, there is an equal and opposite reaction.

Example

A 2.0-kilogram object experiences a net force of 144 newtons. What is its acceleration?

    A. 36 m/s²   B. 72 m/s²   C. 140 m/s²   D. 290 m/s²

B. Use Newton's second law of motion: $F = ma$. (Vectors are unnecessary because the problem only deals with scalars.) Plug in the numbers and solve for a, noting that it will be in meters per square second.

$$F = ma$$

$$144 \text{ N} = (2.0 \text{ kg})a$$

$$a = \frac{144 \text{ } N}{2.0 \text{ } kg} = 72 \text{ } m/s^2$$

Let's Review!

- Motion is the change in an object's position or orientation over time.
- Measurement of motion requires a consistent, accessible standard of distance and time.
- A vector is a quantity with magnitude and direction but no location; a scalar has a magnitude but no direction.
- The standard notation form of a vector is the coordinates of its head when its tail is at the origin of the coordinate system. If the vector is shown elsewhere, subtract the coordinates of the tail from the respective coordinates of the head to get the standard form.
- To multiply a scalar and a vector, multiply each coordinate of the vector by the scalar: $a \times (x, y) = (ax, ay)$.
- To calculate the resultant, or sum, of two vectors, add the respective coordinates of those vectors: $(a, b) + (c, d) = (a + c, b + d)$.
- To find the length of a vector, square its coordinates, add them, and take the square root.
- Vector addition is commutative: $\vec{a} + \vec{b} = \vec{b} + \vec{a}$.
- Velocity is a vector that represents how quickly an object is moving. Speed is the magnitude of that vector (it is a scalar).
- Acceleration is a vector that represents how quickly the velocity is changing.
- Projectile motion is the motion of an object under the influence of gravity. Such an object follows a parabolic path. Its horizontal position at time t, given initial horizontal velocity v_x and initial horizontal position x_i, is $x(t) = x_i + v_x \times t$. Its vertical position at time t, given initial vertical velocity v_y and initial vertical position y_i, is $y(t) = -\frac{1}{2}gt^2 + v_y t + y_i$.

- Newton's laws of motion summarize motion in classical physics.
- Newton's first law is that an object at rest stays at rest and an object in motion stays in motion, unless a net force acts on the object.
- Newton's second law is that the net force, object mass, and acceleration are related by $\vec{F} = m \times \vec{a}$ (or $F = m \times a$ when dealing only in magnitudes).
- Newton's third law is that an object exerting a force on another object feels the same force, but in the opposite direction.

FRICTION AND TYPES OF MOTION

This lesson discusses different types of motion. Then, it examines uniform circular (rotational) motion and centripetal acceleration. It also introduces the concept of friction and its effect on motion in real-world situations.

Types of Motion

According to Newton's first law of motion, an object moving with a given velocity (even if it is zero) will maintain that velocity indefinitely unless some net force acts on it. Absent any net force, the object will move in one direction along a line (assuming a nonzero speed). In this case, the object exhibits **linear motion** because its movement is in only one spatial dimension. If a force acts on the object and that force is parallel with the dimension in which the object is moving, the acceleration will be parallel or antiparallel (exactly opposite in direction) to the velocity. Thus, even though the object will speed up or slow down, its motion will remain linear.

If a force acts on an object in a direction that is not parallel to the object's velocity, the object no longer moves along a line; it exhibits **nonlinear motion**. Passengers riding in a car, for example, can tell the difference between linear and nonlinear motion by the direction of the force they feel as they ride. If the car speeds up or slows down linearly, they will feel only a backward force (positive acceleration) or a forward force (negative acceleration, or deceleration). If it turns (nonlinear motion), the passengers will feel a force toward either side as the car turns in some direction.

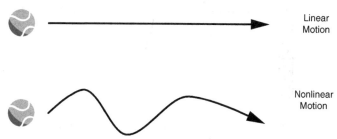

In general, mathematically analyzing nonlinear motion requires vector calculus. However, in certain cases, nonlinear motion can be described using only algebra. One case is **rotational motion**, which involves objects spinning on an axis or moving in a circle around some central point. Because rotational motion involves circular geometry, it is also commonly called **circular motion**.

Example

An object has a constant nonzero speed but a randomly varying velocity. Which term best describes its motion?

A. Linear   B. Nonlinear   C. Rotational   D. Stationary

The correct answer is **B**. If the object has a fixed speed greater than zero but its velocity changes randomly, then its direction of motion changes randomly. Therefore, the object is exhibiting nonlinear motion. Because the changes are random, however, it cannot be rotational motion, which is nonlinear but also determinate with regard to changes in velocity.

Uniform Circular Motion

An object that rotates about an axis or revolves circularly around some point exhibits **rotational motion** (or **circular motion**). A simple case that provides a foundation for more-complex analysis is an object moving in a circle around some point outside its surface. For example, consider a ball tied to the end of a stick by a string. If someone holds the stick and causes the ball to move a circle, the ball will always be a fixed distance from the end of the stick—that distance is the length of the string. If such an object moves with a constant speed, its movement is called **uniform circular motion.**

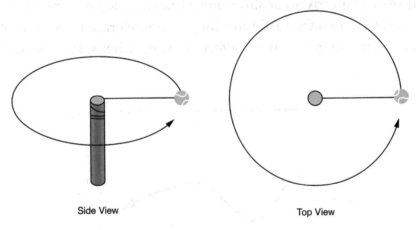

Side View   Top View

The speed of an object in uniform circular motion is, like in linear motion, a distance divided by the time required to traverse that distance. A simple expression is the circumference of the circle divided by the time the object takes to go around one full time. Given a radius r and a time T to go around the circle, the speed v is $v = \frac{2\pi r}{T}$

This time T is also called the object's **period**, and its inverse $\left(\frac{1}{T}\right)$ is the **frequency,** often expressed as f. The frequency measures how often the object completes a revolution around the circle, and its unit (when T is in seconds) is hertz (Hz). Another useful quantity is the **angular frequency,** $2\pi f$, which is often expressed as ω and may also use hertz. Employing this definition, the velocity is ωr. Therefore, the velocity v is also equal to $2\pi f r$.

DID YOU KNOW?

In the case of a ball on a string, if at any point the string is cut, removing the force acting on the ball, the ball will immediately begin moving linearly at the same speed with which it was moving circularly. Its direction will be tangential to the circle—that is, the direction of its velocity at the moment the string is cut.

Example

An electron in a magnetic field moves in a circle of radius 0.030 meters. If the angular frequency of its rotational motion is 2,400 hertz, what is its velocity?

A. 1.3×10^{-5} m/s   B. 72 m/s   C. 452 m/s   D. 80,000 m/s

The correct answer is **B**. The velocity of the electron is the following: $v = \frac{2\pi r}{T}$ Because $\frac{2\pi}{T}$ is equal to $2\pi f$, it is the angular frequency (ω). Thus, the velocity in meters per second is $v = \omega r = (2{,}400 \text{ hertz})(0.030 \text{ m}) = 72 \text{ m/s}$

Centripetal Acceleration

Although the *speed* of an object in uniform circular motion is constant, its *velocity* is always changing: it is at all points tangent to the circular path. By Newton's first law of motion, therefore, the object is experiencing acceleration and thus a force. This acceleration—called **centripetal acceleration**—always points toward the center of the circle. A simple example is a planet, such as Earth, orbiting a star. The star exerts a gravitational force that pulls the planet toward the star, and the planet moves (ideally) in a circle around the star. The derivation of centripetal acceleration (a_c) is complicated, but the formula is simple given a speed v and a radius r: $a_c = \frac{v^2}{r}$

TEST TIP

If you are unsure whether you correctly remember a formula, such as centripetal acceleration, you can increase your confidence by checking the units. For instance, using metric units, acceleration is in units of m/s^2. Velocity squared yields units of m^2/s^2, and the radius is in units of m. Dividing the squared velocity units by the radius units yields m/s^2, which is the same as for acceleration. This check is not sufficient to prove the formula is correct, but it can identify an erroneous formula.

By Newton's second law of motion, the **centripetal force** F_c on an object of mass m is therefore $F_c = ma_c = \frac{mv^2}{r}$

Centrifugal force is a "ghost" force. For example, a passenger in a car that turns right feels a leftward force. But by Newton's first law of motion, the passenger's body tries to keep moving straight when the car turns right, causing the car to push the passenger to the right. The feeling, however, is of another force pushing the passenger leftward into the car rather than the car pushing the passenger rightward toward the center of rotational motion. The centrifugal force is therefore equal in magnitude but opposite in direction to the centripetal force.

Example

A 75-kilogram passenger on a rotating theme-park ride experiences a centripetal force of 230 newtons. If she is 12 meters from the center of rotation, what is her velocity?

    A. 6.1 m/s   B. 6.2 m/s   C. 37 m/s   D. 38 m/s

The correct answer is **A**. Use the formula for centripetal force with respect to mass, velocity, and radius of rotation: $F_c = \frac{mv^2}{r}$ $v^2 = \frac{F_c r}{m}$ $v = \sqrt{\frac{F_c r}{m}}$ Use the given quantities to get the velocity in meters per second: $v = \sqrt{\frac{(230)(12)}{75}} = \sqrt{37} = 6.1$ m/s

Friction

Newton's first law of motion seems to break down in everyday life: rolling cars come to a stop, falling objects stop accelerating at a certain speed despite the force of gravity, and so on. The cause of the apparent breakdown is another force that resists the motion of objects: **friction**. For example, a plane that turns off its engines loses horizontal speed because of **air resistance**, which is a type of friction. A heavy piece of furniture is often difficult to slide across a floor because it experiences friction wherever it touches the floor. Friction can also act on nonmoving objects. For instance, it can prevent an object from sliding down an incline despite the force of gravity.

Because friction is a force, it causes acceleration. For moving objects, the friction force generally has a direction opposite that of the velocity. When an object decelerates because of friction, byproducts of this deceleration can be motion of something else (such as waves or eddies when the object is moving in water) or **heat**. Heat is another type of motion that involves movement of the atoms and molecules that constitute matter. For example, people with cold hands may rub them together briskly to warm them. For stationary objects, the force of friction is opposite to what would otherwise be a net force, such as gravity.

> **KEEP IN MIND**
>
> Calculating the friction force can be difficult because it involves many factors, such as the roughness of surfaces (in the case of sliding objects) and the fluid characteristics of air (in the case of air resistance). For this reason, problems often assume friction is negligible—an assumption that often still allows a good approximation of the solution.

A common example of friction is an object sliding on a surface. The force due to friction is proportional to the object's mass because the mass determines the object's **weight** (which is the force it experiences from gravity). The weight of an object causes it to "push" against the surface, and when the object slides, that vertical push creates the resistance to horizontal motion (that is, friction) because of surface imperfections and irregularities.

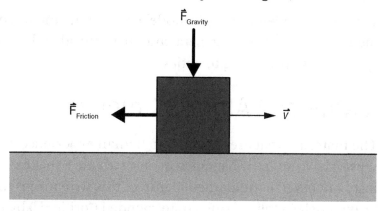

Example

A car is moving east at 20 meters per second. In what direction is the force of friction?

  A. East   B. North   C. South   D. West

The correct answer is **D**. Friction is generally in the direction opposite to the direction of motion—hence, a car that coasts in neutral, for example, will slow down without changing direction. For a car moving east, the friction force is directed west. The car's speed is unimportant to determining the direction of the force of friction.

Let's Review!

- Linear motion is movement along a line; the velocity and acceleration may vary, but they are always parallel to the line.
- Nonlinear motion is movement that is not confined to a line; the velocity and acceleration can be any quantity.
- Rotational (circular) motion is movement around an axis or along a circular path.
- The period (T) of an object in uniform circular motion is the time it takes to travel once around the circle. The inverse of the period is the frequency (f), and the angular frequency (ω) is $2\pi f$.
- Centripetal acceleration (a_c) is the acceleration an object experiences when in uniform circular motion. It is equal to $\frac{v^2}{r}$, where v is the object's velocity and r is the radius of the circle of motion.
- The centripetal force on an object in uniform circular motion is the object's mass times its centripetal acceleration.
- Centrifugal force is a "ghost force" in which an object undergoing centripetal acceleration "feels" like it is being pushed away from the center of rotation.
- Friction is resistance to motion. It is a force that is generally directed opposite to a moving object's velocity.
- Friction causes heat and/or motion of surrounding materials as a byproduct of its force on a moving object.
- Friction can prevent motion by acting opposite to other forces, such as gravity.

WAVES AND SOUND

This lesson reviews a simple model of the atom and its role in the materials of everyday life. It then discusses waves in general and mechanical and electromagnetic waves in particular and applies these principles to optics.

Matter and Atomic Structure

The materials that are common to human experience (through sight, touch, and the other senses) have an invisible, microscopic structure that experimenters can probe using scientific instruments. The fundamental unit of this structure is the **atom,** which comprises a central, heavy **nucleus** (plural **nuclei**) surrounded ("orbited") by lighter **electrons.** The nucleus is composed of **protons,** which carry a positive electric charge, and **neutrons,** which carry no electric charge (they are electrically neutral). Together, the protons and neutrons are sometimes called **nucleons.** Electrons carry a negative electric charge. Below is a simple representation of the structure of an atom.

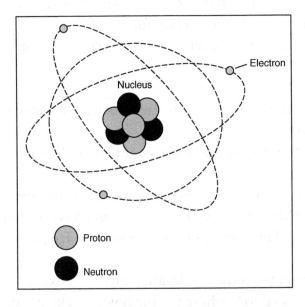

Electric charge (or just "charge") is a property of matter that relates to attraction or repulsion through the **electric force.** Charge comes in two known varieties; although scientists use *positive* and *negative* to describe charge, these terms are just conventions that have some mathematical utility. They do not describe a fundamental "signed" property of charge. The main qualitative rule is that like charges repel and unlike charges attract.

The electric force holds the atom together through the attraction of the negatively charged electrons to the positively charged nucleus. When an atom has the same number of electrons as protons, it is electrically neutral because the amount of charge on an electron is the same as that on a proton, but they are unlike, causing electrical attraction. The result is the simplistic model of an atom that shows electrons orbiting the nucleus like planets orbit the sun.

The number of protons in a nucleus determines the **element** that the atom represents: hydrogen (1 proton), helium (2), carbon (6), oxygen (8), iron (26), and so on. The number of neutrons in a nucleus can vary. Instances of an element with different neutron counts are called **isotopes** of that element. As a rule, isotopes of common elements have about as many neutrons as protons.

If the number of electrons in an atom differs from the number of protons, that atom has a net electric charge: positive if it has more protons than electrons, and negative if it has more electrons than protons. An atom with a net electric charge is called an **ion**.

Although not all matter is composed of atoms—physicists claim to have discovered a variety of particles that can exist apart from atoms—an understanding of atomic structure informs numerous fields, including chemistry and semiconductor physics. Moreover, the nucleons of an atom appear to have a deeper internal structure, a topic that researchers are exploring.

Example

A certain isotope of magnesium has 13 neutrons and 12 protons. If an atom of this isotope is electrically neutral, how many electrons does it have?

A. 12 B. 13 C. 25 D. 50

The correct answer is **A**. An electrically neutral atom must have the same number of protons as electrons. Because they carry no charge, neutrons have no electrical effect on the atom.

Properties of Waves

A universally recognizable example of waves is in water—whether in the ocean, a pool, or a small container. It is possible to visualize many aspects of invisible and conceptual, or mathematical, waves by observing how waves act in water. For example, the highest part of an ocean wave is the **crest** (or **peak**), the lowest part is the **trough,** and half the distance between these two points is the **amplitude**. (The full distance between the crest and trough is called the **peak-to-peak amplitude**.) The distance between successive peaks or successive troughs is called the **wavelength**. These parameters describe the spatial (space-related) characteristics of the wave. But waves also generally have temporal (time-related) characteristics. For example, given some fixed point in space, the time between the arrival of successive waves is the **period**, and its reciprocal is the **frequency**—often expressed in hertz (Hz), or inverse seconds (s^{-1}).

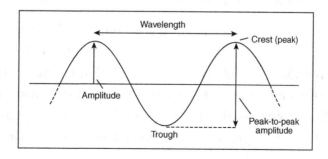

The wavelength (λ), frequency (f), and **wave speed** (v) are related by the equation $v = \lambda f$.

Although these spatial and temporal properties are the most intuitive, waves can have other, less intuitive properties. For instance, if a light source increases and decreases in intensity over time, its intensity can be described as a wave whose frequency is temporal and whose amplitude is intensity (rather than height). Mechanical (e.g., sound and water) and electromagnetic (e.g., visible light and radio) waves are additional examples.

Water waves also demonstrate some of the general behaviors of waves. When they strike a wall or other fairly stationary object, for example, the result is **reflection**: some or all of the wave "bounces" off the object. Waves that pass through a medium with changing material properties may bend, a phenomenon called **refraction**. The changing depth of the ocean floor, for instance, causes ocean waves to bend and usually arrive perpendicular to shore, regardless of their original direction. Another behavior of waves is **diffraction**: waves traveling in a certain direction can "turn" around sharp edges.

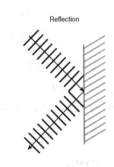

Reflection

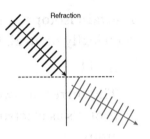

Refraction

Example

An oceanographer has set a post in the water near shore to study waves before a hurricane. If she finds that the waves are 75 feet apart and a trough arrives every 25 seconds, what is the frequency?

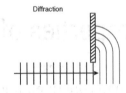

Diffraction

    A. 0.013 Hz   C. 25 Hz

    B. 0.040 Hz   D. 75 Hz

The correct answer is **B**. The frequency of a wave is the reciprocal of its period: the time between arrival of successive troughs or peaks. In this case, the frequency is $\frac{1}{25\text{ s}} = 0.040\text{ s}^{-1} = 0.040$ Hz.

Mechanical Waves

Waves that propagate in matter—for example, water waves—are called **mechanical waves**. They can involve variation in height, as in water waves, or variation in pressure, as in acoustic/sound waves. Earthquakes involve mechanical waves similar to sound waves: these seismic waves cause the ground to shake as they travel from the source of the quake.

In the case of sound, what the ear detects as **pitch** is essentially the frequency of the wave, and the **volume** is essentially the amplitude. Characteristics of the wave, including its speed, depend on the properties of the **medium** (or substance/material) that carries it. In the case of sound, for example, the wave speed depends on the **density** of the medium—how many atoms are packed into a unit volume—and the **compressibility** of the medium—how much the medium can be compacted given a certain force or pressure. The denser and less compressible a material, the faster sound waves will travel through it. Because water is denser and less compressible than air, for instance, sound travels faster in the former than in the latter. Similarly, waves in a rope will travel faster if the rope is taut than if it is loose.

Depending on the type of mechanical wave and the medium through which it travels, the wave speed may be apparent to the human senses. For example, at a sufficiently large distance from the observer, an event such as a hammer strike or gunfire is visible before it is audible. This delay occurs because light travels much faster than sound. Therefore, distant events are often seen before they are heard.

Mechanical waves exhibit the same phenomena as other waves, such as reflection, refraction, and diffraction.

Example

If a sound wave in air at a certain temperature and humidity has a frequency of 125 Hz and a wavelength of 9.00 feet, what is its wave speed?

A. 0.0720 feet per second

B. 13.9 feet per second

C. 134 feet per second

D. 1,125 feet per second

The correct answer is **D**. The wave speed v is related to the frequency f and wavelength λ by the formula $v = \lambda f$. Multiply the frequency (which is in hertz, or inverse seconds) by the wavelength to get the wave speed in feet per second.

Electromagnetic (Light) Waves

Electromagnetic waves exhibit the same behavior as other waves, but unlike mechanical waves, they require no medium to propagate. (That is, they can propagate in a vacuum.) Electromagnetic waves result from the movement—specifically, the acceleration—of a charge. Examples include visible light, radio waves, X-rays, microwaves, and infrared radiation.

As their name implies, electromagnetic waves involve variation in the **electric field** and the **magnetic field** around the source charge(s). These fields mutually oscillate in a manner similar to that of mechanical waves, although the oscillation is in field intensity and direction rather than, for example, wave height or material pressure.

In a vacuum, the speed of an electromagnetic wave (or the **speed of light,** sometimes labeled c) is a constant: approximately 186,000 miles per second, which is much faster than the speed of sound in air—roughly 0.2 miles per second, or about 770 miles per hour. When traveling in a material, the speed of an electromagnetic wave

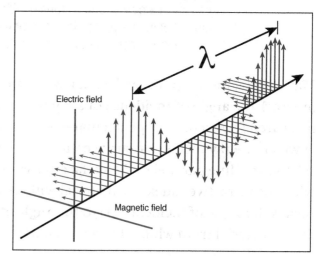

325

decreases by a factor of $1/n$, where n is the material's **refractive index** (or **index of refraction**). Therefore, the speed of light v in a material of refractive index n is $v = c/n$. The refractive index depends on the electrical and magnetic properties of the material.

> **CONNECTIONS**
> Electromagnetic wave behaviors include reflection (e.g., looking in a mirror), refraction (e.g., looking through a prism and seeing objects at off angles), and diffraction (e.g., shifting multicolored patterns on a compact disc).

Example

A radio wave is passing through a material with a refractive index of 2.00. What is its speed?

    A. 2,000 miles per second

    B. 93,000 miles per second

    C. 186,000 miles per second

    D. 372,000 miles per second

The correct answer is **B**. The speed of light in a medium (material) is the speed of light in a vacuum (c = 186,000 miles per second) divided by the refractive index (2.00, in this case). The result is 93,000 miles per second.

Optics

In situations where the dimensions of a problem are much larger than the wavelength of the electromagnetic waves, those waves can often be accurately approximated as **rays**: directed line segments that represent the waves. Some simple rules enable analysis of electromagnetic-wave behavior in media that involve mirrors and in materials with different refractive indices. This model is a straightforward, often effective way to study **optics**, which is the subset of physics that examines the behavior of light.

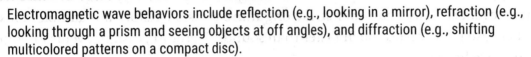

> **DID YOU KNOW?**
> A laser acts as like nearly ideal ray because it maintains a very narrow beam over long distances. When used with caution (specifically, eye protection), low-power lasers are excellent for clearly seeing the principles of optics in action.

Many problems in optics can be analyzed using two simple rules. First, for a reflective surface (mirror), the **angle of incidence** of a ray is equal to the **angle of reflection**. Both angles are measured from a line perpendicular—or **normal**—to the surface and passing through the point at which the ray meets that surface. In the case of reflection, the angles can also be measured relative to a line parallel to the surface at that point. Second, for a ray passing from a material with one refractive index to a material with a different refractive index, the formula below relates the angle of incidence (θ_i) to the **angle of refraction** (θ_r), where n_i is the refractive index of the material from which the ray originates and n_r is the refractive index of the material into which the ray transmits. This relationship is called **Snell's law** and is responsible for the magnification of objects using lenses.

$$\frac{\sin\theta_i}{\sin\theta_r} = \frac{n_r}{n_i}$$

Example

If a light ray hits a mirror with a 30° angle of incidence relative to the normal, what is its angle of reflection relative to the normal?

A. 30°   C. 60°

B. 40°   D. 90°

The correct answer is **A**. The angle of incidence is equal to the angle of reflection, as long as both angles are measured from the same line (normal or parallel).

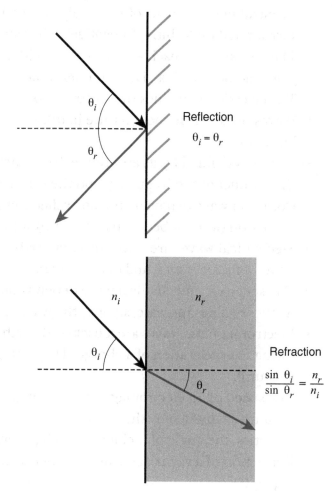

Let's Review!

- The matter that appears in everyday life is largely composed of atoms; each atom has a central nucleus made of positively charged protons and uncharged neutrons that is surrounded by "orbiting" negatively charged electrons.
- The elements are each a type of atom with a different number of protons in its nucleus. A given element with a given number of neutrons is an isotope.
- The electric force binds the electrons to the nucleus of an atom.
- Waves occur throughout nature in different forms, but they have common properties and behaviors.
- A wave is defined by its amplitude, frequency, and wavelength. The wave speed is equal to the product of the frequency and the wavelength ($v = \lambda f$).
- Common wave behaviors include reflection (when the wave "bounces" off an object), refraction (when it bends in a medium), and diffraction (when it turns around an edge).
- Mechanical waves are waves in a material—solid, liquid, or gas. Examples include sound waves, seismic waves, and ocean waves.
- The speed of a mechanical wave depends on the compressibility and density of a material. As these values increase, so does the wave speed.
- Electromagnetic waves are a back-and-forth oscillation of the electric and magnetic fields owing to acceleration of a charge. They can propagate without a medium (that is, in a vacuum).
- The speed of an electromagnetic wave in a material is equal to the speed of light in a vacuum (c) divided by the refractive index of that material.
- In optics, the angle of incidence of a light ray is equal to the angle of reflection.
- Refraction of a ray is described by Snell's law:
- $$\frac{\sin\theta_i}{\sin\theta_r} = \frac{n_r}{n_i},$$
- where θ_i is the angle of incidence, θ_r is the angle of refraction, n_i is the refractive index in the material from which the ray is traveling, and n_r is the refractive index in the material to which the ray is traveling.

KINETIC ENERGY

This lesson introduces the concept of mechanical energy as the sum of kinetic energy and potential energy. The lesson also examines objects in motion and the effects of changing velocities and forces on moving objects. Finally, the lesson discusses how the force of gravitation affects objects in the universe.

Mechanical Energy

Energy is the ability to do work. Mechanical energy can be divided into two types: kinetic energy and potential energy.

Kinetic energy of an object is represented by the equation $KE = \frac{1}{2}mv^2$, where m is the mass of the object and v is the velocity. The kinetic energy is proportional to the object's mass. A 7.26 kg shot thrown through the air has much more kinetic energy than a 145 g baseball with the same velocity. The kinetic energy of an object is also proportional to the square of the velocity of the object. A car traveling at 40 m/s has four times the kinetic energy of the same car moving at 20 m/s. This is the result of the squared velocity term in the formula. Kinetic energy, like work, is measured in **joules**.

Consider a group of boulders perched high on a cliff. These boulders have energy in a stored condition because gravity could cause them to fall. This is called gravitational potential energy (there are other types of stored energy, such as chemical and electrical). Potential energy of an object is stored energy due to the object's configuration or position relative to a force acting on it. The formula for calculating gravitational potential energy is $PE = mgh$, where m is the mass of the object, g is the acceleration of gravity on Earth (9.8 m/s²), and h is the object's height above Earth's surface. The unit for potential energy is also **joules**. Potential energy is an energy of position because much of the way this quantity can be changed is due to height.

Falling objects provide an interesting case for mechanical energy calculations. If we assume that there is no wind resistance, then all potential energy an object has before falling turns into kinetic energy as the object falls. Once the object impacts Earth's surface, there are different calculations to be done. We will simplify things by considering the object at the moment before impact.

Example

If a boulder falls off a 65 m high cliff, at what height, in meters, does the boulder have zero potential energy?

A. 0	B. 0.010	C. 32	D. 65

The correct answer is **A**. Potential energy is defined as $PE = mgh$. Only at $h = 0$ will the equation equal 0.

Linear Momentum and Impulse

The **momentum** of an object depends upon its mass and velocity. **Momentum** is defined as $p = mv$, where m is the mass and v is the velocity. The unit for momentum is kg·m/s and does not have a special name. This concept can be illustrated by a simple example: Most people would rather try stopping a child's tricycle rolling at 0.5 miles per hour than a loaded dump truck at the same speed. The difference is the dump truck's greater momentum as a result of its much larger mass.

Newton's second law of motion explains how the momentum of an object is changed by a net force acting upon it. Newton's second law of motion, $F = ma$, can be rewritten by using the definition of acceleration as the change in velocity divided by the time interval.

$$F = ma = m\left(\frac{\Delta v}{\Delta t}\right)$$

Multiplying both sides of the equation by the time interval results in the following equation:

$$F\Delta t = m\Delta v$$

The left side, $F\Delta t$, is the product of the average force and the time interval over which it acts. This product is called the **impulse**, and an impulse is found by determining the area under the curve of a force-time graph, as shown below.

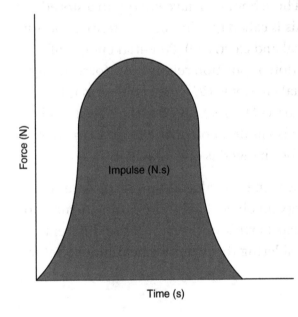

Impulse-Momentum Theorem: $F\Delta t = p2 - p1$

This equation is called the **impulse-momentum theorem**. The impulse on an object is equal to the change in momentum that it causes. If the force is constant, the impulse is just the product of the force and the time interval over which it acts.

What happens to a driver when a crash suddenly stops a car? An impulse is needed to bring the driver's momentum to zero. The steering wheel can exert a large force during a short period of time. An airbag reduces the force exerted on the driver by greatly increasing the length of the time over which the force is exerted.

Refer to the equation: $F = (m\Delta v)/\Delta t$. In the equation, Δv is the same with or without the airbag. However, the airbag reduces F by increasing Δt. Less force on a person during a crash is a good thing.

Example

What is the mass of a student's phone, in grams, if a pillow on the floor provides 7.71 N in 0.100 s while reducing the falling phone's speed from 4.43 m/s to rest?

   A. 0.174   B. 1.74   C. 17.4   D. 174

The correct answer is **D.** Use the impulse-momentum theorem to solve for mass.

$$\frac{F \cdot \Delta t}{v} = m; \quad \frac{7.71 \text{ N} \cdot 0.100 \text{ s}}{4.43 \frac{\text{m}}{\text{s}}} = 0.174 \text{ kg} = 174 \text{ g}$$

Universal Gravitation

Newton used mathematical arguments to show that if the path of a planet is an ellipse, then the magnitude of the force, F, on the planet resulting from the sun must vary inversely with the square of the distance between the center of the planet and center of the sun.

Newton later stated that the sight of a falling apple made him think about the motion of planets. He recognized that the apple fell straight down because Earth attracted it. He wondered whether this force might extend beyond the trees to the clouds, to the moon, and beyond. Could gravity also be the force that attracts the planets to the sun? Newton hypothesized that the force on the apple must be proportional to its mass. In addition, according to Newton's third law of motion, the apple would also attract Earth. Thus, the force of attraction must be proportional to the mass of Earth. The attractive force that exists between all objects is known as **gravitational force**.

Newton assumed that the same force of attraction would act between any two masses, m1 and m2. He proposed his **law of universal gravitation**, which is represented by the following equation:

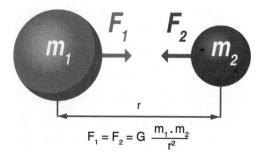

In the equation, r is the distance between the centers of the masses, and G is a universal constant—that is, it is the same everywhere. The gravitational constant $G = 6.67 \times 10^{-11}$ N·m²/kg². The force of gravitation is directly proportional to the masses of the objects. However, force is inversely proportional to the square of the distance between the objects.

Example

What is the force of gravitational attraction, in newtons, between Mars (6.39 × 10²³ kg) and its inner moon Phobos (10.6 × 10¹⁵ kg) 6.00 × 10⁶ m away?

A. 1.25×10^{16} B. 4.37×10^{16} C. 2.42×10^{17} D. 8.93×10^{18}

The correct answer is **A.** Use the formula to calculate the force: $F = G\left(\frac{m_1 m_2}{r^2}\right)$ $F =$ Skipping unsupported tag: span$\left(6.67 \times 10^{-11} \frac{N \cdot m^2}{kg^2}\right)\left(\frac{(6.39 \times 10^{23} kg)(10.6 \times 10^{15} kg)}{(6.00 \times 10^6 m)^2}\right) = 1.25 \times 10^{16} N$.

Let's Review!

- Kinetic energy, or the energy of motion, of an object is represented by the equation $KE = \frac{1}{2}mv^2$.
- The potential energy of an object is stored energy due to the object's configuration or position relative to a force acting on it. Gravitational potential energy is defined as $PE = mgh$. Near Earth's surface, gravitational acceleration is measured to be $g = 9.8$ m/s².
- Newton's second law of motion explains how the momentum of an object is changed by a net force action on it.
- The impulse on an object is equal to the change in momentum that it causes.
- The attractive force that exists between all objects is known as gravitational force. That force is directly related to the product of the two masses and inversely related to the square of the distance between the masses.
- $F = G\left(\frac{m_1 m_2}{r^2}\right)$ where $G = 6.67 \times 10^{-11} \frac{N \cdot m^2}{kg^2}$

ELECTRICITY AND MAGNETISM

This lesson reviews the nature and relationship of electricity and magnetism and how these forces enable many modern technologies.

Electric Forces and Fields

Objects that have an **electric charge** attract or repel other electrically charged objects depending on whether the charges are like (repel) or unlike (attract). **Coulomb's law** describes the **electric force** F_E that an object carrying charge Q_1 exerts on an object carrying charge Q_2:

$$F_E = k\frac{Q_1 Q_2}{r^2}$$

where r is the distance between the objects and k is the electric constant. When using SI units—that is, the force is measured in newtons (N), distance in meters (m), and charge in coulombs (C)—k is approximately 9×10^9. To aid the math, electric charge is described as either positive (like the charge on a proton) or negative (like the charge on an electron).

When studying and describing light (and other electromagnetic waves), defining the **electric field** is helpful. The electric field is the force that an object with a charge of 1 coulomb experiences at a given distance r from an object with charge Q. The formula for this field (E) is similar to Coulomb's law:

$$E = k\frac{Q}{r^2}$$

The field is measured in newtons per coulomb.

Generally, the electric force and field are vectors, meaning they have both a magnitude and direction. Correctly adding forces therefore requires adding the vectors, not just the magnitudes. As a result, for example, if two forces acting on a charged object have equal magnitudes but opposite directions, their sum is zero—the object experiences no net force.

> **BE CAREFUL!**
>
> Charged objects only exert a force on other charged objects. Uncharged objects—for example, neutrons and many everyday objects—neither experience nor exert an electric force (at least under typical conditions).

> **KEEP IN MIND**
>
> Generally, if Coulomb's law yields a negative value for the electric force, that force is attractive; if it yields a positive value, that force is repulsive.

Example

What is the magnitude of the attractive electric force, in newtons, that an object with a charge 5.0 C exerts on another object with a charge −8.0 C that is 1.2×10^2 meters away?

A. -2.7×10^{-3}　　　　B. -3.3×10^{-1}　　　　C. -2.6×10^7　　　　D. -3.0×10^9

The correct answer is C. Using Coulomb's law: $F_E = k\frac{Q_1 Q_2}{r^2}$ $F_E = \left(9 \times 10^9\right)\frac{(5.0) \times (-8.0)}{(1.2 \times 10^2)^2}$ $F_E = (9 \times 10^9)\frac{-40}{1.4 \times 10^4} = -2.6 \times 10^7$ *newtons*

Magnetism

Magnetism manifests through forces and fields in a manner similar to electricity, but the mathematics are more complicated. Qualitatively, a simple model of magnetism is relatively easy to understand. **Magnetic fields** and **magnetic forces** arise from moving charges—that is, any charged object with a nonzero velocity produces a magnetic field (and thus can exert a magnetic force on another moving charge). For instance, a wire that carries an **electric current**—which is the movement of negatively charged electrons through the wire—creates a magnetic field around that wire. The movement of electrons around the nucleus of an atom also creates a magnetic field, and in some elements (such as iron), the result can be powerful magnetic properties. Earth has a magnetic field that allows navigation using a compass, which uses a small magnetic needle to detect the direction of the field.

Like electric charge, magnetism has two "polarities" (or **poles**) called **north** and **south**. Unlike electric charge, however, a magnetic object (or **magnet**) always has a magnetic north and a magnetic south—north and south never exist by themselves. (Positive and negative electric charges can exist by themselves.) In addition, like polarities repel, and unlike polarities attract.

BE CAREFUL!
Remember that any motion of charge creates a magnetic field, but only charge *acceleration* creates electromagnetic waves.

DID YOU KNOW?
Because electric currents create magnetic fields, they can deflect a compass needle. For instance, if you connect a wire across the terminals of a battery, causing an electric current to flow, you can see the effect of magnetism if you bring a compass near it. An accidental observation of this phenomenon led to the discovery of the link between electric current and magnetism.

Example

Which of the following events produces a magnetic field?

A. An accelerating electron

B. A wire in an electric field

C. A neutron moving through space

D. A positively charged object in a stationary position

The correct answer is **A**. Magnetic fields result from moving charges. Of the possible choices, only A involves a charged object (neutrons have no net charge) that is also in motion.

Electric and Magnetic Flux

Electric flux is the "flow" of the electric field through a given surface. To envision this concept, drawing **electric field lines** is helpful. Field lines show the direction of the electric force in space—specifically, the path a positive "test charge" would follow if it were initially stationary at some arbitrary point in space. By convention, field lines are generally shown flowing out from positive charges and in to negative charges. The illustration below shows a positive charge in empty space, a negative charge in empty space, and a positive and negative charge in close proximity.

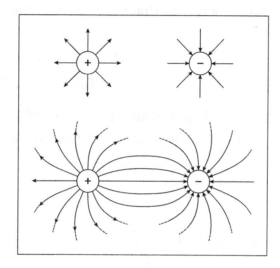

The more field lines that flow through an area, the greater the flux. Higher field-line density indicates a stronger field or force in that region. Although field lines are conceptual rather than physical, they are a helpful way to represent how electricity and magnetism permeate the space around charged objects.

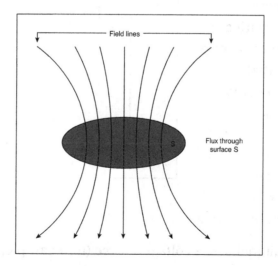

Magnetic flux and **magnetic field lines** are analogous to electric flux and field lines, but they represent magnetism rather than electricity. The same general principles apply.

One aspect of electricity and magnetism underlying much of today's technology is **electromagnetic induction.** This phenomenon occurs when an electrical conductor such as a wire experiences a changing magnetic field: the result is an electric force in that conductor. The strength of the electric force around a conducting loop is proportional to the rate at which the magnetic flux through that loop is changing. For example, spinning a coil of wire positioned between powerful magnets (or vice versa) is essentially how power companies produce electricity. Electrically driven motors apply the same principles, but in reverse.

Example

A positively charged object is inside a sphere that has no effect on electric fields. In what direction will the electric flux be?

A. Into the sphere

B. Out of the sphere

C. Along the surface of the sphere

D. Both into and out of the sphere

The correct answer is **B.** The electric flux is the "flow" of the electric field and is closely related to the field lines. Because the field lines go out from positive charges, the flux will be out of the sphere in this case.

Electric Circuits

Electric circuits are a critical component of many modern technologies, including computing technology and electrical power distribution. An **electric circuit** (or just *circuit*) is a closed "loop" in which electric charge experiences an electric force around the loop. Important parameters in a circuit are voltage, current, and resistance. **Voltage,** also called the **electric potential difference,** is the amount of energy required to move a unit of charge between two points in a circuit. **Current** is the amount of charge flowing through a given surface per second. **Resistance** is a measure of how much an electrical component impedes the flow of current.

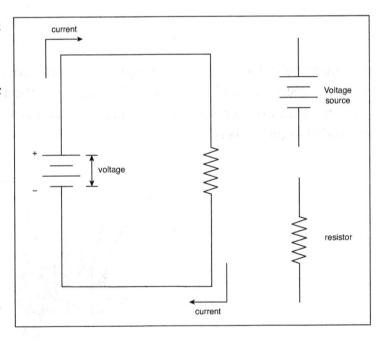

A simple example of a circuit includes a **voltage source** (for example, a battery) and a **resistor** (for example, a light bulb) connected by metal wires. A simple voltage source has two **terminals:** it maintains an electric potential difference across those terminals so that charge will try to flow from the higher-voltage ("positive") terminal to the lower-voltage ("negative") terminal.

Voltage is usually measured in **volts** (V); current is usually measured in **amperes** (A) or **amps**, which are coulombs per second; and resistance is usually measured in **ohms** (Ω). Materials, such as metal, that allow the free flow of electric charge are called **conductors**. Materials, such as many plastics, that do *not* allow the free flow of electric charge are called **insulators**.

DID YOU KNOW?

By convention, current is defined as the flow of positive charge. But because *negative* charge (electrons) is what actually flows in basic circuits, the mathematical assignment of a negative sign to the electron's charge created a historical dilemma. Mathematically, the flow of positive charge in one direction is equal to the flow of negative charge in the opposite direction, so the common practice is to discuss the flow of positive charge even though electrons often constitute the current.

Example

Which of the following best describes an electric current?

A. The storage of electric charge

B. The movement of electric charge

C. The energy required to move electric charge

D. The impedance of electric charge's movement

The correct answer is **B**. Electric current is the flow of electric charge.

Ohm's Law

Circuit analysis can become extremely complex when the circuit involves many components, but a ew basic principles can aid the process, especially for simple circuits. One example is **Ohm's law**, which relates the current *I* through and voltage *V* across a component with a given resistance *R*: $V = IR$.

FOR EXAMPLE

If a circuit involves a 10-volt battery connected to a 100-ohm resistor, you can find the current through the resistor using Ohm's law:

$$V = IR$$
$$I = \frac{V}{R} = \frac{10 \text{ volts}}{100 \text{ ohms}} = 0.1 \text{ amps}$$

Two important rules also help in analyzing circuits. The first rule is that at any point (or **node**) in the circuit, the current flowing into that point must equal the current flowing out of that point. Thus, if three wires join at a node, the sum of the currents flowing in must equal the sum of the currents flowing out. The second rule is that for any closed loop in the circuit, the sum of the voltages around the loop must equal zero. For this rule, going around the entire loop in the same direction is critical. One convention is that going from a higher voltage to a lower voltage represents a positive voltage change (or voltage "drop"), whereas going from a lower voltage to a higher voltage represents a negative voltage change. Thus, in a circuit containing just a battery and a resistor, the voltage change across the resistor must be equal in magnitude but opposite in sign to the voltage change across the battery (when going either clockwise or counterclockwise around the circuit).

Example

If 0.2 amps are flowing through a 1,000-ohm resistor, what is the voltage across that resistor?

A. 0.0002 volts   B. 200 volts   C. 1,000 volts   D. 5,000 volts

The correct answer is **B**. Use Ohm's law: $V = IR$ $V = (0.2 \text{ amps}) \times (1{,}000 \text{ ohms}) = 200 \text{ volts}$

Let's Review!

- Electric charges, which can be either positive or negative, create electric fields and exert an electric force on other charges.
- The electric force between two charges (Q_1 and Q_2) obeys Coulomb's law: $F_E = k\frac{Q_1 Q_2}{r^2}$, where k is the electric constant (about 9×10^9 when working in SI units) and r is the distance between the charges.
- The electric field from a charge Q is $E = k\frac{Q}{r^2}$.
- Magnetic fields and forces result from moving charges (an electric current). Magnets have north and south polarities, but unlike electricity where negative and positive charges can appear separately, these magnetic polarities always appear together.
- Electric flux is the "flow" of the electric field, which can be visualized using electric field lines.
- Magnetic flux is the "flow" of the magnetic field, which can be visualized using magnetic field lines.
- Changing magnetic flux through a surface creates an electric field through that surface—a phenomenon that enables electricity generation.
- Electric circuits involve current flowing through resistors and other electrical components, driven by an electric potential difference (voltage).
- The voltage across a resistor is equal to the product of the resistance and the current (Ohm's law). Common units for these parameters are volts, amperes, and ohms.

Chapter 16 Physics Practice Quiz

1. A vector has its tail at (9, 4) and its head at (0, 3). Which representation of the vector is correct?

    A. (−9, −1)   C. (−9, 7)

    B. (−9, 1)   D. (−9, 12)

2. Which statement about an object undergoing projectile motion is true? (Assume ideal conditions with no friction.)

    A. The object's vertical velocity is constant.

    B. The object's vertical acceleration is zero.

    C. The object's horizontal velocity is constant.

    D. The object's horizontal acceleration is nonzero.

3. Which of the following best describes the behavior of an object in uniform circular motion?

    A. Constant speed, constant velocity, constant acceleration vector

    B. Changing speed, changing velocity, constant acceleration vector

    C. Constant speed, constant velocity, changing acceleration vector

    D. Constant speed, changing velocity, changing acceleration vector

4. Surface imperfections cause a horizontally sliding block to come to a halt. Which of the following remains as a result?

    A. Heat   C. Air resistance

    B. Velocity   D. Horizontal force

5. Which term best describes two atoms that have the same number of protons but different numbers of neutrons?

    A. Elements   C. Isotopes

    B. Ions   D. Nuclei

6. Which statement about a magnesium ion is correct?

    A. The number of protons differs from the number of neutrons.

    B. The number of protons differs from the number of electrons.

    C. The number of electrons differs from the number of neutrons.

    D. The numbers of protons, electrons, and neutrons are all the same.

7. What did Newton hypothesize when he watched the apple fall to the ground?

    A. The force on the apple must be equal to its mass.

    B. The force on the apple must be unrelated to its mass.

    C. The force on the apple must be proportional to its mass.

    D. The force on the apple must be inversely proportional to its mass.

8. The chemical bonds found in sugar are an example of what type of energy?

   A. Kinetic   C. Potential

   B. Magnetic   D. Thermal

9. Which situation represents an attractive magnetic force?

   A. Two north poles in close proximity

   B. Two south poles in close proximity

   C. Any two magnetic poles in close proximity

   D. A north pole and a south pole in close proximity

10. A scientist is using a compass to detect magnetic fields. Which experiment will deflect the compass needle?

   A. Holding a charged object stationary near the compass

   B. Moving a charged object quickly away from the compass

   C. Holding an uncharged object stationary near the compass

   D. Moving an uncharged object quickly away from the compass

CHAPTER 16 PHYSICS
PRACTICE QUIZ – ANSWER KEY

1. A. The standard form of a vector is the head coordinates minus the tail coordinates: $(0 - 9, 3 - 4) = (-9, -1)$. **See Lesson: Nature of Motion.**

2. C. An object undergoing projectile motion (in ideal conditions) has a constant horizontal velocity but a changing vertical velocity due to gravity. Thus, its horizontal acceleration is zero, but its vertical acceleration is nonzero. Only answer C is true. **See Lesson: Nature of Motion.**

3. D. An object in uniform circular motion has a constant speed, but as it moves, its velocity and its acceleration vector change direction. **See Lesson: Friction.**

4. A. Once the block has come to a stop, it no longer has any velocity or acceleration. It is therefore experiencing no net force. Likewise, without any velocity, air resistance no longer applies. But as the block slowed, it created heat because of friction, and that heat remains—just like when people who feel cold rub their hands together briskly to warm them up. **See Lesson: Friction.**

5. C. If two atoms have the same number of protons, they are the same element. If two atoms of the same element have different numbers of neutrons, they are isotopes. **See Lesson: Waves and Sounds.**

6. B. An ion is an atom with a net electric charge. Therefore, the number of protons must be different from the number of electrons. Neutrons have no electric charge and therefore have no bearing on the atom's net charge. **See Lesson: Waves and Sounds.**

7. C. He hypothesized that the force on the apple must be proportional to its mass. **See Lesson: Kinetic Energy.**

8. C. When the bonds are broken, the potential energy stored in them is converted to kinetic energy. **See Lesson: Kinetic Energy.**

9. D. As with electric charge, magnetic polarities (or poles) attract if they are different and repel if they are like. Therefore, a north pole attracts a south pole (and vice versa), but north poles repel each another, as do south poles. **See Lesson: Electricity and Magnetism.**

10. B. A magnetic field will deflect the compass needle. Magnetic fields result from moving charges, eliminating answers C and D (which involve uncharged objects). Answer B involves a moving charged object, which will deflect the compass needle. **See Lesson: Electricity and Magnetism.**

CHAPTER 17 EARTH AND SPACE SCIENCES

ASTRONOMY

Are you ready to embark upon a journey through space and time? For centuries, scientists have sought to answer questions about our planet and its place in the universe. Astronomy is the study of the moon, stars, and other objects in space. Modern astronomy can be dated back to the time of the ancient Greeks, when scientists began using mathematics to explain what they observed in the night sky.

The Solar System

Our solar system is made up primarily of the sun and eight planets. All of the objects in our solar system revolve around the sun. By mass alone, the sun makes up 99.8 percent of our solar system.

The eight planets of our solar system are categorized in two groups. The inner planets, the four planets closest to the sun, are small and dense and have rocky surfaces, while the outer planets are larger, are farther away from the sun, and do not have solid surfaces. Pluto, once considered one of the outer planets, is now categorized as a dwarf planet.

- Inner planets: Mercury, Venus, Earth, and Mars
- Outer planets: Jupiter, Saturn, Uranus, and Neptune

Stars

When humans began observing the night sky, they imagined that the twinkling lights they saw formed pictures of people and animals. Today, we call these lights, stars, and the patterns that they form constellations.

Stars are balls of very hot gases that form when gravity pulls a cloud of gas, called a nebula, together with dust. When the mass of gas and dust becomes dense enough, enormous amounts of energy are released, resulting in the light that we see from Earth. Scientists characterize stars based on their color, temperature, size, and chemical composition.

Stars are grouped together in clusters called star systems. Galaxies are large groups of stars and star systems bound together with dust and gas by gravity. Our solar system is located in a galaxy called the Milky Way. Many galaxies, including the Milky Way, are bound by gravity to hundreds or even thousands of other galaxies in regions of space called galaxy clusters.

Most of the stars in our galaxy are main sequence stars, or stars that are in their longest stage of life. Most are also dwarf stars, or small stars with relatively low luminosity. Giant stars, in contrast, are very large and are brighter than the sun.

The Universe

Astronomers define the universe as all of space and everything in it, such as planets, stars, galaxies, and other matter. Most of the matter in the universe is actually dark matter, so called because it does not interact with light and is therefore difficult to measure. The universe also contains cosmic phenomena called black holes, or regions in space with gravity so intense that nothing—not even light—can escape.

How did it all start? The leading theory, called the Big Bang Theory, is that the universe began in an instant, billions of years ago, with an explosion or a big bang. After that explosion, the universe cooled and expanded, inflating over time to become the cosmos that we know today.

Because the distances between objects in space are so large, astronomers use a special unit of measurement, called a light-year, to evaluate them. A light-year is the distance that light travels in space in one Earth year, about 9.5 trillion kilometers. The sun is approximately 150 million kilometers, or 8 light-minutes, away from Earth, whereas the North Star, also called Polaris, is 2 billion kilometers or 320 light-years away.

Let's Review!

- The solar system is made up of the sun and eight planets: Mercury, Venus, Earth, Mars, Jupiter, Saturn, Uranus, and Neptune.
- Stars are made up of gas and dust that have been pulled together by gravity.
- The universe consists of space and everything in it, such as planets, stars, galaxies, and other matter.

GEOLOGY

Geology is the study of Earth and its physical components and how these components interact over time. Geologists use the information they learn to better understand Earth's history and predict future geological processes.

Earth's Spheres

Earth is made up of four distinct zones, or spheres, that each have unique characteristics: geosphere (land), hydrosphere (water), biosphere (living things), and atmosphere (air).

Geosphere

The geosphere is the region of Earth that contains the crust and core of the planet and everything within them. This includes all of the natural, lifeless matter from the rocks at the top of Mount Everest, to the sand at the bottom of the ocean floor, to the molten magma in Earth's center.

Hydrosphere

The hydrosphere is all of the water on the planet, whether it is in liquid, solid, or gaseous form. Ninety-seven percent of the water on the planet is saltwater, while the remaining three percent is freshwater in the form of rivers, streams, groundwater, and glaciers.

Biosphere

If it is alive, it is part of Earth's biosphere. This includes humans, plants, animals, bacteria, fungi, protists, and microorganisms, as well as any organic matter that has not yet decomposed.

Atmosphere

The atmosphere contains all of Earth's gases, including the air we breathe. The atmosphere absorbs the heat from the sun that is reflected off Earth, controlling the temperature as well as weather patterns on the planet.

Earth's Internal Layers

Earth's internal layers are divided into three sections: the crust, the mantle, and the core.

Crust

The crust is Earth's outermost layer. It is further divided into two categories—the thin oceanic crust that lies under the ocean basins and the thicker continental crust that forms the foundation for land on Earth.

Mantle

Earth's mantle is the filling sandwiched between the crust and the core. It is 2,890 kilometers thick and can be divided into the upper mantle and the lower mantle. The upper mantle is closer to the crust. The temperatures in this region are cooler, resulting in rocks that are hard and brittle. The lower mantle is characterized by warmer temperatures and rock that is hot and soft.

Core

The core is the innermost region of the planet. It is divided into the outer core, which contains molten rock, and the inner core, which is under so much pressure that it prevents rock from becoming liquid. The core is Earth's source of internal heat.

Plate Tectonics

Plate tectonics is the geological theory that the geosphere can be broken down into seven distinct large plates—the African, North American, South American, Eurasian, Australian, Antarctic, and Pacific plates—as well as several smaller plates.

According to the plate tectonics theory, these plates are all moving in different directions and at different speeds in such a way that they sometimes crash into or pull away from one another, causing such phenomena as earthquakes, volcanic eruptions, and rifts.

The regions where plates crash into one another are called convergent boundaries, while divergent boundaries occur when plates pull apart from one another. Places where plates slide past, or "side-swipe," one another are called transform boundaries.

Let's Review!

- Earth is made up of four distict zones: the geosphere, the hydrosphere, the biosphere, and the atmosphere.
- The Earth is divided into three sections: the crust, the mantle, and the core.
- Plate tectonics is the theory that divides the geosphere into seven distict large plates: the African, North American, South American, Eurasian, Australian, Antarctic, and Pacific plates, as well as several smaller plates.

METEOROLOGY

Meteorology is the study of Earth's atmosphere with a focus on predicting weather patterns.

Earth's Resources

All of the resources on Earth can be classified into two categories: renewable and nonrenewable. Renewable resources are natural resources that can be replenished over time, while nonrenewable resources cannot. All fossil fuels, a significant source of energy for people around the world, are nonrenewable and are therefore finite.

Renewable Energy Resources

- Biomass
- Hydropower
- Geothermal
- Wind
- Solar

Nonrenewable Energy Resources

- Crude oil
- Natural gas
- Coal
- Uranium

The Water Cycle

The water cycle describes how water changes form and moves throughout Earth's spheres. The cycling of water into and out of the atmosphere plays a major role in Earth's weather patterns. The three main phases of the water cycle are evaporation, condensation, and precipitation.

Evaporation

In its liquid form, water can be found in rivers, lakes, streams, and oceans. When heat from the sun causes the water on Earth to warm up, some of it may evaporate into its gaseous form and enter the atmosphere. This is called evaporation.

Condensation

Once in the atmosphere, gaseous water begins to cool and change back into its liquid form. This process is called condensation, and it is responsible for the development of clouds.

Precipitation

When enough water has accumulated in the atmosphere, it may fall back to Earth in the form of precipitation. This precipitation may return directly to the oceans, lakes, and rivers, or it may fall on land where it will become groundwater that plants and animals (including humans) drink.

Weather vs. Climate

Weather and climate are often confused, but the terms describe two different phenomena. Weather is what is happening in the atmosphere right now and what will happen in the near future. It is defined in terms of temperature, humidity, precipitation, cloud cover, and wind speed and direction.

In contrast, climate is an accumulation of weather statistics that occur over months or years. Meteorologists use climate data to explain daily weather and make predictions about extreme weather patterns.

Climate Patterns

A climate pattern is any regular cycle that occurs within climate over a period of time. Climate patterns include regular occurrences, such as the yearly change of seasons, and more periodic events, such as El Niño.

The circulation of the atmosphere in the form of wind is the result of Earth's rotation in combination with the influx of energy from the sun. As hot air rises around the equator, it travels north and south toward Earth's poles and circulates within distinct cells.

Together with the tides, or the rise and fall of sea levels produced by gravity and Earth's rotation, atmospheric circulation transfers energy and heat throughout the planet.

Erosion sometimes occurs as a result of this flow of wind and water. When earthen materials, such as soil or rock, are transferred from one location to another as a result of wind or water, it is called erosion.

Let's Review!

- There are two types of resources on Earth: renewable and nonrenewable.
- Renewable resources can be replenished over time, while nonrenewable resources cannot.
- Water changes forms as it moves through Earth's spheres in a water cycle.
- The three main phases of the water cycle are: evaporation, condensation, and precipitation.
- Weather is the term used to define what is happening in the atmosphere right now and what will happen in the near future.
- Climate is the term used to define the accumulation of weather statistics that occur over months and years.
- A climate pattern is a regular cycle that occurs within climate over a period of time.

CHAPTER 17 EARTH AND SPACE SCIENCE PRACTICE QUIZ

1. What is the name for the four planets in our solar system that are closest to the sun?

    A. Inner planets

    B. Outer planets

    C. Interior planets

    D. Adjacent planets

2. What are main sequence stars?

    A. Stars that are very small and dim

    B. Stars that are in their longest stage of life

    C. Stars that are very large and brighter than the sun

    D. Groups of stars and star systems that are bound together by gravity

3. Which components are part of the geosphere?

    A. The gases on Earth

    B. The water on Earth

    C. The living things on Earth

    D. The crust and core of Earth

4. What is the name for Earth's innermost layer?

    A. Core

    C. Center

    B. Crust

    D. Mantle

5. Which of the following is a renewable energy resource?

    A. Coal

    C. Crude oil

    B. Wind

    D. Natural gas

6. What is climate?

    A. The rise and fall of sea levels

    B. The circulation of the atmosphere

    C. Current and future happening in the atmosphere

    D. An accumulation of weather statistics over months or years

CHAPTER 17 EARTH AND SPACE SCIENCE PRACTICE QUIZ – ANSWER KEY

1. A. Mercury, Venus, Earth, and Mars are the four planets closest to the sun and are called the inner planets. **See Lesson: Astronomy.**

2. B. Main sequence stars are stars that are in their longest stage of life. **See Lesson: Astronomy.**

3. D. The geosphere comprises the crust and the core of Earth and everything within them. **See Lesson: Geology.**

4. A. The core is the innermost region of the planet. **See Lesson: Geology.**

5. B. Wind is not finite and is therefore a renewable resource. **See Lesson: Meteorology.**

6. D. Climate describes the accumulation of weather statistics that occurs over months or years. **See Lesson: Meteorology.**

SECTION VI. MATHEMATICAL REASONING

CHAPTER 18 NUMBER AND QUANTITY

BASIC ADDITION AND SUBTRACTION

This lesson introduces the concept of numbers and their symbolic and graphical representations. It also describes how to add and subtract whole numbers.

Numbers

A **number** is a way to quantify a set of entities that share some characteristic. For example, a fruit basket might contain nine pieces of fruit. More specifically, it might contain three apples, two oranges, and four bananas. Note that a number is a quantity, but a **numeral** is the symbol that represents the number: 8 means the number eight, for instance.

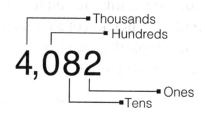

Although number representations vary, the most common is **base 10**. In base-10 format, each **digit** (or individual numeral) in a number is a quantity based on a multiple of 10. The base-10 system designates 0 through 9 as the numerals for zero through nine, respectively, and combines them to represent larger numbers. Thus, after counting from 1 to 9, the next number uses an additional digit: 10. That number means 1 group of 10 ones plus 0 additional ones. After 99, another digit is necessary, this time representing a hundred (10 sets of 10). This process of adding digits can go on indefinitely to express increasingly large numbers. For whole numbers, the rightmost digit is the ones place, the next digit to its left is the tens place, the next is the hundreds place, then the thousands place, and so on.

Classifying numbers can be convenient. The chart below lists a few common number sets.

Sets of Numbers	Members	Remarks
Natural numbers	1, 2, 3, 4, 5,...	The "counting" numbers
Whole numbers	0, 1, 2, 3, 4,...	The natural numbers plus 0
Integers	..., −3, −2, −1, 0, 1, 2, 3,...	The whole numbers plus all negative whole numbers
Real numbers	All numbers	The integers plus all fraction/decimal numbers in between
Rational numbers	All real numbers that can be expressed as p/q, where p and q are integers and q is nonzero	The natural numbers, whole numbers, and integers are all rational numbers
Irrational numbers	All real numbers that are not rational	The rational and irrational numbers together constitute the entire set of real numbers

Example

Jane has 4 pennies, 3 dimes, and 7 dollars. How many cents does she have?

A. 347   B. 437   C. 734   D. 743

The correct answer is **C**. The correct solution is 734. A penny is 1 cent. A dime (10 pennies) is 10 cents, and a dollar (100 pennies) is 100 cents. Place the digits in base-10 format: 7 hundreds, 3 tens, 4 ones, or 734.

The Number Line

The **number line** is a model that illustrates the relationships among numbers. The complete number line is infinite and includes every real number—both positive and negative. A ruler, for example, is a portion of a number line that assigns a **unit** (such as inches or centimeters) to each number. Typically, number lines depict smaller numbers to the left and larger numbers to the right. For example, a portion of the number line centered on 0 might look like the following:

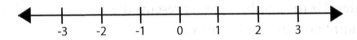

Because people learn about numbers in part through counting, they have a basic sense of how to order them. The number line builds on this sense by placing all the numbers (at least conceptually) from least to greatest. Whether a particular number is greater than or less than another is determined by comparing their relative positions. One number is greater than another if it is farther right on the number line. Likewise, a number is less than another if it is farther left on the number line. Symbolically, < means "is less than" and > means "is greater than." For example, 5 > 1 and 9 < 25.

Example

Place the following numbers in order from greatest to least: 5, –12, 0.

A. 0, 5, –12   C. 5, 0, –12

B. –12, 5, 0   D. –12, 0, 5

> **BE CAREFUL!**
>
> When ordering negative numbers, think of the number line. Although –10 > –2 may seem correct, it is incorrect. Because –10 is to the left of –2 on the number line, –10 < –2.

The correct answer is **C**. The correct solution is 5, 0, –12. Use the number line to order the numbers. Note that the question says *from greatest to least.*

Addition

Addition is the process of combining two or more numbers. For example, one set has 4 members and another set has 5 members. To combine the sets and find out how many members are in the new set, add 4 and 5 to get the **sum**. Symbolically, the expression is 4 + 5, where + is the **plus sign.** Pictorially, it might look like the following:

$$\underset{\circ\,\circ}{\circ\,\circ} \quad + \quad \underset{\circ\,\circ\,\circ}{\circ\,\circ} \quad = \quad \underset{\circ\,\circ\,\circ\,\circ\,\circ}{\circ\,\circ\,\circ\,\circ}$$

To get the sum, combine the two sets of circles and then count them. The result is 9.

KEY POINT

The order of the numbers is irrelevant when adding.

Another way to look at addition involves the number line. When adding 4 + 5, for example, start at 4 on the number line and take 5 steps to the right. The stopping point will be 9, which is the sum.

Counting little pictures or using the number line works for small numbers, but it becomes unwieldy for large ones—even numbers such as 24 and 37 would be difficult to add quickly and accurately. A simple algorithm enables much faster addition of large numbers. It works with two or more numbers.

STEP BY STEP

Step 1. Stack the numbers, vertically aligning the digits for each place.

Step 2. Draw a plus sign (+) to the left of the bottom number and draw a horizontal line below the last number.

Step 3. Add the digits in the ones place.

Step 4. If the sum from Step 3 is less than 10, write it in the same column below the horizontal line. Otherwise, write the first (ones) digit below the line, then **carry** the second (tens) digit to the top of the next column.

Step 5. Going from right to left, repeat Steps 3–4 for the other places.

Step 6. If applicable, write the remaining carry digit as the leftmost digit in the sum.

Example

Evaluate the expression 154 + 98.

   A. 250   B. 252   C. 352   D. 15,498

The correct answer is **B**. The correct solution is 252. Carefully follow the addition algorithm (see below). The process involves carrying a digit twice.

$$
\begin{array}{r}
154 \\
+\ 98 \\
\hline
\end{array}
\ \longrightarrow\
\begin{array}{r}
\overset{1}{} \\
154 \\
+\ 98 \\
\hline
2
\end{array}
\ \longrightarrow\
\begin{array}{r}
\overset{11}{} \\
154 \\
+\ 98 \\
\hline
52
\end{array}
\ \longrightarrow\
\begin{array}{r}
\overset{11}{} \\
154 \\
+\ 98 \\
\hline
252
\end{array}
$$

Subtraction

Subtraction is the inverse (opposite) of addition. Instead of representing the sum of numbers, it represents the difference between them. For example, given a set containing 15 members, subtracting 3 of those members yields a **difference** of 12. Using the **minus sign**, the expression for this operation is 15 − 3 = 12. As with addition, two approaches are counting pictures and using the number line. The first case might involve drawing 15 circles and then crossing off 3 of them; the difference is the number of remaining circles (12). To use the number line, begin at 15 and move left 3 steps to reach 12.

Again, these approaches are unwieldy for large numbers, but the subtraction algorithm eases evaluation by hand. This algorithm is only practical for two numbers at a time.

STEP BY STEP

Step 1. Stack the numbers, vertically aligning the digits in each place. Put the number you are subtracting *from* on top.

Step 2. Draw a minus sign (−) to the left of the bottom number and draw a horizontal line below the stack of numbers.

Step 3. Start at the ones place. If the digit at the top is larger than the digit below it, write the difference under the line. Otherwise, **borrow** from the top digit in the next-higher place by crossing it off, subtracting 1 from it, and writing the difference above it. Then add 10 to the digit in the ones place and perform the subtraction as normal.

Step 4. Going from right to left, repeat Step 3 for the rest of the places. If borrowing was necessary, make sure to use the new digit in each place, not the original one.

When adding or subtracting with negative numbers, the following rules are helpful. Note that x and y are used as placeholders for any real number.

$x + (-y) = x - y$

$-x - y = -(x + y)$

$(-x) + (-y) = -(x + y)$

$x - y = -(y - x)$

BE CAREFUL!

When dealing with numbers that have units (such as weights, currencies, or volumes), addition and subtraction are only possible when the numbers have the same unit. If necessary, convert one or more of them to equivalent numbers with the same unit.

Example

Kevin has 120 minutes to complete an exam. If he has already used 43, how many minutes does he have left?

   A. 43   B. 77   C. 87   D. 163

The correct answer is **B**. The correct solution is 77. The first step is to convert this problem to a math expression. The goal is to find the difference between how many minutes Kevin has for the exam and how many he has left after 43 minutes have elapsed. The expression would be 120 − 43. Carefully follow the subtraction algorithm (see below). The process will involve borrowing a digit twice.

$$
\begin{array}{c}
120 \\
-\ 43 \\
\hline
\end{array}
\longrightarrow
\begin{array}{c}
{}^{1\ 10} \\
12\!\!\!/0 \\
-\ 43 \\
\hline
7
\end{array}
\longrightarrow
\begin{array}{c}
{}^{0\ 1110} \\
1\!\!\!/2\!\!\!/0 \\
-\ 43 \\
\hline
77
\end{array}
$$

Let's Review!

- Numbers are positive and negative quantities and often appear in base-10 format.
- The number line illustrates the ordering of numbers.
- Addition is the combination of numbers. It can be performed by counting objects or pictures, moving on the number line, or using the addition algorithm.
- Subtraction is finding the difference between numbers. Like addition, it can be performed by counting, moving on the number line, or using the subtraction algorithm

BASIC MULTIPLICATION AND DIVISION

This lesson describes the process of multiplying and dividing numbers and introduces the order of operations, which governs how to evaluate expressions containing multiple arithmetic operations.

Multiplication

Addition can be tedious if it involves multiple instances of the same numbers. For example, evaluating 29 + 29 is easy, but evaluating 29 + 29 + 29 + 29 + 29 is laborious. Note that this example contains five instances—or multiples—of 29. **Multiplication** replaces the repeated addition of the same number with a single, more concise operation. Using the **multiplication (or times) symbol** ($\times$), the expression is

$$29 + 29 + 29 + 29 + 29 = 5 \times 29$$

The expression contains 5 multiples of 29. These numbers are the **factors** of multiplication. The result is called the **product**. In this case, addition shows that the product is 145. As with the other arithmetic operations, multiplication is easy for small numbers. Below is the multiplication table for whole numbers up to 12.

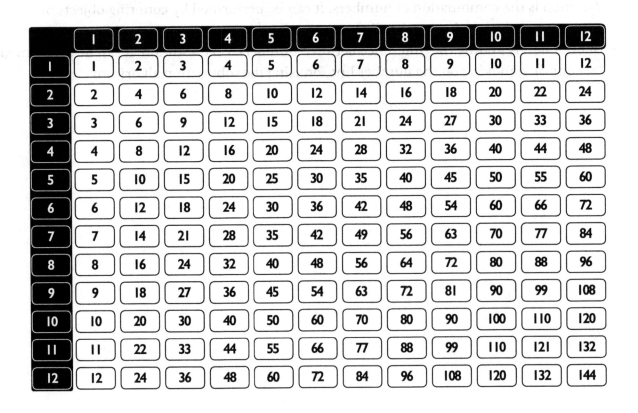

	1	2	3	4	5	6	7	8	9	10	11	12
1	1	2	3	4	5	6	7	8	9	10	11	12
2	2	4	6	8	10	12	14	16	18	20	22	24
3	3	6	9	12	15	18	21	24	27	30	33	36
4	4	8	12	16	20	24	28	32	36	40	44	48
5	5	10	15	20	25	30	35	40	45	50	55	60
6	6	12	18	24	30	36	42	48	54	60	66	72
7	7	14	21	28	35	42	49	56	63	70	77	84
8	8	16	24	32	40	48	56	64	72	80	88	96
9	9	18	27	36	45	54	63	72	81	90	99	108
10	10	20	30	40	50	60	70	80	90	100	110	120
11	11	22	33	44	55	66	77	88	99	110	121	132
12	12	24	36	48	60	72	84	96	108	120	132	144

When dealing with large numbers, the multiplication algorithm is more practical than memorization. The ability to quickly recall the products in the multiplication table is nevertheless crucial to using this algorithm.

STEP BY STEP

Step 1. Stack the two factors, vertically aligning the digits in each place.

Step 2. Draw a multiplication symbol (×) to the left of the bottom number and draw a horizontal line below the stack.

Step 3. Begin with the ones digit in the lower factor. Multiply it with the ones digit from the top factor.

Step 4. If the product from Step 3 is less than 10, write it in the same column below the horizontal line. Otherwise, write the first (ones) digit below the line and carry the second (tens) digit to the top of the next column.

Step 5. Perform Step 4 for each digit in the top factor, adding any carry digit to the result. If an extra carry digit appears at the end, write it as the leftmost digit in the product.

Step 6. Going right to left, repeat Steps 3–4 for the other places in the bottom factor, starting a new line in each case.

Step 7. Add the numbers below the line to get the product.

Example

A certain type of screw comes in packs of 35. If a contractor orders 52 packs, how many screws does he receive?

A. 2   B. 57   C. 245   D. 1,820

The correct answer is **D**. The first step is to convert this problem to a math expression. The goal is to find how many screws the contractor receives if he orders 52 packs of 35 each. The expression would be 52×35 (or 35×52). Carefully follow the multiplication algorithm (see below).

$$
\begin{array}{c}
52 \\
\times\ 35 \\
\hline
\end{array}
\rightarrow
\begin{array}{c}
{}^{1}2 \\
52 \\
\times\ 35 \\
\hline
0
\end{array}
\rightarrow
\begin{array}{c}
{}^{1}2 \\
52 \\
\times\ 35 \\
\hline
260
\end{array}
\rightarrow
\begin{array}{c}
{}^{1}2 \\
52 \\
\times\ 35 \\
\hline
260 \\
6
\end{array}
\rightarrow
\begin{array}{c}
{}^{1}{}^{1}2 \\
52 \\
\times\ 35 \\
\hline
260 \\
56
\end{array}
\rightarrow
\begin{array}{c}
{}^{1}{}^{1}2 \\
52 \\
\times\ 35 \\
\hline
260 \\
156
\end{array}
\rightarrow
\begin{array}{c}
{}^{1}{}^{1}2 \\
52 \\
\times\ 35 \\
\hline
260 \\
+\ 156 \\
\hline
1,820
\end{array}
$$

KEY POINT

As with addition, the order of numbers in a multiplication expression is irrelevant to the product. For example, $6 \times 9 = 9 \times 6$.

Division

Division is the inverse of multiplication, like subtraction is the inverse of addition. Whereas multiplication asks how many individuals are in 8 groups of 9 ($8 \times 9 = 72$), for example, division asks how many groups of 8 (or 9) are in 72. Division expressions use either the / or ÷ symbol. Therefore, $72 \div 9$ means: How many groups of 9 are in 72, or how many times does 9 go into 72? Thinking about the meaning of multiplication shows that $72 \div 9 = 8$ and $72 \div 8 = 9$. In the expression $72 \div 8 = 9$, 72 is the **dividend,** 8 is the **divisor,** and 9 is the **quotient.**

When the dividend is unevenly divisible by the divisor (e.g., $5 \div 2$), calculating the quotient with a **remainder** can be convenient. The quotient in this case is the maximum number of times the divisor goes into the dividend plus how much of the dividend is left over. To express the remainder, use an R. For example, the quotient of $5 \div 2$ is 2R1 because 2 goes into 5 twice with 1 left over.

Knowing the multiplication table allows quick evaluation of simple whole-number division. For larger numbers, the division algorithm enables evaluation by hand.

Unlike multiplication—but like subtraction—the order of the numbers in a division expression is important. Generally, changing the order changes the quotient.

STEP BY STEP	
Step 1.	Write the divisor and then the dividend on a single line.
Step 2.	Draw a vertical line between them, connecting to a horizontal line over the dividend.
Step 3.	If the divisor is smaller than the leftmost digit of the dividend, perform the remainder division and write the quotient (without the remainder) above that digit. If the divisor is larger than the leftmost digit, use the first two digits (or however many are necessary) until the number is greater than the divisor. Write the quotient over the rightmost digit in that number.
Step 4.	Multiply the quotient digit by the divisor and write it under the dividend, vertically aligning the ones digit of the product with the quotient digit.
Step 5.	Subtract the product from the digits above it.
Step 6.	Bring down the next digit from the quotient.
Step 7.	Perform Steps 3–6, using the most recent difference as the quotient.
Step 8.	Write the remainder next to the quotient.

Example

Evaluate the expression 468 ÷ 26.

    A. 18   B. 18R2   C. 494   D. 12,168

The correct answer is **A.** Carefully follow the division algorithm. In this case, the answer has no remainder.

$$26\overline{)468} \rightarrow \begin{array}{r} 1 \\ 26\overline{)468} \\ 26 \end{array} \rightarrow \begin{array}{r} 1 \\ 26\overline{)468} \\ -26 \\ \hline 20 \end{array} \rightarrow \begin{array}{r} 1 \\ 26\overline{)468} \\ -26\downarrow \\ \hline 208 \end{array} \rightarrow \begin{array}{r} 18 \\ 26\overline{)468} \\ -26\downarrow \\ \hline 208 \\ -208 \\ \hline 0 \end{array}$$

KEY POINT

Division by 0 is undefined. If it appears in an expression, something is wrong.

Signed Multiplication and Division

Multiplying and dividing signed numbers is simpler than adding and subtracting them because it only requires remembering two simple rules. First, if the two numbers have the same sign, their product or quotient is positive. Second, if they have different signs, their product or quotient is negative.

As a result, negative numbers can be multiplied or divided as if they are positive. Just keep track of the sign separately for the product or quotient. Note that negative numbers are sometimes written in parentheses to avoid the appearance of subtraction.

For Example:

$5 \times (-3) = -15$

$(-8) \times (-8) = 64$

$(-12) \div 3 = -4$

$(-100) \div (-25) = 4$

Example

Evaluate the expression (−7) × (−9).

    A. −63   B. −16   C. 16   D. 63

The correct answer is **D.** Because both factors are negative, the product will be positive. Because the product of 7 and 9 is 63, the product of −7 and −9 is also 63.

Order of Operations

By default, math expressions work like most Western languages: they should be read and evaluated from left to right. However, some operations take precedence over others, which can change this default evaluation. Following this **order of operations** is critical. The mnemonic **PEMDAS** (Please Excuse My Dear Aunt Sally) helps in remembering how to evaluate an expression with multiple operations.

> **STEP BY STEP**
>
> **P.** Evaluate operations in parentheses (or braces/brackets). If the expression has parentheses within parentheses, begin with the innermost ones.
>
> **E.** Evaluate exponential operations. (For expressions without exponents, ignore this step.)
>
> **MD.** Perform all multiplication and division operations, going through the expression from left to right.
>
> **AS.** Perform all addition and subtraction operations, going through the expression from left to right.

Because the order of numbers in multiplication and addition does not affect the result, the PEMDAS procedure only requires going from left to right when dividing or subtracting. At those points, going in the correct direction is critical to getting the right answer.

Calculators that can handle a series of numbers at once automatically evaluate an expression according to the order of operations. When available, calculators are a good way to check the results.

> **BE CAREFUL!**
>
> When evaluating an expression like $4 - 3 + 2 \times 5$, remember to go from left to right when adding and subtracting or when multiplying and dividing. The first step in this case (MD) yields $4 - 3 + 10$. Avoid the temptation to add first in the next step; instead, go from left to right. The result is $1 + 10 = 11$, *not* $4 - 13 = -9$.

Example

Evaluate the expression $8 \times (3 + 6) \div 3 - 2 + 5$.

A. 13   B. 17   C. 27   D. 77

The correct answer is **C**. Use the PEMDAS mnemonic. Start with parentheses. Then, do multiplication/division from left to right. Finally, do addition/subtraction from left to right.

$8 \times (3 + 6) \div 3 - 2 + 5$

$8 \times 9 \div 3 - 2 + 5$

$72 \div 3 - 2 + 5$

24−2 + 5

22 + 5

27

Working with Exponents

When following the order of operations, the second operation to evaluate within an expression are the exponents. Exponents imply an expression of repeated multiplication, otherwise known as a power. The exponent is a superscripted number for the number of times the base is multiplied. For example, 6^2 is the same as 6 times 6, or 36.

It is important to understand that any base to a power of 0 will equal 1. Otherwise written as a rule $n^0 = 1$. For example, $3^0 = 1$.

When exponents are written as negative values, these expressions are considered fractions or decimals. The value will be one portion of the base number and the exponent as a positive number. For example, $2^{-2} = \frac{1}{2^2} = \frac{1}{4}$.

Negative exponents are commonly used to represent small decimal numbers with a base of 10. For example, the expression 10^{-3} is equivalent to $\frac{1}{1000}$ or 0.001.

These rules are summarized in the chart below.

Property	Definition	Examples
Zero Exponent Rule	$a^0 = 1$	$64^0 = 1$ $y^0 = 1$
Negative Exponent Rule	$a^{-m} = \frac{1}{a^m}$	$3^{-3} = \frac{1}{3^3} = \frac{1}{27}$ $\frac{1}{x^{-3}} = x^3$

Let's Review!

- The multiplication table is important to memorize for both multiplying and dividing small whole numbers (up to about 12).
- Multiplication and division of large numbers by hand typically requires the multiplication and division algorithms.
- Multiplying and dividing signed numbers follows two simple rules: If the numbers have the same sign, the product or quotient is positive. If they have different signs, the product or quotient is negative.
- When evaluating expressions with several operations, carefully follow the order of operations; PEMDAS is a helpful mnemonic.

FACTORS AND MULTIPLES

This lesson shows the relationship between factors and multiples of a number. In addition, it introduces prime and composite numbers and demonstrates how to use prime factorization to determine all the factors of a number.

Factors of a Number

Multiplication converts two or more factors into a product. A given number, however, may be the product of more than one combination of factors; for example, 12 is the product of 3 and 4 and the product of 2 and 6. Limiting consideration to the set of whole numbers, a **factor of a number** (call it x) is a whole number whose product with any other whole number is equal to x. For instance, 2 is a factor of 12 because $12 \div 2$ is a whole number (6). Another way of expressing it is that 2 is a factor of 12 because 12 is **divisible** by 2.

> **BE CAREFUL!**
>
> The term *factor* can mean any number being multiplied by another number, or it can mean a number by which another number is divisible. The two uses are related but slightly different. The context will generally clarify which meaning applies.

A whole number always has at least two factors: 1 and itself. That is, for any whole number y, $1 \times y = y$. To test whether one number is a factor of a second number, divide the second by the first. If the quotient is whole, it is a factor. If the quotient is not whole (or it has a remainder), it is not a factor.

Example

Which number is not a factor of 54?

A. 1   B. 2   C. 4   D. 6

The correct answer is **C**. A number is a factor of another number if the latter is divisible by the former. The number 54 is divisible by 1 because $54 \times 1 = 54$, and it is divisible by 2 because $27 \times 2 = 54$. Also, $6 \times 9 = 54$. But $54 \div 4 = 13.5$ (or 13R2). Therefore, 4 is not a factor.

Multiples of a Number

Multiples of a number are related to factors of a number. A **multiple of a number** is that number's product with some integer. For example, if a hardware store sells a type of screw that only comes in packs of 20, customers must buy these screws in *multiples* of 20: that is, 20, 40, 60, 80, and so on. (Technically, 0 is also a multiple.) These numbers are equal to 20×1, 20×2, 20×3, 20×4, and so on. Similarly, measurements in feet represent multiples of 12 inches. A (whole-number) measurement in feet would be equivalent to 12 inches, 24 inches, 36 inches, and so on.

When counting by twos or threes, multiples are used. But because the multiples of a number are the product of that number with the integers, multiples can also be negative. For the number 2, the multiples are the set {…, −6, −4, −2, 0, 2, 4, 6,…}, where the ellipsis dots indicate that the set continues the pattern indefinitely in both directions. Also, the number can be any real number: the multiples of π (approximately 3.14) are {…, −3π, −2π, −1π, 0, 1π, 2π, 3π,…}. Note that the notation 2π, for example, means 2 × π.

The positive multiples (along with 0) of a whole number are all numbers for which that whole number is a factor. For instance, the positive multiples of 5 are 0, 5, 10, 15, 20, 25, 30, and so on. That full set contains all (whole) numbers for which 5 is a factor. Thus, one number is a multiple of a second number if the second number is a factor of the first.

Example

If a landowner subdivides a parcel of property into multiples of 7 acres, how many acres can a buyer purchase?

A. 1   B. 15   C. 29   D. 42

The correct answer is **D.** Because the landowner subdivides the property into multiples of 7 acres, a buyer must choose an acreage from the list 7 acres, 14 acres, 21 acres, and so on. That list includes 42 acres. Another way to solve the problem is to find which answer is divisible by 7 (that is, which number has 7 as a factor).

Prime and Composite Numbers

For some real-world applications, such as cryptography, factors and multiples play an important role. One important way to classify whole numbers is by whether they are prime or composite. A **prime** number is any whole (or natural) number greater than 1 that has only itself and 1 as factors. The smallest example is 2: because 2 only has 1 and 2 as factors, it is prime. **Composite** numbers have at least one factor other than 1 and themselves. The smallest composite number is 4: in addition to 1 and 4, it has 2 as a factor.

Determining whether a number is prime can be extremely difficult—hence its value in cryptography. One simple test that works for some numbers is to check whether the number is even or odd. An **even number** is divisible by 2; an **odd number** is not. To determine whether a number is even or odd, look at the last (rightmost) digit.

> **BE CAREFUL!**
>
> Avoid the temptation to call 1 a prime number. Although it only has itself and 1 as factors, those factors are the same number. Hence, 1 is fundamentally different from the prime numbers, which start at 2.

If that digit is even (0, 2, 4, 6, or 8), the number is even. Otherwise, it is odd. Another simple test works for multiples of 3. Add all the digits in the number. If the sum is divisible by 3, the original number is also divisible by 3. This rule can be successively applied multiple times until the sum of digits is manageable. That number is then composite.

Example

Which number is prime?

   A. 6   B. 16   C. 61   D. 116

The correct answer is **C**. When applicable, the easiest way to identify a number greater than 2 as composite rather than prime is to check whether it is even. All even numbers greater than 2 are composite. By elimination, 61 is prime.

Prime Factorization

Determining whether a number is prime, even for relatively small numbers (less than 100), can be difficult. One tool that can help both solve this problem and identify all factors of a number is **prime factorization**. One way to do prime factorization is to make a **factor tree.**

The procedure below demonstrates the process.

STEP BY STEP

Step 1. Write the number you want to factor.

Step 2. If the number is prime, stop. Otherwise, go to Step 3.

Step 3. Find any two factors of the number and write them on the line below the number.

Step 4. "Connect" the factors and the number using line segments. The result will look somewhat like an inverted tree, particularly as the process continues.

Step 5. Repeat Steps 2–4 for all composite factors in the tree.

The numbers in the factor tree are either "branches" (if they are connected downward to other numbers) or "leaves" (if they have no further downward connections). The leaves constitute all the prime factors of the original number: when multiplied together, their product is that number. Moreover, any product of two or more of the leaves is a factor of the original number. Thus, using prime factorization helps find any and all factors of a number, although the process can be tedious when performed by hand (particularly for large numbers). Below is a factor tree for the number 96. All the leaves are circled for emphasis.

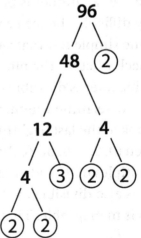

Example

Which list includes all the unique prime factors of 84?

   A. 2, 3, 7   .   C. 3, 5, 7

   B. 3, 4, 7   D. 1, 2, 3, 7

$2 \times 2 \times 3 \times 2 \times 2 \times 2 = 96$

The correct answer is **A**. One approach is to find the prime factorization of 84. The factor tree shows that 84 = 2 × 2 × 3 × 7. Alternatively, note that answer D includes 1, which is not prime. Answer B includes 4, which is a composite number. Since answer C includes 5, which is not a factor of 84, the only possible answer is A.

Let's Review!

- A whole number is divisible by all of its factors, which are also whole numbers by definition.
- Multiples of a number are all possible products of that number and the integers.
- A prime number is a whole number greater than 1 that has no factors other than itself and 1.
- A composite number is a whole number greater than 1 that is not prime (that is, it has factors other than itself and 1).
- Even numbers are divisible by 2; odd numbers are not.
- Prime factorization yields all the prime factors of a number. The factor-tree method is one way to determine prime factorization.

STANDARDS OF MEASURE

This lesson discusses the conversion within and between the standard system and the metric system and between 12-hour clock time and military time.

Length Conversions

The basic units of measure of length in the standard measurement system are inches, feet, yards, and miles. There are 12 inches (in.) in 1 foot (ft.), 3 feet (ft.) in 1 yard (yd.), and 5,280 feet (ft.) in 1 mile (mi.).

The basic unit of measure of metric length is meters. There are 1,000 millimeters (mm), 100 centimeters (cm), and 10 decimeters (dm) in 1 meter (m). There are 10 meters (m) in 1 dekameter (dam), 100 meters (m) in 1 hectometer (hm), and 1,000 meters (m) in 1 kilometer (km).

BE CAREFUL!
There are some cases where multiple conversions must be performed to determine the correct units.

To convert from one unit to the other, multiply by the appropriate factor.

Examples

1. **Convert 27 inches to feet.**

   A. 2 feet   B. 2.25 feet   C. 3 feet   D. 3.25 feet

   The correct answer is **B**. The correct solution is 2.25 feet. $27 \text{ in} \times \frac{1 \text{ ft}}{12 \text{ in}} = \frac{27}{12} = 2.25$ ft.

2. **Convert 67 millimeters to centimeters.**

   A. 0.0067 centimeters   C. 0.67 centimeters

   B. 0.067 centimeters   D. 6.7 centimeters

   The correct answer is **D**. The correct solution is 6.7 centimeters. $67 \text{ mm} \times \frac{1 \text{ cm}}{10 \text{ mm}} = \frac{67}{10} = 6.7$ cm.

Volume and Weight Conversions

There are volume conversion factors for standard and metric volumes.

The volume conversions for standard volume are shown in the table.

Measurement	Conversion
Pints (pt.) and fluid ounces (fl. oz.)	1 pint equals 16 fluid ounces
Quarts (qt.) and pints (pt.)	1 quart equals 2 pints
Quarts (qt.) and gallons (gal.)	1 gallon equals 4 quarts

The basic unit of volume for the metric system is liters. There are 1,000 milliliters (mL) in 1 liter (L) and 1,000 liters (L) in 1 kiloliter (kL).

There are weight conversion factors for standard and metric weights.

The basic unit of weight for the standard measurement system is pounds. There are

16 ounces (oz.) in 1 pound (lb.) and

2,000 pounds (lb.) in 1 ton (T).

The basic unit of weight for the metric system is grams.

KEEP IN MIND
The conversions within the metric system are multiples of 10.

Measurement	Conversion
Milligrams (mg) and grams (g)	1,000 milligrams equals 1 gram
Centigrams (cg) and grams (g)	100 centigrams equals 1 gram
Kilograms (kg) and grams (g)	1 kilogram equals 1,000 grams
Metric tons (t) and kilograms (kg)	1 metric ton equals 1,000 kilograms

Examples

1. **Convert 8 gallons to pints.**

   A. 1 pint   B. 4 pints   C. 16 pints   D. 64 pints

   The correct answer is **D**. The correct solution is 64 pints. $8 \text{ gal} \times \frac{4 \text{ qt}}{1 \text{ gal}} \times \frac{2 \text{ pt}}{1 \text{ qt}} = 64 \text{ pt}$.

2. **Convert 7.5 liters to milliliters.**

   A. 75 ml   B. 750 ml   C. 7,500 ml   D. 75,000 m

   The correct answer is **C**. The correct solution is 7,500 milliliters. $7.5 \text{ L} \times \frac{1,000 \text{ mL}}{1 \text{ L}} = 7,500 \text{ mL}$.

3. **Convert 12.5 pounds to ounces.**

   A. 142 ounces   B. 150 ounces   C. 192 ounces   D. 200 ounces

   The correct answer is **D**. The correct solution is 200 ounces. $12.5 \text{ lb} \times \frac{16 \text{ oz}}{1 \text{ lb}} = 200 \text{ oz}$.

4. **Convert 84 grams to centigrams.**

   A. 0.84 cg   B. 8.4 cg   C. 840 cg   D. 8,400 cg

   The correct answer is **D**. The correct solution is 8,400 centigrams. $84 \text{ g} \times \frac{100 \text{ cg}}{1 \text{ g}} = 8,400 \text{ cg}$.

Conversions between Standard and Metric Systems

The table shows the common conversions of length, volume, and weight between the standard and metric systems.

Measurement	Conversion
Centimeters (cm) and inches (in.)	2.54 centimeters equals 1 inch
Meters (m) and feet (ft.)	1 meter equals 3.28 feet
Kilometers (km) and miles (mi.)	1.61 kilometers equals 1 mile
Quarts (qt.) and liters (L)	1.06 quarts equals 1 liter
Liters (L) and gallons (gal.)	3.79 liters equals 1 gallon
Grams (g) and ounces (oz.)	28.3 grams equals 1 ounce
Kilograms (kg) and pounds (lb.)	1 kilogram equals 2.2 pounds

There are many additional conversion factors, but this lesson uses only the common ones. Most factors have been rounded to the nearest hundredth for accuracy.

STEP BY STEP

Step 1. Choose the appropriate conversion factor within each system, if necessary.

Step 2. Choose the appropriate conversion factor from the standard and metric conversion.

Step 3. Multiply and simplify to the nearest hundredth.

Examples

1. **Convert 12 inches to centimeters.**

   A. 4.72 centimeters
   B. 14.54 centimeters
   C. 28.36 centimeters
   D. 30.48 centimeters

   The correct answer is **D**. The correct solution is 30.48 centimeters. $12 \text{ in} \times \frac{2.54 \text{ cm}}{1 \text{ in}} = 30.48$ cm.

2. **Convert 8 kilometers to feet.**

   A. 13,118.01 feet
   B. 26,236.02 feet
   C. 34,003.20 feet
   D. 68,006.40 feet

   The correct answer is **B**. The correct solution is 26,236.02 feet. $8 \text{ km} \times \frac{1 \text{ mi}}{1.61 \text{ km}} \times \frac{5,280 \text{ ft}}{1 \text{ mi}} = \frac{42,240}{1.61} = 26,236.02$ ft.

3. **Convert 2 gallons to milliliters.**

   A. 527 milliliters
   B. 758 milliliters
   C. 5,270 milliliters
   D. 7,580 milliliters

   The correct answer is **D**. The correct solution is 7,580 milliliters.
   $2 \text{ gal} \times \frac{3.79 \text{ L}}{1 \text{ gal}} \times \frac{1,000 \text{ mL}}{1 \text{ L}} = 7,580$ mL.

4. **Convert 16 kilograms to pounds.**

   A. 7.27 pounds   B. 18.2 pounds   C. 19.27 pounds   D. 35.2 pounds

   The correct answer is **D**. The correct solution is 35.2 pounds. $16 \text{ kg} \times \frac{2.2 \text{ lb}}{1 \text{ kg}} = 35.2$ lb.

Time Conversions

Two ways to keep time are 12-hour clock time using a.m. and p.m. and military time based on a 24-hour clock. Keep these three key points in mind:

> **KEEP IN MIND**
> Midnight (12:00 a.m.) is 2400 or 0000 in military time.

- The hours from 1:00 a.m. to 12:59 p.m. are the same in both methods. For example, 9:15 a.m. in 12-hour clock time is 0915 in military time.
- From 1:00 p.m. to 11:59 p.m., add 12 hours to obtain military time. For example, 4:07 p.m. in 12-hour clock time is 1607 in military time.
- From 12:01 a.m. to 12:59 a.m. in 12-hour clock time, military time is from 0001 to 0059.

Example

Identify 9:27 p.m. in military time.

   A. 0927   B. 1927   C. 2127   D. 2427

The correct answer is **C**. The correct solution is 2127. Add 1200 to the time, 1200 + 927 = 2127.

Let's Review!

- To convert from one unit to another, choose the appropriate conversion factors.
- In many cases, it is necessary to use multiple conversion factors.

	Metric	English
Volume	1 cubic centimeter = 1 milliliter	30 milliliters = 1 ounce
	1,000 milliliters = 1 liter	8 ounces = 1 cup
		2 cups = 1 pint
		2 pints = 1 quart
		4 quarts = 1 gallon
Weight	1,000 milligrams = 1 gram	16 ounces = 1 pound
	100 centigrams = 1 gram	2.2 pounds = 1 kilogram
	1,000 grams = 1 kilogram	2,000 pounds = 1 ton
	1,000 kilograms = 1 ton	
Distance	10 millimeters = 1 centimeter	12 inches = 1 foot
	2.54 centimeters = 1 inch	3 feet = 1 yard
	100 centimeters = 1 meter	5, 280 feet = 1,760 yards = 1 mile
	1,000 meters = 1 kilometer	

CHAPTER 18 NUMBER AND QUANTITY PRACTICE QUIZ

1. Evaluate the expression 8 – 27.

   A. –35

   B. –19

   C. 0

   D. 19

2. Evaluate the expression 102 + 3 + 84 + 27.

   A. 105

   B. 216

   C. 250

   D. 513

3. How much change should a customer expect if she is buying a $53 item and hands the cashier two $50 bills?

   A. $3

   B. $47

   C. $57

   D. $100

4. When dealing with a series of multiplication and division operations, which is the correct approach to evaluating them?

   A. Evaluate all division operations first.

   B. Evaluate the expression from left to right.

   C. Evaluate all multiplication operations first.

   D. None of the above.

5. Evaluate the expression 28 × 43.

   A. 71

   B. 196

   C. 1,204

   D. 1,960

6. Evaluate the expression 3 + 1 – 5 + 2 – 6.

   A. –9

   B. –5

   C. 0

   D. 17

7. Which number is a factor of 128?

   A. 3

   B. 6

   C. 12

   D. 16

8. How many prime factors does 42 have?

   A. 1

   B. 2

   C. 3

   D. 4

9. If a factor tree for a prime factorization has four leaves—3, 2, 5, and 7—what is the number being factored?

   A. 7

   B. 5

   C. 210

   D. Not enough information

10. Convert 16,000 ounces to tons.

    A. 0.5 ton

    B. 1 ton

    C. 1.5 tons

    D. 2 tons

11. Convert 99 meters to kilometers.

    A. 0.0099 kilometers

    B. 0.099 kilometers

    C. 0.9 centimeters

    D. 9.9 centimeters

12. Identify 12:45 a.m. in military time.

    A. 0045

    B. 0145

    C. 1245

    D. 1345

CHAPTER 18 NUMBER AND QUANTITY PRACTICE QUIZ – ANSWER KEY

1. B. The correct solution is −19. Because the subtraction algorithm does not apply directly in this case (the first number is smaller than the second), first use the rule that $x - y = -(y - x)$. So, $8 - 27 = -(27 - 8)$. Applying the algorithm to $27 - 8$ yields 19, then $-(27 - 8) = -19$. **See Lesson: Basic Addition and Subtraction.**

2. B. The correct solution is 216. Use the addition algorithm. Add the numbers two at a time or all at once. The latter approach will involve two carry digits. **See Lesson: Basic Addition and Subtraction.**

3. B. The correct solution is $47. The customer gives the cashier $100, which is the sum of $50 and $50. To find out how much change she receives, calculate the difference between $100 and $53, which is $47. **See Lesson: Basic Addition and Subtraction.**

4. B. Multiplication and division have equivalent priority in the order of operations. In this case, the expression must be evaluated from left to right. **See Lesson: Basic Multiplication and Division.**

5. C. Use the multiplication algorithm. It involves adding 84 and 1,120 to get the product of 1,204. **See Lesson: Basic Multiplication and Division.**

6. B. This expression only involves addition and subtraction, but its evaluation must go from left to right. **See Lesson: Basic Multiplication and Division.**

$$3 + 1 - 5 + 2 - 6$$
$$4 - 5 + 2 - 6$$
$$(-1) + 2 - 6$$
$$1 - 6$$
$$-5$$

7. D. To determine whether a number is a factor of another number, divide the second number by the first number. If the quotient is whole, the first number is a factor. In this case, 128 is only divisible by 16. **See Lesson: Factors and Multiples.**

8. C. The prime factorization—for example, using a factor tree—shows that 42 has the prime factors 2, 3, and 7 because $2 \times 3 \times 7 = 42$. **See Lesson: Factors and Multiples.**

9. C. The number being factored in a prime factorization is the product of all its prime factors. The leaves in a factor tree are these prime factors. Therefore, the number is their product. In this case, it is $3 \times 2 \times 5 \times 7 = 210$. **See Lesson: Factors and Multiples.**

10. **A.** The correct solution is 0.5 ton. $16{,}000\ oz \times \frac{1\ lb}{16\ oz} \times \frac{1\ T}{2{,}000\ lb} = \frac{16{,}000}{32{,}000} = 0.5\ T$. **See Lesson: Standards of Measure.**

11. **B.** The correct solution is 0.099 kilometers. $99\ m \times \frac{1\ km}{1{,}000\ m} = \frac{99}{1{,}000} = 0.099\ km$. **See Lesson: Standards of Measure.**

12. **A.** The correct solution is 0045. Subtract 1200 from the time, 1245 − 1200 = 0045. **See Lesson: Standards of Measure.**

CHAPTER 19 ALGEBRA

DECIMALS AND FRACTIONS

This lesson introduces the basics of decimals and fractions. It also demonstrates changing decimals to fractions, changing fractions to decimals, and converting between fractions, decimals, and percentages.

Introduction to Fractions

A fraction represents part of a whole number. The top number of a fraction is the **numerator,** and the bottom number of a fraction is the **denominator.** The numerator is smaller than the denominator for a **proper fraction.** The numerator is larger than the denominator for an **improper fraction.**

Proper Fractions	Improper Fractions
$\frac{2}{5}$	$\frac{5}{2}$
$\frac{7}{12}$	$\frac{12}{7}$
$\frac{19}{20}$	$\frac{20}{19}$

An improper fraction can be changed to a **mixed number.** A mixed number is a whole number and a proper fraction. To write an improper fraction as a mixed number, divide the denominator into the numerator. The result is the whole number.

KEEP IN MIND

When comparing fractions, the denominators of the fractions must be the same.

The remainder is the numerator of the proper fraction, and the value of the denominator does not change. For example, $\frac{5}{2}$ is $2\frac{1}{2}$ because 2 goes into 5 twice with a remainder of 1. To write an improper fraction as a mixed number, multiply the whole number by the denominator and add the result to the numerator. The results become the new numerator. For example, $2\frac{1}{2}$ is $\frac{5}{2}$ because 2 times 2 plus 1 is 5 for the new numerator.

When comparing fractions, the denominators must be the same. Then, look at the numerator to determine which fraction is larger. If the fractions have different denominators, then a **least common denominator** must be found. This number is the smallest number that can be divided evenly into the denominators of all fractions being compared.

To determine the largest fraction from the group $\frac{1}{3}, \frac{3}{5}, \frac{2}{3}, \frac{2}{5}$ the first step is to find a common denominator. In this case, the least common denominator is 15 because 3 times 5 and 5 times 3 is 15. The second step is to convert the fractions to a denominator of 15.

The fractions with a denominator of 3 have the numerator and denominator multiplied by 5, and the fractions with a denominator of 5 have the numerator and denominator multiplied by 3, as shown below:

$$\frac{1}{3} \times \frac{5}{5} = \frac{5}{15}, \frac{3}{5} \times \frac{3}{3} = \frac{9}{15}, \frac{2}{3} \times \frac{5}{5} = \frac{10}{15}, \frac{2}{5} \times \frac{3}{3} = \frac{6}{15}$$

Now, the numerators can be compared. The largest fraction is $\frac{2}{3}$ because it has a numerator of 10 after finding the common denominator.

Examples

1. **Which fraction is the least?**

   A. $\frac{3}{5}$ B. $\frac{3}{4}$ C. $\frac{1}{5}$ D. $\frac{1}{4}$

   The correct answer is **C**. The correct solution is $\frac{1}{5}$ because it has the smallest numerator compared to the other fractions with the same denominator. The fractions with a common denominator of 20 are $\frac{3}{5} = \frac{12}{20}, \frac{3}{4} = \frac{15}{20}, \frac{1}{5} = \frac{4}{20}, \frac{1}{4} = \frac{5}{20}$.

2. **Which fraction is the greatest?**

   A. $\frac{5}{6}$ B. $\frac{1}{2}$ C. $\frac{2}{3}$ D. $\frac{1}{6}$

   The correct answer is **A**. The correct solution is $\frac{5}{6}$ because it has the largest numerator compared to the other fractions with the same denominator. The fractions with a common denominator of 6 are $\frac{5}{6} = \frac{5}{6}, \frac{1}{2} = \frac{3}{6}, \frac{2}{3} = \frac{4}{6}, \frac{1}{6} = \frac{1}{6}$.

Introduction to Decimals

A **decimal** is a number that expresses part of a whole. Decimals show a portion of a number after a decimal point. Each number to the left and right of the decimal point has a specific place value. Identify the place values for 645.3207.

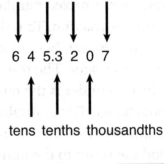

6 4 5.3 2 0 7

tens tenths thousandths

When comparing decimals, compare the numbers in the same place value. For example, determine the greatest decimal from the group 0.4, 0.41, 0.39, and 0.37. In these numbers, there is a value to the right of the decimal point. Comparing the tenths places, the numbers with 4 tenths (0.4 and 0.41) are greater than the numbers with three tenths (0.39 and 0.37).

0.4

0.41

0.39

0.37

KEEP IN MIND

When comparing decimals, compare the place value where the numbers are different.

Then, compare the hundredths in the 4 tenths numbers. The value of 0.41 is greater because there is a 1 in the hundredths place versus a 0 in the hundredths place.

Here is another example: determine the least decimal of the group 5.23, 5.32, 5.13, and 5.31. In this group, the ones value is 5 for all numbers. Then, comparing the tenths values, 5.13 is the smallest number because it is the only value with 1 tenth.

Examples

1. **Which decimal is the greatest?**

   A. 0.07   B. 0.007   C. 0.7   D. 0.0007

   The correct answer is **C**. The solution is 0.7 because it has the largest place value in the tenths.

2. **Which decimal is the least?**

   A. 0.0413   B. 0.0713   C. 0.0513   D. 0.0613

   The correct answer is **A**. The correct solution is 0.0413 because it has the smallest place value in the hundredths place.

0.4

0.41

5.23

5.32

5.13

5.31

HELPFUL TIPS

The multiplication and division algorithms can be used, even with decimal numbers. With the multiplication algorithm, count the total number of place values to the right the decimal must move in the multiplier numbers. Simply place the decimal the total number of place values to the *left* in the sum. For example, 0.5 × 0.5, the decimal must move one place value to the *right* for each number and a total of two place values. Place the decimal two place values to the *left* in the answer. After completing the algorithm, 25 becomes 0.25 from the decimal.

For the division algorithm, move the decimal to the right as many place values as needed to make the divisor and dividend whole numbers. The place value should be moved the same amount of times in both numbers. For example, 180 ÷ 0.2, the divisor must have the place value moved one place value to the right to become 2. Move the decimal from 180 (180.0) the same amount, to complete long division with whole numbers: 1800 ÷ 2 = 900, which is equal to 180 ÷ 0.2 = 900.

Changing Decimals and Fractions

Three steps change a decimal to a fraction.

> **STEP BY STEP**
>
> **Step 1.** Write the decimal divided by 1 with the decimal as the numerator and 1 as the denominator.
>
> **Step 2.** Multiply the numerator and denominator by 10 for every number after the decimal point. (For example, if there is 1 decimal place, multiply by 10. If there are 2 decimal places, multiply by 100).
>
> **Step 3.** Reduce the fraction completely.

To change the decimal 0.37 to a fraction, start by writing the decimal as a fraction with a denominator of one, $\frac{0.37}{1}$. Because there are two decimal places, multiply the numerator and denominator by 100, $\frac{0.37 \times 100}{1 \times 100} = \frac{37}{100}$. The fraction does not reduce, so $\frac{37}{100}$ is 0.37 in fraction form.

Similarly, to change the decimal 2.4 to a fraction start by writing the decimal as a fraction with a denominator of one, $\frac{0.4}{1}$, and ignore the whole number. Because there is one decimal place, multiply the numerator and denominator by 10, $\frac{0.4 \times 10}{1 \times 10} = \frac{4}{10}$. The fraction does reduce: $2\frac{4}{10} = 2\frac{2}{5}$ is 2.4 in fraction form.

The decimal $0.\overline{3}$ as a fraction is $\frac{0.\overline{3}}{1}$. In the case of a repeating decimal, let $n = 0.\overline{3}$ and $10n = 3.\overline{3}$. Then, $10n - n = 3.\overline{3} - 0.\overline{3}$, resulting in $9n = 3$ and solution of $n = \frac{3}{9} = \frac{1}{3}$. The decimal $0.\overline{3}$ is $\frac{1}{3}$ as a fraction.

Examples

1. **Change 0.38 to a fraction. Simplify completely.**

   A. $\frac{3}{10}$ B. $\frac{9}{25}$ C. $\frac{19}{50}$ D. $\frac{2}{5}$

   The correct answer is **C**. The correct solution is $\frac{19}{50}$ because $\frac{0.38}{1} = \frac{38}{100} = \frac{19}{50}$.

2. **Change 1.$\overline{1}$ to a fraction. Simplify completely.**

   A. $1\frac{1}{11}$ B. $1\frac{1}{9}$ C. $1\frac{1}{6}$ D. $1\frac{1}{3}$

   The correct answer is **B**. The correct solution is $1\frac{1}{9}$. Let $n = 1.\overline{1}$ and $10n = 11.\overline{1}$. Then, $10n - n = 11.\overline{1} - 1.\overline{1}$, resulting in $9n = 10$ and solution of $n = \frac{10}{9} = 1\frac{1}{9}$.

Two steps change a fraction to a decimal.

STEP BY STEP

Step 1. Divide the numerator by the denominator . Add zeros after the decimal point as needed.

Step 2. Complete the process when there is no remainder or the decimal is repeating.

To convert $\frac{1}{5}$ to a decimal, rewrite $\frac{1}{5}$ as a long division problem and add zeros after the decimal point, $1.0 \div 5$. Complete the long division and $\frac{1}{5}$ as a decimal is 0.2. The division is complete because there is no remainder.

To convert $\frac{8}{9}$ to a decimal, rewrite $\frac{8}{9}$ as a long division problem and add zeros after the decimal point, $8.00 \div 9$. Complete the long division, and $\frac{8}{9}$ as a decimal is $0.\overline{8}$. The process is complete because the decimal is complete.

To rewrite the mixed number $2\frac{3}{4}$ as a decimal, the fraction needs changed to a decimal. Rewrite $\frac{3}{4}$ as a long division problem and add zeros after the decimal point, $3.00 \div 4$. The whole number is needed for the answer and is not included in the long division. Complete the long division, and $2\frac{3}{4}$ as a decimal is 2.75.

Examples

1. **Change $\frac{9}{10}$ to a decimal. Simplify completely.**

    A. 0.75   B. 0.8   C. 0.85   D. 0.9

    The correct answer is **D**. The correct answer is 0.9 because $\frac{9}{10} = 9.0 \div 10 = 0.9$.

2. **Change $\frac{5}{6}$ to a decimal. Simplify completely.**

    A. 0.73   B. $0.7\overline{6}$ C. $0.8\overline{3}$ D. 0.86

    The correct answer is **C**. The correct answer is $0.8\overline{3}$ because $\frac{5}{6} = 5.000 \div 6 = 0.8\overline{3}$.

Convert among Fractions, Decimals, and Percentages

Fractions, decimals, and percentages can change forms, but they are equivalent values.

There are two ways to change a decimal to a percent. One way is to multiply the decimal by 100 and add a percent sign. 0.24 as a percent is 24%.

Another way is to move the decimal point two places to the right. The decimal 0.635 is 63.5% as a percent when moving the decimal point two places to the right.

Any decimal, including repeating decimals, can change to a percent. $0.\overline{3}$ as a percent is $0.\overline{3} \times 100 = 33.\overline{3}\%$.

Example

Write 0.345 as a percent.

A. 3.45%   B. 34.5%   C. 345%   D. 3450%

The correct answer is **B**. The correct answer is 34.5% because 0.345 as a percent is 34.5%.

There are two ways to change a percent to a decimal. One way is to remove the percent sign and divide the decimal by 100. For example, 73% as a decimal is 0.73.

Another way is to move the decimal point two places to the left. For example, 27.8% is 0.278 as a decimal when moving the decimal point two places to the left.

Any percent, including repeating percents, can change to a decimal. For example, $44.\overline{4}\%$ as a decimal is $44.\overline{4} \div 100 = 0.\overline{4}$.

Example

Write 131% as a decimal.

A. 0.131   B. 1.31   C. 13.1   D. 131

The correct answer is **B**. The correct answer is 1.31 because 131% as a decimal is 131 ÷ 100 = 1.31.

Two steps change a fraction to a percent.

> **STEP BY STEP**
> **Step 1.**   Divide the numerator and denominator.
> **Step 2.**   Multiply by 100 and add a percent sign.

To change the fraction $\frac{3}{5}$ to a decimal, perform long division to get 0.6. Then, multiply 0.6 by 100 and $\frac{3}{5}$ is the same as 60%.

To change the fraction $\frac{7}{8}$ to a decimal, perform long division to get 0.875. Then, multiply 0.875 by 100 and $\frac{7}{8}$ is the same as 87.5%.

Fractions that are repeating decimals can also be converted to a percent. To change the fraction $\frac{2}{3}$ to a decimal, perform long division to get $0.\overline{6}$. Then, multiply $0.\overline{6}$ by 100 and the percent is $66.\overline{6}\%$.

Example

Write $2\frac{1}{8}$ as a percent.

A. 21.2%   B. 21.25%   C. 212%   D. 212.5%

The correct answer is **D**. The correct answer is 212.5% because $2\frac{1}{8}$ as a percent is 2.125 x 100 = 212.5%.

Two steps change a percent to a fraction.

> **STEP BY STEP**
> **Step 1.** Remove the percent sign and write the value as the numerator with a denominator of 100.
> **Step 2.** Simplify the fraction.

Remove the percent sign from 45% and write as a fraction with a denominator of 100, $\frac{45}{100}$. The fraction reduces to $\frac{9}{20}$.

Remove the percent sign from 22.8% and write as a fraction with a denominator of 100, $\frac{22.8}{100}$. The fraction reduces to $\frac{228}{1000} = \frac{57}{250}$.

Repeating percentages can change to a fraction. Remove the percent sign from $16.\overline{6}\%$ and write as a fraction with a denominator of 100, $\frac{16.\overline{6}}{100}$. The fraction simplifies to $\frac{0.1\overline{6}}{1} = \frac{1}{6}$.

Example

Write 72% as a fraction.

A. $\frac{27}{50}$ B. $\frac{7}{10}$ C. $\frac{18}{25}$ D. $\frac{3}{4}$

The correct answer is **C**. The correct answer is $\frac{18}{25}$ because 72% as a fraction is $\frac{72}{100} = \frac{18}{25}$.

It is useful to see how these numbers compare on a number line when working between fractions, decimals, and percentages. Use the table and number line below as a quick reference to draw comparisons.

0	$\frac{1}{8}$	$\frac{1}{5}$	$\frac{1}{4}$	$\frac{1}{3}$	$\frac{3}{8}$	$\frac{2}{5}$	$\frac{1}{2}$	$\frac{3}{5}$	$\frac{5}{8}$	$\frac{2}{3}$	$\frac{3}{4}$	$\frac{7}{8}$	$\frac{1}{1}$
0	0.125	0.2	0.25	0.333	0.375	0.4	0.5	0.6	0.625	0.666	0.75	0.875	1.00
0	12.5%	20%	25%	33.3%	37.5%	40%	50%	60%	62.5%	66.6%	75%	87.5%	100%

Let's Review!

- A fraction is a number with a numerator and a denominator. A fraction can be written as a proper fraction, an improper fraction, or a mixed number. Changing fractions to a common denominator enables you to determine the least or greatest fraction in a group of fractions.
- A decimal is a number that expresses part of a whole. By comparing the same place values, you can find the least or greatest decimal in a group of decimals.

MULTIPLICATION AND DIVISION OF FRACTIONS

This lesson introduces how to multiply and divide fractions.

Multiplying a Fraction by a Fraction

The multiplication of fractions does not require changing any denominators like adding and subtracting fractions do. To multiply a fraction by a fraction, multiply the numerators together and multiply the denominators together. For example, $\frac{2}{3} \times \frac{4}{5}$ is $2 \times \frac{4}{3} \times 5$, which is $\frac{8}{15}$.

Sometimes, the final solution reduces. For example, $\frac{3}{5} \times \frac{1}{9} = 3 \times \frac{1}{5} \times 9 = \frac{3}{45}$. The fraction $\frac{3}{45}$ reduces to $\frac{1}{15}$.

Simplifying fractions can occur before completing the multiplication. In the previous problem, the numerator of 3 can be simplified with the denominator of 9: $\frac{\cancel{3}^{1}}{5} \times \frac{1}{\cancel{9}_{3}} = \frac{1}{15}$. This method of simplifying only occurs with the multiplication of fractions.

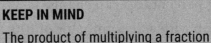

Examples

1. **Multiply $\frac{1}{2} \times \frac{3}{4}$.**

   A. $\frac{1}{4}$ B. $\frac{1}{2}$ C. $\frac{3}{8}$ D. $\frac{2}{3}$

   The correct answer is **C**. The correct solution is $\frac{3}{8}$ because $\frac{1}{2} \times \frac{3}{4} = \frac{3}{8}$.

2. **Multiply $\frac{2}{3} \times \frac{5}{6}$.**

   A. $\frac{1}{9}$ B. $\frac{5}{18}$ C. $\frac{5}{9}$ D. $\frac{7}{18}$

   The correct answer is **C**. The correct solution is $\frac{5}{9}$ because $\frac{2}{3} \times \frac{5}{6} = \frac{10}{18} = \frac{5}{9}$.

Multiply a Fraction by a Whole or Mixed Number

Multiplying a fraction by a whole or mixed number is similar to multiplying two fractions. When multiplying by a whole number, change the whole number to a fraction with a denominator of 1. Next, multiply the numerators together and the denominators together. Rewrite the final answer as a mixed number.

For example: $\frac{9}{10} \times 3 = \frac{9}{10} \times \frac{3}{1} = \frac{27}{10} = 2\frac{7}{10}$.

When multiplying a fraction by a mixed number or multiplying two mixed numbers, the process is similar.

For example, multiply $\frac{10}{11} \times 3\frac{1}{2}$. Change the mixed number to an improper fraction, $\frac{10}{11} \times \frac{7}{2}$. Multiply the numerators together and multiply the denominators together, $\frac{70}{22}$. Write the improper fraction as a mixed number, $3\frac{4}{22}$. Reduce if necessary, $3\frac{2}{11}$.

This process can also be used when multiplying a whole number by a mixed number or multiplying two mixed numbers.

Examples

1. **Multiply $4 \times \frac{5}{6}$.**

   A. $\frac{5}{24}$ 　　　　　 B. $2\frac{3}{4}$ 　　　　　 C. $3\frac{1}{3}$ 　　　　　 D. $4\frac{5}{6}$

   The correct answer is **C**. The correct solution is $3\frac{1}{3}$ because $\frac{4}{1} \times \frac{5}{6} = \frac{20}{6} = 3\frac{2}{6} = 3\frac{1}{3}$.

2. **Multiply $1\frac{1}{2} \times 1\frac{1}{6}$.**

   A. $1\frac{1}{12}$ 　　　　　 B. $1\frac{1}{4}$ 　　　　　 C. $1\frac{3}{8}$ 　　　　　 D. $1\frac{3}{4}$

   The correct answer is **D**. The correct solution is $1\frac{3}{4}$ because $\frac{3}{2} \times \frac{7}{6} = \frac{21}{12} = 1\frac{9}{12} = 1\frac{3}{4}$.

Dividing a Fraction by a Fraction

Some basic steps apply when dividing a fraction by a fraction. The information from the previous two sections is applicable to dividing fractions.

STEP BY STEP

Step 1. Leave the first fraction alone.

Step 2. Find the reciprocal of the second fraction.

Step 3. Multiply the first fraction by the reciprocal of the second fraction.

Step 4. Rewrite the fraction as a mixed number and reduce the fraction completely.

Divide, $\frac{3}{10} \div \frac{1}{2}$. Find the reciprocal of the second fraction, which is $\frac{2}{1}$.

Now, multiply the fractions, $\frac{3}{10} \times \frac{2}{1} = \frac{6}{10}$. Reduce $\frac{6}{10}$ to $\frac{3}{5}$.

Divide, $\frac{4}{5} \div \frac{3}{8}$. Find the reciprocal of the second fraction, which is $\frac{8}{3}$.

Now, multiply the fractions, $\frac{4}{5} \times \frac{8}{3} = \frac{32}{15}$. Rewrite the fraction as a mixed number, $\frac{32}{15} = 2\frac{2}{15}$.

Examples

1. **Divide** $\frac{1}{2} \div \frac{5}{6}$.

    A. $\frac{5}{12}$ B. $\frac{3}{5}$ C. $\frac{5}{6}$ D. $1\frac{2}{3}$

    The correct answer is **B**. The correct solution is $\frac{3}{5}$ because $\frac{1}{2} \times \frac{6}{5} = \frac{6}{10} = \frac{3}{5}$.

2. **Divide** $\frac{2}{3} \div \frac{3}{5}$.

    A. $\frac{2}{15}$ B. $\frac{2}{5}$ C. $1\frac{1}{15}$ D. $1\frac{1}{9}$

    The correct answer is **D**. The correct solution is $1\frac{1}{9}$ because $\frac{2}{3} \times \frac{5}{3} = \frac{10}{9} = 1\frac{1}{9}$.

Dividing a Fraction and a Whole or Mixed Number

Some basic steps apply when dividing a fraction by a whole number or a mixed number.

> **STEP BY STEP**
>
> **Step 1.** Write any whole number as a fraction with a denominator of 1. Write any mixed numbers as improper fractions.
>
> **Step 2.** Leave the first fraction (improper fraction) alone.
>
> **Step 3.** Find the reciprocal of the second fraction.
>
> **Step 4.** Multiply the first fraction by the reciprocal of the second fraction.
>
> **Step 5.** Rewrite the fraction as a mixed number and reduce the fraction completely.

Divide, $\frac{3}{10} \div 3$. Rewrite the expression as $\frac{3}{10} \div \frac{3}{1}$. Find the reciprocal of the second fraction, which is $\frac{1}{3}$. Multiply the fractions, $\frac{3}{10} \times \frac{1}{3} = \frac{3}{30} = \frac{1}{10}$. Reduce $\frac{3}{30}$ to $\frac{1}{10}$.

Divide, $2\frac{4}{5} \div 1\frac{3}{8}$. Rewrite the expression as $\frac{14}{5} \div \frac{11}{8}$. Find the reciprocal of the second fraction, which is $\frac{8}{11}$.

Multiply the fractions, $\frac{14}{5} \times \frac{8}{11} = \frac{112}{55} = 2\frac{2}{55}$. Reduce $\frac{112}{55}$ to $2\frac{2}{55}$.

Examples

1. **Divide** $\frac{2}{3} \div 4$.

    A. $\frac{1}{12}$ B. $\frac{1}{10}$ C. $\frac{1}{8}$ D. $\frac{1}{6}$

    The correct answer is **D**. The correct answer is $\frac{1}{6}$ because $\frac{2}{3} \times \frac{1}{4} = \frac{2}{12} = \frac{1}{6}$.

2. **Divide** $1\frac{5}{12} \div 1\frac{1}{2}$.

    A. $\frac{17}{18}$ B. $1\frac{5}{24}$ C. $1\frac{5}{6}$ D. $2\frac{1}{8}$

    The correct answer is **A**. The correct answer is $\frac{17}{18}$ because $\frac{17}{12} \div \frac{3}{2} = \frac{17}{12} \times \frac{2}{3} = \frac{34}{36} = \frac{17}{18}$.

Let's Review!

- The process to multiply fractions is to multiply the numerators together and multiply the denominators together. When there is a mixed number, change the mixed number to an improper fraction before multiplying.
- The process to divide fractions is to find the reciprocal of the second fraction and multiply the fractions. As with multiplying, change any mixed numbers to improper fractions before dividing.

EQUATIONS WITH ONE VARIABLE

This lesson introduces how to solve linear equations and linear inequalities.

One-Step Linear Equations

A **linear equation** is an equation where two expressions are set equal to each other. The equation is in the form $ax + b = c$, where a is a non-zero constant and b and c are constants. The exponent on a linear equation is always 1, and there is no more than one solution to a linear equation.

There are four properties to help solve a linear equation.

Property	Definition	Example with Numbers	Example with Variables
Addition Property of Equality	Add the same number to both sides of the equation.	$x - 3 = 9$ $x - 3 + 3 = 9 + 3$ $x = 12$	$x - a = b$ $x - a + a = b + a$ $x = a + b$
Subtraction Property of Equality	Subtract the same number from both sides of the equation.	$x + 3 = 9$ $x + 3 - 3 = 9 - 3$ $x = 6$	$x + a = b$ $x + a - a = b - a$ $x = b - a$
Multiplication Property of Equality	Multiply both sides of the equation by the same number.	$\frac{x}{3} = 9$ $\frac{x}{3} \times 3 = 9 \times 3$ $x = 27$	$\frac{x}{a} = b$ $\frac{x}{a} \times a = b \times a$ $x = ab$
Division Property of Equality	Divide both sides of the equation by the same number.	$3x = 9$ $\frac{3x}{3} = \frac{9}{3}$ $x = 3$	$ax = b$ $\frac{ax}{a} = \frac{b}{a}$ $x = \frac{b}{a}$

Example

Solve the equation for the unknown, $\frac{w}{2} = -6$.

A. -12 B. -8 C. -4 D. -3

The correct answer is **A**. The correct solution is -12 because both sides of the equation are multiplied by 2.

Two-Step Linear Equations

A two-step linear equation is in the form $ax + b = c$, where a is a non-zero constant and b and c are constants. There are two basic steps in solving this equation.

STEP BY STEP

Step 1. Use addition and subtraction properties of an equation to move the variable to one side of the equation and all number terms to the other side of the equation.

Step 2. Use multiplication and division properties of an equation to remove the value in front of the variable.

Examples

1. **Solve the equation for the unknown, $\frac{x}{-2} - 3 = 5$.**

   A. −16   B. −8   C. 8   D. 16

   The correct answer is **A.** The correct solution is −16.

   $\frac{x}{-2} = 8$ Add 3 to both sides of the equation.

   $x = -16$ Multiply both sides of the equation by −2.

2. **Solve the equation for the unknown, $4x + 3 = 8$.**

   A. −2   B. $-\frac{5}{4}$ C. $\frac{5}{4}$ D. 2

   The correct answer is **C.** The correct solution is $\frac{5}{4}$.

   $4x = 5$ Subtract 3 from both sides of the equation.

   $x = \frac{5}{4}$ Divide both sides of the equation by 4.

3. **Solve the equation for the unknown w, $P = 2l + 2w$.**

   A. $2P - 2l = w$ B. $\frac{P - 2l}{2} = w$ C. $2P + 2l = w$ D. $\frac{P + 2l}{2} = w$

   The correct answer is **B.** The correct solution is $\frac{P - 2l}{2} = w$.

   $P - 2l = 2w$ Subtract 2l from both sides of the equation.

   $\frac{P - 2l}{2} = w$ Divide both sides of the equation by 2.

Multi-Step Linear Equations

In these basic examples of linear equations, the solution may be evident, but these properties demonstrate how to use an opposite operation to solve for a variable. Using these properties, there are three steps in solving a complex linear equation.

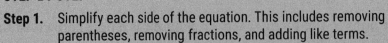

STEP BY STEP

Step 1. Simplify each side of the equation. This includes removing parentheses, removing fractions, and adding like terms.

Step 2. Use addition and subtraction properties of an equation to move the variable to one side of the equation and all number terms to the other side of the equation.

Step 3. Use multiplication and division properties of an equation to remove the value in front of the variable.

In Step 2, all of the variables may be placed on the left side or the right side of the equation. The examples in this lesson will place all of the variables on the left side of the equation.

When solving for a variable, apply the same steps as above. In this case, the equation is not being solved for a value, but for a specific variable.

Examples

1. **Solve the equation for the unknown, $2(4x + 1)-5 = 3-(4x-3)$.**

   A. $\frac{1}{4}$　　　　　B. $\frac{3}{4}$　　　　　C. $\frac{4}{3}$　　　　　D. 4

   The correct answer is **B**. The correct solution is $\frac{3}{4}$.

$8x + 2-5 = 3-4x + 3$	Apply the distributive property.
$8x-3 = -4x + 6$	Combine like terms on both sides of the equation.
$12x-3 = 6$	Add $4x$ to both sides of the equation.
$12x = 9$	Add 3 to both sides of the equation.
$x = \frac{3}{4}$	Divide both sides of the equation by 12.

2. **Solve the equation for the unknown, $\frac{2}{3}x + 2 = -\frac{1}{2}x + 2(x + 1)$.**

   A. 0　　　　　B. 1　　　　　C. 2　　　　　D. 3

   The correct answer is **A**. The correct solution is 0.

$\frac{2}{3}x + 2 = -\frac{1}{2}x + 2x + 2$	Apply the distributive property.
$4x + 12 = -3x + 12x + 12$	Multiply all terms by the least common denominator of 6 to eliminate the fractions.
$4x + 12 = 9x + 12$	Combine like terms on the right side of the equation.
$-5x = 12$	Subtract $9x$ from both sides of the equation.
$-5x = 0$	Subtract 12 from both sides of the equation.
$x = 0$	Divide both sides of the equation by -5.

3. **Solve the equation for the unknown for** x, $y-y_1 = m(x-x_1)$.

   A. $y-y_1 + mx_1$ B. $my - my_1 + mx_1$ C. $\frac{y-y_1 + x_1}{m}$ D. $\frac{y-y_1 + mx_1}{m}$

The correct answer is **D**. The correct solution is $\frac{y-y_1 + mx_1}{m}$

$y-y_1 = mx - mx_1$	Apply the distributive property.
$y-y_1 + mx_1 = mx$	Add mx_1 to both sides of the equation.
$\frac{y-y_1 + mx_1}{m} = x$	Divide both sides of the equation by m.

Solving Linear Inequalities

A **linear inequality** is similar to a linear equation, but it contains an inequality sign ($<, >, \leq, \geq$). Many of the steps for solving linear inequalities are the same as for solving linear equations. The major difference is that the solution is an infinite number of values. There are four properties to help solve a linear inequality.

Property	Definition	Example
Addition Property of Inequality	Add the same number to both sides of the inequality.	$x-3 < 9$ $x-3+3 < 9+3$ $x < 12$
Subtraction Property of Inequality	Subtract the same number from both sides of the inequality.	$x+3 > 9$ $x+3-3 > 9-3$ $x > 6$
Multiplication Property of Inequality (when multiplying by a positive number)	Multiply both sides of the inequality by the same number.	$\frac{x}{3} \geq 9$ $\frac{x}{3} \times 3 \geq 9 \times 3$ $x \geq 27$
Division Property of Inequality (when multiplying by a positive number)	Divide both sides of the inequality by the same number.	$3x \leq 9$ $\frac{3x}{3} \leq \frac{9}{3}$ $x \leq 3$
Multiplication Property of Inequality (when multiplying by a negative number)	Multiply both sides of the inequality by the same number.	$\frac{x}{-3} \geq 9$ $\frac{x}{-3} \times -3 \geq 9 \times -3$ $x \leq -27$
Division Property of Inequality (when multiplying by a negative number)	Divide both sides of the inequality by the same number.	$-3x \leq 9$ $\frac{-3x}{-3} \leq \frac{9}{-3}$ $x \geq -3$

Multiplying or dividing both sides of the inequality by a negative number reverses the sign of the inequality.In these basic examples, the solution may be evident, but these properties demonstrate how to use an opposite operation to solve for a variable. Using these properties, there are three steps in solving a complex linear inequality.

STEP BY STEP

Step 1. Simplify each side of the equation. This includes removing parentheses, removing fractions, and adding like terms.

Step 2. Use addition and subtraction properties of an equation to move the variable to one side of the equation and all number terms to the other side of the equation.

Step 3. Use multiplication and division properties of an equation to remove the value in front of the variable.

In Step 2, all of the variables may be placed on the left side or the right side of the inequality.

The examples in this lesson will place all of the variables on the left side of the inequality.

Examples

1. **Solve the inequality for the unknown, $3(2 + x) < 2(3x–1)$.**

   A. $x < -\frac{8}{3}$ B. $x > -\frac{8}{3}$ C. $x < \frac{8}{3}$ D. $x > \frac{8}{3}$

   The correct answer is **D**. The correct solution is $x > \frac{8}{3}$.

$6 + 3x < 6x–2$	Apply the distributive property.
$6–3x < -2$	Subtract $6x$ from both sides of the inequality.
$-3x < -8$	Subtract 6 from both sides of the inequality.
$x > \frac{8}{3}$	Divide both sides of the inequality by -3.

2. **Solve the inequality for the unknown, $\frac{1}{2}(2x–3) \geq \frac{1}{4}(2x + 1)–2$.**

   A. $x > -7$ B. $x > -3$ C. $x \geq -\frac{3}{2}$ D. $x \geq -\frac{1}{2}$

   The correct answer is **D**. The correct solution is $x \geq -\frac{1}{2}$.

$2(2x–3) \geq 2x + 1–8$	Multiply all terms by the least common denominator of 4 to eliminate the fractions.
$4x–6 \geq 2x + 1–8$	Apply the distributive property.
$4x–6 \geq 2x–7$	Combine like terms on the right side of the inequality.
$2x–6 \geq -7$	Subtract $2x$ from both sides of the inequality.
$2x \geq -1$	Add 6 to both sides of the inequality.
$x \geq -\frac{1}{2}$	Divide both sides of the inequality by 2.

Let's Review!

- A linear equation is an equation with one solution. Using opposite operations solves a linear equation.
- The process to solve a linear equation or inequality is to eliminate fractions and parentheses and combine like terms on the same side of the sign. Then, solve the equation or inequality by using inverse operations.

EQUATIONS WITH TWO VARIABLES

This lesson discusses solving a system of linear equations by substitution, elimination, and graphing, as well as solving a simple system of a linear and a quadratic equation.

Solving a System of Equations by Substitution

A **system of linear equations** is a set of two or more linear equations in the same variables. A solution to the system is an ordered pair that is a solution in all the equations in the system. The ordered pair (1, -2) is a solution for the system of equations $\begin{aligned} 2x + y &= 0 \\ -x + 2y &= -5 \end{aligned}$ because $\begin{aligned} 2(1) + (-2) &= 0 \\ -1 + 2(-2) &= -5 \end{aligned}$ makes both equations true.

One way to solve a system of linear equations is by substitution.

STEP BY STEP

Step 1. Solve one equation for one of the variables.

Step 2. Substitute the expression from Step 1 into the other equation and solve for the other variable.

Step 3. Substitute the value from Step 2 into one of the original equations and solve.

All systems of equations can be solved by substitution for any one of the four variables in the problem. The most efficient way of solving is locating the $1x$ or $1y$ in the equations because this eliminates the possibility of having fractions in the equations.

Examples

1. **Solve the system of equations,** $\begin{aligned} x &= y + 6 \\ 4x + 5y &= 60 \end{aligned}$.

   A. (10, 12)   B. (6, 12)   C. (6, 4)   D. (10, 4)

   The correct answer is **D**. The correct solution is (10, 4).

   The first equation is already solved for x.

$4(y + 6) + 5y = 60$	Substitute $y + 6$ in for x in the first equation.
$4y + 24 + 5y = 60$	Apply the distributive property.
$9y + 24 = 60$	Combine like terms on the left side of the equation.
$9y = 36$	Subtract 24 from both sides of the equation.
$y = 4$	Divide both sides of the equation by 9.
$x = 4 + 6$	Substitute 4 in the first equation for y.
$x = 10$	Simplify using order of operations.

2. **Solve the system of equations,** $\begin{array}{l} 3x + 2y = 41 \\ -4x + y = -18 \end{array}$.

A. (5, 13) B. (6, 6) C. (7, 10) D. (10, 7)

The correct answer is **C.** The correct solution is (7, 10).

$y = 4x{-}18$	Solve the second equation for y by adding $4x$ to both sides of the equation.
$3x + 2(4x{-}18) = 41$	Substitute $4x{-}18$ in for y in the first equation.
$3x + 8x{-}36 = 41$	Apply the distributive property.
$11x{-}36 = 41$	Combine like terms on the left side of the equation.
$11x = 77$	Add 36 to both sides of the equation.
$x = 7$	Divide both sides of the equation by 11.
$-4(7) + y = -18$	Substitute 7 in the second equation for x.
$-28 + y = -18$	Simplify using order of operations.
$y = 10$	Add 28 to both sides of the equation.

Solving a System of Equations by Elimination

Another way to solve a system of linear equations is by elimination.

STEP BY STEP

Step 1. Multiply, if necessary, one or both equations by a constant so at least one pair of like terms has opposite coefficients.

Step 2. Add the equations to eliminate one of the variables.

Step 3. Solve the resulting equation.

Step 4. Substitute the value from Step 3 into one of the original equations and solve for the other variable.

All system of equations can be solved by the elimination method for any one of the four variables in the problem. One way of solving is locating the variables with opposite coefficients and adding the equations. Another approach is multiplying one equation to obtain opposite coefficients for the variables.

Examples

1. **Solve the system of equations,** $\begin{array}{l} 3x + 5y = 28 \\ -4x - 5y = -34 \end{array}$.

    A. (12, 6) B. (6, 12) C. (6, 2) D. (2, 6)

    The correct answer is **C**. The correct solution is (6, 2).

$-x = -6$	Add the equations.
$x = 6$	Divide both sides of the equation by -1.
$3(6) + 5y = 28$	Substitute 6 in the first equation for x.
$18 + 5y = 28$	Simplify using order of operations.
$5y = 10$	Subtract 18 from both sides of the equation.
$y = 2$	Divide both sides of the equation by 5.

2. **Solve the system of equations,** $\begin{array}{l} -5x + 5y = 0 \\ 2x - 3y = -3 \end{array}$.

    A. (2, 2) B. (3, 3) C. (6, 6) D. (9, 9)

    The correct answer is **B**. The correct solution is (3, 3).

$-10x + 10y = 0$	Multiply all terms in the first equation by 2.
$10x - 15y = -15$	Multiply all terms in the second equation by 5.
$-5y = -15$	Add the equations.
$y = 3$	Divide both sides of the equation by -5.
$2x - 3(3) = -3$	Substitute 3 in the second equation for y.
$2x - 9 = -3$	Simplify using order of operations.
$2x = 6$	Add 9 to both sides of the equation.
$x = 3$	Divide both sides of the equation by 2.

Solving a System of Equations by Graphing

Graphing is a third method of a solving system of equations. The point of intersection is the solution for the graph. This method is a great way to visualize each graph on a coordinate plane.

STEP BY STEP

Step 1. Graph each equation in the coordinate plane.

Step 2. Estimate the point of intersection.

Step 3. Check the point by substituting for x and y in each equation of the original system.

The best approach to graphing is to obtain each line in slope-intercept form. Then, graph the y-intercept and use the slope to find additional points on the line.

Example

Solve the system of equations by graphing, $\begin{array}{l} y = 3x-2 \\ y = x-4 \end{array}$.

A.

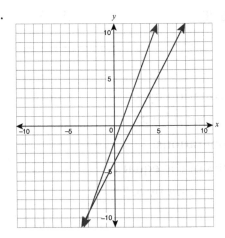

C.

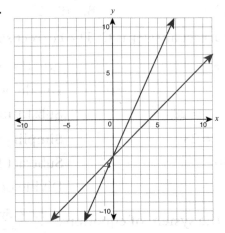

B.

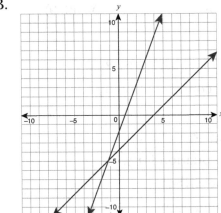

D.

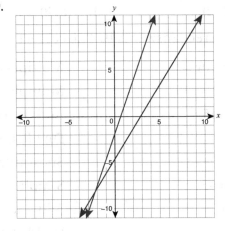

The correct answer is **B**. The correct graph has the two lines intersect at (-1, -5).

Solving a System of a Linear Equation and an Equation of a Circle

There are many other types of systems of equations. One example is the equation of a line $y = mx$ and the equation of a circle $x^2 + y^2 = r^2$ where r is the radius. With this system of equations, there can be two ordered pairs that intersect between the line and the circle. If there is one ordered pair, the line is tangent to the circle.

This system of equations is solved by substituting the expression mx in for y in the equation of a circle. Then, solve the equation for x. The values for x are substituted into the linear equation to find the value for y.

KEEP IN MIND

There will be two solutions in many cases with the system of a linear equation and an equation of a circle.

Example

Solve the system of equations, $\begin{array}{l} y = -3x \\ x^2 + y^2 = 10 \end{array}$.

A. (1, 3) and (−1, −3)

B. (1, −3) and (−1, 3)

C. (−3, 10) and (3, −10)

D. (3, 10) and (−3, −10)

The correct answer is **B.** The correct solutions are (1, −3) and (−1, 3).

$x^2 + (-3x)^2 = 10$	Substitute −3x in for y in the second equation.
$x^2 + 9x^2 = 10$	Apply the exponent.
$10x^2 = 10$	Combine like terms on the left side of the equation.
$x^2 = 1$	Divide both sides of the equation by 10.
$x = \pm 1$	Apply the square root to both sides of the equation.
$y = -3(1) = -3$	Substitute 1 in the first equation and multiply.
$y = -3(-1) = 3$	Substitute −1 in the first equation and multiply.

Let's Review!

- There are three ways to solve a system of equations: graphing, substitution, and elimination. Using any method will result in the same solution for the system of equations.
- Solving a system of a linear equation and an equation of a circle uses substitution and usually results in two solutions.

SOLVING REAL-WORLD MATHEMATICAL PROBLEMS

This lesson introduces solving real-world mathematical problems by using estimation and mental computation. This lesson also includes real-world applications involving integers, fractions, and decimals.

Estimating

Estimations are rough calculations of a solution to a problem. The most common use for estimation is completing calculations without a calculator or other tool. There are many estimation techniques, but this lesson focuses on integers, decimals, and fractions.

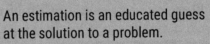

KEEP IN MIND
An estimation is an educated guess at the solution to a problem.

To round a whole number, round the value to the nearest ten or hundred. The number 142 rounds to 140 for the nearest ten and to 100 for the nearest hundred. The context of the problem determines the place value to which to round.

In most problems with fractions and decimals, the context of the problem requires rounding to the nearest whole number. Rounding these values makes calculation easier and provides an accurate estimation to the solution of the problem.

Other estimation strategies include the following:

- Using friendly or compatible numbers
- Using numbers that are easy to compute
- Adjusting numbers after rounding

Example

There are 168 hours in a week. Carson does the following:

- Sleeps 7.5 hours each day of the week
- Goes to school 6.75 hours five days a week
- Practices martial arts and basketball 1.5 hours each three times a week
- Reads and studies 1.75 hours every day
- Eats 1.5 hours every day

Estimate the remaining number of hours.

A. 20   B. 30   C. 40   D. 50

The correct answer is **C**. The correct solution is 40. He sleeps about 56 hours, goes to school for 35 hours, practices for 12 hours, reads and studies for about 14 hours, and eats for about 14 hours. This is 131 hours. Therefore, Carson has about 40 hours remaining.

Real-World Integer Problems

The following five steps can make solving word problems easier:

1. Read the problem for understanding.
2. Visualize the problem by drawing a picture or diagram.
3. Make a plan by writing an expression to represent the problem.
4. Solve the problem by applying mathematical techniques.
5. Check the answer to make sure it answers the question asked.

> **BE CAREFUL!**
> Make sure that you read the problem fully before visualizing and making a plan.

In basic problems, the solution may be evident, but make sure to demonstrate knowledge of writing the expression. In multi-step problems, first make a plan with the correct expression. Then, apply the correct calculation.

Examples

1. **The temperature on Monday was –9°F, and on Tuesday it was 8°F. What is the difference in temperature, in °F?**

    A. –17°   B. –1°   C. 1°   D. 17°

    The correct answer is **D**. The correct solution is 17° because 8–(–9) = 17°F.

2. **A golfer's last 12 rounds were –2, +4, –3, –1, +5, +3, –4, –5, –2, –6, –1, and 0. What is the average of these rounds?**

    A. –12   B. –1   C. 1   D. 12

    The correct answer is **B**. The correct solution is –1. The total of the scores is –12. The average is –12 divided by 12, which is –1.

Real-World Fraction and Decimal Problems

The five steps in the previous section are applicable to solving real-world fraction and decimal problems. The expressions with one step require only one calculation: addition, subtraction, multiplication, or division. The problems with multiple steps require writing out the expressions and performing the correct calculations.

> **KEEP IN MIND**
> Estimating the solution first can help determine if a calculation is completed correctly.

Examples

1. The length of a room is $7\frac{2}{3}$ feet. When the length of the room is doubled, what is the new length in feet?

    A. $14\frac{2}{3}$ B. $15\frac{1}{3}$ C. $15\frac{2}{3}$ D. $16\frac{1}{3}$

    The correct answer is **B**. The correct solution is $15\frac{1}{3}$. The length is multiplied by 2, $7\frac{2}{3} \times 2 = \frac{23}{3} \times \frac{2}{1} = \frac{46}{3} = 15\frac{1}{3}$ feet.

2. A fruit salad is a mixture of $1\frac{3}{4}$ pounds of apples, $2\frac{1}{4}$ pounds of grapes, and $1\frac{1}{4}$ pounds of bananas. After the fruit is mixed, $1\frac{1}{2}$ pounds are set aside, and the rest is divided into three containers. What is the weight in pounds of one container?

    A. $1\frac{1}{5}$ B. $1\frac{1}{4}$ C. $1\frac{1}{3}$ D. $1\frac{1}{2}$

    The correct answer is **B**. The correct solution is $1\frac{1}{4}$. The amount available for the containers is $1\frac{3}{4} + 2\frac{1}{4} + 1\frac{1}{4} - 1\frac{1}{2} = 5\frac{1}{4} - 1\frac{1}{2} = 5\frac{1}{4} - 1\frac{2}{4} = 4\frac{5}{4} - 1\frac{2}{4} = 3\frac{3}{4}$. This amount is divided into three containers, $3\frac{3}{4} \div 3 = \frac{15}{4} \times \frac{15}{12} = 1\frac{3}{12} = 1\frac{1}{4}$ pounds.

3. In 2016, a town had 17.4 inches of snowfall. In 2017, it had 45.2 inches of snowfall. What is the difference in inches?

    A. 27.2   B. 27.8   C. 28.2   D. 28.8

    The correct answer is **B**. The correct solution is 27.8 because $45.2 - 17.4 = 27.8$ inches.

4. Mike bought items that cost $4.78, $3.49, $6.79, $9.78, and $14.05. He had a coupon worth $5.00. If he paid with a $50.00 bill, then how much change does he receive?

    A. $16.11   B. $18.11   C. $21.11   D. $23.11

    The correct answer is **A**. The correct solution is $16.11. The total bill is $38.89, less the coupon is $33.89. The amount of change is $50.00 - $33.89 = $16.11.

Let's Review!

- Using estimation is beneficial to determine an approximate solution to the problem when the numbers are complex.
- When solving a word problem with integers, fractions, or decimals, first read and visualize the problem. Then, make a plan, solve, and check the answer.

CHAPTER 19 ALGEBRA PRACTICE QUIZ

1. Which decimal is the greatest?

   A. 1.7805

   C. 1.7085

   B. 1.5807

   D. 1.8057

2. Change $0.\overline{63}$ to a fraction. Simplify completely.

   A. $\frac{5}{9}$

   C. $\frac{2}{3}$

   B. $\frac{7}{11}$

   D. $\frac{5}{6}$

3. Write $0.\overline{1}$ as a percent.

   A. $0.\overline{1}\%$

   C. $11.\overline{1}\%$

   B. $1.\overline{1}\%$

   D. $111.\overline{1}\%$

4. Solve the equation for the unknown, $4x + 3 = 8$.

   A. -2

   C. $\frac{5}{4}$

   B. $-\frac{5}{4}$

   D. 2

5. Solve the inequality for the unknown, $3x + 5 - 2(x + 3) > 4(1-x) + 5$.

   A. $x > 2$

   C. $x > 10$

   B. $x > 9$

   D. $x > 17$

6. Solve the equation for h, $SA = 2\pi rh + 2\pi r^2$.

   A. $2\pi rSA - 2\pi r^2 = h$

   B. $2\pi rSA + 2\pi r^2 = h$

   C. $\frac{SA - 2\pi r^2}{2\pi r} = h$

   D. $\frac{SA + 2\pi r^2}{2\pi r} = h$

7. Solve the system of equations,
   $y = -2x + 3$
   $y + x = 5$.

   A. $(-2, 7)$

   C. $(2, -7)$

   B. $(-2, -7)$

   D. $(2, 7)$

8. Solve the system of equations,
   $2x - 3y = -1$
   $x + 2y = 24$.

   A. $(7, 10)$

   C. $(6, 8)$

   B. $(10, 7)$

   D. $(8, 6)$

9. Divide $1\frac{5}{6} \div 1\frac{1}{3}$.

   A. $1\frac{5}{18}$

   C. $2\frac{4}{9}$

   B. $1\frac{3}{8}$

   D. $3\frac{1}{6}$

10. Multiply $1\frac{1}{4} \times 1\frac{1}{2}$.

    A. $1\frac{1}{8}$

    C. $1\frac{2}{3}$

    B. $1\frac{1}{3}$

    D. $1\frac{7}{8}$

11. Divide $\frac{1}{10} \div \frac{2}{3}$.

    A. $\frac{1}{15}$

    C. $\frac{3}{20}$

    B. $\frac{1}{10}$

    D. $\frac{3}{5}$

12. A store has 75 pounds of bananas. Eight customers buy 3.3 pounds, five customers buy 4.25 pounds, and one customer buys 6.8 pounds. How many pounds are left in stock?

    A. 19.45

    C. 20.45

    B. 19.55

    D. 20.55

13. A rectangular garden needs a border. The length is $15\frac{3}{5}$ feet, and the width is $3\frac{2}{3}$ feet. What is the perimeter in feet?

    A. $18\frac{5}{8}$

    C. $37\frac{1}{4}$

    B. $19\frac{4}{15}$

    D. $38\frac{8}{15}$

14. Solve the system of equations by graphing, $\begin{array}{l} 3x + y = -1 \\ 2x - y = -4 \end{array}$.

A.

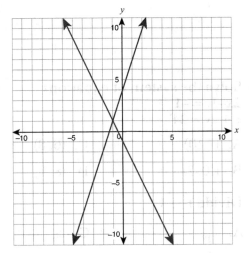

C.

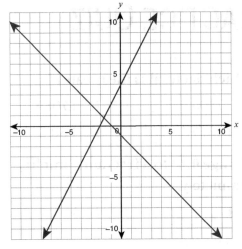

B.

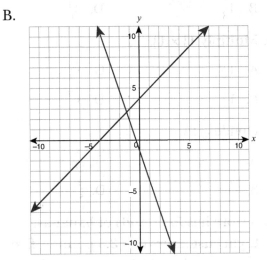

D.

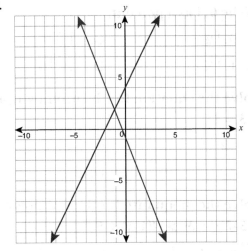

15. A historical society has 8 tours daily 5 days a week, with 32 people on each tour. Estimate the number of people who can be on the tour in 50 weeks.

A. 25,000

C. 75,000

B. 50,000

D. 100,000

CHAPTER 19 ALGEBRA
PRACTICE QUIZ – ANSWER KEY

1. D. The correct solution is 1.8057 because 1.8075 contains the largest value in the tenths place. **See Lesson: Decimals and Fractions.**

2. B. The correct solution is $\frac{7}{11}$. Let $n = 0.\overline{63}$ and $100n = 63.\overline{63}$ Then, $100n-n = 63.\overline{63}-0.\overline{63}$ resulting in $99n = 63$ and solution of $n = \frac{63}{99} = \frac{7}{11}$. **See Lesson: Decimals and Fractions.**

3. C. The correct answer is $11.\overline{1}\%$ because $0.\overline{1}$ as a percent is $0.\overline{1} \times 100 = 11.\overline{1}\%$. **See Lesson: Decimals and Fractions.**

4. C. The correct solution is $\frac{5}{4}$.

$4x = 5$	Subtract 3 from both sides of the equation.
$x = \frac{5}{4}$	Divide both sides of the equation by 4.

See Lesson: Equations with One Variable.

5. A. The correct solution is $x > 2$.

$3x + 5-2x-6 > 4-4x + 5$	Apply the distributive property.
$x-1 > -4x + 9$	Combine like terms on both sides of the inequality.
$5x-1 > 9$	Add $4x$ to both sides of the inequality.
$5x > 10$	Add 1 to both sides of the inequality.
$x > 2$	Divide both sides of the inequality by 5.

See Lesson: Equations with One Variable.

6. C. The correct solution is $\frac{SA-2\pi r^2}{2\pi r} = h$.

$SA-2\pi r^2 = 2\pi rh$	Subtract $2\pi r^2$ from both sides of the equation.
$\frac{SA-2\pi r^2}{2\pi r} = h$	Divide both sides of the equation by $2\pi r$.

See Lesson: Equations with One Variable.

7. A. The correct solution is (-2, 7).

	The first equation is already solved for y.
$-2x + 3 + x = 5$	Substitute $-2x + 3$ in for y in the second equation.
$-x + 3 = 5$	Combine like terms on the left side of the equation.
$-x = 2$	Subtract 3 from both sides of the equation.
$x = -2$	Divide both sides of the equation by -1.
$y = -2(-2) + 3$	Substitute -2 in the first equation for x.
$y = 4 + 3 = 7$	Simplify using order of operations.

See Lesson: Equations with Two Variables.

8. B. The correct solution is (10, 7).

$-2x{-}4y = -48$	Multiply all terms in the second equation by -2.
$-7y = -49$	Add the equations.
$y = 7$	Divide both sides of the equation by -7.
$x + 2(7) = 24$	Substitute 7 in the second equation for y.
$x + 14 = 24$	Simplify using order of operations.
$x = 10$	Subtract 14 from both sides of the equation.

See Lesson: Equations with Two Variables.

9. B. The correct answer is $1\frac{3}{8}$ because $\frac{11}{6} \div \frac{4}{3} = \frac{11}{6} \times \frac{3}{4} = \frac{33}{24} = 1\frac{9}{24} = 1\frac{3}{8}$. **See Lesson: Multiplication and Division of Fractions.**

10. D. The correct solution is $1\frac{7}{8}$ because $\frac{5}{4} \times \frac{3}{2} = \frac{15}{8} = 1\frac{7}{8}$. **See Lesson: Multiplication and Division of Fractions.**

11. C. The correct solution is $\frac{3}{20}$ because $\frac{1}{10} \times \frac{3}{2} = \frac{3}{20}$. **See Lesson: Multiplication and Division of Fractions.**

12. D. The correct solution is 20.55 because the number of pounds purchased is $8(3.3) + 5(4.25) + 6.8 = 26.4 + 21.25 + 6.8 = 54.55$ pounds. The number of pounds remaining is $75{-}54.45 = 20.55$ pounds. **See Lesson: Solving Real World Mathematical Problems.**

13. D. The correct solution is $38\frac{8}{15}$ because $15\frac{3}{5} + 3\frac{2}{3} = 15\frac{9}{15} + 3\frac{10}{15} = 18\frac{19}{15}(2) = \frac{289}{15} \times \frac{2}{1} = \frac{578}{15} = 38\frac{8}{15}$ feet. **See Lesson: Solving Real World Mathematical Problems.**

14. D. The correct graph has the two lines intersect at (-1, 2). **See Lesson: Equations with Two Variables.**

15. C. The correct solution is 75,000 because by estimation $10(5)(30)(50) = 75,000$ people can be on the tour in 50 weeks. **See Lesson: Solving Real World Mathematical Problems.**

CHAPTER 20 FUNCTIONS

SOLVING QUADRATIC EQUATIONS

This lesson introduces solving quadratic equations by the square root method, completing the square, factoring, and using the quadratic formula.

Solving Quadratic Equations by the Square Root Method

A **quadratic equation** is an equation where the highest variable is squared. The equation is in the form $ax^2 + bx + c = 0$, where a is a non-zero constant and b and c are constants. There are at most two solutions to the equation because the highest variable is squared. There are many methods to solve a quadratic equation.

This section will explore solving a quadratic equation by the square root method. The equation must be in the form of $ax^2 = c$, or there is no x term.

> **STEP BY STEP**
>
> **Step 1.** Use multiplication and division properties of an equation to remove the value in front of the variable.
>
> **Step 2.** Apply the square root to both sides of the equation.

Note: The positive and negative square root make the solution true. For the equation $x^2 = 9$, the solutions are –3 and 3 because $3^2 = 9$ and $(-3)^2 = 9$.

Example

Solve the equation by the square root method, $4x^2 = 64$.

A. 4   B. 8   C. ±4   D. ±8

The correct answer is **C**. The correct solution is ±4.

$x^2 = 16$	Divide both sides of the equation by 4.
$x = \pm4$	Apply the square root to both sides of the equation.

Solving Quadratic Equations by Completing the Square

A quadratic equation in the form $x^2 + bx$ can be solved by a process known as completing the square. The best time to solve by completing the square is when the b term is even.

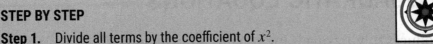

STEP BY STEP

Step 1. Divide all terms by the coefficient of x^2.

Step 2. Move the number term to the right side of the equation.

Step 3. Complete the square $\left(\frac{b}{2}\right)^2$ and add this value to both sides of the equation.

Step 4. Factor the left side of the equation.

Step 5. Apply the square root to both sides of the equation.

Step 6. Use addition and subtraction properties to move all number terms to the right side of the equation.

Examples

1. **Solve the equation by completing the square, $x^2 - 8x + 12 = 0$.**

   A. -2 and -6 B. 2 and -6 C. -2 and 6 D. 2 and 6

   The correct answer is **D**. The correct solutions are 2 and 6.

$x^2 - 8x = -12$	Subtract 12 from both sides of the equation.
$x^2 - 8x + 16 = -12 + 16$	Complete the square, $\left(-\frac{8}{2}\right)^2 = (-4)^2 = 16$.
	Add 16 to both sides of the equation.
$x^2 - 8x + 16 = 4$	Simplify the right side of the equation.
$(x-4)^2 = 4$	Factor the left side of the equation.
$x - 4 = \pm 2$	Apply the square root to both sides of the equation.
$x = 4 \pm 2$	Add 4 to both sides of the equation.
$x = 4 - 2 = 2, \ x = 4 + 2 = 6$	Simplify the right side of the equation.

2. **Solve the equation by completing the square, $x^2 + 6x - 8 = 0$.**

   A. $-3 \pm \sqrt{17}$ B. $3 \pm \sqrt{17}$ C. $-3 \pm \sqrt{8}$ D. $3 \pm \sqrt{8}$

   The correct answer is **A**. The correct solutions are $-3 \pm \sqrt{17}$.

$x^2 + 6x = 8$	Add 8 to both sides of the equation.
$x^2 + 6x + 9 = 8 + 9$	Complete the square, $\left(\frac{6}{2}\right)^2 = 3^2 = 9$. Add 9 to both sides of the equation.
$x^2 + 6x + 9 = 17$	Simplify the right side of the equation.
$(x + 3)^2 = 17$	Factor the left side of the equation.
$x + 3 = \pm\sqrt{17}$	Apply the square root to both sides of the equation.
$x = -3 \pm \sqrt{17}$	Subtract 3 from both sides of the equation.

Solving Quadratic Equations by Factoring

Factoring can only be used when a quadratic equation is factorable; other methods are needed to solve quadratic equations that are not factorable.

> **STEP BY STEP**
> **Step 1.** Simplify if needed by clearing any fractions and parentheses.
> **Step 2.** Write the equation in standard form, $ax^2 + bx + c = 0$.
> **Step 3.** Factor the quadratic equation.
> **Step 4.** Set each factor equal to zero.
> **Step 5.** Solve the linear equations using inverse operations.

The quadratic equation will have two solutions if the factors are different or one solution if the factors are the same.

Examples

1. **Solve the equation by factoring, $x^2 - 13x + 42 = 0$.**

   A. $-6, -7$ B. $-6, 7$ C. $6, -7$ D. $6, 7$

   The correct answer is **D**. The correct solutions are 6 and 7.

$(x-6)(x-7) = 0$	Factor the equation.
$(x-6) = 0$ or $(x-7) = 0$	Set each factor equal to 0.
$x-6 = 0$	Add 6 to both sides of the equation to solve for the first factor.
$x = 6$	
$x-7 = 0$	Add 7 to both sides of the equation to solve for the second factor.
$x = 7$	

2. **Solve the equation by factoring, $9x^2 + 30x + 25 = 0$.**

   A. $-\frac{5}{3}$ B. $-\frac{3}{5}$ C. $\frac{3}{5}$ D. $\frac{5}{3}$

   The correct answer is **A**. The correct solution is $-\frac{5}{3}$.

$(3x + 5)(3x + 5) = 0$	Factor the equation.
$(3x + 5) = 0$ or $(3x + 5) = 0$	Set each factor equal to 0.
$(3x + 5) = 0$	Set one factor equal to zero since both factors are the same.
$3x + 5 = 0$	Subtract 5 from both sides of the equation and divide both sides of the equation by 3 to solve.
$3x = -5$	
$x = -\frac{5}{3}$	

Solving Quadratic Equations by the Quadratic Formula

Many quadratic equations are not factorable. Another method of solving a quadratic equation is by using the quadratic formula. This method can be used to solve any quadratic equation in the form . Using the coefficients a, b, and c, the quadratic formula is $x = \frac{-b \pm \sqrt{b^2 - 4ac}}{2a}$. The values are substituted into the formula, and applying the order of operations finds the solution(s) to the equation.

The solution of the quadratic formula in these examples will be exact or estimated to three decimal places. There may be cases where the exact solutions to the quadratic formula are used.

KEEP IN MIND

Watch the negative sign in the formula. Remember that a number squared is always positive.

Examples

1. **Solve the equation by the quadratic formula, $x^2 - 5x - 6 = 0$.**

    A. –6 and –1   B. 6 and –1   C. –6 and 1   D. 6 and 1

    The correct answer is **B**. The correct solutions are 6 and –1.

    $x = \frac{-(-5) \pm \sqrt{(-5)^2 - 4(1)(-6)}}{2(1)}$ Substitute 1 for a, –5 for b, and –6 for c.

    $x = \frac{5 \pm \sqrt{25 - (-24)}}{2}$ Apply the exponent and perform the multiplication.

    $x = \frac{5 \pm \sqrt{49}}{2}$ Perform the subtraction.

    $x = \frac{5 \pm 7}{2}$ Apply the square root.

    $x = \frac{5 + 7}{2}$, $x = \frac{5 - 7}{2}$ Separate the problem into two expressions.

    $x = \frac{12}{2} = 6$, $x = \frac{-2}{2} = -1$ Simplify the numerator and divide.

2. **Solve the equation by the quadratic formula, $2x^2 + 4x - 5 = 0$.**

    A. –0.87 and –2.87   B. 0.87 and –2.87   C. –0.87 and 2.87   D. 0.87 and 2.87

    The correct answer is **B**. The correct solutions are –0.87 and –2.87.

    $x = \frac{-4 \pm \sqrt{4^2 - 4(2)(-5)}}{2(2)}$ Substitute 2 for a, 4 for b, and –5 for c.

    $x = \frac{-4 \pm \sqrt{16 - (-40)}}{4}$ Apply the exponent and perform the multiplication.

    $x = \frac{-4 \pm \sqrt{56}}{4}$ Perform the subtraction.

    $x = \frac{-4 \pm 7.48}{4}$ Apply the square root.

    $x = \frac{-4 + 7.48}{4}$, $x = \frac{-4 - 7.48}{4}$ Separate the problem into two expressions.

    $x = \frac{3.48}{4} = 0.87$, $x = \frac{-11.48}{4} = -2.87$ Simplify the numerator and divide.

Let's Review!

There are four methods to solve a quadratic equation algebraically:

- The square root method is used when there is a squared variable term and a constant term.
- Completing the square is used when there is a squared variable term and an even variable term.
- Factoring is used when the equation can be factored.
- The quadratic formula can be used for any quadratic equation.

POLYNOMIALS

This lesson introduces adding, subtracting, and multiplying polynomials. It also explains polynomial identities that describe numerical expressions.

Adding and Subtracting Polynomials

A **polynomial** is an expression that contains exponents, variables, constants, and operations. The exponents of the variables are only whole numbers, and there is no division by a variable. The operations are addition, subtraction, multiplication, and division. Constants are terms without a variable. A polynomial of one term is a **monomial**; a polynomial of two terms is a **binomial**; and a polynomial of three terms is a **trinomial**.

KEEP IN MIND

The solution is an expression, and a value is not calculated for the variable.

To add polynomials, combine like terms and write the solution from the term with the highest exponent to the term with the lowest exponent. To simplify, first rearrange and group like terms. Next, combine like terms.

$$(3x^2 + 5x{-}6) + (4x^3{-}3x + 4) = 4x^3 + 3x^2 + (5x{-}3x) + ({-}6 + 4) = 4x^3 + 3x^2 + 2x{-}2$$

To subtract polynomials, rewrite the second polynomial using an additive inverse. Change the minus sign to a plus sign, and change the sign of every term inside the parentheses. Then, add the polynomials.

$$(3x^2 + 5x{-}6){-}(4x^3{-}3x + 4) = (3x^2 + 5x{-}6) + ({-}4x^3 + 3x{-}4) = {-}4x^3 + 3x^2 + (5x + 3x) + ({-}6{-}4)$$
$$= {-}4x^3 + 3x^2 + 8x{-}10$$

Examples

1. **Perform the operation, $(2y^2{-}5y + 1) + ({-}3y^2 + 6y + 2)$.**

   A. $y^2 + y + 3$ B. $-y^2{-}y + 3$ C. $y^2{-}y + 3$ D. $-y^2 + y + 3$

   The correct answer is **D**. The correct solution is $-y^2 + y + 3$.

   $$(2y^2{-}5y + 1) + ({-}3y^2 + 6y + 2) = (2y^2{-}3y^2) + ({-}5y + 6y) + (1 + 2) = -y^2 + y + 3$$

2. **Perform the operation, $(3x^2y + 4xy{-}5xy^2){-}(x^2y{-}3xy{-}2xy^2)$.**

   A. $2x^2y{-}7xy + 3xy^2$ C. $2x^2y + 7xy{-}3xy^2$

   B. $2x^2y + 7xy + 3xy^2$ D. $2x^2y{-}7xy{-}3xy^2$

   The correct answer is **C**. The correct solution is $2x^2y + 7xy{-}3xy^2$.

   $$(3x^2y + 4xy{-}5xy^2){-}(x^2y{-}3xy{-}2xy^2) = (3x^2y + 4xy{-}5xy^2) + ({-}x^2y + 3xy + 2xy^2)$$
   $$= (3x^2y{-}x^2y) + (4xy + 3xy) + ({-}5xy^2 + 2xy^2) = 2x^2y + 7xy{-}3xy^2$$

408

Multiplying Polynomials

Multiplying polynomials comes in many forms. When multiplying a monomial by a monomial, multiply the coefficients and apply the multiplication rule for the power of an exponent.

$$4xy(3x^2y) = 12x^3y^2.$$

When multiplying a monomial by a polynomial, multiply each term of the polynomial by the monomial.

$$4xy(3x^2y-2xy^2) = 4xy(3x^2y) + 4xy(-2xy^2) = 12x^3y^2-8x^2y^3.$$

When multiplying a binomial by a binomial, apply the distributive property and combine like terms.

$$(3x-4)(2x + 5) = 3x(2x + 5)-4(2x + 5) = 6x^2 + 15x-8x-20 = 6x^2 + 7x-20$$

When multiplying a binomial by a trinomial, apply the distributive property and combine like terms.

$$(x + 2)(3x^2-2x + 3) = (x + 2)(3x^2) + (x + 2)(-2x) + (x + 2)(3) = 3x^3 + 6x^2-2x^2-4x + 3x + 6 = 3x^3 +$$

$$4x^2-x + 6$$

Examples

1. **Multiply, $3xy^2(2x^2y)$.**

   A. $6x^2y^2$ B. $6x^3y^2$ C. $6x^3y^3$ D. $6x^2y^3$

   The correct answer is **C**. The correct solution is $6x^3y^3$. $3xy^2(2x^2y) = 6x^3y^3$.

2. **Multiply, $-2xy(3xy-4x^2y^2)$.**

   A. $-6x^2y^2 + 8x^3y^3$ B. $-6x^2y^2-8x^3y^3$ C. $-6xy + 8x^3y^3$ D. $-6xy-8x^3y^3$

   The correct answer is **A**. The correct solution is $-6x^2y^2 + 8x^3y^3$.

   $$-2xy(3xy-4x^2y^2) = -2xy(3xy)-2xy(-4x^2y^2) = -6x^2y^2 + 8x^3y^3$$

Polynomial Identities

There are many polynomial identities that show relationships between expressions.

- Difference of two squares: $a^2-b^2 = (a-b)(a + b)$
- Square of a binomial: $(a + b)^2 = a^2 + 2ab + b^2$
- Square of a binomial: $(a-b)^2 = a^2-2ab + b^2$
- Sum of cubes: $a^3 + b^3 = (a + b)(a^2-ab + b^2)$
- Difference of two cubes: $a^3-b^3 = (a-b)(a^2 + ab + b^2)$

Examples

1. **Apply the polynomial identity to rewrite $x^2 + 6x + 9$.**

   A. $x^2 + 9$ B. $(x^2 + 3)^2$ C. $(x + 3)^2$ D. $(3x)^2$

   The correct answer is **C**. The correct solution is $(x + 3)^2$. The expression $x^2 + 6x + 9$ is rewritten as $(x + 3)^2$ because the value of a is x and the value of b is 3.

2. **Apply the polynomial identity to rewrite $x^3 - 1$.**

   A. $(x - 1)(x^2 + x + 1)$

   B. $(x - 1)(x^2 - x - 1)$

   C. $(x + 1)(x^2 + x + 1)$

   D. $(x + 1)(x^2 - x - 1)$

   The correct answer is **A**. The expression $x^3 - 1$ can be rewritten with the value a as x and the value of b as 1 using the polynomial identity of the difference of two cubes.

3. **Apply the polynomial identity to rewrite $x^3 - 1$.**

   A. $(x + 1)(x^2 + x + 1)$

   B. $(x-1)(x^2 + x - 1)$

   C. $(x + 1)(x^2 + x - 1)$

   D. $(x-1)(x^2 + x + 1)$

   The correct answer is **D**. The correct solution is $(x-1)(x^2 + x + 1)$ because the value of a and the value of b is 1. Refer to the polynomial identity for the difference of two cubes equation.

Let's Review!

- Adding, subtracting, and multiplying are commonly applied to polynomials. The key step in applying these operations is combining like terms.
- Polynomial identities require rewriting polynomials into different form

RATIOS, PROPORTIONS, AND PERCENTAGES

This lesson reviews percentages and ratios and their application to real-world problems. It also examines proportions and rates of change.

Percentages

A **percent** or **percentage** represents a fraction of some quantity. It is an integer or decimal number followed by the symbol %. The word *percent* means "per hundred." For example, 50% means 50 per 100. This is equivalent to half, or 1 out of 2.

Converting between numbers and percents is easy. Given a number, multiply by 100 and add the % symbol to get the equivalent percent. For instance, 0.67 is equal to $0.67 \times 100 = 67\%$, meaning 67 out of 100. Given a percent, eliminate the % symbol and divide by 100. For instance, 23.5% is equal to $23.5 \div 100 = 0.235$.

Although percentages between 0% and 100% are the most obvious, a percent can be any real number, including a negative number. For example, $1.35 = 135\%$ and $-0.872 = -87.2\%$. An example is a gasoline tank that is one-quarter full: one-quarter is $\frac{1}{4}$ or 0.25, so the tank is 25% full. Another example is a medical diagnostic test that has a certain maximum normal result. If a patient's test exceeds that value, its representation can be a percent greater than 100%. For instance, a reading that is 1.22 times the maximum normal value is 122% of the maximum normal value. Likewise, when measuring increases in a company's profits as a percent from one year to the next, a negative percent can represent a decline. That is, if the company's profits fell by one-tenth, the change was −10%.

Example

If 15 out of every 250 contest entries are winners, what percentage of entries are winners?

   A. 0.06%   B. 6%   C. 15%   D. 17%

The correct answer is **B**. First, convert the fraction $\frac{15}{250}$ to a decimal: 0.06. To get the percent, multiply by 100% (that is, multiply by 100 and add the % symbol). Of all entries, 6% are winners.

Ratios

A **ratio** expresses the relationship between two numbers and is expressed using a colon or fraction notation. For instance, if 135 runners finish a marathon but 22 drop out, the ratio of finishers to non-finishers is 135:22 or $\frac{135}{22}$. These expressions are equal.

> **BE CAREFUL!**
>
> Avoid confusing standard ratios with odds (such as "3:1 odds"). Both may use a colon, but their meanings differ. In general, a ratio is the same as a fraction containing the same numbers.

Ratios also follow the rules of fractions. Performing arithmetic operations on ratios follows the same procedures as on fractions. Ratios should also generally appear in lowest terms. Therefore, the constituent numbers in a ratio represent the relative quantities of each side, not absolute quantities. For example, because the ratio 1:2 is equal to 2:4, 5:10, and 600:1,200, ratios are insufficient to determine the absolute number of entities in a problem.

Example

If the ratio of women to men in a certain industry is 5:4, how many people are in that industry?

A. 9   B. 20   C. 900   D. Not enough information

The correct answer is **D**. The ratio 5:4 is the industry's relative number of women to men. But the industry could have 10 women and 8 men, 100 women and 80 men, or any other breakdown whose ratio is 5:4. Therefore, the question provides too little information to answer. Had it provided the total number of people in the industry, it would have been possible to determine how many women and how many men are in the industry.

> **KEY POINT**
>
> Mathematically, ratios act just like fractions. For example, the ratio 8:13 is mathematically the same as the fraction $\frac{8}{13}$.

Proportions

A **proportion** is an equation of two ratios. An illustrative case is two equivalent fractions:

$$\frac{21}{28} = \frac{3}{4}$$

This example of a proportion should be familiar: going left to right, it is the conversion of one fraction to an equivalent fraction in lowest terms by dividing the numerator and denominator by the same number (7, in this case).

Equating fractions in this way is correct, but it provides little information. Proportions are more informative when one of the numbers is unknown. Using a question mark (?) to represent an unknown number, setting up a proportion can aid in solving problems involving different scales. For instance, if the ratio of maple saplings to oak saplings in an acre of young forest is 7:5 and that acre contains 65 oaks, the number of maples in that acre can be determined using a proportion: $\frac{7}{5} = \frac{?}{65}$

Note that to equate two ratios in this manner, the numerators must contain numbers that represent the same entity or type, and so must the denominators. In this example, the numerators represent maples and the denominators represent oaks.

$$\frac{7 \text{ maples}}{5 \text{ oaks}} = \frac{? \text{ maples}}{65 \text{ oaks}}$$

Recall from the properties of fractions that if you multiply the numerator and denominator by the same number, the result is an equivalent fraction. Therefore, to find the unknown in this proportion, first divide the denominator on the right by the denominator on the left. Then, multiply the quotient by the numerator on the left.

$$65 \div 5 = 13$$
$$7 \times \frac{13}{5} \times 13 = \frac{?}{65}$$

The unknown (?) is $7 \times 13 = 91$. In the example, the acre of forest has 91 maple saplings.

> **DID YOU KNOW?**
> When taking the reciprocal of both sides of a proportion, the proportion still holds. When setting up a proportion, ensure that the numerators represent the same type and the denominators represent the same type.

Example

If a recipe calls for 3 parts flour to 2 parts sugar, how much sugar does a baker need if she uses 12 cups of flour?

A. 2 cups   B. 3 cups   C. 6 cups   D. 8 cups

The correct answer is **D**. The baker needs 8 cups of sugar. First, note that "3 parts flour to 2 parts sugar" is the ratio 3:2. Set up the proportion using the given amount of flour (12 cups), putting the flour numbers in either the denominators or the numerators (either will yield the same answer): $\frac{3}{2} = \frac{12}{?}$. Since $12 \div 3 = 4$, multiply 2×4 to get 8 cups of sugar.

Rates of Change

Numbers that describe current quantities can be informative, but how they change over time can provide even greater insight into a problem. The rate of change for some quantity is the ratio of the quantity's difference over a specific time period to the length of that period. For example, if an automobile increases its speed from 50 mph to 100 mph in 10 seconds, the rate of change of its speed (its acceleration) is

$$\frac{100 \text{ mph} - 50 \text{ mph}}{10 \text{ s}} = \frac{50 \text{ mph}}{10 \text{ s}} = 5 \text{ mph per second} = 5 \text{ mph/s}$$

The basic formula for the rate of change of some quantity is

$$\frac{x_f - x_i}{t_f - t_i}$$

x_f = final quantity
x_i = initial quantity
t_f = final time
t_i = initial time

where t_f is the "final" (or ending) time and t_i is the "initial" (or starting) time. Also, x_f is the (final) quantity at (final) time t_f, and x_i is the (initial) quantity at (initial) time t_i.

In this formula, the numerator is the difference between the two quantities and the denominator is the difference in time.

In the example above, the final time is 10 seconds and the initial time is 0 seconds—hence the omission of the initial time from the calculation.

Consider that the final quantity occurs at the final time, and the initial quantity occurs at the initial time. As long as both quantities stay consistent in comparison, like with proportions, the order of the terms in the formula can be reversed.

$$\frac{x_f - x_i}{t_f - t_i} = \frac{x_i - x_f}{t_i - t_f}$$

This concept stays consistent with the rules of fractions, because multiplying the equation by -1 will result in the reversible formula.

The key to getting the correct rate of change is to ensure that the first number in the numerator and the first number in the denominator correspond to each other (that is, the quantity from the numerator corresponds to the time from the denominator). This must also be true for the second number

Example

If the population of an endangered frog species fell from 2,250 individuals to 2,115 individuals in a year, what is that population's annual rate of increase?

A. −135% B. −6% C. 6% D. 135%

The correct answer is **B**. The population's rate of increase was −6%. The solution in this case involves two steps. First, calculate the population's annual rate of change using the formula. It will yield the change in the number of individuals.

$$\frac{2,115 - 2,250}{1 \text{ year} - 0 \text{ year}} = -135 \text{ per year}$$

Second, divide the result by the initial population. Finally, convert to a percent.

$$\frac{-135 \text{ per year}}{2,250} = -0.06 \text{ per year}$$

$(-0.06 \text{ per year}) \times 100\% = -6\% \text{ per year}$

Since the question asks for the *annual* rate of increase, the "per year" can be dropped. Also, note that the answer must be negative to represent the decreasing population.

Let's Review!

- A percent—meaning "per hundred"—represents a relative quantity as a fraction or decimal. It is the absolute number multiplied by 100 and followed by the % symbol.
- A ratio is a relationship between two numbers expressed using fraction or colon notation (for example, $\frac{3}{2}$ or 3:2). Ratios behave mathematically just like fractions.
- An equation of two ratios is called a proportion. Proportions are used to solve problems involving scale
- Rates of change are the speeds at which quantities increase or decrease. The formula $\frac{x_f - x_i}{t_f - t_i}$ provides the rate of change of quantity x over the period between some initial (i) time and final (f) time.

POWERS, EXPONENTS, ROOTS, AND RADICALS

This lesson introduces how to apply the properties of exponents and examines square roots and cube roots. It also discusses how to estimate quantities using integer powers of 10.

Properties of Exponents

An expression that is a repeated multiplication of the same factor is a **power**. The **exponent** is the number of times the **base** is multiplied. For example, 6^2 is the same as 6 times 6, or 36. There are many rules associated with exponents.

Property	Definition	Examples
Product Rule (Same Base)	$a^m \times a^n = a^{m+n}$	$4^1 \times 4^4 = 4^{1+4} = 4^5 = 1024$
		$x^1 \times x^4 = x^{1+4} = x^5$
Product Rule (Different Base)	$a^m \times b^m = (a \times b)^m$	$2^2 \times 3^2 = (2 \times 3)^2 = 6^2 = 36$
		$3^3 \times x^3 = (3 \times x)^3 = (3x)^3 = 27x^3$
Quotient Rule (Same Base)	$\frac{a^m}{a^n} = a^{m-n}$	$\frac{4^4}{4^2} = 4^{4-2} = 4^2 = 16$
		$\frac{x^6}{x^3} = x^{6-3} = x^3$
Quotient Rule (Different Base)	$\frac{a^m}{b^m} = \left(\frac{a}{b}\right)^m$	$\frac{4^4}{3^4} = \left(\frac{4}{3}\right)^4$
		$\frac{x^6}{y^6} = \left(\frac{x}{y}\right)^6$
Power of a Power Rule	$(a^m)^n = a^{mn}$	$(2^2)^3 = 2^{2\times3} = 2^6 = 64$
		$(x^5)^8 = x^{5\times8} = x^{40}$
Zero Exponent Rule	$a^0 = 1$	$64^0 = 1$
		$y^0 = 1$
Negative Exponent Rule	$a^{-m} = \frac{1}{a^m}$	$3^{-3} = \frac{1}{3^3} = \frac{1}{27}$
		$\frac{1}{x^{-3}} = x^3$

For many exponent expressions, it is necessary t use multiplication rules to simplify the expression completely.

Examples

1. **Simplify $(3^2)^3$.**

   A. 18

   C. 243

   B. 216

   D. 729

   The correct answer is **D**. The correct solution is 729 because $(3^2)^3 = 3^{2\times3} = 3^6 = 729$.

> **KEEP IN MIND**
>
> The expressions
> $(-2)^2 = (-2) \times (-2) = 4$ and
> $-2^2 = -(2 \times 2) = -4$ have different results because of the location of the negative signs and parentheses. For each problem, focus on each detail to simplify completely and correctly.

2. **Simplify $(2x^2)^4$.**

   A. $2x^8$ B. $4x^4$ C. $8x^6$ D. $16x^8$

   The correct answer is **D**. The correct solution is $16x^8$ because $(2x^2)^4 = 2^4(x^2)^4 = 2^4 x^{2 \times 4} = 16x^8$.

3. **Simplify $\left(\frac{x^{-2}}{y^2}\right)^3$.**

   A. $\frac{1}{x^6 y^6}$ B. $\frac{x^6}{y^6}$ C. $\frac{y^6}{x^6}$ D. $x^6 y^6$

   The correct answer is **A**. The correct solution is $\frac{1}{x^6 y^6}$ because $\left(\frac{x^{-2}}{y^2}\right)^3 = \left(\frac{1}{x^2 y^2}\right)^3 = \frac{1}{x^{2 \times 3} y^{2 \times 3}} = \frac{1}{x^6 y^6}$.

Square Root and Cube Roots

The **square** of a number is the number raised to the power of 2. The **square root** of a number, when the number is squared, gives that number. $10^2 = 100$, so the square of 100 is 10, or $\sqrt{100} = 10$. **Perfect squares** are numbers with whole number square roots, such as 1, 4, 9, 16, and 25.

Squaring a number and taking a square root are opposite operations, meaning that the operations undo each other. This means that $\sqrt{x^2} = x$ and $(\sqrt{x})^2 = x$. When solving the equation $x^2 = p$, the solutions are $x = \pm\sqrt{p}$ because a negative value squared is a positive solution.

The **cube** of a number is the number raised to the power of 3. The **cube root** of a number, when the number is cubed, gives that number. $10^3 = 1000$, so the cube of 1,000 is 10, or $\sqrt[3]{1000} = 10$. **Perfect cubes** are numbers with whole number cube roots, such as 1, 8, 27, 64, and 125.

KEEP IN MIND

Most square roots and cube roots are not perfect roots.

Cubing a number and taking a cube root are opposite operations, meaning that the operations undo each other. This means that $\sqrt[3]{x^3} = x$ and $\left(\sqrt[3]{x}\right)^3 = x$. When solving the equation $x^3 = p$, the solution is $x = \sqrt[3]{p}$.

If a number is not a perfect square root or cube root, the solution is an approximation. When this occurs, the solution is an irrational number. For example, $\sqrt{2}$ is the irrational solution to $x^2 = 2$.

Examples

1. **Solve $x^2 = 121$.**

   A. –10, 10 B. –11, 11 C. –12, 12 D. –13, 13

   The correct answer is **B**. The correct solution is –11, 11 because the square root of 121 is 11. The values of –11 and 11 make the equation true.

2. **Solve $x^3 = 125$.**

   A. 1 B. 5 C. 10 D. 25

   The correct answer is **B**. The correct solution is 5 because the cube root of 125 is 5.

Express Large or Small Quantities as Multiples of 10

Scientific notation is a large or small number written in two parts. The first part is a number between 1 and 10. In these problems, the first digit will be a single digit. The number is followed by a multiple to a power of 10. A positive integer exponent means the number is greater than 1, while a negative integer exponent means the number is smaller than 1.

> **KEEP IN MIND**
>
> A positive exponent in scientific notation represents a large number, while a negative exponent represents a small number.

The number 3×10^4 is the same as $3 \times 10,000 = 30,000$.

The number 3×10^{-4} is the same as $3 \times 0.0001 = 0.0003$.

For example, the population of the United States is about 3×10^8, and the population of the world is about 7×10^9. The population of the United States is 300,000,000, and the population of the world is 7,000,000,000. The world population is about 20 times larger than the population of the United States.

Examples

1. **The population of China is about 1×10^9, and the population of the United States is about 3×10^8. How many times larger is the population of China than the population of the United States?**

   A. 2   B. 3   C. 4   D. 5

   The correct answer is **B**. The correct solution is 3 because the population of China is about 1,000,000,000 and the population of the United States is about 300,000,000. So the population is about 3 times larger.

2. **A red blood cell has a length of 8×10^{-6} meter, and a skin cell has a length of 3×10^{-5} meter. How many times larger is the skin cell?**

   A. 1   B. 2   C. 3   D. 4

   The correct answer is **D**. The correct solution is 4 because 3×10^{-5} is 0.00003 and 8×10^{-6} is 0.000008. So, the skin cell is about 4 times larger.

Let's Review!

- The properties and rules of exponents are applicable to generate equivalent expressions.
- Only a few whole numbers out of the set of whole numbers are perfect squares. Perfect cubes can be positive or negative.
- Numbers expressed in scientific notation are useful to compare large or small numbers.

CHAPTER 20 FUNCTIONS PRACTICE QUIZ

1. Multiply, $(x-1)(x^2 + 2x + 3)$.

   A. $x^3 + x^2 + x-3$

   B. $x^3 - x^2 - x - 3$

   C. $x^3 + x^2 - x - 3$

   D. $x^3 - x^2 + x - 3$

2. Apply the polynomial identity to rewrite $9x^2 - 30x + 25$.

   A. $(3x + 5)(3x-5)$

   B. $(3x-5)^2$

   C. $(3x-5)(3x-1)$

   D. $(3x-5)(3x + 1)$

3. Perform the operation, $(3y^2 + 4y)-(5y^3 - 2y^2 + 3)$.

   A. $-5y^3 + y^2 + 4y - 3$

   B. $-5y^3 + 5y^2 + 4y + 3$

   C. $-5y^3 + y^2 + 4y + 3$

   D. $-5y^3 + 5y^2 + 4y - 3$

4. Solve $x^3 = 343$.

   A. 6

   B. 7

   C. 8

   D. 9

5. One online seller has about 6×10^8 online orders, and another online seller has about 5×10^7 online orders. How many times more orders does the first company have?

   A. 12

   B. 15

   C. 20

   D. 32

6. Simplify $\frac{x^2y^{-2}}{x^{-3}y^3}$.

   A. $\frac{x^5}{y^5}$

   B. $\frac{y^5}{x^5}$

   C. $\frac{1}{x^5y^5}$

   D. x^5y^5

7. What is 15% of 64?

   A. 5:48

   B. 15:64

   C. 48:5

   D. 64:15

8. Which number satisfies the proportion $\frac{378}{?} = \frac{18}{7}$?

   A. 18

   B. 147

   C. 972

   D. 2,646

9. If a tree grows an average of 4.2 inches in a day, what is the rate of change in its height per month? Assume a month is 30 days.

   A. 0.14 inches per month

   B. 4.2 inches per month

   C. 34.2 inches per month

   D. 126 inches per month

10. Solve the equation by the quadratic formula, $11x^2 - 14x + 4 = 0$.

    A. -0.84 and -0.43

    B. 0.84 and -0.43

    C. -0.84 and 0.43

    D. 0.84 and 0.43

11. Solve the equation by any method, $3x^2 - 5 = 22$.

    A. 0

    B. ± 1

    C. ± 2

    D. ± 3

12. Solve the equation by the square root method, $5x^2 + 10 = 10$.

    A. 0

    B. 1

    C. 2

    D. 3

CHAPTER 20 FUNCTIONS
PRACTICE QUIZ – ANSWER KEY

1. A. The correct solution is $x^3 + x^2 + x - 3$.

$(x-1)(x^2 + 2x + 3) = (x-1)(x^2) + (x-1)(2x) + (x-1)(3)$
$= x^3 - x^2 + 2x^2 - 2x + 3x - 3 = x^3 + x^2 + x - 3$

See Lesson: Polynomials.

2. B. The correct solution is $(3x-5)^2$. The expression $9x^2 - 30x + 25$ is rewritten as $(3x-5)^2$ because the value of a is $3x$ and the value of b is 5. **See Lesson: Polynomials.**

3. D. The correct solution is $-5y^3 + 5y^2 + 4y - 3$.

$(3y^2 + 4y) - (5y^3 - 2y^2 + 3) = (3y^2 + 4y) + (-5y^3 + 2y^2 - 3)$
$= -5y^3 + (3y^2 + 2y^2) + 4y - 3 = -5y^3 + 5y^2 + 4y - 3$

See Lesson: Polynomials.

4. B. The correct solution is 7 because the cube root of 343 is 7. **See Lesson: Powers, Exponents, Roots, and Radicals.**

5. A. The correct solution is 12 because the first company has about 600,000,000 orders and the second company has about 50,000,000 orders. So, the first company is about 12 times larger. **See Lesson: Powers, Exponents, Roots, and Radicals.**

6. A. The correct solution is $\frac{x^5}{y^5}$ because $\frac{x^2 y^2}{x^{-3} y^3} = x^{2-(-3)} y^{-2-3} = x^5 y^{-5} = \frac{x^5}{y^5}$. **See Lesson: Powers, Exponents, Roots, and Radicals.**

7. C. Either set up a proportion or just note that this question is asking for a fraction of a specific number: 15% (or $\frac{3}{20}$) of 64. Multiply $\frac{3}{20}$ by 64 to get $\frac{48}{5}$, or 48:5. **See Lesson: Ratios, Proportions, and Percentages.**

8. B. The number 147 satisfies the proportion. First, divide 378 by 18 to get 21. Then, multiply 21 by 7 to get 147. Check your answer by dividing 147 by 7: the quotient is also 21, so 147 satisfies the proportion. **See Lesson: Ratios, Proportions, and Percentages.**

9. D. The rate of change is 126 inches per month. One approach is to set up a proportion.

$$\frac{1\ day}{4.2\ inches} = \frac{30\ days}{?}$$

Since 1 month is equivalent to 30 days, multiply the rate of change per day by 30 to get the rate of change per month. 4.2 inches multiplied by 30 is 126 inches. Thus, the growth rate is 126 inches per month. **See Lesson: Ratios, Proportions, and Percentages.**

10. D. The correct solutions are 0.84 and 0.43.

$$x = \frac{-(-14) \pm \sqrt{(-14)^2 - 4(11)(4)}}{2(11)}$$ Substitute 11 for a, –14 for b, and 4 for c.

$$x = \frac{14 \pm \sqrt{196 - 176}}{22}$$ Apply the exponent and perform the multiplication.

$$x = \frac{14 \pm \sqrt{20}}{22}$$ Perform the subtraction.

$$x = \frac{14 \pm 4.47}{22}$$ Apply the square root.

$$x = \frac{14 + 4.47}{22}, \ x = \frac{14 - 4.47}{22}$$ Separate the problem into two expressions.

$$x = \frac{18.47}{22} = 0.84, \ x = \frac{9.53}{22} = 0.43$$ Simplify the numerator and divide.

See Lesson: Solving Quadratic Equations.

11. D. The correct solutions are ± 3. Solve this equation by the square root method.

$3x^2 = 27$ Add 5 to both sides of the equation.

$x^2 = \pm 9$ Divide both sides of the equation by 3.

$x = \pm 3$ Apply the square root to both sides of the equation.

See Lesson: Solving Quadratic Equations.

12. A. The correct solution is 0.

$5x^2 = 0$ Subtract 10 from both sides of the equation.

$x^2 = 0$ Divide both sides of the equation by 5.

$x = 0$ Apply the square root to both sides of the equation.

See Lesson: Solving Quadratic Equations.

CHAPTER 21 GEOMETRY

CONGRUENCE

This lesson discusses basic terms for geometry. Many polygons have the property of lines of symmetry, or rotational symmetry. Rotations, reflections, and translations are ways to create congruent polygons.

Geometry Terms

The terms *point*, *line*, and *plane* help define other terms in geometry. A point is an exact location in space with no size and has a label with a capital letter. A line has location and direction, is always straight, and has infinitely many points that extend in both directions. A plane has infinitely many intersecting lines that extend forever in all directions.

The diagram shows point W, point X, point Y, and point Z. The line is labeled as $\overleftrightarrow{WX}$, and the plane is Plane A or Plane WYZ (or any three points in the plane).

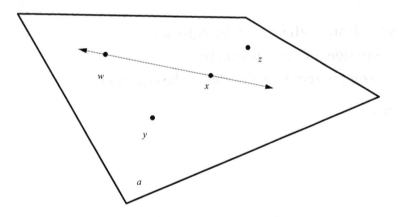

With these definitions, many other geometry terms can be defined. *Collinear* is a term for points that lie on the same line, and *coplanar* is a term for points and/or lines within the same plane. A line segment is a part of a line with two endpoints. For example, $\overline{WX}$ has endpoints W and X. A ray has an endpoint and extends forever in one direction. For example, $\overrightarrow{AB}$ has an endpoint of A, and $\overrightarrow{BA}$ has an endpoint of B. The intersection of lines, planes, segment, or rays is a point or a set of points.

Some key statements that are evident in geometry are

- There is exactly one straight line through any two points.
- There is exactly one plane that contains any three non-collinear points.
- A line with points in the plane lies in the plane.
- Two lines intersect at a point.
- Two planes intersect at a line.

Two rays that share an endpoint form an angle. The vertex is the common endpoint of the two rays that form an angle. When naming an angle, the vertex is the center point. The angle below is named ∠ABC or ∠CBA.

An acute angle has a measure between 0° and 90°, and a 90° angle is a right angle. An obtuse angle has a measure between 90° and 180°, and a 180° angle is a straight angle.

There are two special sets of lines. Parallel lines are at least two lines that never intersect within the same plane. Perpendicular lines intersect at one point and form four angles.

Example

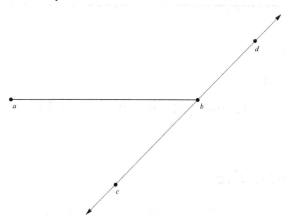

> **BE CAREFUL!**
> Lines are always named with two points, a plane can be named with three points, and an angle is named with the vertex as the center point.

Describe the diagram.

A. Points *A*, *B*, *C*, and *D* are collinear.

B. Points *A*, *C*, and *D* are collinear.

C. $\overline{CD}$ intersects $\overleftrightarrow{AB}$ at point *B*.

D. $\overline{AB}$ intersects $\overleftrightarrow{CD}$ at point *B*.

The correct answer is **D**. The correct solution is $\overline{AB}$ intersects $\overleftrightarrow{CD}$ at point *B*. The segment intersects the line at point *B*.

Line and Rotational Symmetry

Symmetry is a reflection or rotation of a shape that allows that shape to be carried onto itself. Line symmetry, or reflection symmetry, is when two halves of a shape are reflected onto each other across a line. A shape may have none, one, or several lines of symmetry. A kite has one line of symmetry, and a scalene triangle has no lines of symmetry.

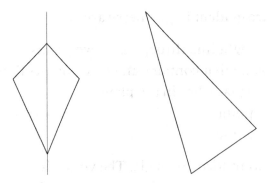

Rotational symmetry is when a figure can be mapped onto itself by a rotation about a point through any angle between 0° and 360°. The order of rotational symmetry is the number of times the object can be rotated. If there is no rotational symmetry, the order is 1 because the object can only be rotated 360° to map the figure onto itself. A square has 90° rotational symmetry and is order 4 because it can be rotated 90°, 180°, 270°, and 360°. A trapezoid has no rotational symmetry and is order 1 because it can only be rotated 360° to map onto itself.

> **KEEP IN MIND**
>
> A polygon can have both, neither, or either reflection and rotational symmetry.

Example

What is the rotational symmetry for a regular octagon?

A. 30°   B. 45°   C. 60°   D. 75°

The correct answer is **B**. The correct solution is 45°. For a regular polygon, divide 360° by the eight sides of the octagon to obtain 45°.

Rotations, Reflections, and Translations

There are three types of transformations: rotations, reflections, and translations. A rotation is a turn of a figure about a point in a given direction. A reflection is a flip over a line of symmetry, and a translation is a slide horizontally, vertically, or both. Each of these transformations produces a congruent image.

A rotation changes ordered pairs (x, y) in the coordinate plane. A 90° rotation counterclockwise about the point becomes $(-y, x)$, a 180° rotation counterclockwise about the point becomes $(-x, -y)$, and a 270° rotation the point becomes $(y, -x)$. Using the point $(6, -8)$,

- 90° rotation counterclockwise about the origin $(8, 6)$
- 180° rotation counterclockwise about the origin $(-6, 8)$
- 270° rotation counterclockwise about the origin $(-8, -6)$

A reflection also changes ordered pairs (x, y) in the coordinate plane. A reflection across the x-axis changes the sign of the y-coordinate, and a reflection across the y-axis changes the sign of the x-coordinate. A reflection over the line $y = x$ changes the points to (y, x), and a reflection over the line $y = -x$ changes the points to $(-y, -x)$. Using the point $(6, -8)$,

- A reflection across the x-axis $(6, 8)$
- A reflection across the y-axis $(-6, -8)$
- A reflection over the line $y = x$ $(-8, 6)$
- A reflection over the line $y = -x$ $(8, -6)$

A translation changes ordered pairs (x, y) left or right and/or up or down. Adding a positive value to an x-coordinate is a translation to the right, and adding a negative value to an x-coordinate is a translation to the left. Adding a positive value to

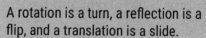

KEEP IN MIND

A rotation is a turn, a reflection is a flip, and a translation is a slide.

a y-coordinate is a translation up, and adding a negative value to a y-coordinate is a translation down. Using the point $(6, -8)$,

- A translation of $(x + 3)$ is a translation right 3 units $(9, -8)$
- A translation of $(x - 3)$ is a translation left 3 units $(3, -8)$
- A translation of $(y + 3)$ is a translation up 3 units $(6, -5)$
- A translation of $(y - 3)$ is a translation down 3 units $(6, -11)$

Example

$\triangle ABC$ has points A $(3, -2)$, B $(2, -1)$, and C $(-1, 4)$, which after a transformation become A' $(2, 3)$, B' $(1, 2)$, and C' $(-4, -1)$. What is the transformation between the points?

A. Reflection across the x-axis

B. Reflection across the y-axis

C. Rotation of 90° counterclockwise

D. Rotation of 270° counterclockwise

The correct answer is **C**. The correct solution is a rotation of 90° counterclockwise because the points (x, y) become $(y, -x)$.

Let's Review!

- The terms *point*, *line*, and *plane* help define many terms in geometry.
- Symmetry allows a figure to carry its shape onto itself. This can be reflectional or rotational symmetry.
- Three transformations are rotation (turn), reflection (flip), and translation (slide).

SIMILARITY, RIGHT TRIANGLES, AND TRIGONOMETRY

This lesson defines and applies terminology associated with coordinate planes. It also demonstrates how to find the area of two-dimensional shapes and the surface area and volume of three-dimensional cubes and right prisms.

Coordinate Plane

The **coordinate plane** is a two-dimensional number line with the horizontal axis called the **x-axis** and the vertical axis called the **y-axis**. Each **ordered pair** or **coordinate** is listed as (x, y). The center point is the origin and has an ordered pair of $(0, 0)$. A coordinate plane has four quadrants.

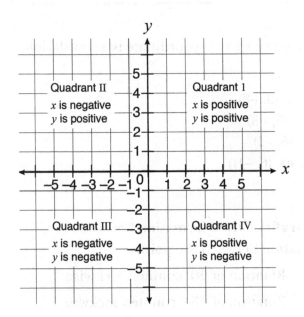

KEEP IN MIND

The x-coordinates are positive to the right of the y-axis. The y-coordinates are positive above the x-axis.

To graph a point in the coordinate plane, start with the x-coordinate. This point states the number of steps to the left (negative) or to the right (positive) from the origin. Then, the y-coordinate states the number of steps up (positive) or down (negative) from the x-coordinate.

Given a set of ordered pairs, points can be drawn in the coordinate plane to create polygons. The length of a segment can be found if the segment has the same first coordinate or the same second coordinate.

Examples

1. Draw a triangle with the coordinates (–2, –1), (–3, 5), (–4, 2).

A.
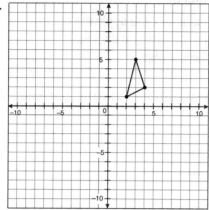

C.
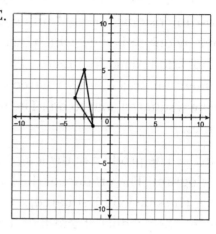

B.
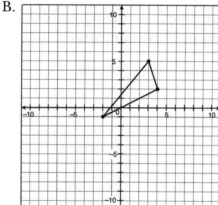

D.
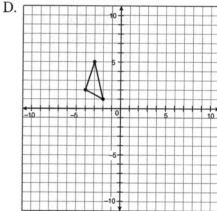

The correct answer is **C**. The first point is in the third quadrant because *x* is negative and *y* is negative, and the last two points are in the second quadrant because *x* is negative and *y* is positive.

2. Given the coordinates for a rectangle (4, 8), (4, –2), (–1, –2), (–1, 8), find the length of each side of the rectangle.

A. 3 units and 6 units

B. 3 units and 10 units

C. 5 units and 6 units

D. 5 units and 10 units

The correct answer is **D**. The correct solution is 5 units and 10 units. The difference between the *x*-coordinates is 4–(–1) = 5 units, and the difference between the *y*-coordinates is 8–(–2) = 10 units.

3. The dimensions for a soccer field are 45 meters by 90 meters. One corner of a soccer field on the coordinate plane is (–45, –30). What could a second coordinate be?

A. (–45, 30)   B. (–45, 45)   C. (–45, 60)   D. (–45, 75)

The correct answer is **C**. The correct solution is (–45, 60) because 90 can be added to the *y*-coordinate, –30 + 90 = 60.

Area of Two-Dimensional Objects

The **area** is the number of unit squares that fit inside a two-dimensional object. A unit square is one unit long by one unit wide, which includes 1 foot by 1 foot and 1 meter by 1 meter. The unit of measurement for area is units squared (or feet

squared, meters squared, and so on). The following are formulas for calculating the area of various shapes.

- Rectangle: The product of the length and the width, $A = lw$.
- Parallelogram: The product of the base and the height, $A = bh$.
- Square: The side length squared, $A = s^2$.
- Triangle: The product of one-half the base and the height, $A = \frac{1}{2}bh$.
- Trapezoid: The product of one-half the height and the sum of the bases, $A = \frac{1}{2}h(b_1 + b_2)$.
- Regular polygon: The product of one-half the **apothem** (a line from the center of the regular polygon that is perpendicular to a side) and the sum of the perimeter, $A = \frac{1}{2}ap$.

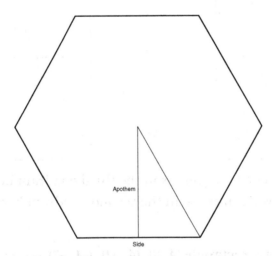

Apothem

Side

Examples

1. **A trapezoid has a height of 3 centimeters and bases of 8 centimeters and 10 centimeters. Find the area in square centimeters.**

   A. 18   B. 27   C. 52   D. 55

   The correct answer is **B**. The correct solution is 27. Substitute the values into the formula and simplify using the order of operations, $A = \frac{1}{2}h(b_1 + b_2) = \frac{1}{2}(3)(8 + 10) = \frac{1}{2}(3)(18) = 27$ square centimeters.

2. A regular decagon has a side length of 12 inches and an apothem of 6 inches. Find the area in square inches.

   A. 120　　　　　B. 360　　　　　C. 720　　　　　D. 960

   The correct answer is **B**. The correct solution is 360. Simplify using the order of operations, $A = \frac{1}{2}ap = \frac{1}{2}(6)(12(10)) = 360$ square inches.

3. Two rectangular rooms need to be carpeted. The dimensions of the first room are 18 feet by 19 feet, and the dimensions of the second room are 12 feet by 10 feet. What is the total area to be carpeted in square feet?

   A. 118　　　　　B. 236　　　　　C. 342　　　　　D. 462

   The correct answer is **D**. The correct solution is 462. Substitute the values into the formula and simplify using the order of operations, $A = lw + lw = 18(19) + 12(10) = 342 + 120 = 462$ square feet.

4. A picture frame is in the shape of a right triangle with legs 9 centimeters and 12 centimeters and hypotenuse of 15 centimeters. What is the area in square centimeters?

   A. 54　　　　　B. 90　　　　　C. 108　　　　　D. 180

   The correct answer is **A**. The correct solution is 54. Substitute the values into the formula and simplify using the order of operations, $A = \frac{1}{2}bh = \frac{1}{2}(9)(12) = 54$ square centimeters.

Surface Area and Volume of Cubes and Right Prisms

A three-dimensional object has length, width, and height. **Cubes** are made up of six congruent square faces. A **right prism** is made of three sets of congruent faces, with at least two sets of congruent rectangles.

> **BE CAREFUL!**
> Surface area is a two-dimensional calculation, and volume is a three-dimensional calculation.

The **surface area** of any three-dimensional object is the sum of the area of all faces. The formula for the surface area of a cube is $SA = 6s^2$ because there are six congruent faces. For a right rectangular prism, the surface area formula is $SA = 2lw + 2lh + 2hw$ because there are three sets of congruent rectangles. For a triangular prism, the surface area formula is twice the area of the base plus the area of the other three rectangles that make up the prism.

The **volume** of any three-dimensional object is the amount of space inside the object. The volume formula for a cube is $V = s^3$. The volume formula for a rectangular prism is the area of the base times the height, or $V = Bh$.

Examples

1. **A cube has a side length of 5 centimeters. What is the surface area in square centimeters?**

   A. 20   B. 25   C. 125   D. 150

   The correct answer is **D**. The correct solution is 150. Substitute the values into the formula and simplify using the order of operations, $SA = 6s^2 = 6(5^2) = 6(25) = 150$ square centimeters.

2. **A cube has a side length of 5 centimeters. What is the volume in cubic centimeters?**

   A. 20   B. 25   C. 125   D. 180

   The correct answer is **C**. The correct solution is 125. Substitute the values into the formula and simplify using the order of operations, $V = s^3 = 5^3 = 125$ cubic centimeters.

3. **A right rectangular prism has dimensions of 4 inches by 5 inches by 6 inches. What is the surface area in square inches?**

   A. 60   B. 74   C. 120   D. 148

   The correct answer is **D**. The correct solution is 148. Substitute the values into the formula and simplify using the order of operations, $SA = 2lw + 2lh + 2hw = 2(4)(5) + 2(4)(6) + 2(6)(5) = 40 + 48 + 60 = 148$ square inches.

4. **A right rectangular prism has dimensions of 4 inches by 5 inches by 6 inches. What is the volume in cubic inches?**

   A. 60   B. 62   C. 120   D. 124

   The correct answer is **C**. The correct solution is 120. Substitute the values into the formula and simplify using the order of operations, $V = lwh = 4(5)(6) = 120$ cubic inches.

Let's Review!

- The coordinate plane is a two-dimensional number line that is used to display ordered pairs. Two-dimensional shapes can be drawn on the plane, and the length of the objects can be determined based on the given coordinates.
- The area of a two-dimensional object is the amount of space inside the shape. There are area formulas to use to calculate the area of various shapes.
- For a three-dimensional object, the surface area is the sum of the area of the faces and the volume is the amount of space inside the object. Cubes and right rectangular prisms are common three-dimensional solids.

CIRCLES

This lesson introduces concepts of circles, including finding the circumference and the area of the circle.

Circle Terminology

A **circle** is a figure composed of points that are equidistant from a given point. The **center** is the point from which all points are equidistant. A **chord** is a segment whose endpoints are on the circle, and the **diameter** is a chord that goes through the center of the circle. The **radius** is a segment with one endpoint at the center of the circle and one endpoint on the circle. **Arcs** have two endpoints on the circle and all points on a circle between those endpoints.

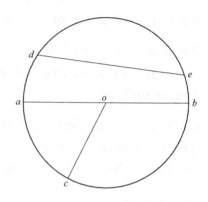

In the circle at the right, O is the center, $\overline{OC}$ is the radius, $\overline{AB}$ is the diameter, $\overline{DE}$ is a chord, and $\overset{\frown}{AD}$ is an arc.

Example

Identify a diameter of the circle.

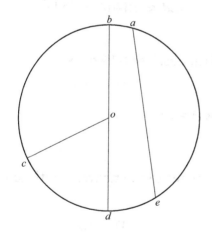

KEEP IN MIND

The radius is one-half the length of the diameter of the circle.

A. $\overline{BD}$	B. $\overline{OC}$	C. $\overline{DO}$	D. $\overline{AE}$

The correct answer is **A**. The correct solution is $\overline{BD}$ because points B and D are on the circle and the segment goes through the center O.

Circumference and Area of a Circle

The **circumference** of a circle is the perimeter, or the distance, around the circle. There are two ways to find the circumference. The formulas are the product of the diameter and pi or the product of twice the radius and pi. In symbol form, the formulas are $C = \pi d$ or $C = 2\pi r$.

BE CAREFUL!

Make sure that you apply the correct formula for circumference and area of a circle.

The **area** of a circle is the amount of space inside a circle. The formula is the product of pi and the radius squared. In symbol form, the formula is $A = \pi r^2$. The area is always expressed in square units.

Given the circumference or the area of a circle, the radius and the diameter can be determined. The given measurement is substituted into the appropriate formula. Then, the equation is solved for the radius or the diameter.

Examples

1. Find the circumference in centimeters of a circle with a diameter of 8 centimeters. Use 3.14 for π.

    A. 12.56   B. 25.12   C. 50.24   D. 100.48

    The correct answer is **B**. The correct solution is 25.12 because $C = \pi d \approx 3.14(8) \approx 25.12$ centimeters.

2. Find the area in square inches of a circle with a radius of 15 inches. Use 3.14 for π.

    A. 94.2   B. 176.63   C. 706.5   D. 828.96

    The correct answer is **C**. The correct solution is 706.5 because $A = \pi r^2 \approx 3.14(15)^2 \approx$

    $3.14(225) \approx 706.5$ square inches.

3. A circle has a circumference of 70 centimeters. Find the diameter to the nearest tenth of a centimeter. Use 3.14 for π.

    A. 11.1   B. 22.3   C. 33.5   D. 44.7

    The correct answer is **B**. The correct solution is 22.3 because $C = \pi d; 70 = 3.14d; d \approx 22.3$ centimeters.

4. A circle has an area of 95 square centimeters. Find the radius to the nearest tenth of a centimeter. Use 3.14 for π.

    A. 2.7   B. 5.5   C. 8.2   D. 10.9

    The correct answer is **B**. The correct solution is 5.5 because $A = \pi r^2; 95 = 3.14 r^2; 30.25 = r^2; r \approx 5.5$ centimeters.

Finding Circumference or Area Given the Other Value

Given the circumference of a circle, the area of the circle can be found. First, substitute the circumference into the formula and find the radius. Substitute the radius into the area formula and simplify.

Reverse the process to find the circumference given the area. First, substitute the area into the area formula and find the radius. Substitute the radius into the circumference formula and simplify.

BE CAREFUL!

Pay attention to the details with each formula and apply them in the correct order.

Examples

1. **The circumference of a circle is 45 inches. Find the area of the circle in square inches. Round to the nearest tenth. Use 3.14 for π.**

   A. 51.8   B. 65.1   C. 162.8   D. 204.5

   The correct answer is **C**. The correct solution is 162.8.

   $C = 2\pi r; 45 = 2(3.14)r; 45 = 6.28r; r \approx 7.2$ inches. $A = \pi r^2 \approx 3.14(7.2)^2 \approx 3.14(51.84) \approx 162.8$ square inches.

2. **The area of a circle is 60 square centimeters. Find the circumference of the circle in centimeters. Round to the nearest tenth. Use 3.14 for π.**

   A. 4.4   B. 13.8   C. 19.1   D. 27.6

   The correct answer is **D**. The correct solution is 27.6.

   $A = \pi r^2; 60 = 3.14 r^2; 19.11 = r^2; r \approx 4.4$ centimeters. $C = 2\pi r; C = 2(3.14)4.4 \approx 27.6$ centimeters.

Let's Review!

- Key terms related to circles are *radius, diameter, chord,* and *arc*. Note that the diameter is twice the radius.
- The circumference or the perimeter of a circle is the product of pi and the diameter or twice the radius and pi.
- The area of the circle is the product of pi and the radius squared.

MEASUREMENT AND DIMENSION

This lesson applies the formulas of volume for cylinders, pyramids, cones, and spheres to solve problems.

Volume of a Cylinder

A **cylinder** is a three-dimensional figure with two identical circular bases and a rectangular lateral face.

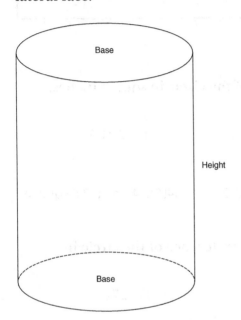

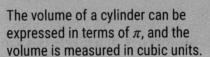

KEEP IN MIND

The volume of a cylinder can be expressed in terms of π, and the volume is measured in cubic units.

The volume of a cylinder equals the product of the area of the base and the height of the cylinder. This is the same formula used to calculate the volume of a right prism. In this case, the area of a base is a circle, so the formula is $V = Bh = \pi r^2 h$. The height is the perpendicular distance between the two circular bases.

Example

Find the volume of a cylinder in cubic centimeters with a radius of 13 centimeters and a height of 12 centimeters.

   A. 156π B. 312π C. $1{,}872\pi$ D. $2{,}028\pi$

The correct answer is **D**. The correct solution is $2{,}028\pi$. Substitute the values into the formula and simplify using the order of operations, $V = \pi r^2 h = \pi 13^2(12) = \pi(169)(12) = 2{,}028\pi$ cubic centimeters.

Volume of a Pyramid and a Cone

A **pyramid** is a three-dimensional solid with one base and all edges from the base meeting at the top, or apex. Pyramids can have any two-dimensional shape as the base. A **cone** is similar to a pyramid, but it has a circle instead of a polygon for the base.

> **BE CAREFUL!**
> Make sure that you apply the correct formula for area of the base for a pyramid.

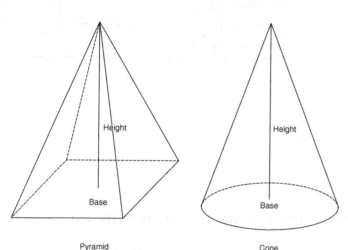

Pyramid   Cone

The formula for the volume of a pyramid is similar to a prism, $V = \frac{1}{3}Bh$ where B is the area of the base; in the case of a hexagonal pyramid B is = to $\frac{1}{2}(apothem)(perimeter)$. The base is a circle for a cone, and the formula for the volume is $V = \frac{1}{3}Bh = \frac{1}{3}\pi r^2 h$.

Examples

1. **A regular hexagonal pyramid has base with side lengths of 5 centimeters and an apothem of 3 centimeters. If the height is 6 centimeters, find the volume in cubic centimeters.**

   A. 90   B. 180   C. 270   D. 360

   The correct answer is **A**. The correct solution is 90. Substitute the values into the formula and simplify using the order of operations, $V = \frac{1}{3}Bh = \frac{1}{3}(\frac{1}{2}ap)h = \frac{1}{3}(\frac{1}{2}(3)(30))6 = 90$ cubic centimeters.

2. **A cone has a radius of 10 centimeters and a height of 9 centimeters. Find the volume in cubic centimeters.**

   A. 270π B. 300π C. 810π D. 900π

   The correct answer is **B**. The correct solution is 300π. Substitute the values into the formula and simplify using the order of operations, $V = \frac{1}{3}\pi r^2 h = \frac{1}{3}\pi 10^2(9) = \frac{1}{3}\pi(100)(9) = 300\pi$ cubic centimeters.

Volume of a Sphere

A **sphere** is a round, three-dimensional solid, with every point on its surface equidistant to the center. The formula for the volume of a sphere is represented by just the radius of the sphere. The volume of a sphere is $V = \frac{4}{3}\pi r^3$. The volume of a hemi (half) of a sphere is $V = \left(\frac{1}{2}\right)\frac{4}{3}\pi r^3 = \frac{2}{3}\pi r^3$.

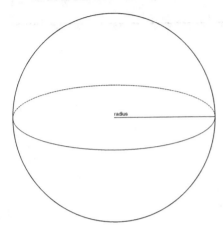

radius

BE CAREFUL!

The radius is cubed, not squared, for the volume of a sphere.

Example

A sphere has a radius of 3 centimeters. Find the volume of a sphere in cubic centimeters.

A. 18π B. 27π C. 36π D. 45π

The correct answer is **C**. The correct solution is 36π. Substitute the values into the formula and simplify using the order of operations, $V = \frac{4}{3}\pi r^3 = \frac{4}{3}\pi 3^3 = \frac{4}{3}\pi(27) = 36\pi$ cubic centimeters.

Let's Review!

- The volume is the capacity of a three-dimensional object and is expressed in cubic units.
- The volume formula for a cylinder is the product of the area of the base (which is a circle) and the height of the cylinder.
- The volume formula for a pyramid or cone is one-third of the product of the area of the base (a circle in the case of the cone) and the height of the pyramid or cone.
- The volume formula for a sphere is $V = \frac{4}{3}\pi r^3$.

CHAPTER 21 GEOMETRY PRACTICE QUIZ

1. The bottom of a plastic pool has an area of 64 square feet. What is the radius to the nearest tenth of a foot? Use 3.14 for π.

   A. 2.3   C. 6.9

   B. 4.5   D. 10.2

2. The area of a circular hand mirror is 200 square centimeters. Find the circumference of the mirror to the nearest tenth of a centimeter. Use 3.14 for π.

   A. 25.1   C. 75.3

   B. 50.2   D. 100.4

3. The circumference of a pie is 300 centimeters. Find the area of one-fourth of the pie to the nearest tenth of a square centimeter. Use 3.14 for π.

   A. 1,793.6   C. 7,174.4

   B. 2,284.8   D. 14,348.8

4. A regular hexagon has a rotational order of 6. What is the smallest number of degrees for the figure to be rotated onto itself?

   A. 30°   C. 90°

   B. 60°   D. 120°

5. A right triangle has a base of 6 inches and a hypotenuse of 10 inches. Find the height in inches of the triangle if the area is 24 square inches.

   A. 4   C. 8

   B. 6   D. 10

6. $\triangle GHI$ has points $G(2, 7)$, $H(-3, -8)$, and $I(-6, 0)$. After a transformation, the points are $G'(7, 2)$, $H'(-8, -3)$, and $I'(0, -6)$. What is the transformation between the points?

   A. Reflection across the x-axis

   B. Reflection across the y-axis

   C. Reflection across the line of $y = x$

   D. Reflection across the line of $y = -x$

7. Name the right angle in the diagram.

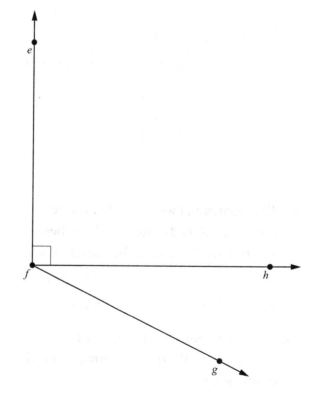

   A. $\angle EHF$ C. $\angle EFH$

   B. $\angle EFG$ D. $\angle EGF$

8. Draw a rectangle with the coordinates $(5,7), (5,1), (1,1), (1,7)$.

A.
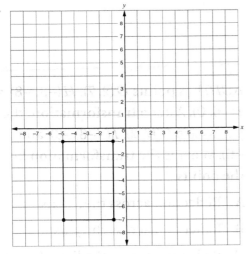

C.
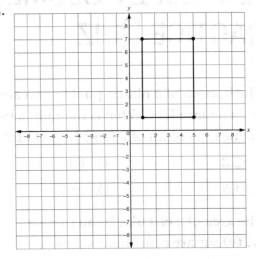

B.
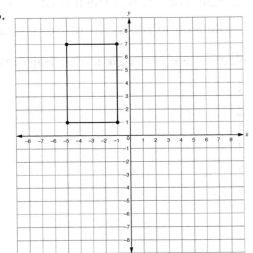

D.
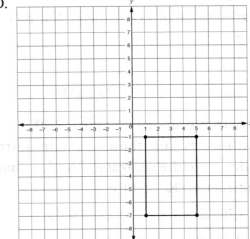

9. The volume of a cone is 28π cubic inches, and its diameter is 2 inches. What is the height of the cone?

   A. 2 inches   C. 6 inches

   B. 4 inches   D. 8 inches

10. A hemi-sphere has a radius of 6 centimeters. Find the volume in cubic centimeters.

    A. 72π C. 288π

    B. 144π D. 576π

11. A rectangular pyramid has a height of 7 meters and a volume of 112 cubic meters. Find the area of the base in square meters.

    A. 16   C. 42

    B. 28   D. 48

12. A right rectangular prism has dimensions of 3 inches by 6 inches by 9 inches. What is the surface area in square inches?

    A. 162   C. 232

    B. 198   D. 286

CHAPTER 21 GEOMETRY PRACTICE QUIZ – ANSWER KEY

1. B. The correct solution is 4.5 because $A = \pi r^2$; $64 = 3.14 r^2$; $20.38 = r^2$; $r \approx 4.5$ feet. **See Lesson: Circles.**

2. B. The correct solution is 50.2. $A = \pi r^2$; $200 = 3.14 r^2$; $63.69 = r^2$; $r \approx 8.0$ centimeters. $C = 2\pi r$; $C = 2$ (3.14)8.0 $\approx$ 50.2 centimeters. **See Lesson: Circles.**

3. A. The correct solution is 1,793.6. $C = 2\pi r$; $300 = 2(3.14)r$; $300 = 6.28r$; $r \approx 47.8$ centimeters. $A = \frac{1}{4}\pi$ $r^2 \approx \frac{1}{4}(3.14)(47.8)^2 \approx \frac{1}{4}3.14(2,284.84) \approx 1793.6$ square centimeters. **See Lesson: Circles.**

4. B. The correct solution is 60°. For a regular hexagon, divide 360° by the six sides to obtain 60°. **See Lesson: Congruence.**

5. C. The correct solution is 8. Substitute the values into the formula, $24 = \frac{1}{2}(6)h$ and simplify the right side of the equation, $24 = 3h$. Divide both sides of the equation by 3, $h = 8$ inches. **See Lesson: Similarity, Right Triangles, and Trigonometry.**

6. C. The correct solution is a reflection across the line of $y = x$ because the points (x, y) become (y, x). **See Lesson: Congruence.**

7. C. The correct solution is $\angle EFH$ because the vertex of the right angle is F and the other two points are E and H. **See Lesson: Congruence.**

8. C. All points are in the first quadrant. **See Lesson: Similarity, Right Triangles, and Trigonometry.**

9. C. The correct solution is 6 inches. Substitute the values into the formula, $2\pi = \frac{1}{3}\pi(1)^2 h$ and simplify using the right side of the equation by applying the exponent and multiplying, $2\pi = \frac{1}{3}\pi$ $(1)h$, $2\pi = \frac{1}{3}\pi h$. Multiply both sides of the equation by 3 to get a solution of 6 inches. **See Lesson: Measurement and Dimension.**

10. B. The correct solution is 144π. Substitute the values into the formula and simplify using the order of operations, $V = \frac{2}{3}\pi r^3 = \frac{2}{3}\pi(6^3) = \frac{2}{3}\pi(216) = 144\pi$ cubic centimeters. **See Lesson: Measurement and Dimension.**

11. D. The correct solution is 48. Substitute the values into the formula, $112 = \frac{1}{3}B(7)$ and simplify the right side of the equation, $112 = \frac{7}{3}B$. Multiply both sides of the equation by the reciprocal, B = 48 square meters. **See Lesson: Measurement and Dimension.**

12. B. The correct solution is 198. Substitute the values into the formula and simplify using the order of operations, $SA = 2lw + 2lh + 2hw = 2(3)(6) + 2(6)(9) + 2(9)(3) = 36 + 108 + 54 = 198$ square inches. **See Lesson: Similarity, Right Triangles, and Trigonometry.**

CHAPTER 22 STATISTICS AND PROBABILITY

INTERPRETING GRAPHICS

This lesson discusses how to create a bar, line, and circle graph and how to interpret data from these graphs. It also explores how to calculate and interpret the measures of central tendency.

Creating a Line, Bar, and Circle Graph

A line graph is a graph with points connected by segments that examines changes over time. The horizontal axis contains the independent variable (the input value), which is usually time. The vertical axis contains the dependent variable (the output value), which is an item that measures a quantity. A line graph will have a title and an appropriate scale to display the data. The graph can include more than one line.

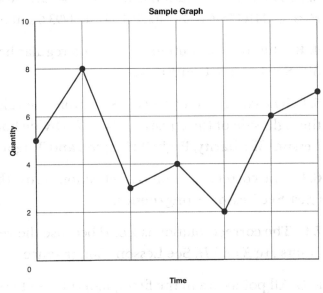

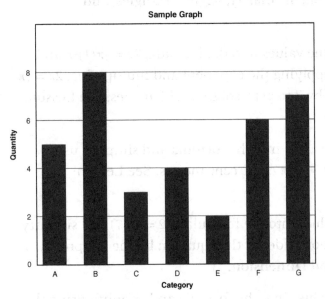

A bar graph uses rectangular horizontal or vertical bars to display information. A bar graph has categories on the horizontal axis and the quantity on the vertical axis. Bar graphs need a title and an appropriate scale for the frequency. The graph can include more than one bar.

BE CAREFUL

Make sure to use the appropriate scale for each type of graph.

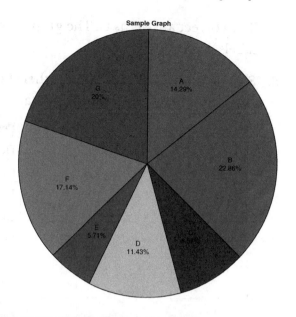

Sample Graph

A circle graph is a circular chart that is divided into parts, and each part shows the relative size of the value. To create a circle graph, find the total number and divide each part by the total to find the percentage. Then, to find the part of the circle, multiply each percent by 360°. Draw each part of the circle and create a title.

Examples

1. The table shows the amount of rainfall in inches. Select the line graph that represents this data.

Day	1	2	3	4	5	6	7	8	9	10	11	12
Rainfall Amount	0.5	0.2	0.4	1.1	1.6	0.9	0.7	1.3	1.5	0.8	0.5	0.1

A.

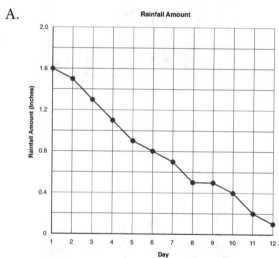

C.

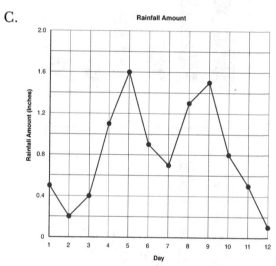

B.

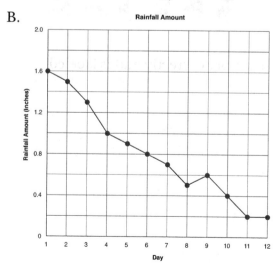

D.

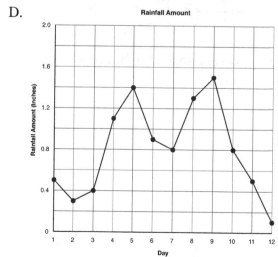

441

The correct answer is **C**. The graph is displayed correctly for the days with the appropriate labels.

2. **Students were surveyed about their favorite pet, and the table shows the results. Select the bar graph that represents this data.**

Pet	Quantity
Dog	14
Cat	16
Fish	4
Bird	8
Gerbil	7
Pig	3

A.

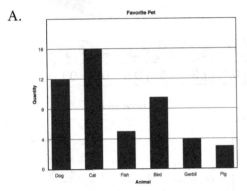

C.

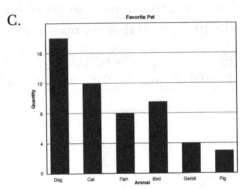

B.

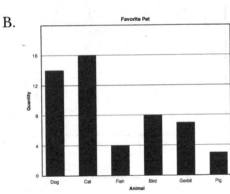

D.

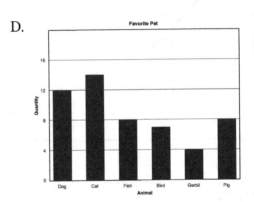

The correct answer is **B**. The bar graph represents each pet correctly and is labeled correctly.

3. The table shows the amount a family spends each month. Select the circle graph that represents the data.

Item	Food/Household Items	Bills	Mortgage	Savings	Miscellaneous
Amount	$700	$600	$400	$200	$100

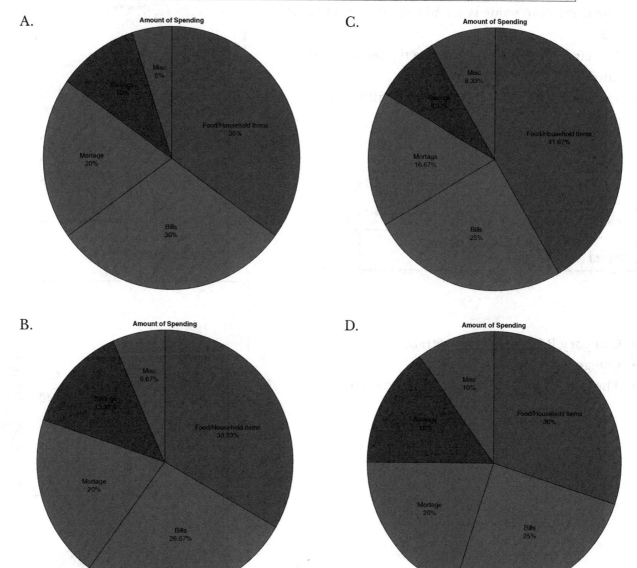

A.

C.

B.

D.

The correct answer is **A**. The total amount spent each month is $2,000. The section of the circle for food and household items is $\frac{700}{2,000} = 0.35 = 35\%$. The section of the circle for bills is $\frac{600}{2,000} = 0.30 = 30\%$. The section of the circle for mortgage is $\frac{400}{2,000} = 0.20 = 20\%$. The section of the circle for savings is $\frac{200}{2,000} = 0.10 = 10\%$. The section of the circle for miscellaneous is $\frac{100}{2,000} = 0.05 = 5\%$.

Interpreting and Evaluating Line, Bar, and Circle Graphs

Graph and charts are used to create visual examples of information, and it is important to be able to interpret them. The examples from Section 1 can show a variety of conclusions.

- The minimum value is 2, and the maximum value is 8.
- The largest decrease is between the second and third points.
- The largest increase is between the fifth and sixth points.

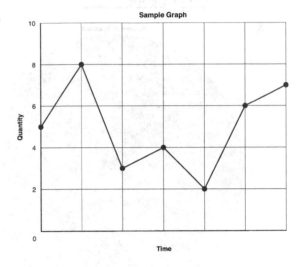

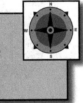

KEEP IN MIND

Read and determine the parts of the graph before answering questions related to the graph.

- Category B is the highest with 8.
- Category E is the lowest with 2.
- There are no categories that are the same.

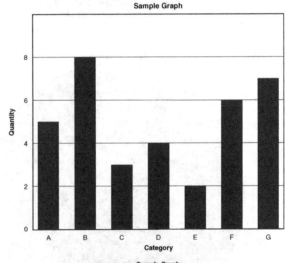

- Category B is the largest with 22.86%.
- Category E is the smallest with 5.71%.
- All of the categories are less than one-fourth of the graph.

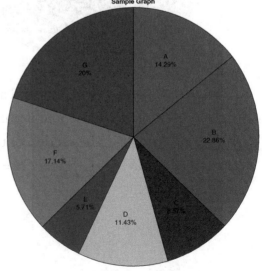

Examples

1. The line chart shows the number of minutes a commuter drove to work during a month. Which statement is true for the line chart?

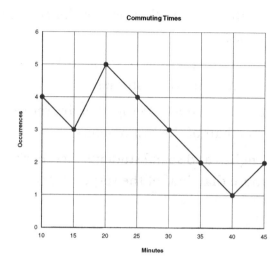

A. The commuter drove 25 minutes to work the most times

B. The commuter drove 25 minutes to work the fewest times.

C. The commuter took 10 minutes and 25 minutes twice during the month.

D. The commuter took 35 minutes and 45 minutes twice during the month.

The correct answer is **D**. The commuter took 35 minutes and 45 minutes twice during the month.

2. The bar chart shows the distance different families traveled for summer vacation. Which statement is true for the bar chart?

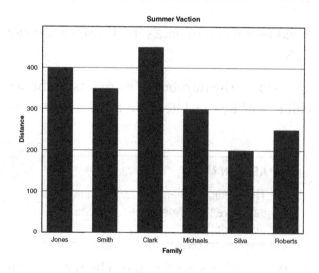

A. All families drove more than 200 miles.

B. The Clark family traveled 250 miles more than the Silva family.

C. The Roberts family traveled more miles than the Michaels family.

D. The Jones family is the only family that traveled 400 miles or more.

The correct answer is **B**. The correct solution is the Clark family traveled 250 miles more than the Silva family. The Clark family traveled 450 miles, and the Silva family traveled 200 miles, making the difference 250 miles.

3. Students were interviewed about their favorite subject in school. The circle graph shows the results. Which statement is true for the circle graph?

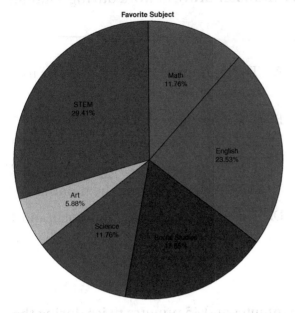

Favorite Subject

Math 11.76%

STEM 29.41%

English 23.53%

Art 5.88%

Science 11.76%

Social Studies 17.65%

A. Math is the smallest percent for favorite subject.

B. The same number of students favor science and social studies.

C. English and STEM together are more than half of the respondents.

D. English and social students together are more than half of the respondents.

The correct answer is **C**. The correct solution is English and STEM together are more than half of the respondents because these values are more than 50% combined.

Mean, Median, Mode, and Range

The mean, median, mode, and range are common values related to data sets. These values can be calculated using the data set 2, 4, 7, 6, 8, 5, 6, and 3.

The mean is the sum of all numbers in a data set divided by the number of elements in the set. The sum of items in the data set is 41. Divide the value of 41 by the 8 items in the set. The mean is 5.125.

The median is the middle number of a data set when written in order. If there are an odd number of items, the median is the middle number. If there are an even number of items, the median is the mean of the middle two numbers. The

KEEP IN MIND

The mean, median, mode, and range can have the same values, depending on the data set.

numbers in order are 2, 3, 4, 5, 6, 6, 7, 8. The middle two numbers are 5 and 6. The mean of the two middle numbers is 5.5, which is the median.

The mode is the number or numbers that occur most often. There can be no modes, one mode, or many modes. In the data set, the number 6 appears twice, making 6 the mode.

The range is the difference between the highest and lowest values in a data set. The highest value is 8 and the lowest value is 2, for a range of 6.

Examples

1. Find the mean and the median for the data set 10, 20, 40, 20, 30, 50, 40, 60, 30, 10, 40, 20, 50, 70, and 80.

    A. The mean is 40, and the median is 38.

    B. The mean is 38, and the median is 40.

    C. The mean is 36, and the median is 50.

    D. The mean is 50, and the median is 36.

    The correct answer is **B**. The correct solution is the mean is 38 and the median is 40. The sum of all items is 570 divided by 15, which is 38. The data set in order is 10, 10, 20, 20, 20, 30, 30, 40, 40, 40, 50, 50, 60, 70, 80. The median number is 40.

2. Find the mode and the range for the data set 10, 20, 40, 20, 30, 50, 40, 60, 30, 10, 40, 20, 50, 70, and 80.

    A. The mode is 20, and the range is 70.

    B. The mode is 40, and the range is 70.

    C. The modes are 20 and 40, and the range is 70.

    D. The modes are 20, 40, and 70, and the range is 70.

    The correct answer is **C**. The correct solution is the modes are 20 and 40 and the range is 70. The modes are 20 and 40 because each of these numbers appears three times. The range is the difference between 80 and 10, which is 70.

Let's Review!

*   A bar graph, line graph, and circle graph are different ways to summarize and represent data.

*   The mean, median, mode, and range are values that can be used to interpret the meaning of a set of numbers.

STATISTICAL MEASURES

This lesson explores the different sampling techniques using random and non-random sampling. The lesson also distinguishes among different study techniques. In addition, it provides simulations that compare results with expected outcomes.

Probability and Non-Probability Sampling

A population includes all items within a set of data, while a sample consists of one or more observations from a population.

The collection of data samples from a population is an important part of research and helps researcher draw conclusions related to populations. Probability sampling creates a sample from a population by using random sampling techniques.

KEEP IN MIND
Probability sampling is random, and non-probability sampling is not random.

Every person within a population has an equal chance of being selected for a sample. Non-probability sampling creates a sample from a population without using random sampling techniques.

There are four types of probability sampling. Simple random sampling is assigning a number to each member of a population and randomly selecting numbers. Stratified sampling uses simple random sampling after the population is split into equal groups. Systematic sampling chooses every n^{th} member from a list or a group. Cluster random sampling uses natural groups in a population: the population is divided into groups, and random samples are collected from groups.

Each type of probability sampling has an advantage and a disadvantage when finding an appropriate sample.

Probability Sampling	Advantage	Disadvantage
Simple random sampling	Most cases have a sample representative of a population	Not efficient for large samples
Stratified random sampling	Creates layers of random samples from different groups representative of a population	Not efficient for large samples
Systematic sampling	Creates a sample representative of population without a random number selection	Not as random as simple random sampling
Cluster random sampling	Relatively easy and convenient to implement	Might not work if clusters are different from one another

There are four types of non-probability sampling. Convenience sampling produces samples that are easy to access. Volunteer sampling asks for volunteers or recommendations for a sample. Purposive sampling bases samples on specific characteristics by selecting samples from a group that meets the qualifications of the study. Quota sampling is choosing samples of groups of the subpopulation.

Examples

1. **A factory is studying the quality of beverage samples. There are 50 bottles randomly chosen from one shipment every 60 minutes. What type of sampling is used?**

    A. Systematic sampling

    B. Simple random sampling

    C. Cluster random sampling

    D. Stratified random sampling

    The correct answer is **C**. The correct solution is cluster random sampling because bottles of beverage are selected within specific boundaries.

2. **A group conducting a survey asks a person for his or her opinion. Then, the group asks the person being surveyed for the names of 10 friends to obtain additional options. What type of sampling is used?**

    A. Quota sampling

    B. Volunteer sampling

    C. Purposive sampling

    D. Convenience sampling

    The correct answer is **B**. The correct solution is volunteer sampling because the group is looking for recommendations.

Census, Surveys, Experiments, Observational Studies

Various sampling techniques are used to collect data from a population. These are in the form of a census, a survey, observational studies, or experiments.

A census collects data by asking everyone in a population the same question. Asking everyone at school or everyone at work are examples of a

> **KEEP IN MIND**
>
> A census includes everyone within a population, and a survey includes every subject of a sample. An observational study involves watching groups randomly, and an experiment involves assigning groups.

census. A survey collects data on every subject within a sample. The subjects can be determined by convenience sampling or by simple random sampling. Examples of surveys are asking sophomores at school or first shift workers at work.

In an observational study, data collection occurs by watching or observing an event. Watching children who play outside and observing if they drink water or sports drinks is an example. An experiment is way of finding information by assigning people to groups and collecting data on observations. Assigning one group of children to drink water and another group to drink sports drinks after playing and making comparisons is an example of an experiment.

Examples

1. **A school wants to create a census to identify students' favorite subject in school. Which group should the school ask?**

   A. All staff

   C. All sophomores

   B. All students

   D. All male students

   The correct answer is **B.** The correct solution is all students because this gathers information on the entire population.

2. **A researcher records the arrival time of employees at a job based on their actual start time. What type of study is this?**

   A. Census

   C. Experiment

   B. Survey

   D. Observational study

   The correct answer is **D.** The correct solution is observational study because the researcher is observing the time the employees arrive at work.

3. **The local county wants to test the water quality of a stream by collecting samples. What should the county collect?**

   A. The water quality at one spot

   C. The water quality under bridges

   B. The water quality under trees

   D. The water quality at different spots

   The correct answer is **D.** The correct solution is the water quality at different spots because this survey allows for the collection of different samples.

Simulations

A simulation enables researchers to study real-world events by modeling events. Advantages of simulations are that they are quick, easy, and inexpensive; the disadvantage is that the results are approximations. The steps to complete a simulation are as follows:

KEEP IN MIND

A simulation is only useful if the results closely mirror real-world outcomes.

- Describe the outcomes.
- Assign a random value to the outcomes.
- Choose a source to generate the outcomes.
- Generate values for the outcomes until a consistent pattern emerges.
- Analyze the results.

Examples

1. A family has two children and wants to simulate the gender of the children. Which object would be beneficial to use for the simulation?

   A. Coin

   B. Four-section spinner

   C. Six-sided number cube

   D. Random number generator

   The correct answer is **B**. The correct solution is a four-section spinner because there are four possible outcomes of the event (boy/boy, boy/girl, girl/boy, and girl/girl).

2. There are six options from which to choose a meal at a festival. A model using a six-sided number cube is used to represent the simulation.

Hamburger	Chicken	Hot Dog	Bratwurst	Pork Chop	Fish	Total
1	2	3	4	5	6	
83	82	85	89	86	75	500

   Choose the statement that correctly answers whether the simulation of using a six-sided number cube is consistent with the actual number of dinners sold and then explains why or why not.

   A. The simulation is consistent because it has six equally likely outcomes.

   B. The simulation is consistent because it has two equally likely outcomes.

   C. The simulation is not consistent because of the limited number of outcomes.

   D. The simulation is not consistent because of the unlimited number of outcomes.

   The correct answer is **A**. The correct solution is the simulation is consistent because it has six equally likely outcomes. The six-sided number cube provides consistent outcomes because there is an equal opportunity to select any dinner.

Let's Review!

- Probability (random) sampling and non-probability (not random) sampling are ways to collect data.
- Censuses, surveys, experiments, and observational studies are ways to collect data from a population.
- A simulation is way to model random events and compare the results to real-world outcomes.

STATISTICS & PROBABILITY: THE RULES OF PROBABILITY

This lesson explores a sample space and its outcomes and provides an introduction to probability, including how to calculate expected values and analyze decisions based on probability.

Sample Space

A **sample space** is the set of all possible outcomes. Using a deck of cards labeled 1–10, the sample space is 1, 2, 3, 4, 5, 6, 7, 8, 9, and 10. An **event** is a subset of the sample space. For example, if a card is drawn and the outcome of the event is an even number, possible results are 2, 4, 6, 8, 10.

The **union** of two events is everything in both events, and the notation is $A \cup B$. The union of events is associated with the word *or*. For example, a card is drawn that is either a multiple of 3 or a multiple of 4. The set containing the multiples of 3 is 3, 6, and 9. The set containing the multiples of 4 is 4 and 8. The union of the set is 3, 4, 6, 8, and 9.

> **KEEP IN MIND**
>
> The intersection of an event can have no values. The intersection of drawing a card that is even and odd is a set with no values because a card cannot be both even and odd. The complement of an event is the "not," or the opposite of, the event.

The **intersection** of two events is all of the events in both sets, and the notation is $A \cap B$. The intersection of events is associated with the word *and*. For example, a card is drawn that is even and a multiple of 4. The set containing even numbers is 2, 4, 6, 8, and 10. The set containing the multiples of 4 is 4 and 8. The intersection is 4 and 8 because these numbers are in both sets.

The **complement** of an event is an outcome that is not part of the set. The complement of an event is associated with the word *not*. A card is drawn and is not a multiple of 5. The set not containing multiples of 5 is 1, 2, 3, 4, 6, 7, 8, and 9. The complement of not a multiple of 5 is 1, 2, 3, 4, 6, 7, 8, and 9.

Examples

Use the following table of the results when rolling two six-sided number cubes.

1, 1	1, 2	1, 3	1, 4	1, 5	1, 6
2, 1	2, 2	2, 3	2, 4	2, 5	2, 6
3, 1	3, 2	3, 3	3, 4	3, 5	3, 6
4, 1	4, 2	4, 3	4, 4	4, 5	4, 6
5, 1	5, 2	5, 3	5, 4	5, 5	5, 6
6, 1	6, 2	6, 3	6, 4	6, 5	6, 6

1. **How many possible outcomes are there for the union of rolling a sum of 3 or a sum of 5?**

    A. 2   B. 4   C. 6   D. 8

    The correct answer is **C.** The correct solution is 6 possible outcomes. There are two options for the first event (2, 1) and (1, 2). There are 4 options for the second event (4, 1), (3, 2), (2, 3), and (1, 4). The union of two events is six possible outcomes.

2. **How many possible outcomes are there for the intersection of rolling a double and a multiple of 3?**

    A. 0   B. 2   C. 4   D. 6

    The correct answer is **B.** The correct solution is 2 possible outcomes. There are six options for the first event (1, 1), (2, 2), (3, 3), (4, 4), (5, 5), and (6, 6). There are 12 options for the second event of the multiple of three. The intersection is (3, 3) and (6, 6) because these numbers meet both requirements.

3. **How many possible outcomes are there for the complement of rolling a 3 and a 5?**

    A. 16   B. 18   C. 27   D. 36

    The correct answer is **A.** The correct solution is 16 possible outcomes. There are 16 options of not rolling a 3 or a 5.

Probability

The **probability** of an event is the number of favorable outcomes divided by the total number of possible outcomes.

BE CAREFUL!

Make sure that you apply the correct formula for the probability of an event.

$$Probability = \frac{number\ of\ favorable\ outcomes}{number\ of\ possible\ outcomes}$$

Probability is a value between 0 (event does not happen) and 1 (event will happen). For example, the probability of getting heads when a coin is flipped is $\frac{1}{2}$ because heads is 1 option out of 2 possibilities. The probability of rolling an odd number on a six-sided number cube is $\frac{3}{6} = \frac{1}{2}$ because there are three odd numbers, 1, 3, and 5, out of 6 possible numbers.

The probability of an "or" event happening is the sum of the events happening. For example, the probability of rolling an odd number or a 4 on a six-sided number cube is $\frac{4}{6}$. The probability of rolling an odd number is $\frac{3}{6}$, and the probability of rolling a 4 is $\frac{1}{6}$. Therefore, the probability is $\frac{3}{6} + \frac{1}{6} = \frac{4}{6} = \frac{2}{3}$.

The probability of an "and" event happening is the product of the probability of two or more events. The probability of rolling 6 three times in a row is $\frac{1}{216}$. The probability of a single event is $\frac{1}{6}$, and this fraction is multiplied three times to find the probability, $\frac{1}{6} \times \frac{1}{6} \times \frac{1}{6}$. There are cases of "with replacement" when the item is returned to the pile and "without replacement" when the item is not returned to the pile.

The probability of a "not" event happening is 1 minus the probability of the event occurring. For example, the probability of not rolling 6 three times in a row is $1 - \frac{1}{216} = \frac{215}{216}$.

Examples

1. A deck of cards contains 40 cards divided into 4 colors: red, blue, green, and yellow. Each group has cards numbered 0–9. What is the probability of selecting an 8?

   A. $\frac{1}{10}$　　　　B. $\frac{1}{8}$　　　　C. $\frac{1}{4}$　　　　D. $\frac{1}{2}$

   The correct answer is **A**. The correct solution is $\frac{1}{10}$. There are 4 cards out of 40 that contain the number 8, making the probability $\frac{4}{40} = \frac{1}{10}$.

2. A deck of cards contains 40 cards divided into 4 colors: red, blue, green, and yellow. Each group has cards numbered 0–9. What is the probability of selecting an even or a red card?

   A. $\frac{1}{4}$　　　　B. $\frac{3}{8}$　　　　C. $\frac{5}{8}$　　　　D. $\frac{3}{4}$

   The correct answer is **C**. The correct solution is $\frac{5}{8}$. There are 20 even cards and 10 red cards. The overlap of 5 red even cards is subtracted from the probability, $\frac{20}{40} + \frac{10}{40} - \frac{5}{40} = \frac{25}{40} = \frac{5}{8}$.

3. A deck of cards contains 40 cards divided into 4 colors: red, blue, green, and yellow. Each group has cards numbered 0–9. What is the probability of selecting a blue card first, replacing the card, and selecting a 9?

   A. $\frac{1}{100}$　　　　B. $\frac{1}{80}$　　　　C. $\frac{1}{40}$　　　　D. $\frac{1}{20}$

   The correct answer is **C**. The correct solution is $\frac{1}{40}$. There are 10 blue cards and 4 cards that contain the number 9. The probability of the event is $\frac{10}{40} \times \frac{4}{40} = \frac{40}{1600} = \frac{1}{40}$.

4. A deck of cards contains 40 cards divided into 4 colors: red, blue, green, and yellow. Each group has cards numbered 0–9. What is the probability of NOT selecting a green card?

   A. $\frac{1}{4}$　　　　B. $\frac{3}{8}$　　　　C. $\frac{1}{2}$　　　　D. $\frac{3}{4}$

   The correct answer is **D**. The correct solution is $\frac{3}{4}$. There are 10 cards that are green, making the probability of NOT selecting a green card $1 - \frac{10}{40} = \frac{30}{40} = \frac{3}{4}$.

Calculating Expected Values and Analyzing Decisions Based on Probability

The **expected value** of an event is the sum of the products of the probability of an event times the payoff of an event. A good example is calculating the expected value for buying a lottery ticket. There is a one in a hundred million chance that a person would win $50 million. Each ticket costs $2. The expected value is

$$\frac{1}{100,000,000}(50,000,000-2) + \frac{99,999,999}{100,000,000}(-2) = \frac{49,999,998}{100,000,000} - \frac{199,999,998}{100,000,000} = -\frac{150,000,000}{100,000,000} = -\$1.50$$

On average, one should expect to lose $1.50 each time the game is played. Analyzing the information, the meaning of the data shows that playing the lottery would result in losing money every time.

> **BE CAREFUL!**
>
> The expected value will not be the same as the actual value unless the probability of winning is 100%.

Examples

1. What is the expected value of an investment if the probability is $\frac{1}{5}$ of losing $1,000, $\frac{1}{4}$ of no gain, $\frac{2}{5}$ of making $1,000, and $\frac{3}{20}$ of making $2,000?

    A. $0
    B. $200
    C. $500
    D. $700

    The correct answer is **C**. The correct solution is $500. The expected value is $\frac{1}{5}(-1,000) + \frac{1}{4}(0) + \frac{2}{5}(1,000) + \frac{3}{20}(2,000) = -200 + 0 + 400 + 300 = \$500$.

2. The table below shows the value of the prizes and the probability of winning a prize in a contest.

Prize	$10	$100	$5,000	$50,000
Probability	1 in 50	1 in 1,000	1 in 50,000	1 in 250,000

    Calculate the expected value.

    A. $0.10
    B. $0.20
    C. $0.50
    D. $0.60

    The correct answer is **D**. The correct solution is $0.60. The probability for each event is

Prize	$10	$100	$5,000	$50,000	Not Winning
Probability	1 in 50 = 0.02	1 in 1,000 = 0.001	1 in 50,000 = 0.00002	1 in 250,000 = 0.000004	0.978976

    The expected value is $0.02(10) + 0.001(100) + 0.00002(5,000) + 0.000004(50,000) + 0.978976(0) =$

    $0.2 + 0.1 + 0.1 + 0.2 + 0 = \$0.60$.

3. Which option results in the largest loss on a product?

    A. 40% of gaining $100,000 and 60% of losing $100,000

    B. 60% of gaining $250,000 and 40% of losing $500,000

    C. 30% of gaining $400,000 and 70% of losing $250,000

    D. 60% of gaining $250,000 and 40% of losing $450,000

    The correct answer is **C**. The correct solution is 30% of gaining $400,000 and 70% of losing $250,000. The expected value is $0.30(400,000) + 0.7(-250,000) = 120,000 + (-175,000) = -55,000$.

Let's Review!

- The sample space is the number of outcomes of an event. The union, the intersection, and the complement are related to the sample space.
- The probability of an event is the number of possible events divided by the total number of outcomes. There can be "and," "or," and "not" probabilities.
- The expected value of an event is based on the payout and probability of an event occurring.

INTERPRETING CATEGORICAL AND QUANTITATIVE DATA

This lesson discusses how to represent and interpret data for a dot plot, a histogram, and a box plot. It compares multiple sets of data by using the measures of center and spread and examines the impact of outliers.

Representing Data on a Number Line

There are two types of data: quantitative and categorical. Quantitative variables are numerical, such as number of people in a household, bank account balance, and number of cars sold. Categorical variables are not numerical, and there is no inherent way to order them. Examples are classes in college, types of pets, and party affiliations. The information for these data sets can be arranged on a number line using dot plots, histograms, and box plots.

A dot plot is a display of data using dots. The dots represent the number of times an item appears. Below is a sample of a dot plot.

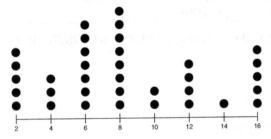

The mean and median can be determined by looking at a dot plot. The mean is the sum of all items divided by the number of dots. The median is the middle dot or the average of the middle two dots.

A histogram is a graphical display that has bars of various heights. It is similar to a bar chart, but the numbers are grouped into ranges. The bins, or ranges of values, of a histogram have equal lengths, such as 10 or 50 units. Continuous data such as weight, height, and amount of time are examples of data shown in a histogram. In the histogram to the right, the bin length is 8 units.

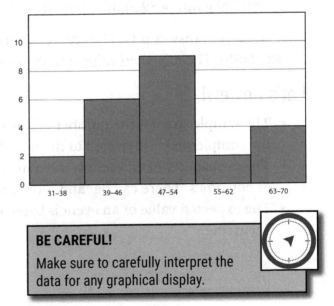

It is not possible to calculate the mean and median by looking at a histogram because there is a bin size rather than a single value on the horizontal axis. Histograms are beneficial when working with a large set of data.

BE CAREFUL!
Make sure to carefully interpret the data for any graphical display.

A box plot (or box-and-whisker plot) is a graphical display of the minimum, first quartile, median, third quartile, and maximum of a set of data. Recall the minimum is the smallest value and the maximum is the largest value in a set of data. The median is the middle number when the data set is written in order. The first quartile is the middle number between the minimum and the median. The third quartile is the middle number between the median and the maximum.

In the data display below, the minimum is 45, the first quartile is 50, the median is 57, the third quartile is 63, and the maximum is 75. With most box-and-whisker plots, the data is not symmetrical.

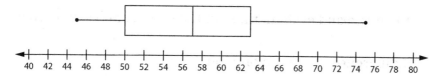

Example

The histogram below shows a basketball team's winning margin during the season. Which statement is true for the histogram?

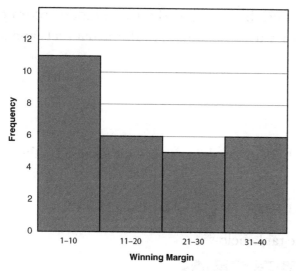

A. The team played a total of 30 games.

B. The frequency for 20–30 points is the same as for 30–40 points.

C. The sum of the frequency for the last two bins is the same as the first bin.

D. The frequency for 0–10 is twice the frequency for any other winning margin.

The correct answer is **C**. The correct solution is the sum of the frequency for the last two bins is the same as the first bin. The frequency of the first bin is 11, the frequency of the third bin is 5, and the frequency of the fourth bin is 6. The sum of the frequency of the last two bins is the same as the first bin.

Comparing Center and Spread of Multiple Data Sets

The measures of center are the mean (average) and median (middle number when written in order). These values describe the expected value of a data set. Very large or very small numbers affect the mean, but they do not affect the median.

The measures of spread are standard deviation (how far the numbers of a data set are from the mean) and interquartile range (the difference between the third and first quartile values).

To find the standard deviation:

- Find the mean.
- Find the difference between the mean and each member of the date set and square that result.
- Find the mean of the squared differences from the previous step.
- Apply the square root.

The larger the value for the standard deviation, the greater the spread of values from the mean. The larger the value for the interquartile range, the greater the spread of the middle 50% of values from the median.

Symmetric data has values that are close together, and the mean, median, and mode occur near the same value. The mean and standard deviation are used to explain multiple data sets and are evident in dot plots.

For example, consider this data set.

10, 10, 11, 11, 11, 12, 12, 12, 12, 12, 13, 13, 13, 14, 14

The mean is found by finding the sum of the numbers in the data set and dividing it by the number of items in the set, as follows:

$10 + 10 + 11 + 11 + 11 + 12 + 12 + 12 + 12 + 12 + 13 + 13 + 13 + 14 + 14 = 180 \div 15 = 12.$

The standard deviation calculation is shown in the table below.

Data	Data – Mean	(Data – Mean)^2
10	−2	4
10	−2	4
11	−1	1
11	−1	1
11	−1	1
12	0	0
12	0	0
12	0	0
12	0	0

Data	Data – Mean	(Data – Mean)²
12	0	0
13	1	1
13	1	1
13	1	1
14	2	4
14	2	4

The sum of the last column is 22. The standard deviation is $\sqrt{\frac{22}{15}} \approx 1.211$.

Next, consider this data set.

8, 8, 9, 10, 11, 12, 12, 12, 12, 12, 13, 14, 15, 16, 16

The mean is $8 + 8 + 9 + 10 + 11 + 12 + 12 + 12 + 12 + 12 + 13 + 14 + 15 + 16 + 16 = 180 \div 15 = 12$.

The standard deviation calculation is shown in the table below.

Data	Data – Mean	(Data – Mean)²
8	−4	16
8	−4	16
9	−3	9
10	−2	4
11	−1	1
12	0	0
12	0	0
12	0	0
12	0	0
12	0	0
13	1	1
14	2	4
15	3	9
16	4	16
16	4	16

The sum of the last column is 92. The standard deviation is $\sqrt{\frac{92}{15}} \approx 2.476$.

Therefore, the second set of data has values that are farther from the mean than the first data set.

When data is skewed, a group of its values are close and the remaining values are evenly spread. The median and interquartile range are used to explain multiple data sets and are evident in dot plots and box plots.

KEEP IN MIND

Compare the same measure of center or variation to draw accurate conclusions when comparing data sets.

The data set 10, 10, 11, 11, 11, 11, 11, 11, 12, 12, 12, 13, 13, 14, 15 has a median of 11 and an interquartile range of 2. The data set 10, 11, 12, 12, 13, 13, 14, 14, 14, 14, 14, 14, 14, 15, 15 has a median of 14 and an interquartile range of 2. The median is greater in the second data set, but the spread of data is the same for both sets of data.

Example

The box plots below show the heights of students in inches for two classes. Choose the statement that is true for the median and the interquartile range.

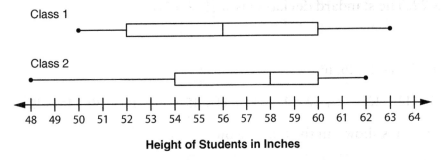

Class 1

Class 2

48 49 50 51 52 53 54 55 56 57 58 59 60 61 62 63 64

Height of Students in Inches

A. The median and interquartile range are greater for class 1.

B. The median and interquartile range are greater for class 2.

C. The median is greater for class 1, and the interquartile range is greater for class 2.

D. The median is greater for class 2, and the interquartile range is greater for class 1.

The correct answer is **D**. The correct solution is the median is greater for class 2, and the interquartile range is greater for class 1. The median is 58 inches for class 2 and 56 inches for class 1. The interquartile range is 8 inches for class 1 and 6 inches for class 2.

Determining the Effect of Extreme Data Points

An outlier is a value that is much smaller or much larger than rest of the values in a data set. This value has an impact on the mean and standard deviation values and occasionally has an impact on the median and interquartile range values.

The data set of 10, 10, 11, 11, 11, 12, 12, 12, 12, 12, 13, 13, 13, 14, 14 has a mean of 12 and a standard deviation of 1.211. If an outlier of 50 is added, the data set has a mean of has a mean of 14.38 and a standard deviation of 9.273. The outlier has increased the mean by more than 2, and the spread of the data has increased significantly.

BE CAREFUL!

There may be a high outlier and a low outlier that may not have an impact on data.

The data set 10, 10, 11, 11, 11, 11, 11, 11, 12, 12, 12, 13, 13, 14, 15 has a median of 11 and an interquartile range of 2. If an outlier of 50 is added, the median slightly increases to 11.5 and the interquartile range remains 2.

Example

A little league basketball team scores 35, 38, 40, 36, 41, 42, 39, 35, 29, 32, 37, 33 in its first 12 games. In its next game, the team scores 12 points. Which statement describes the mean and standard deviation?

    A. The mean increases, and the standard deviation increases.

    B. The mean decreases, and the standard deviation increases.

    C. The mean increases, and the standard deviation decreases.

    D. The mean decreases, and the standard deviation decreases.

The correct answer is **B**. The correct solution is the mean decreases, and the standard deviation increases. The outlier value is lower than all other values, which results in a decrease for the mean. The standard deviation increases because the outlier of 12 is a value far away from the mean.

Let's Review!

- Dot plots, histograms, and box plots summarize and represent data on a number line.
- The mean and standard deviation are used to compare symmetric data sets.
- The median and interquartile range are used to compare skewed data sets.
- Outliers can impact measures of center and spread, particularly mean and standard deviation.

CHAPTER 22 STATISTICS AND PROBABILITY PRACTICE QUIZ

1. Two companies have made a chart of paid time off. Which statement describes the mean and standard deviation?

Paid Time off for Employees at Company A   Paid Time off for Employees at Company B

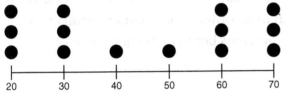
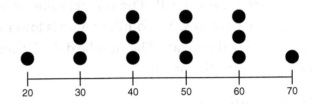
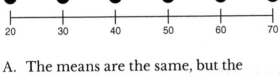

A. The means are the same, but the standard deviation is smaller for Company B.

B. The means are the same, but the standard deviation is smaller for Company A.

C. The mean is greater for Company A, and the standard deviation is smaller for Company A.

D. The mean is greater for Company B, and the standard deviation is smaller for Company B.

2. A basketball player scores 18, 17, 20, 23, 15, 24, 22, 28, 5. What is the effect of removing the outlier on the mean and standard deviation?

A. The mean and the standard deviation increase.

B. The mean and the standard deviation decrease.

C. The standard deviation increases, but the mean decreases.

D. The standard deviation decreases, but the mean increases.

3. Find the median from the dot plot.

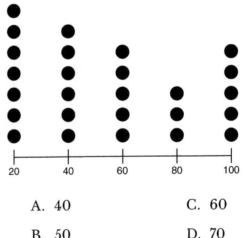

A. 40   C. 60

B. 50   D. 70

4. The table shows the number of students in grades kindergarten through sixth grade. Select the correct bar graph for this data.

Grade	Kindergarten	1st	2nd	3rd	4th	5th	6th
Number of Students	135	150	140	155	145	165	170

A.

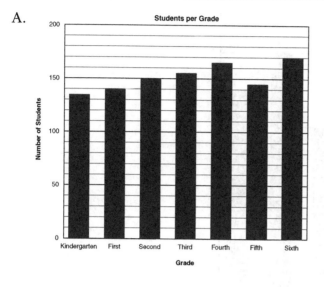

C.

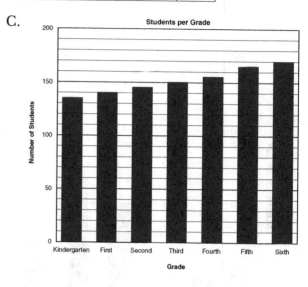

B.

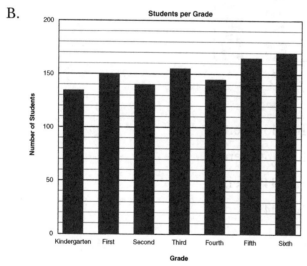

D.

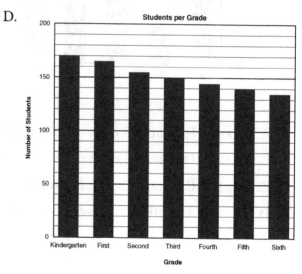

5. The bar chart shows the number of items collected for a charity drive. Which statement is true for the bar chart?

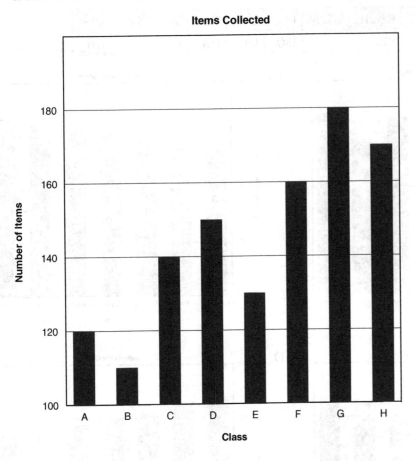

A. Classes F, G, and H each collected more than 150 items.

B. Classes D, F, and G each collected more than 150 items.

C. Classes C, D, and E each collected more than 140 items.

D. Classes A, B, and C each collected more than 140 items.

6. The circle graph shows the number of votes for each candidate. How many votes were cast for candidate D if there were 25,000 voters?

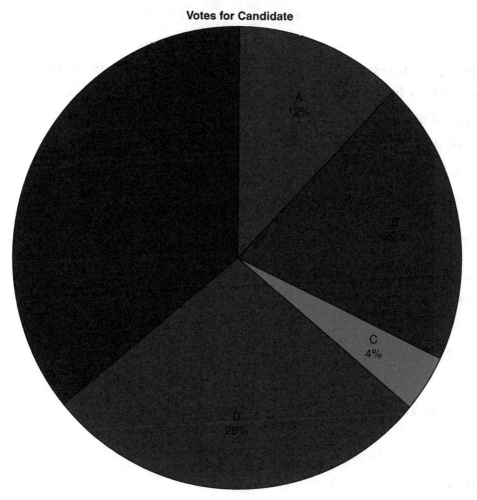

Votes for Candidate

A. 3,000 votes

B. 5,000 votes

C. 7,000 votes

D. 9,000 votes

7. A factory is investigating defects in screwdrivers that have been placed in containers to be shipped to stores. Random containers are selected for the team leader to review. What type of sampling is used?

A. Systematic sampling

B. Simple random sampling

C. Cluster random sampling

D. Stratified random sampling

8. A study looked at a random sample of people and watched their use of social media on mobile devices. The researcher looked at which group of users were happier. What type of study is this?

A. Census

B. Survey

C. Experiment

D. Observational study

9. There are four available pen colors to choose. A simulation is used to represent the number of times each pen is used.

Red	Blue	Black	Green	Total
1,248	1,260	1,247	1,245	5,000

Choose the statement that correctly explains why or why not seeing these results questions the probability of one out of four for each color.

A. Yes, because of the limited number of outcomes

B. Yes, because not enough simulations were completed

C. No, because the probability of each color is not exactly one out of four

D. No, because the probability of each color is very close to one out of four

10. A bag contains 10 red marbles, 8 black marbles, and 7 white marbles. What is the probability of selecting a black marble first and a red marble second with no replacement?

A. $\frac{8}{25}$

B. $\frac{16}{125}$

C. $\frac{2}{15}$

D. $\frac{7}{75}$

11. Which option results in the greatest gain on an investment?

A. 100% of gaining $1,000

B. 60% of gaining $2,500 and 40% of gaining $0

C. 75% of gaining $1,000 and 25% of gaining $1,500

D. 70% of gaining $1,500 and 30% of gaining $1,000

12. There are 60 students attending classes in town. There are 40 students in dance class and 30 students in art class. Find the number of students in either dance or art class.

A. 30

B. 40

C. 50

D. 60

Chapter 22 Statistics and Probability Practice Quiz – Answer Key

1. A. The correct solution is the means are the same, but the standard deviation is smaller for Company B. The standard deviation is smaller for Company B because more values are closer to the mean. **See Lesson: Interpreting Categorical and Quantitative Data.**

2. D. The correct solution is the standard deviation decreases, but the mean increases. The standard deviation from 6.226 and 3.951 when the low outlier is removed. The mean increases from 19.11 to 20.88 because the outlier, 5, is the lowest value. **See Lesson: Interpreting Categorical and Quantitative Data.**

3. B. The correct solution is 50. The middle two values are 40 and 60, and the average of these values is 50. **See Lesson: Interpreting Categorical and Quantitative Data.**

4. B. The correct solution is B because the number of students for each grade is correct. **See Lesson: Interpreting Graphics.**

5. A. The correct solution is classes F, G, and H collected more than 150 items. Class F collected 160 items, class G collected 180 items, and class H collected 170 items. **See Lesson: Interpreting Graphics.**

6. C. The correct solution is 7,000 votes because 28% of 25,000 is 7,000 voters. **See Lesson: Interpreting Graphics.**

7. D. The correct solution is stratified random sampling because the screwdrivers are placed into containers and the containers are randomly selected. **See Lesson: Statistical Measures.**

8. D. The correct solution is observational study because people were not randomly assigned to group and their behaviors were observed. **See Lesson: Statistical Measures.**

9. D. The correct solution is no, because the probability of each color is very close to one out of four. The more simulations, the closer the results will be to the actual probability of one out of four for each color. **See Lesson: Statistical Measures.**

10. C. The correct solution is $\frac{2}{15}$. There are 8 marbles out of 25 for the first event and 10 marbles out of 24 for the second event. The probability of the event is $\frac{8}{25} \times \frac{10}{24} = \frac{80}{600} = \frac{2}{15}$. **See Lesson: Statistics & Probability: The Rules of Probability.**

11. B. The correct solution is 60% of gaining $2,500 and 40% of gaining $0. The expected value is $0.60(2,500) + 0.40(0) = \$1,500$. **See Lesson: Statistics & Probability: The Rules of Probability.**

12. C. The correct solution 50 because there are 70 students in both classes less the total students is 10 students. Then, subtract 10 students from the total, which is 50 students. **See Lesson: Statistics & Probability: The Rules of Probability.**

SECTION VII. FULL-LENGTH PRACTICE EXAMS

TASC PRACTICE EXAM 1

Section I. Writing

(35 minutes)

1. Which of the following spellings is correct?

   A. Depindant   C. Dependunt

   B. Dependint   D. Dependent

2. What is the correct plural of quiz?

   A. Quizs   C. Quizies

   B. Quizes   D. Quizzes

3. Which of the following is correct?

   A. fourth of July   C. Fourth of july

   B. Fourth of July   D. Fourth Of July

4. Which word(s) in the following sentence should be capitalized?

   she asked, "do you like indian food?"

   A. she and do   C. she and indian

   B. do and indian   D. she, do, and indian

5. What is the sentence with the correct use of punctuation?

   A. The bookstore has three types of books: fiction, nonfiction, and biography.

   B. The bookstore has three types of books, fiction, nonfiction, and biography.

   C. The bookstore: has three types of books fiction, nonfiction, and biography.

   D. The bookstore has three: types of books fiction, nonfiction, and biography.

6. What is the mistake in the following sentence?

   Today the new movie premiered, and it was a hit.

   A. The comma is misplaced.

   B. There should be a comma after *today*.

   C. There should be a colon after *premiered*.

   D. There should be a semicolon after *today*.

7. Which of the following sentences is correct?

   A. It was good, wasn't it?

   B. Anne did you like the movie?

   C. It had action drama and romance.

   D. Before the movie we went to dinner.

8. Which of the following nouns can be made plural by simply adding *-s*?

   A. Fox   C. Cherry

   B. Frog   D. Potato

9. What part of speech is the underlined in the following sentence?

   Douglas served on the <u>Supreme Court</u> for 36 years.

   A. Noun   C. Adjective

   B. Pronoun   D. Preposition

10. Identify the nouns in the following sentence.

    Marie Curie won the Nobel Prize in 1911.

    A. won, in, 1911

    B. won, Nobel Prize, 1911

    C. Marie Curie, won, Nobel Prize

    D. Marie Curie, Nobel Prize, 1911

11. Which word in the following sentence is a pronoun?

    The driver checked her side mirror.

    A. The   C. side

    B. her   D. driver

12. What part of speech is the underlined word in the following sentence?

    The dog wagged its tail.

    A. Noun   C. Pronoun

    B. Adverb   D. Adjective

13. Select the word that is a possessive pronoun.

    A. It's   C. That

    B. Who   D. Ours

14. Which word in the following sentence is an adjective?

    Mrs. Washington loves red roses.

    A. Mrs. Washington   C. red

    B. loves   D. roses

15. Select the part of speech of the underlined words in the following sentence.

    Thousands of young people showed up to meet the teen idol.

    A. Adverb   C. Noun

    B. Adjective   D. Pronoun

16. Which word does the underlined adverb describe?

    She played beautifully in the recital.

    A. She   C. in

    B. played   D. recital

17. Which word is not a conjunction?

    A. Or   C. So

    B. The   D. But

18. Select another conjunction with the same meaning as the underlined conjunction.

    History is my favorite subject, but I did not do well on the test.

    A. so   C. yet

    B. since   D. if

19. Identify the preposition in the following sentence.

    It's really hot in that room.

    A. It   C. in

    B. hot   D. that

20. Select the verb that best completes the following sentence.

    Katharina didn't ____ her job as an accountant, so she decided to change careers.

    A. like   C. liken

    B. likes   D. liked

21. What tense are the underlined verbs in the following sentence?

    We read a book and wrote a paper about it.

    A. Simple past   C. Simple present

    B. Past perfect   D. Present perfect

22. **What is the main verb in the following sentence?**

Can I ask you another question?

A. Can

C. another

B. ask

D. question

23. **Which of the following options correctly fixes the run-on sentence below?**

Being able to drive cross-country is an incredible opportunity there is so much to experience.

A. Being able to drive cross-country is an incredible opportunity, there is so much to experience.

B. Being able to drive cross-country. Is an incredible opportunity there is so much to experience.

C. Being able to drive cross-country is an incredible opportunity, for there is so much to experience.

D. Being able to drive cross-country is an incredible opportunity and there is so much to experience.

24. **Which of the following is an example of a simple sentence?**

A. Calcium for bones.

B. Calcium makes bones strong.

C. Calcium is necessary it makes bones strong.

D. Calcium is good for bones, so people need it.

25. **Which of the following options would complete the sentence below to make it a complex sentence?**

I enjoy watching the snow fall
_____.

A. the winters are brutally cold.

B. but, the winters can be brutally cold.

C. however, the winters can be brutally cold.

D. even though the winters can be brutally cold.

26. **How would you connect the following clauses?**

The trial must begin.

She shows up or not.

A. The trial must begin and she shows up or not.

B. The trial must begin which she shows up or not.

C. The trial must begin because she shows up or not.

D. The trial must begin whether she shows up or not.

27. **Identify the independent clause in the following sentence.**

The mother could not take her kids to school because it snowed all night.

A. The mother could not take her kids

B. It snowed all night

C. Because it snowed all night

D. The mother could not take her kids to school

28. Fill in the blank with the correct subordinating conjunction.

We will throw a pizza party _____ you win the game.

A. If

B. That

C. Since

D. Because

29. Select the correct verbs to complete the following sentence.

My dentist, who I ____ visited for years, ____ suddenly disappeared.

A. has, has

B. have, has

C. has, have

D. have, have

30. Which part of the following sentence is the predicate?

My granddaughter was born on January 18.

A. My granddaughter

B. was

C. was born on January 18

D. January 18

31. Select the subject with which the underlined verb must agree.

On Memorial Day, which is the last Monday in May, Americans <u>honor</u> those who have died for their country.

A. Memorial Day

B. which

C. Americans

D. died

32. Which word does the underlined modifier describe?

I looked up to Marvin, <u>who was a year older</u>.

A. I

B. looked

C. up

D. Marvin

33. Identify the dangling or misplaced modifier in the following sentence.

When six years old, our family was transferred overseas by my father's company.

A. When six years old

B. our family

C. was transferred overseas

D. by my father's company

34. How many modifiers are in the following sentence?

They carried sleeping bags, tents, and backpacks.

A. 0

B. 1

C. 2

D. 3

35. What type of error can be found in the following sentence?

The report earned an A that I wrote on the Korean War.

A. Run-on sentence

B. Incorrect subject-verb agreement

C. Misplaced modifier

D. Pronoun error

36. Select the direct object of the underlined verb.

Andrei was happy to help his daughter and her fiancé <u>plan</u> their wedding.

A. was happy

B. to help

C. his daughter and her fiancé

D. their wedding

37. **Identify the direct object in the following sentence, if there is one.**

Max tried so hard, but he did not succeed.

A. so
B. hard
C. not
D. There is no direct object.

38. **What part of speech correctly describes the underlined phrase in the following sentence?**

Leo watched his older brother walk to the bus stop on the first day of school.

A. Direct object
B. Indirect object
C. Subject
D. Object of the preposition

39. **Which of the following suffixes means in a manner of or resembling?**

A. -ful
B. -able
C. -less
D. -esque

40. **Which of the following root words means people?**

A. ject
B. fasc
C. dem
D. cycl

41. **The use of the root mers in the word immerse indicates which the following?**

A. Something is dipped in liquid
B. Something is heated in liquid
C. Something got sprayed with liquid
D. Something is kept away from liquid

42. **Irascible most nearly means**

A. easily angered
B. easily swayed
C. easily amused
D. easily embarrassed

43. **Select the correct definition of the underlined word that has multiple meanings in the sentence.**

The copy machine had a paper jam, and the technician had to come fix it.

A. A backup in traffic
B. An awkward situation or predicament
C. An instance of a machine seizing or getting stuck
D. An informal gathering of musicians improvising together

44. **Select the context clue from the following sentence that helps you define the multiple meaning word solution.**

Claude used a solution of ammonia and water to clean the mess that was on the floor.

A. "Claude used"
B. "ammonia and water"
C. "to clean"
D. "the floor"

45. **Select the word from the following sentence that has more than one meaning.**

The flu has the ability to strike millions of people each year and some do not survive.

A. Ability
B. Strike
C. Year
D. Survive

46. Select the meaning of the underlined word in the sentence based on the context clues.

    The school has a policy to <u>confiscate</u> all student cell phones before an exam so they are unable to cheat.

    A. Seize
    B. Hide
    C. Protect
    D. Store

47. The following words have the same denotation. Which word has a positive connotation?

    A. Assertive
    B. Dictatorial
    C. Domineering
    D. Overbearing

48. Which word in the list of synonyms shows the strongest degree of the word?

    A. Light
    B. Vivid
    C. Bright
    D. Dazzling

49. Pundit : Apprentice :: Flux :

    _____

    A. Stability
    B. Increase
    C. Decrease
    D. Variation

50. Adding which prefix to <u>intentional</u> would make the antonym of the word?

    A. De-
    B. Un-
    C. Dis-
    D. Mis-

SECTION II. READING

(60 minutes)

Please read the text below and answer questions 1-5.

Most people have had the pleasure of tasting a delicious chocolate chip cookie at some point in their lives. But what most folks do not know is that chocolate chip cookies were invented by accident. Ruth Graves Wakefield, owner of the popular Toll House Inn in Whitman, Massachusetts, prepared all the food for her guests. People came from all over to stay at the Toll House Inn and eat her famous Chocolate Butter Drop Do cookies. These chocolate cookies were such a hit that Ruth found herself baking them on a daily basis. One day, when she was preparing the recipe, she realized she had run out of baker's chocolate. She decided to break up a block of Nestle semi-sweet chocolate instead, expecting them to melt and disperse through the cookie dough. To her surprise, when she took the cookies out of the oven, the chocolate morsels retained their shape as "chips" in the cookie, thereby making them the first batch of chocolate chip cookies every baked. Ruth's chocolate chip cookies were so popular that they ended up permanently replacing her chocolate butter drop do cookies. Thanks to this happy accident, people all over the world get to enjoy one of the best desserts ever invented!

1. **Which sentence is the topic sentence?**
   A. Most people have had the pleasure of tasting a delicious chocolate chip cookie at some point in their lives.
   B. But what most folks do not know is that chocolate chip cookies were invented by accident.
   C. She decided to break up a block of Nestle semi-sweet chocolate instead, expecting them to melt and disperse through the cookie dough.
   D. Ruth's chocolate chip cookies were so popular that they ended up permanently replacing her chocolate butter drop do cookies.

2. **In the paragraph above, the chocolate chip cookie is:**
   A. the topic.
   B. the main idea.
   C. a supporting detail.
   D. the topic sentence.

3. **Which sentence summarizes the main idea of the paragraph?**
   A. Chocolate chip cookies are more popular than chocolate butter drop do cookies.
   B. Ruth Graves Wakefield became famous for her chocolate chip cookie recipe.
   C. One of the most classic and popular desserts came about unexpectedly.
   D. It takes a whole lot of work to create something long-lasting.

4. Which of the following sentences from the paragraph is a supporting detail of the topic sentence?

   A. Ruth Graves Wakefield, owner of the popular Toll House Inn in Whitman, Massachusetts, prepared all the food for her guests on a daily basis.

   B. People came from all over to stay at the Toll House Inn and eat her famous Chocolate Butter Drop Do cookies.

   C. These chocolate cookies were such a hit that Ruth found herself baking them on a daily basis.

   D. She decided to break up a block of Nestle semi-sweet chocolate instead, expecting them to melt and disperse through the cookie dough.

5. Which sentence would *best* function as a supporting detail in this paragraph?

   A. The Nestle Company now owns the rights to Ruth Graves Wakefield's chocolate chip cookie recipe.

   B. Ruth Graves Wakefield tasted the cookies with the chocolate morsels in them and realized immediately how delicious they were.

   C. Today people buy pre-packaged chocolate chips instead of breaking off pieces of chocolate from a Nestle bar.

   D. Ruth Graves Wakefield sold her recipe in exchange for a lifetime of free chocolate.

Read the text below and answer questions 6-7.

Carving a pumpkin is a fun activity that can create family memories to last a lifetime.

You Will Need

A pumpkin

A knife or kid-safe cutting tool

A bowl

A large spoon

A marker

Old newspapers or plastic sheeting (optional)

Your imagination!

What to Do

Before you start carving a pumpkin, choose your workspace carefully. Spread newspapers or plastic sheeting over the floor if desired.

First, hollow the pumpkin out. Do this by using your knife or kid-safe cutting tool to make a circular cut on the pumpkin around the stem. Carefully pull off the outer rind and reach into the pumpkin to scoop out the pulp and seeds. Scrape the bottom and inside edges of the pumpkin with the spoon to remove as much pulp as possible. A jack-o-lantern with a wet, pulpy interior is difficult to carve and rots quickly once it is on display.

Now it is time to create your jack-o-lantern's face. Clean the surface of the pumpkin if necessary and decide which side you'll use for the face. Errors cannot easily be fixed once you start to carve, so for best results, draw the design onto the pumpkin before making any cuts. Then use your knife or cutting tool to carefully carve your jack-o-lantern's features.

6. **Which step comes just before the creation of the jack-o-lantern's face?**

   A. Scooping out the pulp

   B. Cutting around the stem

   C. Rotting while on display

   D. Preparing the workspace

7. **Why is it best to draw a design onto the pumpkin before cutting?**

   A. It prevents injury.

   B. It prevents errors.

   C. It prevents rotting.

   D. It prevents messes.

Read the following text and its summary and answer questions 8-9.

Text: In the late 1800s, life was terrible for some children. The Industrial Revolution was in full effect and factories sprang up in urban areas all over the country. Many innocent children left the comforts of home for the big cities to make money for their families. Children as young as 6 were forced to work long hours with dangerous equipment for little pay. A lot of children grew ill or even died on the job. Factory owners justified this abominable treatment by claiming they fed, clothed, and provided shelter for these children.

Summary: The author argues that children led awful lives during the Industrial Revolution due to long work hours, dangerous equipment, and little pay. Factory owners justified this treatment even though children were becoming ill or dying.

8. **Is this summary effective or not? Why or why not?**

   A. The summary is effective because it captures the emotional component of the text.

   B. The summary is effective because it restates the key points in a new way.

   C. The summary is ineffective because it makes its own claims and judgments.

   D. The summary is ineffective because it is structurally the same as the original.

9. **If the first line of the summary were replaced, which of the following lines would make the summary ineffective?**

   A. The author claims that in the late 1800s, life was terrible for some children.

   B. The author states that during the Industrial Revolution, children faced many hardships.

   C. The author claims that life was difficult for children during the Industrial Revolution.

   D. The author states that children who worked during the Industrial Revolution had it tough.

Read the following passage and answer questions 10-13.

Adelia stood on the porch in her bathrobe.

"Mr. Snuggles?" she called. "Mr. Snuggles! Come on in, you little vermin."

She peered up and down the street. Sighing, she went back inside and, a moment later, emerged with a metal bowl and a spoon. She rapped on the bowl several times.

"Mr. Snuggles? Breakfast!"

When Mr. Snuggles did not appear, Adelia reached inside and grabbed some keys off a low table. Cinching her bathrobe tightly around her waist, she climbed into the car.

"It's not like I have anything better to do than look for you again," she said.

10. **From the text above, you can infer that Adelia is:**

    A. looking for a pet.

    B. calling her son home.

    C. a kindhearted person.

    D. unconcerned for Mr. Snuggles.

11. **Which detail does not provide evidence to back up the conclusion that Adelia is feeling frustrated?**

    A. She calls Mr. Snuggles "you little vermin."

    B. She has not yet gotten dressed for the day.

    C. She complains about having to search for Mr. Snuggles.

    D. She sighs when Mr. Snuggles does not immediately appear.

12. **Which detail from the text supports the inference that Adelia cares what happens to Mr. Snuggles, even if she is angry at him?**

    A. She goes out to look for him.

    B. She keeps her car keys near the door.

    C. She is joking when she calls him "vermin."

    D. She says she wants to be doing something else.

13. **Which sentence of dialogue, if added to the passage, would support the conclusion that Mr. Snuggles actually belongs to someone else?**

    A. "What ever possessed me to adopt a cat?"

    B. "You shed on my sheets, you pee on my couch, and now *this*."

    C. "Next time Raul goes out of town, I'm going to babysit his plants instead."

    D. "If you make me late again, I'm going to lose my job. Then how will we eat?"

14. **Which of the following sentences uses the MOST formal language?**

    A. Congrats!

    B. Congratulations!

    C. Congratulations on your recent success.

    D. Congrats to you.

15. **Which of the following sentences uses the MOST informal language?**

    A. Where's the best café in these parts?

    B. Could you direct me to a nice café in the area?

    C. Would you be able to show me to a nice café?

    D. Could you tell me where a nice café is around here?

16. **In which of the following situations would it be best to use informal language?**

    A. At brunch.

    B. Talking to a professor.

    C. Giving a presentation.

    D. Giving a professional talk.

17. **Which of the following sentences uses the MOST formal language?**

    A. This essay claims that sugar is bad for people.

    B. I think that sugar is bad for people.

    C. I believe that sugar is bad for people.

    D. I say that sugar is bad for people.

Read the passage and answer questions 18-21.

Dear Mr. O'Hara,

I am writing to let you know how much of a positive impact you have made on our daughter. Before being in your algebra class, Violet was math phobic. She would shut down when new concepts would not come to her easily. As a result, she did not pass many tests. Despite this past struggle, she has blossomed in your class! Your patience and dedication have made all the difference in the world. Above all, your one-on-one sessions with her have truly helped her in ways you cannot imagine. She is a more confident and capable math student, thanks to you. We cannot thank you enough.

Fondly,

Bridgette Foster

18. **Which adjective best describes the tone of this passage?**

    A. Arrogant   C. Friendly

    B. Hopeless   D. Appreciative

19. **Which phrase from the passage has an openly appreciative and warm tone?**

    A. I am writing to let you now

    B. you have made on our daughter

    C. made all the difference

    D. We cannot thank you enough

20. **What mood would this passage most likely evoke in the math teacher, Mr. O'Hara?**

    A. Calm

    B. Grateful

    C. Sympathetic

    D. Embarrassment

21. **Which transition word or phrase from the passage adds emphasis to the writer's point?**

    A. Being   C. Despite

    B. As a result   D. Above all

Read the following text and answer questions 22-24.

As Time Goes On is a painfully realistic depiction of what life is like for some senior citizens in the twilight of their lives. Tabitha Reynolds artfully captures the harsh reality people face when they grow old. From one's physical limitations to the emotional toll of letting go of one's former self, Reynolds pays homage to this fragile yet meaningful time in a person's life.

The book chronicles the final years of Audrey Lacoste's life. A former prima ballerina, Audrey is now a prisoner to her rheumatoid arthritis. The disease has limited Audrey's body in ways she could never have imagined. Her physical ailment coupled with the loss of her beloved husband causes her two self-involved children to move her into *Sunshine Cove,* an assisted living facility. The facility is anything but sunny, but slowly the light in Audrey's life begins to flicker once again when she makes an unexpected friend.

A New York Times best seller for seven consecutive weeks, *As Time Goes On* is a must read. The words will make you laugh, cry, gasp and sigh as you travel along the rocky road to the end of Audrey's life.

22. **The purpose of this passage is to:**

    A. decide.

    B. inform.

    C. persuade.

    D. entertain.

23. **Which detail from the passage is factual?**

    A. *As Time Goes On* is a painfully realistic depiction of what life is like for some senior citizens...

    B. Tabitha Reynolds artfully captures the harsh reality people face as they grow old.

    C. The book chronicles the final years of Audrey Lacoste's life.

    D. *...As Time Goes On* is a must read.

24. **The author of the passage includes details about Audrey Lacoste's life in order to appeal to the reader's:**

    A. reason.   C. feelings.

    B. trust.   D. knowledge.

Read the following paragraphs and answer questions 25-28.

The idea of getting rid of homework at the elementary school level is debatable, but giving young children a well-needed break after school is undoubtedly beneficial. A study of elementary age children and homework showed that daily homework causes high rates of anxiety and depression in young people. In contrast, schools that have gotten rid of the homework requirement have reported a drop in depression and anxiety among students.

According to a nationwide analysis of standardized testing scores, schools that have gotten rid of homework have seen benefits. Test scores have gone up incrementally from year to year. On the contrary, schools that mandate daily homework have seen stagnant test scores. Therefore, it is safe to say that homework does nothing to enhance student learning at all.

25. Which statement expresses an opinion?

A. The idea of getting rid of homework at the elementary school level is debatable, but giving young children a well-needed break after school is undoubtedly beneficial.

B. A study of elementary age children and homework showed that daily homework causes high rates of anxiety and depression in young people.

C. In contrast, schools that have gotten rid of the homework requirement have reported a drop in depression and anxiety among students.

D. According to a nationwide analysis of standardized testing scores, schools that have gotten rid of homework have seen benefits.

26. Consider the following sentence from the passage:

On the contrary, schools that mandate daily homework have seen stagnant test scores.

Is this statement a fact or an opinion? Why?

A. An opinion because it focuses on the beliefs of the schools involved.

B. An opinion because it expresses how the author feels about standardized test scores.

C. A fact because it shares test score results which is something that can be verified.

D. A fact because it relies on the schools' projected test score results.

27. What is the primary argument of the passage?

A. Schools need to change the type of homework they give to elementary school students.

B. There are no clear benefits from giving elementary aged students daily homework.

C. A school's standardized test scores is a good measure of how the school is performing overall.

D. Schools with stagnant test scores would benefit from giving students more homework.

28. Which sentence in the passage displays faulty reasoning?

A. According to a nationwide analysis of standardized testing scores, schools that have gotten rid of homework have seen benefits.

B. Test scores have gone up incrementally from year to year.

C. On the contrary, schools that mandate daily homework have seen stagnant test scores.

D. Therefore, it is safe to say that homework does nothing to enhance student learning at all.

Read the map below and answer questions 29-33.

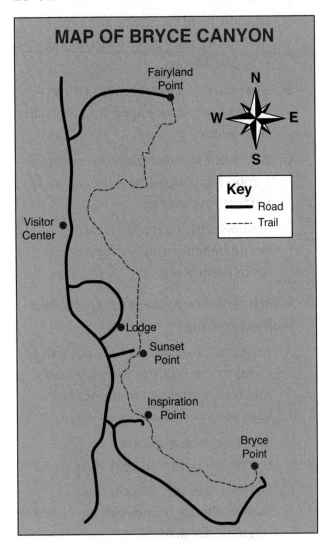

MAP OF BRYCE CANYON

Fairyland Point

N
W E
S

Key
—— Road
----- Trail

Visitor Center

Lodge

Sunset Point

Inspiration Point

Bryce Point

29. A person could get from the Lodge to Fairyland Point by:

A. driving east on the road.

B. driving west on the road.

C. walking north on the Rim Trail.

D. walking south on the Rim Trail.

30. Which feature on the map is between Sunset Point and Bryce Point?

A. Sunrise Point

B. Fairyland Point

C. Visitor's Center

D. Inspiration Point

31. How could a person travel from the Visitor's Center to Bryce Point without touching Sunset Point?

A. By keeping to the main road

B. By walking along the Rim Trail

C. By taking the route to Fairyland Point

D. By driving the loop road near the Lodge

32. Which feature on the map is farthest west?

A. Bryce Point

B. Sunrise Point

C. Fairyland Point

D. Visitor's Center

33. The legend shows:

A. how to differentiate between a road and a trail.

B. where visitors can leave a parked vehicle while hiking.

C. which point is the Visitor's Center and which is the Lodge.

D. how to see all the viewpoints in Bryce Canyon on a single visit.

Read both of the following texts and answer questions 34-38.

1. Once when a Lion was asleep a little Mouse began running up and down upon him; this soon wakened the Lion, who placed his huge paw upon him, and opened his big jaws to swallow him. "Pardon, O King," cried the little Mouse: "forgive me this time, I shall never forget it: who knows but what I may be able to do you a turn some of these days?" The Lion was so tickled at the idea of the Mouse being able to help him, that he lifted up his paw and let him

go. Sometime after the Lion was caught in a trap, and the hunters who desired to carry him alive to the King, tied him to a tree while they went in search of a wagon to carry him on. Just then the little Mouse happened to pass by, and seeing the sad plight in which the Lion was, went up to him and soon gnawed away the ropes that bound the King of the Beasts. "Was I not right?" said the little Mouse.

Little friends may prove great friends.

2. Beast left his mark on the fence.

It was lime green and slate gray and beautiful, so of course my father was outraged. If Beast hadn't had talent, Dad would have left it a while, but as it was, he got two of his parishioners to paint the thing over. Within the hour, the fence was back to being as white as the everlasting soul. My father's anger lasted longer than the tag.

The funny thing was, Beast loved my father. I don't know why. Life had knocked that kid down so hard so often he should have hated everything with the name of God stamped on it. But he loved my preacher father more than anyone else in the world. Maybe it was the dark suits and the white collars. Beast liked a pretty picture.

So there was my dad, ministering to the people in the worst parts of town, charging straight into drug dens and whorehouses to save people when they called him. He acted like he had no fear whatsoever. Plenty of the neighbors, the hardest-put ones, hated him for that. Lots of times he came close to getting his throat cut. More than once it was Beast who saved him.

And every time Beast saved my dad, he left his mark on the fence.

Dad couldn't stand it.

34. **What type of writing is used in the passages?**

   A. Both are narrative.

   B. Passage 1 is narrative and passage 2 is expository.

   C. Passage 1 is expository and passage 2 is narrative.

   D. Both are expository.

35. **Which term describes the structure of both passages?**

   A. Sequence

   B. Description

   C. Cause/effect

   D. Problem-solution

36. **Which statement accurately describes the genre of the passages?**

   A. Both are definitely fiction.

   B. Both are definitely nonfiction.

   C. Passage 1 is definitely nonfiction, and passage 2 is definitely fiction.

   D. Passage 1 is definitely fiction, and passage 2 could be fiction or nonfiction.

37. **Which label accurately describes the genre of passage 1?**

   A. Myth

   B. Fable

   C. Legend

   D. Mystery

38. **Which label could *not* accurately describe the genre of passage 2?**

   A. Legend

   B. Memoir

   C. Short story

   D. Autobiography

485

Study the outline below and answer questions 39-43.

I. Introduction - We need more racial and gender diversity in our superheroes.

II. The lack of diversity in comics means kids get the message that only white males can be heroic.

   A. Quote from Sid Markell (pg. 213): "When I was a kid, imagining myself saving the world meant imagining I was white."

   B. Quote from Lydia Green (kenswicktimes.com): "I remember people seeing my comments and saying, 'You like reading *that*?' I heard, 'You think you can be *important*?'"

   C. Markell and Green aren't just interacting with superhero comics as fiction; they're seeing them as messages from a real world that excludes them.

III. Conclusion

   A. Recap main points.

   B. Let's create a world where all kids are invited to imagine they can be heroes.

39. **Which statement from the outline will be the main idea of the essay?**

   A. We need more racial and gender diversity in our superheroes.

   B. Kids get the message that only white males can be heroic.

   C. Markell and Green aren't just interacting with superhero comics as fiction.

   D. Let's create a world where all kids are invited to imagine they can be heroes.

40. **What does the writer of this outline still need to do?**

   A. Collect evidence to back up the main idea.

   B. Figure out how to end the essay.

   C. Create an attention-grabbing opening statement.

   D. Decide how to organize the ideas in the essay.

41. **The writer of this outline wants to add this sentence:**

This world needs all the heroes it can get.

Where would it fit best?

   A. In the introduction, before the thesis statement.

   B. In the introduction, after the thesis statement.

   C. In the body, before the topic sentence.

   D. In the body, after the first quotation.

42. **The writer of this outline wants to add a second body paragraph. Which statement could function as a topic sentence that clearly adds new information to support the main idea?**

A. Girls and women tend to gravitate away from careers our society associates with heroic actions.

B. Green writes, "As a kid I wanted to be a firefighter, but people always laughed at me when I said so."

C. If our fiction presented more women and people of color as superheroes, more kids would likely grow up aspiring to save others.

D. Superhero characters in comics and the movies are almost all white and male, sending fans the message that these traits are necessary for heroism.

43. **The information in parentheses under II.A. and II.B. is most likely:**

A. a visual element the writer wants to add while drafting.

B. intended to remind the writer to look up different quotations.

C. source information the writer will later use to create citations.

D. an error that will need to be fixed at a later stage in the writing process.

Read the following draft essay and answer questions 44-49.

Last week I saw a bad television commercial. (1) It said that women need more "self-confidence," and that breast augmentation surgery can give it to them. (2) I do not think plastic surgery leads to self-confidence. (3) True self-confidence comes from the belief in our accomplishments, not from the belief that we look good. (4)

Our society sends the message that women need to look like fashion models, but fashion models' body types aren't normal. (5) Many suffer from anorexia, and some have undergone plastic surgery to conform to a false ideal of beauty. (6) And what is the point of aiming for that unattainable ideal? (7) It takes time and energy that could be focused on more important matters. (8)

Women are told they need to look perfect, but nobody actually looks perfect. (9) Even the pictures in magazines are airbrushed and augmented. (10) They are not real. (11) And the women in those pictures are unusually pretty, plus they have professional help to keep their bodies looking as close to our false ideal of beauty as possible. (12) Ordinary women who have to spend time working every day and caring for their families have no chance of attaining anything close to that level of beauty. (13)

If you're like me, you may feel a pressure to measure up to society's false ideal of beauty. (14) But you shouldn't. (15) As women, we need to focus on making the world better, not on making our faces prettier. (16)

44. **The word *bad* in Sentence 1 is poor word choice because it is not:**

A. simple. C. positive.

B. precise. D. inclusive.

45. **Which revision of Sentence 1 leads the reader more precisely toward the author's main idea?**

   A. Last week I saw a television commercial that left me outraged.

   B. Last week I saw a television commercial that should be banned.

   C. Last week I saw a commercial that was not aiming to sell anything.

   D. Last week I saw a poorly acted and directed television commercial.

46. **If Sentence 4 is the thesis statement, which statement accurately expresses a problem the writer should address in revision?**

   A. The thesis has nothing to do with television.

   B. The thesis contains spelling and grammar errors.

   C. The body paragraphs do not clearly defend the thesis.

   D. The thesis directly contradicts the conclusion paragraph.

47. **Which thesis statement should replace Sentence 4 to align more clearly with the points the author makes in the body of the essay?**

   A. The media's ideal of beauty cannot be achieved.

   B. Fashion models are often victims of eating disorders.

   C. More women need to get involved in business and politics.

   D. Television commercials about breast augmentation should be banned.

48. **How would you change the following sentence to active voice?**

   The books were returned to the library by the student.

   A. The student returned the books to the library.

   B. By the student, the books were returned to the library.

   C. To the library, the books were returned by the student.

   D. It is already in active voice.

49. **Which of the following sentences is passive?**

   A. The cashier helped the customer.

   B. She filled the container with water.

   C. Steve answered the phone when it rang.

   D. The computer was turned on by the technician.

50. **Fill in the blank with the correct active or passive verb.**

   I _____ to become a police officer.

   A. Have always wanted

   B. Am always wanting

   C. Was always wanted

   D. Have always wanting

Section III. Social Studies

(70 minutes)

1. **Why did the American colonists revolt against Great Britain?**
   A. They wanted a president.
   B. They wanted a different monarch.
   C. They wanted to govern themselves.
   D. They wanted to live without government.

2. **A government run by all of the people governed is called a(n) _____.**
   A. oligarchy
   B. monarchy
   C. democracy
   D. constitution

3. **In a constitutional democracy, the constitution _____ the power of the government.**
   A. stops
   B. holds
   C. describes
   D. symbolizes

4. **Who first introduced the idea of natural rights?**
   A. John Locke
   B. The colonists
   C. The Founders
   D. King George III

5. **According to John Locke, what is the principal role of government?**
   A. To develop rules and laws
   B. To take care of the environment
   C. To protect people's natural rights
   D. To rule so people do not break laws

6. **According to the rule of law, all people are _____ in the eyes of the law.**
   A. equal
   B. honorable
   C. innocent
   D. punishable

7. **Which detail about the legislative branch is TRUE?**
   A. Senators are appointed by the president.
   B. The House and Senate are equal in power.
   C. Representatives in the House serve 10-year terms.
   D. Each state has the same number of representatives in Congress.

8. **Which of the following is often called the Upper House?**
   A. U.S. Senate
   B. White House
   C. Supreme Court
   D. House of Representatives

9. **Which position has a two-year term?**
   A. United States Senator
   B. Supreme Court Justice
   C. Representative in the House
   D. President of the United States

10. **How many amendments have been ratified?**
    A. 8
    B. 10
    C. 12
    D. 27

11. **Who is allowed to propose an amendment?**
    A. Congress
    B. Any state
    C. Any citizen
    D. The president

12. **What does a proposed amendment need to become a law?**

    A. Approval by the president

    B. Approval by a majority of citizens

    C. Approval by three-fourths of state legislatures

    D. Approval by two-thirds of representatives in the House and Senate

13. **Which of the following is an example of U.S. public policy?**

    A. How the legislature works

    B. How colleges teach American history

    C. How Supreme Court justices are appointed

    D. How justice is delivered to those accused of crimes

14. **What is the purpose of a primary election?**

    A. To allow all citizens to register

    B. To ensure all voting machines work

    C. To elect the president of the country

    D. To choose a candidate to run for a party

15. **Which of the following is a general election?**

    A. An election to see who will take office

    B. An election decided by the Electoral College

    C. An election including two people in the same party

    D. An election in which representatives vote for a leader

The next three questions relate to the following passage from John Winthrop. Winthrop was a Puritan leader in the Massachusetts Colony and delivered this message to his followers in 1630.

"...if we shall neglect the observation of these articles...the Lord will surely break out in wrath against us, and be revenged of such a people, and make us know the price of the breach of such a covenant. Now the only way to avoid this shipwreck, and to provide for our posterity, is to follow the counsel of Micah, to do justly, to love mercy, to walk humbly with our God. For this end, we must be knit together, in this work, as one man...We must uphold a familiar commerce together in all meekness, gentleness, patience and liberality. We must delight in each other; make others' conditions our own; rejoice together, mourn together, labor and suffer together, always having before our eyes our commission and community in the work, as members of the same body. So shall we keep the unity of the spirit in the bond of peace...We shall find that the God of Israel is among us, when ten of us shall be able to resist a thousand of our enemies; when He shall make us a praise and glory that men shall say of succeeding plantations, "may the Lord make it like that of New England." *For we must consider that we shall be as a city upon a hill.*

16. **Winthrop ends the passage by saying that they "shall be as a city upon a hill." What does Winthrop mean by this?**

    A. God will favor them.

    B. They will be very rich.

    C. They will work very hard.

    D. They will be an example to others.

17. **Based on what Winthrop says, which of the following statements MOST ACCURATELY describes the Puritans' beliefs about God?**

    A. Sinners could earn God's forgiveness.

    B. God punished those who disobeyed his laws.

    C. Those who followed God's laws would be rich.

    D. God was kind even to those who broke his laws.

18. **Which of the following is the MOST LIKELY explanation for how Puritan society embraced Winthrop's ideas?**

    A. New Englanders embraced a desire for wealth.

    B. New Englanders became less religious over time.

    C. New Englanders wanted to go to war with France.

    D. New Englanders were tight-knit socially and worked together.

The next two questions are based on the following passage, which is an excerpt from the Declaration of Independence, written in 1776 by Thomas Jefferson.

"We hold these truths to be self-evident, that all men are created equal, that they are endowed by their Creator with certain unalienable Rights, that among these are Life, Liberty and the pursuit of Happiness.--That to secure these rights, Governments are instituted among Men, deriving their just powers from the consent of the governed, --That whenever any Form of Government becomes destructive of these ends, it is the Right of the People to alter or to abolish it, and to institute new Government, laying its foundation on such principles and organizing its powers in such form, as to them shall seem most likely to effect their Safety and Happiness. Prudence, indeed, will dictate that Governments long established should not be changed for light and transient causes; and accordingly all experience hath shewn, that mankind are more disposed to suffer, while evils are sufferable, than to right themselves by abolishing the forms to which they are accustomed. But when a long train of abuses and usurpations, pursuing invariably the same Object evinces a design to reduce them under absolute Despotism, it is their right, it is their duty, to throw off such Government, and to provide new Guards for their future security."

19. **According to Jefferson, what is the basis for why governments are formed?**

    A. Governments are created solely by dictators.

    B. Governments are created to protect private property.

    C. Subjects give their freedom in exchange for government protection.

    D. People form governments to protect themselves from hostile powers.

20. Much of the Declaration of Independence is a long list of the grievances the colonists had toward King George III. Why, based on what you read here, would Jefferson have felt the need to list these?

    A. Jefferson believed that the British did not understand the grievances.

    B. Jefferson wanted to demonstrate that the colonies were right to leave Britain.

    C. Jefferson feared that the American colonists would refuse to accept the declaration.

    D. Jefferson hoped that Parliament could be persuaded to accept the American grievances.

The next two questions are based on the following passage, which is an excerpt from Captain Park Holland's reminiscences of Shays' Rebellion, written in 1834.

"As I have had ocation to mention the Shay Rebellion it may not be impropper for me to indeavour to explain the cause which gave rise to this very unfortunate affair but this will be a difficult Task fully to & clearly to explain for there were more causes than one but the main cause may be said to arrise from a Sudden Flow of hard Money and an uncommon large importation of Forreign Goods... the general opinion was that Money was growing verry plenty & all kinds of good being scarce during the War and now being Varry plenty the Money (espetially that in the Hands of the poorer sort of People) was soon spent and many of them were in debt as much as their credit would admit of and to add to this there was a large Tax out & generally unpaid.

These circumstance with some others put together mad Money as extraordinary scarce as it had ben plenty - sometime in the year 1786 the scarcity of Money became quite alarming and those who were the most distressed or otherways most in debt began to hold Town & County convention & corresponded with each so as to be as uniform in their proceedings as possible and the amount of their deliberations seemed to be that it was best to stop the setting of the Courts of Common Pleas for there was a verry unusual number of sutes to be brought before their Court which were now about Setting and when the Court began to assemble at Northampton within & for the County of Hamshere there assembled a large body of People..."

21. To what does Holland attribute the discontent in Massachusetts?

    A. Excessive borrowing of money by the wealthy

    B. The debt that people were in because of scarce money

    C. The excessive taxes coming from the federal government

    D. The downturn in trade after the Revolutionary War ended

22. **How would the discontent described in this passage have been attributed to the federal government under the Articles of Confederation?**

    A. The federal government's taxes were too high.

    B. The federal government hadn't printed enough money.

    C. The federal government couldn't stabilize the economy.

    D. The federal government was oppressing the state government.

23. **What was Andrew Johnson's goal for Reconstruction?**

    A. Restoring slavery in the South

    B. Quickly reintegrating the South

    C. Giving African Americans rights

    D. Punishing the South for starting the war

The next two questions are based on an excerpt from *Uncle Tom's Cabin* by Harriet Beecher Stowe. In it, Senator John Bird and his wife debate a law.

"You ought to be ashamed, John! Poor, homeless, houseless creatures! It's a shameful, wicked, abominable law, and I'll break it, for one, the first time I get a chance; and I hope I *shall* have a chance, I do! Things have got to a pretty pass, if a woman can't give a warm supper and a bed to poor, starving creatures, just because they are slaves, and have been abused and oppressed all their lives, poor things!"

"But, Mary, just listen to me. Your feelings are all quite right, dear, and interesting, and I love you for them; but, then, dear, we mustn't suffer our feelings to run away with our judgment; you must consider it's not a matter of private feeling,—there are great public interests involved,—there is such a state of public agitation rising, that we must put aside our private feelings."

"Now, John, I don't know anything about politics, but I can read my Bible; and there I see that I must feed the hungry, clothe the naked, and comfort the desolate; and that Bible I mean to follow."

"But in cases where your doing so would involve a great public evil—"

"Obeying God never brings on public evils. I know it can't. It's always safest, all round, to *do as He* bids us.

"Now, listen to me, Mary, and I can state to you a very clear argument, to show—"

"O, nonsense, John! —you can talk all night, but you wouldn't do it. I put it to you, John,—would *you* now turn away a poor, shivering, hungry creature from your door, because he was a runaway? *Would* you, now?"

24. **Which political event created the fugitive slave law that the senator and his wife are debating?**

    A. The Compromise of 1850

    B. The Kansas-Nebraska Act

    C. The attack on Fort Sumter

    D. The Missouri Compromise

25. Based on the passage, how did the fugitive slave law affect Northern attitudes toward slavery and the South?

    A. Northerners stopped aiding escaped enslaved people.

    B. Northerners felt that the law was necessary to save the United States.

    C. Northerners had grown tired of aiding enslaved people as they left the South.

    D. Northerners were angered by the inhumanity of slavery and being unable to aid enslaved people.

The following three questions are based on the passage below. It is an excerpt from the Treaty of Versailles.

"Germany acknowledges and will respect strictly the independence of Austria, within the frontiers which may be fixed in a Treaty between that State and the Principal Allied and Associated Powers; she agrees that this independence shall be inalienable, except with the consent of the Council of the League of Nations.

...

The Allied and Associated Governments affirm and Germany accepts the responsibility of Germany and her allies for causing all the loss and damage to which the Allied and Associated Governments and their nationals have been subjected as a consequence of the war imposed upon them by the aggression of Germany and her allies."

...

By a date which must not be later than March 31, 1920, the German Army must not comprise more than seven divisions of infantry and three divisions of cavalry.

After that date the total number of effectives in the Army of the States constituting Germany must not exceed one hundred thousand men, including officers and establishments of depots. The Army shall be devoted exclusively to the maintenance of order within the territory and to the control of the frontiers."

26. Which of the following countries would have been MOST LIKELY to want to change the German army into an exclusively defensive one?

    A. France   C. Austria

    B. Turkey   D. Hungary

27. What is the MOST LIKELY explanation for why the victorious Entente wanted to prevent a union between Germany and Austria?

    A. Germany was dependent on Austria as a power.

    B. Austria was openly making plans to go to war again.

    C. The Entente wanted to stop them from allying again.

    D. They knew that Austria was tired of being controlled by Germany.

28. **How did Germans react to the clause establishing German guilt for the war?**

    A. Germans were angered by having to agree to this.

    B. Germans initially agreed but later came to resent it.

    C. Germans agreed that they bore responsibility for the war.

    D. Germans generally ignored it and went on with their lives.

The following three questions are based on the passage below. It is an excerpt of a speech given by Ronald Reagan in 1983.

"It took one kind of military force to deter an attack when, we had far more nuclear weapons than any other power; it takes another kind now that the Soviets, for example, have enough accurate and powerful nuclear weapons to destroy virtually all of our missiles on the ground. Now, this is not to say that the Soviet Union is planning to make war on us. Nor do I believe a war is inevitable—quite the contrary. But what must be recognized is that our security is based on being prepared to meet all threats.

...

The calls for cutting back the defense budget come in nice, simple arithmetic. They're the same kind of talk that led the democracies to neglect their defenses in the 1930s and invited the tragedy of World War II. We must not let that grim chapter of history repeat itself through apathy or neglect.

...

I call upon the scientific community in our country, those who gave us nuclear weapons, to turn their great talents now to the cause of mankind and world peace, to give us the means of rendering these nuclear weapons impotent and obsolete.

Tonight, consistent with our obligations of the ABM treaty and recognizing the need for closer consultation with our allies, I'm taking an important first step. I am directing a comprehensive and intensive effort to define a long-term research and development program to begin to achieve our ultimate goal of eliminating the threat posed by strategic nuclear missiles."

29. **Why did the Soviet Union fear the creation of a nuclear defense system?**

    A. It would require the Soviet Union to develop new nuclear weapons.

    B. It would force the Soviet Union to negotiate with the United States.

    C. It would enable the United States to attack without fear of Soviet retribution.

    D. It would prevent the Soviet Union from attacking the United States preemptively.

30. **Why did Reagan oppose cuts to the defense budget?**

    A. He felt cuts would alienate NATO members.

    B. He thought it would embolden the Soviet Union.

    C. He wanted the United States to attack the Soviet Union.

    D. He argued that the defense spending was good for the economy.

31. What nuclear policy does Reagan propose to change with this speech?

    A. Détente

    B. Containment

    C. The Truman Doctrine

    D. Mutually Assured Destruction

32. Trade promotes economic progress because it _____

    A. makes larger outputs possible as a result of specialization.

    B. benefits all countries in the world, even those with little to trade.

    C. allows countries with absolute advantage to trade more products.

    D. moves goods and services from one group to another so sellers prosper.

33. Which country gains when trading goods?

    A. The seller only.

    B. The buyer only.

    C. Both the seller and the buyer.

    D. The buyer, but the seller gets rid of unwanted goods

34. What do the terms of trade measure?

    A. Opportunity costs for both countries

    B. Probability of trade deals in the future

    C. The rate of exchange of one product for another

    D. The amount of economic progress made by both countries

35. Which resource is sold by households and bought by firms in a resource market?

    A. Labor   C. Wages

    B. Stock   D. Interest

36. With a monopoly, there is/are _____

    A. few buyers.

    B. one company in the market.

    C. no supply but great demand.

    D. too much competition to balance supply and demand.

37. Law of demand states that _____

    A. without supply, there is no demand.

    B. quantity increases as the price increases.

    C. quantity decreases as the price increases.

    D. the market determines demand, but not price, when there is equilibrium.

38. If a country's GDP is rising, _____

    A. the economy is healthy.

    B. prices are stable, but unemployment is high.

    C. the country needs to produce fewer goods and services.

    D. growth is slowing, and more intermediate goods need to be consumed.

39. Who tracks the price changes in the United States that are presented in the Consumer Price Index?

    A. Banks

    B. Government

    C. Private companies

    D. Consumer advisory board

The following two questions are based on the map.

40. What is the name of the current country that was part of the Roman Empire?

A. Italy

B. Egypt

C. Turkey

D. Greece

41. What body of water surrounded the empire ruled by the ancient Greeks?

A. Red Sea

B. Black Sea

C. Atlantic Ocean

D. Mediterranean Sea

42. What happens when the government prints too much money?

A. GDP rises.

B. Inflation occurs.

C. Too many goods are produced.

D. The number of employed individuals increases.

43. What was the start of the United States' debt?

A. Poor free trade policies

B. Paying off debts to the mother country

C. Too much trade with European countries

D. Paying for the American Revolutionary War

44. What was the state of the economy in the 13 colonies after they won the American Revolutionary War?

A. Low debt

B. High inflation

C. Free trade equilibrium

D. More supply than demand

497

45. **What is one characteristic of a republic?**

   A. There is no monarch.

   B. The country's founders hold power.

   C. Trade is limited to European countries

   D. Economic policy ensures that the country's firms can demand the highest prices.

46. **Russia lies in which two continents?**

   A. Asia and Africa

   B. Asia and Europe

   C. Africa and Europe

   D. Antarctica and Asia

47. **A school district in an example of a(n) _____ region.**

   A. fixed

   B. formal

   C. uniform

   D. functional

48. **The French Quarter in New Orleans, Louisiana, can be described as a(n) _____ region.**

   A. fixed

   B. formal

   C. uniform

   D. functional

49. **The statement that the equator is located at 0°00'00" is an example of a(n) _____ location.**

   A. place

   B. relative

   C. regional

   D. absolute

50. **If Quito, the capital of Ecuador, is described as a city in the central part of Ecuador, a South American country, what type of location has been presented?**

   A. exact

   B. precise

   C. relative

   D. absolute

SECTION IV. SCIENCE

(90 minutes)

1. Why did it take many years for the cell theory to be developed?

   A. Advancements in microscopy took place slowly.

   B. Cells were difficult to isolate for experimental analysis.

   C. Researchers believed a cell formed from preexisting cells.

   D. Scientists already proved that cells were essential for life.

2. Which statement is most strongly supported by the cell theory?

   A. Plant cells have similar cell parts to animal cells.

   B. Cells house their genetic information in the nucleus.

   C. Blood cells arise from stem cells in the bone marrow.

   D. Nonliving things lack a cell and associated organelles.

3. Which cell component is characterized as a jelly-like substance?

   A. Nucleus   C. Cytoplasm

   B. Vacuole   D. Cell membrane

4. If a biochemist isolates a large amount of pyruvate, which part of the cell is he working with?

   A. Chloroplasts   C. Mitochondria

   B. Cytoplasm   D. Nucleus

5. Which of the following characteristics is unique to all prokaryotes?

   A. Creates gametes

   B. Requires meiosis

   C. Uses photosynthesis

   D. Reproduces asexually

6. Mitosis is different from meiosis because mitosis

   A. is a form of asexual reproduction.

   B. leads to the production of gametes.

   C. includes two rounds of cell division.

   D. results in increased genetic diversity.

7. What step of the scientific method relies on logic reasoning to be formulated?

   A. Asking a question

   B. Writing a conclusion

   C. Researching information

   D. Developing a hypothesis

8. When a researcher determines the cause-and-effect relationship between two variables, what part of the scientific method is the researcher performing?

   A. Analysis   C. Experiment

   B. Conclusion   D. Hypothesis

9. What is the purpose of a placebo?

   A. Determine how people respond to treatment

   B. Represent the independent variable in a study

   C. Account for a psychological factor during treatment

   D. Provide an additional way to collect data for analysis

10. Human cells have _____ sets of different chromosomes.

    A. 12   C. 46

    B. 23   D. 50

11. In DNA replication, a DNA strand is separated, and a

    A. complementary strand attaches.

    B. complementary strand is assembled.

    C. complementary strand replicates itself.

    D. complementary strand forms a double helix.

12. An offspring receives _____ allele(s) for a particular trait from each parent.

    A. 1   C. 3

    B. 2   D. 4

13. Which sequence describes the hierarchy level of biological organization?

    A. Kingdom, phylum, class, order, family, genus, and species

    B. Genus, class, kingdom, species, order, phylum, and family

    C. Family, species, genus, order, kingdom, class, and phylum

    D. Species, kingdom, genus, class, family, phylum, and order

14. Which class of biomolecules help transmit genetic information?

    A. Lipids   C. Nucleic acids

    B. Proteins   D. Carbohydrates

15. When using the scientific method, what does a researcher do immediately after proposing a scientific question?

    A. Perform background research on the topic

    B. Analyze data to observe trends or patterns

    C. Collect information or data during an experiment

    D. Communicate results in an article or presentation

16. Which of the following is a characteristic of citrus substances?

    A. Taste sour

    B. Have a pH of 7

    C. Turn litmus blue

    D. Slippery to touch

17. Water can act as an acid or a base. Because of this behavior, it is known to be

    A. amphoteric.   C. ionic.

    B. aqueous.   D. pure.

18. Which is classified as a type of acid-base reaction that produces a salt?

    A. Combination

    B. Decomposition

    C. Hydrolysis

    D. Neutralization

19. Which of the following atoms is an anion?

    A. 12 protons, 12 neutrons, 10 electrons

    B. 16 protons, 16 neutrons, 18 electrons

    C. 19 protons, 20 neutrons, 19 electrons

    D. 26 protons, 30 neutrons, 24 electrons

20. A neutral atom has two electrons in its first energy shell, eight electrons in its second energy shell, and three electrons in its third energy shell. Which electrons will be lost when the atom reacts to become stable?

   A. Electrons in the first shell

   B. Electrons in the second shell

   C. Electrons in the third shell

   D. Electrons in the second or third shell

21. How many potassium and nitrogen ions are needed to form an ionic compound?

   A. One potassium ion and one nitrogen ion

   B. Three potassium ions and one nitrogen ion

   C. One potassium ion and three nitrogen ions

   D. Three potassium ions and three nitrogen ions

22. Which of the following is an example of a homogeneous mixture?

   A. A bowl of cereal with milk

   B. A glass of lemonade with ice

   C. A mixture of silver and gold coins

   D. A pitcher of cherry-flavored beverage

23. The graph below shows the energy of the species involved in a chemical reaction as the reaction proceeds. How much energy is released in this reaction?

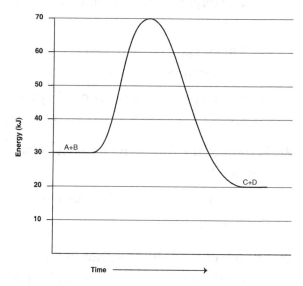

   A. 10 kJ   C. 30 kJ

   B. 20 kJ   D. 40 kJ

24. Which of the following equations shows a single-replacement reaction?

   A. $3H_2 + N_2$ $2NH_3$

   B. $Zn + 2HCl$ $H_2 + ZnCl_2$

   C. $C_2H_4 + 3O_2$ $2CO_2 + 2H_2O$

   D. $2AgNO_3 + CuCl_2$ $2AgCl + Cu(NO_3)_2$

25. Which of the following is an example of a physical property?

   A. Amount   C. Reactivity

   B. Corrosion   D. Rusting

26. The amount of matter that an object contains is _____.

   A. deposition   C. polarity

   B. mass   D. sublimation

27. Why does oxygen diffuse out of lungs into the bloodstream?

   A. The oxygen is repulsed by the blood.

   B. The oxygen is being pulled into the blood.

   C. The oxygen is polar, and the blood has the opposite charge.

   D. The oxygen is going from a higher area of concentration to a lower one.

28. Which of the following parts of an atom has no charge?

   A. Electron

   B. Neutron

   C. Nucleus

   D. Proton

29. Which of the following isotopes of boron should be the most abundant, and why?

   A. Boron-10, because its mass is closer to the average atomic mass in the periodic table.

   B. Boron-11, because its mass is closer to the average atomic mass in the periodic table.

   C. Boron-10, because its mass is farther from the average atomic mass in the periodic table.

   D. Boron-11, because its mass is farther from the average atomic mass in the periodic table.

30. Which of the following atoms will have an overall negative charge?

   A. 9 protons, 10 neutrons, 9 electrons

   B. 12 protons, 13 neutrons, 10 electrons

   C. 14 protons, 14 neutrons, 10 electrons

   D. 15 protons, 16 neutrons, 18 electrons

31. At the end of which phase change will a substance have less energy than it did at the beginning?

   A. Deposition

   B. Melting

   C. Sublimation

   D. Vaporization

32. During which of the following phase changes will the cohesion between the particles in a substance decrease?

   A. Condensation

   B. Deposition

   C. Freezing

   D. Vaporization

33. What happens to the shape and volume of a sample of helium gas when it is transferred from a tank to a balloon?

   A. Both the shape and volume change.

   B. Neither the shape nor the volume changes.

   C. The shape changes, but the volume remains the same.

   D. The volume changes, but the shape remains the same.

34. How many cups are in 22 pints?

   A. 11

   B. 20

   C. 24

   D. 44

35. Which of the following is part of the metric system?

   A. Celsius

   B. Feet

   C. Ounces

   D. Pound

36. A scientist wants to measure how far a person can run in 30 minutes. Which of the following units should she use to record this measurement as a small number?

   A. Gigameters

   B. Kilometers

   C. Megameters

   D. Terameters

37. Which of the following is an example of electromagnetic induction?

   A. A wire loop spinning in a magnetic field

   B. A proton exerting a force on an electron

   C. A battery delivering electric current to a resistor

   D. An accelerating charge creating electromagnetic waves

38. Region X and region Y are approximately the same size, but the magnetic flux through region X is much higher. Which statement about these regions is correct?

   A. The magnetic force in region X is less than in region Y.

   B. The magnetic force in region X is greater than in region Y.

   C. The magnetic force in region X and in region Y is about zero.

   D. The magnetic force in region X is about the same as in region Y.

39. A scientist wants to determine how much current a particular instrument is drawing. If she knows how much voltage the instrument employs and how much resistance it presents, which principle must she use?

   A. Ohm's law

   B. Electric flux

   C. Coulomb's law

   D. Electromagnetic induction

40. Children on a turning bus feel a centrifugal force to the west. What is the direction of the centripetal force?

   A. East   C. South

   B. North   D. West

41. Which of the following can be a result of friction on a moving object?

   A. Centripetal acceleration

   B. An increase in the object's speed

   C. Movement of a fluid surrounding the object

   D. A net force in the direction of the object's velocity

42. A softball player throws a ball at a moderately upward angle to the ground. Which term best describes the motion of the ball?

   A. Linear   C. Stationary

   B. Nonlinear   D. Rotational

43. How is an airbag useful in car accidents?

   A. The airbag increases the force exerted by the driver.

   B. The airbag decreases the force exerted by the driver.

   C. The airbag increases the velocity exerted by the driver.

   D. The airbag decreases the velocity exerted by the driver.

44. A stationary object can possess which of the following?

   A. Impulse   C. Kinetic energy

   B. Momentum   D. Potential energy

45. Which parameter is always a vector?

A. Acceleration   C. Speed

B. Mass   D. Velocity

46. A man applies a force to a wall by pushing on it. What does the wall do in response?

A. The wall applies a greater force in the same direction.

B. The wall applies a smaller force in the opposite direction.

C. The wall applies a force of equal magnitude in the same direction.

D. The wall applies a force of equal magnitude in the opposite direction.

47. Which statement best describes the motion of smooth ball thrown into the air on a calm day?

A. The ball follows a line.

B. The ball follows a circular path.

C. The ball follows an erratic path.

D. The ball follows a parabolic path.

48. Which of the following creates electromagnetic waves?

A. An electron that is stationary

B. An electron that is approaching a proton

C. An electron that is moving at a constant velocity

D. An electron that is moving at a decreasing velocity

49. An observer reports seeing a large, far-off explosion before feeling rumbles in the ground. Which explanation best accounts for this difference?

A. The electromagnetic waves have a greater frequency than the mechanical waves.

B. The electromagnetic waves have a greater amplitude than the mechanical waves.

C. The electromagnetic waves have a greater wavelength than the mechanical waves.

D. The electromagnetic waves have a greater wave speed than the mechanical waves.

50. One isotope of a particular element is neutral, and a different isotope of that element is an ion. Which conclusion is correct?

A. One isotope has more protons than the other.

B. One isotope has more electrons than the other.

C. Both isotopes have the same number of neutrons.

D. Both isotopes have the same number of nucleons.

Section V. Mathematical Reasoning

(115 minutes)

1. How many whole numbers are less than 3 but greater than −3?

   A. 2   C. 4

   B. 3   D. 5

2. Which number will appear farthest right on a standard number line?

   A. −1,024   C. 32

   B. −256   D. 512

3. Which statement best describes a remainder in division?

   A. The quotient minus the divisor

   B. The product of the dividend and divisor

   C. The difference between the dividend and the quotient

   D. The portion of a dividend not evenly divisible by the divisor

4. Evaluate the expression $15 \times (-15)$.

   A. −225   C. −1

   B. −30   D. 0

5. How many prime numbers are less than 20 but greater than 0?

   A. 8   C. 10

   B. 9   D. 11

6. If the term of a mobile-phone contract is in multiples of a year, which duration can a customer choose?

   A. 6 months   C. 24 months

   B. 18 months   D. 32 months

7. Convert 15,000 grams to metric tons.

   A. 0.00015 metric ton

   B. 0.0015 metric ton

   C. 0.015 metric ton

   D. 0.15 metric ton

8. Convert 2.5 miles to feet.

   A. 2,112 feet   C. 10,560 feet

   B. 2,640 feet   D. 13,200 feet

9. Which decimal is the least?

   A. 2.22   C. 2.002

   B. 2.02   D. 2.2

10. Change 0.375 to a fraction. Simplify completely.

    A. $\frac{3}{8}$ C. $\frac{1}{2}$

    B. $\frac{2}{5}$ D. $\frac{7}{16}$

11. Multiply $\frac{3}{16} \times \frac{4}{7}$.

    A. $\frac{3}{28}$ C. $\frac{1}{6}$

    B. $\frac{1}{9}$ D. $\frac{7}{9}$

12. Divide $\frac{8}{9} \div \frac{5}{7}$.

    A. $\frac{11}{45}$ C. $1\frac{11}{45}$

    B. $\frac{40}{63}$ D. $1\frac{40}{63}$

13. Solve the equation for the unknown, $\frac{x}{2} + 5 = 8$.

    A. $\frac{3}{2}$ C. 6

    B. $\frac{5}{2}$ D. 26

14. Solve the inequality for the unknown, $\frac{1}{2}(4x + 3) < \frac{3}{4}x + 2$.

    A. $x < \frac{2}{5}$ C. $x < \frac{6}{5}$

    B. $x > \frac{2}{5}$ D. $x > \frac{6}{5}$

505

15. Solve the system of equations,
    $-2x + 2y = 28$
    $3x + y = -22$.

    A. (9, 5)   C. (9, -5)

    B. (-9, -5)   D. (-9, 5)

16. Solve the system of equations by graphing,
    $y = \frac{1}{3}x + 2$
    $y = \frac{2}{3}x + 5$.

    A.
    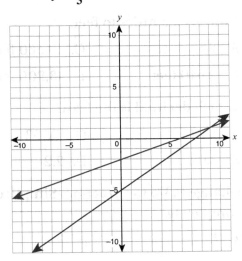

    B.
    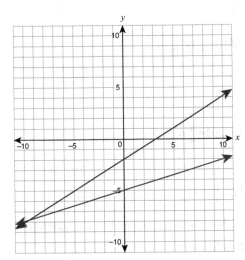

C.
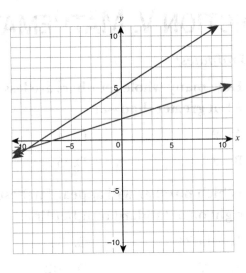

D.
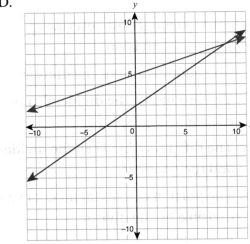

17. Solve the system of equations,
    $y = -3x$
    $x^2 + y^2 = 20$.

    A. (1.4, 4.2) and (-1.4, -4.2)

    B. (-1.4, 4.2) and (1.4, -4.2)

    C. (-2, 6) and (2, -6)

    D. (2, 6) and (-2, -6)

18. A person has $250 in a checking account and writes checks for $70, $85, $60, and $100. There is also a fee of $20. What is the balance of the account?

    A. −$335   C. $335

    B. −$85   D. $685

19. A small landscaping company mows lawns and has three 5.4-gallon gas cans. One day, the landscapers empty the gas cans three times. How many gallons of gas did they use?

    A. 10.8

    B. 16.2

    C. 32.4

    D. 48.6

20. A pair of jeans with tax costs $39.97, and a shirt with tax costs $18.49. What is the amount of change for a pair of jeans and two shirts if playing with a $100 bill?

    A. $23.05

    B. $36.98

    C. $41.54

    D. $60.03

21. Solve the equation by any method, $2x^2 - 70 = 2$.

    A. ±2

    B. ±4

    C. ±6

    D. ±8

22. Solve the equation by completing the square, $x^2 - 2x - 37 = 0$.

    A. $-1 \pm \sqrt{37}$

    B. $1 \pm \sqrt{37}$

    C. $-1 \pm \sqrt{38}$

    D. $1 \pm \sqrt{38}$

23. Solve the equation by factoring, $x^2 - 5x - 50 = 0$.

    A. $-10, -5$

    B. $-10, 5$

    C. $10, -5$

    D. $10, 5$

24. Multiply, $(5x - 3)(5x + 3)$.

    A. $25x^2 - 9$

    B. $25x^2 + 9$

    C. $25x^2 + 30x - 9$

    D. $25x^2 + 30x + 9$

25. Perform the operation, $(-3x^2 - 2xy + 4y^2) + (5x^2 + 3xy - 3y^2)$.

    A. $2x^2 - xy + y^2$

    B. $-2x^2 - xy + y^2$

    C. $-2x^2 + xy + y^2$

    D. $2x^2 + xy + y^2$

26. Apply the polynomial identity to rewrite $x^2 + 20x + 100$.

    A. $x^2 + 100$

    B. $(x + 10)^2$

    C. $(x^2 + 10)^2$

    D. $(10x)^2$

27. If 17 widgets failed but the other 1,273 worked properly, what is the failure rate of that widget?

    A. 1.30%

    B. 1.32%

    C. 1.34%

    D. 1.36%

28. Which is different from the others?

    A. 6.4%

    B. $\frac{8}{125}$

    C. 128:2000

    D. All of the above are equal.

29. Simplify $\left(\dfrac{x^3 y^{-2}}{x^{-2} y^3}\right)^5$.

    A. $\frac{1}{x^{25} y^{25}}$

    B. $\frac{y^{25}}{x^{25}}$

    C. $\frac{x^{25}}{y^{25}}$

    D. $x^{25} y^{25}$

30. One athlete had a salary of about 3×10^7 dollars per year and another athlete had a salary of about 2×10^6 dollars per year. How many times larger is the salary of the first athlete?

    A. 2

    B. 5

    C. 10

    D. 15

31. What is the intersection of two walls in a room?

    A. A ray

    B. A line

    C. A point

    D. A plane

32. What is the order of rotational symmetry for a parallelogram?

    A. 1

    B. 2

    C. 3

    D. 4

33. A regular hexagon has a side length of 5 inches and an apothem of 2 inches. Find the area in square inches.

    A. 30   C. 50

    B. 40   D. 60

34. A wedge of cheese is in the shape of a right triangular prism. The area of the base is 30 square inches. What is the height in inches of the cheese if the volume is 150 cubic inches?

    A. 2.5   C. 7.5

    B. 5   D. 10

35. A box in the shape of a right rectangular prism has dimensions of 6 centimeters by 7 centimeters by 8 centimeters. What is the volume in cubic centimeters?

    A. 280   C. 560

    B. 336   D. 672

36. A circle has an area of 12 square feet. Find the diameter to the nearest tenth of a foot. Use 3.14 for π.

    A. 1.0   C. 3.0

    B. 2.0   D. 4.0

37. Find the area in square centimeters of a circle with a diameter of 16 centimeters. Use 3.14 for π.

    A. 25.12   C. 100.48

    B. 50.24   D. 200.96

38. The area of a half circle is 48 square centimeters. Find the circumference of the curved portion of the half circle to the nearest tenth of a centimeter. Use 3.14 for π.

    A. 17.3   C. 34.5

    B. 24.5   D. 49.0

39. A rectangular pyramid has a length of 10 centimeters, a width of 11 inches, and a height of 12 inches. Find the volume in cubic inches.

    A. 220   C. 660

    B. 440   D. 880

40. A basketball has a diameter of 10 inches. What is the volume in cubic inches inside the ball? Use 3.14 for π.

    A. 261.67   C. 1,046.67

    B. 523.33   D. 2,093.33

41. Find the median for the data set 34, 31, 37, 35, 38, 33, 39, 32, 36, 35, 37, and 33.

    A. 34   C. 36

    B. 35   D. 37

42. Find the range for the data set 34, 45, 27, 29, 36, 60, 52, 48, 41, 65, 44, 50, 64, 58, 47, and 31.

    A. 3   C. 36

    B. 5   D. 38

43. Find the mode the data set 42, 45, 44, 44, 45, 42, 45, 44, 45, 46, 42, 44, 41, 48, 47, 46, 45, 42, 42, and 44.

    A. 42, 43   C. 42, 44, 45

    B. 44, 45   D. 42, 43, 44, 45

44. There is an election at a school where 4 candidates out of 10 will be elected. Which object and results are the most appropriate for a simulation?

    A. Toss a coin

    B. Ten-sided number cube and use multiples of 2

    C. Eight-section spinner and use the odd numbers

    D. Throw two six-sided number cubes and use the results of 1 and 6

45. A group is conducting a survey at a mall asking shoppers their opinion of the mall. What type of sampling is used?

A. Quota sampling

B. Volunteer sampling

C. Purposive sampling

D. Convenience sampling

46. A doctor wants to study the effects of a low-fat diet in patients. What would be needed to create an observational study?

A. Ask how many fat calories were eaten and track weight.

B. Ask about the amount of weight patients have gained or lost.

C. Have one-half of the patients eat a high-fat diet and the other eat a low-fat diet.

D. Select a group of patients with a low-fat diet and ask how they feel being on the diet.

47. If a letter is chosen at random from the word SUBSTITUTE, what is the probability that the letter chosen is "S" or "T"?

A. $\frac{1}{5}$ C. $\frac{2}{5}$

B. $\frac{3}{10}$ D. $\frac{1}{2}$

48. A spinner contains numbers 1–20. What is the probability of spinning a multiple of 3 or a multiple of 5?

A. $\frac{3}{10}$ C. $\frac{9}{20}$

B. $\frac{1}{5}$ D. $\frac{11}{20}$

49. The histogram below shows the amount a family spent on groceries during the year. Which statement is true for the histogram?

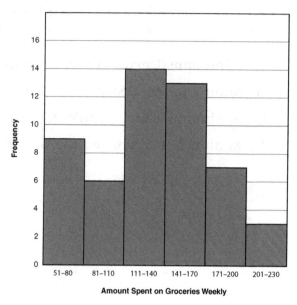

A. The lowest frequency is between $80 and $110.

B. The highest frequency is between $140 and $170.

C. More than half of the amount spent is greater than $140.

D. More than half of the amount spent is between $110 and $170.

509

50. Find the values from the box plot.

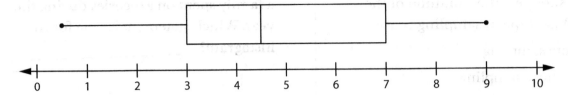

A. Minimum: 0, first quartile: 3, median: 5, third quartile: 7, maximum: 9

B. Minimum: 0.5, first quartile: 3, median: 4.5, third quartile: 7, maximum: 9

C. Minimum: 0, first quartile: 3, median: 5, third quartile: 7, maximum: 10

D. Minimum: 0.5, first quartile: 3, median: 4.5, third quartile: 7, maximum: 10

TASC Practice Exam 1
Answer Key with Explanatory Answers

Section I. Writing

1. D. *Dependent* is the only correct spelling. **See Lesson: Spelling.**

2. D. With words ending in -z, add -es. This one is irregular and needs an extra -z. **See Lesson: Spelling.**

3. B. Fourth of July. Holidays need to be capitalized. **See Lesson: Capitalization.**

4. D. *she, do, and indian.* She is at the beginning of the sentence and needs to be capitalized. Do is at the beginning of a quoted sentence and also needs to be capitalized. Nationalities such as Indian should always be capitalized. **See Lesson: Capitalization.**

5. A. *The bookstore has three types of books: fiction, nonfiction, and biography.* Colons are used after the last word before introducing a list. **See Lesson: Punctuation.**

6. B. *There should be a comma after today.* Commas are used after introductory phrases. **See Lesson: Punctuation.**

7. A. *It was good, wasn't it?* Commas are used before question tags. **See Lesson: Punctuation.**

8. B. To make the word *frog* plural, simply add *-s*. **See Lesson: Nouns.**

9. A. *Supreme Court* is a noun. **See Lesson: Nouns.**

10. D. *Marie Curie, Nobel Prize,* and *1911* are nouns. **See Lesson: Nouns.**

11. B. *Her* is a possessive pronoun. **See Lesson: Pronouns.**

12. C. *Its* is a possessive pronoun; *it* replaces the noun dog. **See Lesson: Pronouns.**

13. D. *Ours* is a possessive pronoun. *It's* is a contraction of *it is. Who* and *That* are relative pronouns. **See Lesson: Pronouns.**

14. C. *Red* is an adjective that describes the noun *roses*. **See Lesson:** Adjectives and Adverbs

15. B. *Young* is an adjective that describes the noun *people,* and *teen* is an adjective that describes the word *idol*. **See Lesson:** Adjectives and Adverbs.

16. B. *Beautifully* is an adverb that describes the verb *played.* **See Lesson:** Adjectives and Adverbs.

17. B. *The* is an article, not a conjunction. **See Lesson: Conjunctions and Prepositions.**

18. C. *But* and *yet* have the same meaning here. **See Lesson: Conjunctions and Prepositions.**

19. C. *In* is a preposition. **See Lesson: Conjunctions and Prepositions.**

20. A. This is a past tense negative, so it takes the helping verb *did* with the base form *like*. **See Lesson: Verbs and Verb Tenses.**

21. A. *Read* and *wrote* are in simple past tense. **See Lesson: Verbs and Verb Tenses.**

22. B. *Ask* is the main verb. **See Lesson: Verbs and Verb Tenses.**

23. C. This sentence correctly fixes the run-on sentence. **See Lesson: Types of Sentences.**

24. B. This is a simple sentence since it contains one independent clause consisting of a simple subject and a predicate. **See Lesson: Types of Sentences.**

25. D. This option would make the sentence a complex one since it has a subordinating conjunction, *even though*, and a dependent clause. **See Lesson: Types of Sentences.**

26. D. The trial must begin whether she shows up or not. With an independent and dependent clause, a subordinating conjunction is used to connect them. "Whether" is the only choice that makes sense. **See Lesson: Types of Clauses.**

27. D. The mother could not take her kids to school. It is independent because it has a subject, verb, and expresses a complete thought. **See Lesson: Types of Clauses.**

28. A. If. The word "if" signifies the beginning of a dependent clause and is the only conjunction that makes sense in the sentence. **See Lesson: Types of Clauses.**

29. B. This sentence has a predicate within a predicate. The "inside" predicate is *who I have visited for years*, and the "outside" predicate is *my dentist has suddenly disappeared*. **See Lesson: Subject and Verb Agreement.**

30. C. The subject is *my granddaughter*, and the predicate is *was born on January 18*. **See Lesson: Subject and Verb Agreement.**

31. C. The verb *honor* must agree with the subject *Americans*. **See Lesson: Subject and Verb Agreement.**

32. D. *Who was a year older* describes *Marvin*. **See Lesson: Modifiers, misplaced modifiers, dangling modifiers.**

33. A. *When six years old* is missing a reference. To add this reference, *I*, the sentence can be rewritten *When I was six years old, our family...* or *When six years old, I experienced our family's transfer....***See Lesson: Modifiers, misplaced modifiers, dangling modifiers.**

34. B. The only modifier is the word *sleeping*, which is an adjective describing *bags*. **See Lesson: Modifiers, misplaced modifiers, dangling modifiers.**

35. C. *That I wrote on the Korean War* should modify *report*, so it should be placed after that word. **See Lesson: Modifiers, misplaced modifiers, dangling modifiers.**

36. D. *Their wedding* is a direct object of the verb *plan*. **See Lesson: Direct Objects and Indirect Objects.**

37. D. Neither the verb *tried* nor the verb *succeed* has a direct object. *So* and *hard* are adverbs. **See Lesson: Direct Objects and Indirect Objects.**

38. A. *His older brother* is a direct object of the verb *watched* in this sentence. **See Lesson: Direct Objects and Indirect Objects.**

39. D. The suffix that means "in a manner of or resembling" is *-esque as in the word grotesque.* **See Lesson: Root Words, Prefixes, and Suffixes.**

40. C. The root that means "people" is *dem as in the word democracy.* **See Lesson: Root Words, Prefixes, and Suffixes.**

41. A. The root *mers* means "dip or dive," so immerse indicates that something is dipped in liquid. **See Lesson: Root Words, Prefixes, and Suffixes.**

42. A. The root *irasc* means "to be angry" and the suffix *-ible* means "able to be," so irascible means easily angered. **See Lesson: Root Words, Prefixes, and Suffixes.**

43. C. The meaning of jam in the context of this sentence is "an instance of a machine seizing or getting stuck." **See Lesson: Context Clues and Multiple Meaning Words**

44. B. The meaning of solution in this context is "a mixture of two or more substances." The phrase "ammonia and water" helps you figure out which meaning of solution is being used. **See Lesson: Context Clues and Multiple Meaning Words**

45. B. The word "strike" has more than one meaning. **See Lesson: Context Clues and Multiple Meaning Words**

46. A. The meaning of confiscate in the context of this sentence is "seize." **See Lesson: Context Clues and Multiple Meaning Words**

47. A. Assertive has a positive connotation. **See Lesson: Synonyms, Antonyms, and Analogies.**

48. D. Dazzling is the word showing the strongest degree. **See Lesson: Synonyms, Antonyms, and Analogies.**

49. A. Pundit and apprentice are antonyms in the same way that flux and stability are antonyms. **See Lesson: Synonyms, Antonyms, and Analogies.**

50. B. Adding the prefix "un" would make the word unintentional, which is an antonym for intentional. **See Lesson: Synonyms, Antonyms, and Analogies.**

Section II. Reading

1. B. The second sentence of this paragraph expresses the main idea that chocolate chip cookies were invented by accident. This makes it the topic sentence. **See Lesson: Main Ideas, Topic Sentences, and Supporting Details.**

2. A. The topic of a sentence is a word or phrase that describes what the text is about. **See Lesson: Main Ideas, Topic Sentences, and Supporting Details.**

3. C. This paragraph presents the story behind the invention of the chocolate chip cookie. It discusses the fact that the dessert was a complete accident. This idea is expressed in a topic sentence at the beginning of the paragraph. **See Lesson: Main Ideas, Topic Sentences, and Supporting Details.**

4. D. The main idea of this paragraph is that chocolate chip cookies were invented by accident. The detail that directly supports this is the one describing what Ruth Graves Wakefield did when she ran out of baker's chocolate – she broke up a block of Nestle semi-sweet chocolate expecting them to melt. This is a supporting detail. **See Lesson: Main Ideas, Topic Sentences, and Supporting Details.**

5. B. All of the above sentences relate to the topic of chocolate chip cookies, but only the sentence about Ruth Graves Wakefield realizing how delicious they were relates directly to the main idea that the chocolate chip cookie was invented by accident. **See Lesson: Main Ideas, Topic Sentences, and Supporting Details.**

6. A. Although the text mentions that a jack-o-lantern can rot once it is on display, this is not a step to follow in the process. Scooping out the pulp is one of the steps. **See Lesson: Summarizing Text and Using Text Features.**

7. B. The text states that drawing a design on the pumpkin helps prevent cutting errors. **See Lesson: Summarizing Text and Using Text Features.**

8. B. This summary is effective because it restates only the key points and it does it using new words. **See Lesson: Summarizing Text and Using Text Features.**

9. A. An ineffective summary would copy the original text word for word and only change one or two words. The first sentence is almost exactly like the first sentence of the original text, so this would be structurally plagiarized. **See Lesson: Summarizing Text and Using Text Features.**

10. A. Adelia is attempting to call a pet, not a child. You can infer this because she calls Mr. Snuggles "vermin" and bangs on a bowl with a spoon to get his attention. **See Lesson: Understanding Primary Sources, Making Inferences and Drawing Conclusions.**

11. B. Adelia's bathrobe is not evidence that she is frustrated at Mr. Snuggles. **See Lesson: Understanding Primary Sources, Making Inferences and Drawing Conclusions.**

12. A. Adelia tries repeatedly to call Mr. Snuggles, and when he does not come, she goes out to look for him. This implies that she does care about him, even if she is angry at him. **See Lesson: Understanding Primary Sources, Making Inferences and Drawing Conclusions.**

13. C. The line about Raul and his plants does not explicitly say Adelia is babysitting Mr. Snuggles, but it suggests that she is caring for the pet for someone else. **See Lesson: Understanding Primary Sources, Making Inferences and Drawing Conclusions.**

14. C. Congratulations on your recent success. It is the sentence with the most formal language and no slang. **See Lesson: Formal and Informal Language.**

15. A. Where's the best café in these parts? The sentence is informal because it has a contraction and uses more colloquial language. **See Lesson: Formal and Informal Language.**

16. A. At brunch. It is an informal setting that a person goes to with their friends. **See Lesson: Formal and Informal Language.**

17. A. This essay claims that sugar is bad for people. In academic writing, pronouns such as I should not be used. **See Lesson: Formal and Informal Language.**

18. D. The tone of this letter is appreciative as the author openly thanks the teacher for all he has done for her daughter. **See Lesson: Tone, Mood, and Transition Words.**

19. D. The author of the letter uses a lot of respectful and admiring language, but the line "We cannot thank you enough" has an especially appreciative and warm tone. **See Lesson: Tone, Mood, and Transition Words.**

20. B. A teacher receiving a note like this would likely feel grateful. **See Lesson: Tone, Mood, and Transition Words.**

21. D. The phrase "above all" adds emphasis to the writer's point that the teacher has made a significant impact on the daughter. **See Lesson: Tone, Mood, and Transition Words.**

22. C. This is a book review. Although it includes some information about the story, its primary purpose is to convince you to read it. This makes it a persuasive text. **See Lesson: Understanding Author's Purpose, Point of View, and Rhetorical Strategies.**

23. C. Most of the information despite the second paragraph is not verifiable, but the fact that the book chronicles the final years of Audrey Lacoste's life is a fact. **See Lesson: Understanding Author's Purpose, Point of View, and Rhetorical Strategies.**

24. C. This is a book review. The author includes details about Audrey Lacoste's life to personalize the idea of getting old by telling one individual's struggle. This is meant to appeal to the reader's emotions. **See Lesson: Understanding Author's Purpose, Point of View, and Rhetorical Strategies.**

25. A. The argument that getting rid of homework is undoubtedly beneficial is an opinion statement because it makes a judgment. **See Lesson: Facts, Opinions, and Evaluating an Argument.**

26. C. The statement is a fact because it discusses the results of standardized test scores, which can be measured. **See Lesson: Facts, Opinions, and Evaluating an Argument.**

27. B. The main argument in this passage is that there are no clear benefits from giving elementary aged students daily homework. **See Lesson: Facts, Opinions, and Evaluating an Argument.**

28. D. The sentence about homework doing nothing to enhance student learning at all is an overgeneralization. The term "at all" makes a big over-arching claim that cannot be verified, as the author does not even explore some of the potential benefits of daily homework. **See Lesson: Facts, Opinions, and Evaluating an Argument.**

29. C. The Rim Trail is the dotted line running generally north-south past the Lodge in the middle. Fairyland Point is in the far north, so a walk north on the trail would get you there. **See Lesson: Evaluating and Integrating Data.**

30. D. Inspiration Point is between Sunset Point and Bryce Point along the Rim Trail. **See Lesson: Evaluating and Integrating Data.**

31. A. The main road parallels the Rim Trail but only touches the northernmost and southernmost viewpoints; it does not touch Sunset Point. **See Lesson: Evaluating and Integrating Data.**

32. D. The compass shows that the left-hand side of the page is west. The Visitor's Center is the westernmost labeled point on the map. **See Lesson: Evaluating and Integrating Data.**

33. A. The legend explains what the solid and dotted lines represent. In this case, the dotted line is a trail and the solid line is a road. **See Lesson: Evaluating and Integrating Data.**

34. A. Both passages tell stories. That makes this narrative writing. **See Lesson: Types of Passages, Text Structures, Genre and Theme.**

35. A. Both passages say what happened first, second, third, and so on, in chronological order. This is a sequential structure. **See Lesson: Types of Passages, Text Structures, Genre and Theme.**

36. D. Passage 1, with its talking animal characters, is definitely fiction. Passage 2 could be nonfiction (memoir or autobiography) or fiction (short story or novel). **See Lesson: Types of Passages, Text Structures, Genre and Theme.**

37. B. Passage 1 is a short fantastical tale for children that teaches an explicit lesson. This makes it a fable. **See Lesson: Types of Passages, Text Structures, Genre and Theme.**

38. A. Passage 2 could be a novel excerpt, a short story, or a section from an autobiography or memoir. It is least likely to be a legend. **See Lesson: Types of Passages, Text Structures, Genre and Theme.**

39. A. The main point is the unifying idea. Here, that is the argument that there is a need for diverse superheroes. **See Lesson: The Writing Process.**

40. C. The author of this outline has not yet figured out how to grab the attention and set up the topic in the introductory paragraph. The introduction in this outline contains only the thesis statement. **See Lesson: The Writing Process.**

41. A. The sentence about the world needing more heroes is a surprising statement that could grab the reader's attention at the beginning of the essay. **See Lesson: The Writing Process.**

42. C. A new body paragraph needs to say something new, not just restate the points already made. However, it must also stay focused on the main point about superheroes, not veer off onto a related side topic. **See Lesson: The Writing Process.**

43. C. This outline contains information from research, and the writer has made a note of where the quotations came from. This will help later when it is time to create citations. **See Lesson: The Writing Process.**

44. B. The author needs more precise word choice in Sentence 1. A "bad" commercial could have poor acting or be unconvincing; in this case, the author is implying that the commercial is harmful to society. **See Lesson: Essay Revision and Transitions.**

45. A. The author's point is not necessarily that the TV commercial she saw should be banned. Rather, she is trying to convince women to share her outrage about the way society pressures them to look. **See Lesson: Essay Revision and Transitions.**

46. C. The thesis suggests that women should base their self-esteem on their accomplishments, but the body paragraphs mainly defend the point that the media presents unrealistic images of beauty. **See Lesson: Essay Revision and Transitions.**

47. A. The author does not actually defend the point that women should base their self-esteem on their accomplishments. Rather, the body paragraphs focus on the idea that the media's image of beauty is false. **See Lesson: Essay Revision and Transitions.**

48. A. *The student returned the books to the library.* The sentence is active because the subject is performing the action of the verb, and not being acted on. **See Lesson: Active and Passive Voice.**

49. D. *The computer was turned on by the technician.* This sentence is passive because the subject is receiving the action of the verb. There is a "to be" verb (was) and the words "by the" indicates that the sentence is passive. **See Lesson: Active and Passive Voice.**

50. A. *Have always wanted.* The sentence is active because the subject is performing the action of the verb, and not being acted on. **See Lesson: Active and Passive Voice.**

Section III. Social Studies

1. C. The colonists were tired of being governed by a government that did not listen to their concerns. They wanted to govern themselves. **See Lesson: Types of Governments.**

2. C. A government in which the people being governed hold the ultimate power is called a democracy. **See Lesson: Types of Governments.**

3. C. In a constitutional democracy, government powers are described in the constitution. **See Lesson: Types of Governments.**

4. A. The philosopher John Locke introduced the principle of natural rights. **See Lesson: Principles of American Constitutional Democracy.**

5. C. John Locke believed the principal role of a government was to protect its citizens' natural rights. **See Lesson: Principles of American Constitutional Democracy.**

6. A. The rule of law states that all human beings are equal in the eyes of the law. Even a government official can be punished if he or she is proven to have broken the law. **See Lesson: Principles of American Constitutional Democracy.**

7. B. The legislative branch is made up of two houses in Congress that have equal power. **See Lesson: The Structure of the United States Government.**

8. A. The U.S. Senate is often called the Upper House. **See Lesson: The Structure of the United States Government.**

9. C. Representatives in the House serve two-year terms. **See Lesson: The Structure of the United States Government.**

10. D. There are currently 27 amendments to the U.S. Constitution. **See Lesson: Individual Rights and Civic Responsibilities.**

11. A. Either Congress or a group of state legislatures can propose an amendment if it meets certain requirements. **See Lesson: Individual Rights and Civic Responsibilities.**

12. C. When three-fourths of state legislatures approve an amendment, it is ratified, or becomes law. **See Lesson: Individual Rights and Civic Responsibilities.**

13. D. How justice is delivered to those charged with crimes is an example of public policy. How the legislature and Supreme Court work is laid out in the Constitution. The federal government does not decide how colleges should teach U.S. history. **See Lesson: Political Parties, Campaigns, and Elections in American Politics.**

14. D. Leading up to an election, parties hold a primary election to determine who will run for their party in the general election. **See Lesson: Political Parties, Campaigns, and Elections in American Politics.**

15. A. The general election is the election to determine who will take office. **See Lesson: Political Parties, Campaigns, and Elections in American Politics.**

16. D. Winthrop is saying that that they have a chance to act as a moral example to the rest of the world. **See Lesson: The Earliest Americans and the Age of Exploration.**

17. **B.** Winthrop focuses on the fact that disobeying God would lead to divine vengeance. **See Lesson: The Earliest Americans and the Age of Exploration.**

18. **D.** New Englanders formed close communities that tended to work together. **See Lesson: The Earliest Americans and the Age of Exploration.**

19. **C.** Jefferson believed that governments are formed when individuals voluntarily surrender some freedoms in exchange for government protection of their rights. **See Lesson: The American Revolution and the Growth of a Nation.**

20. **B.** Jefferson used the list of grievances to justify claims of natural law for leaving the British Empire. **See Lesson: The American Revolution and the Growth of a Nation.**

21. **B.** Holland attributed the discontent to the declining supply of money. **See Lesson: The American Revolution and the Growth of a Nation.**

22. **C.** The federal government's inaction caused the economy to suffer. **See Lesson: The American Revolution and the Growth of a Nation.**

23. **B.** Johnson wanted to reintegrate the South into the Union as quickly as possible. **See Lesson: Civil War Times.**

24. **A.** The Compromise of 1850 included a Fugitive Slave Act to mollify Southerners. **See Lesson: Civil War Times.**

25. **D.** The fugitive slave law helped turn Northern opinion against the South. **See Lesson: Civil War Times.**

26. **A.** France would have been most interested in limiting the capabilities of the German army because it had borne much of the fighting during the war. **See Lesson: Becoming a World Power.**

27. **C.** Preventing a union would likely prevent another alliance and stop Germany from becoming too powerful. **See Lesson: Becoming a World Power.**

28. **A.** The war guilt clause was extremely unpopular in Germany and contributed to German resentment of the Treaty of Versailles. **See Lesson: Becoming a World Power.**

29. **C.** The premise of MAD was that the attacker would suffer as much as the defender, and a defensive system would end that. **See Lesson: The Twentieth Century and Beyond.**

30. **B.** Reagan draws a direct comparison between the 1930s and then to illustrate potential vulnerability. **See Lesson: The Twentieth Century and Beyond.**

31. **D.** Reagan is proposing to change the policy of Mutually Assured Destruction. **See Lesson: The Twentieth Century and Beyond.**

32. **A.** Trade allows for specialization so countries (and people) can spend their time doing what they do best. **See Lesson: The Fundamentals of Economics.**

33. C. Each country negotiates conditions of trade until a deal is made that benefits both countries. **See Lesson: The Fundamentals of Economics.**

34. C. When trade takes place between two countries, the terms of trade measure the rate of exchange of one product for another. **See Lesson: The Fundamentals of Economics.**

35. A. Households supply and sell labor, capital, land, and entrepreneurial activity, and firms buy it in a resource market. **See Lesson: Microeconomics.**

36. B. A monopoly is a company that is the only provider of a good or service. Sometimes, it is beneficial for a company to have no competition. The government awards utilities a market to ensure production and delivery. **See Lesson: Microeconomics.**

37. C. The law of demand states that when the price of an item goes up, consumers buy less of that item. **See Lesson: Microeconomics.**

38. A. GDP measures economic progress. If GDP is rising, the country is moving forward. **See Lesson: Macroeconomics.**

39. B. In the United States, the government issues the CPI every month. **See Lesson: Macroeconomics.**

40. A. Rome is the capital of Italy. The Roman Empire included present-day Italy. **See Lesson: World Geography: Human/Environment Interaction.**

41. D. The Mediterranean Sea allowed the Greeks to conquer and settle lands. **See Lesson: World Geography: Human/Environment Interaction.**

42. B. The rate of inflation increases when the money supply increases quickly. The increase in money makes goods more expensive for consumers and businesses. **See Lesson: Macroeconomics.**

43. D. The United States had a poor economy during its first years as a republic because of war debt. **See Lesson: Economics Through History.**

44. B. The inflation rate was high. Debt was enormous after the Revolutionary War, and the purchasing power of Continental currency fell dramatically. **See Lesson: Economics Through History.**

45. A. A republic is a form of government under which the head of state is not a monarch. **See Lesson: Economics Through History.**

46. B. Russia includes territory in both Europe and Asia. **See Lesson: World Geography: Human/Environment Interaction.**

47. D. A school district is an example of a functional region because it is based on activities (schooling). **See Lesson: Global Connections: Cultures & Society.**

48. C. It is a uniform region because of its shared French traditions and culture. **See Lesson: Global Connections: Cultures & Society.**

49. D. When a longitude/latitude/parallel is provided in the description for a location, it is a specific or absolute location. **See Lesson: Global Connections: Cultures & Society.**

50. C. It is a relative location because it is described in relation to something else (the country of Ecuador and the continent of South America). It is not an exact location. **See Lesson: Global Connections: Cultures & Society.**

Section IV. Science

1. A. The cell theory is a theory because it is supported by a significant number of experimental findings. The cell theory took many years to be developed because microscopes were not powerful enough to make such observations. **See Lesson: Cell Structure, Function, and Type**

2. C. One characteristic of the cell theory is that cells arise from preexisting cells. This is the case for blood cells, which arise from stem progenitor cells. **See Lesson: Cell Structure, Function, and Type.**

3. C. The cytoplasm is a jelly-like fluid in the cell where many organelles are found. **See Lesson: Cell Structure, Function, and Type.**

4. B. Pyruvate is produced during the process of glycolysis. Because glycolysis happens in the cytoplasm of the cell, the chemist is most likely working with this structure. **See Lesson: Cellular Reproduction, Cellular Respiration, and Photosynthesis.**

5. D. All prokaryotes reproduce asexually. This means they require only one parent cell to produce two daughter cells. **See Lesson: Cellular Reproduction, Cellular Respiration, and Photosynthesis.**

6. A. Mitosis and meiosis are both ways that cells divide to produce new cells. However, mitosis can produce new cells asexually by using one parent cell. Meiosis requires two parent cells to produce daughter cells. **See Lesson: Cellular Reproduction, Cellular Respiration, and Photosynthesis.**

7. D. Researchers must use inductive and deductive reasoning to formulate a plausible hypothesis. **See Lesson: Designing an Experiment.**

8. A. During experimental analysis, results from data collection are analyzed for cause-and-effect relationships. **See Lesson: Designing an Experiment.**

9. C. Placebos are false treatments given during an experimental study to account for the placebo effect. A placebo group is also a type of control group. **See Lesson: Designing an Experiment.**

10. B. Humans have 23 sets of chromosomes. **See Lesson: Genetics and DNA.**

11. B. After the DNA strand is separated, a complementary strand is assembled. **See Lesson: Genetics and DNA.**

12. A. Each offspring receives 1 allele for a particular trait from each parent. **See Lesson: Genetics and DNA.**

13. A. Taxonomy is the process of classifying, describing, and naming organisms. There are seven levels in the Linnaean taxonomic system, starting with the broadest level, kingdom, and ending with the species level. **See Lesson: An Introduction to Biology.**

14. C. Nucleic acids such as DNA and RNA are a class of biomolecules that play a role in the transmission of genetic information. **See Lesson: An Introduction to Biology.**

15. A. The first step in the scientific method is to state a question or problem based on an observation. The next step is to research and learn more about the topic from which the question originates. **See Lesson: An Introduction to Biology.**

16. A. Because citrus substances are acidic, they taste sour, which is a property of acidic substances dissolved in water. **See Lesson: Acids and Bases.**

17. A. Pure water is classified as a neutral solution. However, water is also known to be amphoteric because it can function as either an acid or a base. **See Lesson: Acids and Bases.**

18. D. A neutralization reaction is a type of acid-base reaction where an acid and base react to form a salt and water. **See Lesson: Acids and Bases.**

19. B. Because it has more electrons than protons, this atom has a negative charge and can be classified as an anion. **See Lesson: Chemical Bonds.**

20. C. Electrons in the third shell are the valence electrons for this atom, which are the electrons involved in bonding. **See Lesson: Chemical Bonds.**

21. B. To become stable, a potassium atom will lose one electron to form an ion with a +1 charge, and a nitrogen atom will gain three electrons to form an ion with a -3 charge. Because ionic compounds are neutral, it will require three potassium ions to balance the charge of one nitrogen ion. **See Lesson: Chemical Bonds.**

22. D. The cherry-flavored beverage is the only mixture described in which the components are mixed evenly. In the other mixtures, the individual components of the mixture can be seen because substances did not mix completely. **See Lesson: Chemical Solutions.**

23. A. The amount of energy released is the difference in energy between the reactants and the products. Overall, the reactants released 10 kJ to get from 30 kJ to 20 kJ in the products. **See Lesson: Chemical Solutions.**

24. B. In this reaction, one element (Zn) replaces another (hydrogen in HCl) to form an element (H_2) and a different compound ($ZnCl_2$). **See Lesson: Chemical Solutions.**

25. A. The amount of a substance does not change the substance's chemical composition. **See Lesson: Properties of Matter.**

26. B. The amount of matter that an object contains is mass. **See Lesson: Properties of Matter.**

27. D. In the lungs, oxygen diffuses into the bloodstream because there is a higher concentration of oxygen molecules in the lungs' air sacs than there is in the blood. **See Lesson: Properties of Matter.**

28. B. The neutron is the only part of an atom that is neutral. **See Lesson: Scientific Notation.**

29. B. Often, though not always, the isotope that has a mass closest to the average atomic mass is most abundant. Because the average atomic mass of boron is 10.81 amu, the isotope with the closest mass is boron-11. **See Lesson: Scientific Notation.**

30. D. For an atom to carry a negative charge, it must have more negatively charged electrons than positively charged protons. **See Lesson: Scientific Notation.**

31. A. During deposition, a gas turns to a solid. The particles will have less energy as a solid at the end of the phase change than as a gas at the beginning. **See Lesson: States of Matter.**

32. D. If the cohesion between particles decreases, then the particles must be undergoing a phase change that allows particles to move farther apart. This happens when a substance vaporizes and turns from liquid to gas. **See Lesson: States of Matter.**

33. A. Because helium is a gas, the particles are so far away from one another that the gas takes both the shape and the volume of its container. **See Lesson: States of Matter.**

34. D. There are 2 cups in 1 pint. Thus, 22 pints is 44 cups. **See Lesson: Temperature and the Metric System.**

35. A. Celsius is part of metric system of measurement. It is a universally accepted way to record temperature values in science. **See Lesson: Temperature and the Metric System.**

36. B. The smallest unit of the available answer choices is kilometers. There are 1,000 meters in 1 kilometer. **See Lesson: Temperature and the Metric System.**

37. A. Electromagnetic induction is the creation of an electric force in a conductor by a changing magnetic field. In the case of a wire loop spinning in a magnetic field, the magnetic flux through the loop changes as the loop spins, creating the electric force. **See Lesson: Electricity and Magnetism.**

38. B. The greater the magnetic flux in a given region (alternatively, the denser the field lines in that region), the greater the magnetic force. Answer C is therefore correct. **See Lesson: Electricity and Magnetism.**

39. A. Ohm's law relates the voltage, current, and resistance of a component in an electric circuit. Therefore, the scientist can use it to calculate how much current the instrument is drawing. **See Lesson: Electricity and Magnetism.**

40. A. The centripetal force is equal in magnitude but opposite in direction to the centrifugal force, which is a ghost force. Thus, the children are experiencing a centripetal force to the east. **See Lesson: Friction.**

41. C. Because friction is a force that generally acts in the direction opposite to an object's velocity, answers B and D are incorrect. Centripetal acceleration is a force perpendicular to velocity, eliminating answer A. Friction can cause movement of a fluid surrounding the object, such as in the case of a boat moving in the water. **See Lesson: Friction.**

42. B. When a player throws a ball, it will (under ideal conditions with no friction) undergo projectile motion, following a parabola. That motion is neither linear nor rotational; the best description in this case is nonlinear. **See Lesson: Friction.**

43. B. The airbag decreases the force exerted by the driver by extending the length of time over which the force is exerted. **See Lesson: Kinetic Energy.**

44. D. When velocity is zero, impulse, momentum, and kinetic energy are zero. However, a stationary object could have a height above ground and therefore possess potential energy. **See Lesson: Kinetic Energy.**

45. D. Mass and speed are always scalars. Acceleration can be a vector or a scalar, depending on the context. Velocity is always a vector; speed is the magnitude of the velocity. **See Lesson: Nature of Motion.**

46. D. According to Newton's third law, every action has an equal and opposite reaction—meaning the wall applies a force of equal magnitude but opposite in direction to the force that the man applies. **See Lesson: Nature of Motion.**

47. D. A ball thrown into the air undergoes projectile motion once released. The shape of the path it follows is a parabola (that is, the path is parabolic). **See Lesson: Nature of Motion.**

48. D. Acceleration of a charge creates electromagnetic waves. Because the electrons in answers A and C are experiencing no acceleration, they do not create waves. In general, neither does an electron approaching a proton. An electron with a decreasing velocity is experiencing acceleration, creating electromagnetic waves. **See Lesson: Waves and Sounds.**

49. D. Because electromagnetic waves travel much faster than mechanical waves, observers at a great distance will see events before they hear or feel them. **See Lesson: Waves and Sounds.**

50. B. If two isotopes are of the same element, they have the same number of protons but different numbers of neutrons (and, therefore, different numbers of nucleons). Because one is charged and one is neutral, one must have more electrons than the other. **See Lesson: Waves and Sounds.**

Section V. Mathematical Reasoning

1. B. The correct solution is 3. The whole numbers include 0, 1, 2, 3,.... All whole numbers are greater than −3, but only 0, 1, and 2 are less than 3. **See Lesson: Basic Addition and Subtraction.**

2. D. The correct solution is 512. A standard number line orders numbers from lesser (on the left) to greater (on the right). Remember that negatives are to the left of 0 and positives are to the right. Since 512 > 32, 512 is the greatest number in this list and will appear farthest right on the number line. **See Lesson: Basic Addition and Subtraction.**

3. D. When dividing whole numbers, the remainder is the portion of the dividend left over after finding the whole-number part of the quotient. The remainder is always smaller than the divisor. **See Lesson: Basic Multiplication and Division.**

4. A. When multiplying signed numbers, remember that the product of a negative and a positive is negative. Other than the sign, the process is the same as multiplying whole numbers. **See Lesson: Basic Multiplication and Division.**

5. A. Start by eliminating 1, which is not a prime number. The number 2 is the only even prime; the other even numbers are composite. Therefore, consider only odd numbers greater than 2. The prime numbers less than 20 but greater than 2 are 3, 5, 7, 11, 13, 17, and 19. The total is eight. **See Lesson: Factors and Multiples.**

6. C. A year-long contract is also 12 months long. Multiples of 12 months are 24 months, 36 months, 48 months, and so on. **See Lesson: Factors and Multiples.**

7. C. The correct solution is 0.015 metric ton. $15,000 \ g \times \frac{1 \ kg}{1,000 \ g} \times \frac{1 \ t}{1,000 \ kg} = \frac{15,000}{1,000,000} = 0.015 \ t$. **See Lesson: Standards of Measure.**

8. D. The correct solution is 13,200 feet. $2.5 \ mi \times \frac{5280 \ ft}{1 \ mi} = 13,200 \ ft$. **See Lesson: Standards of Measure.**

9. C. The correct solution is 2.002 because 2.002 contains the smallest values in the tenths and hundredths places. **See Lesson: Decimals and Fractions.**

10. A. The correct solution is $\frac{3}{8}$ because $\frac{0.375}{1} = \frac{375}{1000} = \frac{3}{8}$. **See Lesson: Decimals and Fractions.**

11. A. The correct solution is $\frac{3}{28}$ because $\frac{3}{16} \times \frac{4}{7} = \frac{12}{112} = \frac{3}{28}$. **See Lesson: Multiplication and Division of Fractions.**

12. C. The correct solution is $1\frac{11}{45}$ because $\frac{8}{9} \times \frac{7}{5} = \frac{56}{45} = 1\frac{11}{45}$. **See Lesson: Multiplication and Division of Fractions.**

13. C. The correct solution is 6.

$\frac{x}{2} = 3$ Subtract 5 from both sides of the equation.

$x = 6$ Multiply both sides of the equation by 2.

See Lesson: Equations with One Variable.

14. A. The correct solution is $x < \frac{2}{5}$.

$2(4x + 3) < 3x + 8$ Multiply all terms by the least common denominator of 4 to eliminate the fractions.

$8x + 6 < 3x + 8$ Apply the distributive property.

$5x + 6 < 8$ Subtract $3x$ from both sides of the inequality.

$5x < 2$ Subtract 6 from both sides of the inequality.

$x < \frac{2}{5}$ Divide both sides of the inequality by 5.

See Lesson: Equations with One Variable.

15. D. The correct solution is (-9, 5).

$-6x{-}2y = 44$ Multiply all terms in the second equation by -2.

$-8x = 72$ Add the equations.

$x = -9$ Divide both sides of the equation by -8.

$3(-9) + y = -22$ Substitute -9 in the second equation for x.

$-27 + y = -22$ Simplify using order of operations.

$y = 5$ Add 27 to both sides of the equation.

See Lesson: Equations with Two Variables.

16. C. The correct graph has the two lines intersect at (-9, -1). **See Lesson: Equations with Two Variables.**

17. B. The correct solutions are (-1.4, 4.2) and (1.4, -4.2).

$x^2 + (-3x)^2 = 20$ Substitute $-3x$ in for y in the second equation.

$x^2 + 9x^2 = 20$ Apply the exponent.

$10x^2 = 20$ Combine like terms on the left side of the equation.

$x^2 = 2$ Divide both sides of the equation by 10.

$x = \pm 1.4$ Apply the square root to both sides of the equation.

$y = -3(1.4) = -4.2$ Substitute 1.4 in the first equation and multiply.

$y = -3(-1.4) = 4.2$ Substitute -1.4 in the first equation and multiply.

See Lesson: Equations with Two Variables.

18. B. The correct solution is -$85 because $250{-}(70 + 85 + 60 + 100 + 20) = 250 - 335 = -\$85$. **See Lesson: Solving Real World Mathematical Problems.**

19. D. The correct solution is 48.6 because $5.4(3)(3) = 48.6$ gallons. **See Lesson: Solving Real World Mathematical Problems.**

20. A. The correct solution is $23.05 because the total cost is $18.49(2) + 39.97 = 36.98 + 39.97 = 76.95$. The amount of change is $100 – 76.95 = 23.05. **See Lesson: Solving Real World Mathematical Problems.**

21. C. The correct solutions are ± 6. Solve this equation by the square root method.

$2x^2 = 72$	Add 70 to both sides of the equation.
$x^2 = 36$	Divide both sides of the equation by 2.
$x = \pm 6$	Apply the square root to both sides of the equation.

See Lesson: Solving Quadratic Equations.

22. D. The correct solutions are $1 \pm \sqrt{38}$.

$x^2 – 2x = 37$	Add 37 to both sides of the equation.
$x^2 – 2x + 1 = 37 + 1$	Complete the square, $\left(\frac{2}{2}\right)^2 = 1^2 = 1$. Add 1 to both sides of the equation.
$x^2 – 2x + 1 = 38$	Simplify the right side of the equation.
$(x–1)^2 = 38$	Factor the left side of the equation.
$x – 1 = \pm\sqrt{38}$	Apply the square root to both sides of the equation.
$x = 1 \pm \sqrt{38}$	Add 1 to both sides of the equation.

See Lesson: Solving Quadratic Equations.

23. B. The correct solutions are –10 and 5.

$(x + 10)(x–5) = 0$	Factor the equation.
$(x + 10) = 0$ *and* $(x–5) = 0$	Set each factor equal to 0.
$x + 10 = 0$	Subtract 10 from both sides of the equation to solve for the first factor.
$x = –10$	
$x–5 = 0$	Add 5 to both sides of the equation to solve for the second factor.
$x = 5$	

See Lesson: Solving Quadratic Equations.

24. A. The correct solution is $25x^2 – 9$.

$$(5x–3)(5x + 3) = 5x(5x + 3) – 3(5x + 3) = 25x^2 + 15x – 15x – 9 = 25x^2 – 9$$

See Lesson: Polynomials.

25. **D.** The correct solution is $2x^2 + xy + y^2$.

$(-3x^2 - 2xy + 4y^2) + (5x^2 + 3xy - 3y^2) = (-3x^2 + 5x^2) + (-2xy + 3xy) + (4y^2 - 3y^2) = 2x^2 + xy + y^2$

See Lesson: Polynomials.

26. **B.** The correct solution is $(x + 10)^2$. The expression $x^2 + 20x + 100$ is rewritten as $(x + 10)^2$ because the value of a is x and the value of b is 10. **See Lesson: Polynomials.**

27. **B.** The failure rate is 1.32%. The failure rate is the fraction of all widgets that failed. In this case, the total number of widgets is $17 + 1{,}273 = 1{,}290$. The failure rate is therefore $\frac{17}{1290}$, which is about 1.32%. **See Lesson: Ratios, Proportions, and Percentages.**

28. **D.** All of the answer choices are equal. Although answer C is not in lowest terms, it is equal to $\frac{8}{125}$, which is equal to 0.064 or 6.4%. **See Lesson: Ratios, Proportions, and Percentages.**

29. **C.** The correct solution is $\frac{x^{25}}{y^{25}}$ because $\left(\frac{x^3 y^{-2}}{x^{-2} y^3}\right)^5 = (x^{3-(-2)} y^{-2-3})^5 = (x^5 y^{-5})^5 = x^{5\times5} y^{-5\times5} = x^{25} y^{-25} = \frac{x^{25}}{y^{25}}$. **See Lesson: Powers, Exponents, Roots, and Radicals.**

30. **D.** The correct solution is 15 because the first athlete's salary is about \$30,000,000 and the second athlete's salary is about \$2,000,000. So, the first athlete's salary is about 15 times larger. **See Lesson: Powers, Exponents, Roots, and Radicals.**

31. **B.** The correct solution is a line. The walls are two planes, and two planes intersect at a line. **See Lesson: Congruence.**

32. **B.** The correct solution is 2. For a parallelogram, there is rotational symmetry every $180°$. **See Lesson: Congruence.**

33. **A.** The correct solution is 30. Substitute the values into the formula and simplify using the order of operations, $A = \frac{1}{2}ap = \frac{1}{2}(2)(6(5)) = 30$ square inches. **See Lesson: Similarity, Right Triangles, and Trigonometry.**

34. **B.** The correct solution is 5. Substitute the values into the formula, $150 = 30h$. Divide both sides of the equation by 30, $h = 5$ inches. **See Lesson: Similarity, Right Triangles, and Trigonometry.**

35. **B.** The correct solution is 336. Substitute the values into the formula and simplify using the order of operations, $V = lwh = 6(7)(8)$ cubic centimeters. **See Lesson: Similarity, Right Triangles, and Trigonometry.**

36. **D.** The correct solution is 4.0 because $A = \pi r^2$; $12 = 3.14 r^2$; $3.82 = r^2$; $r \approx 2.0$. The diameter is twice the radius, or about 4.0 feet. **See Lesson: Circles.**

37. **D.** The correct solution is 200.96. The radius is 8 centimeters and $A = \pi r^2 \approx 3.14(8)^2 \approx 3.14(64) \approx 200.96$ square centimeters. **See Lesson: Circles.**

38. **A.** The correct solution is 17.3. $A = \frac{1}{2}\pi r^2$; $48 = \frac{1}{2}(3.14) r^2$; $48 = 1.57 r^2$; $30.57 = r^2$; $r \approx 5.5$ centimeters. $C = \frac{1}{2}(2\pi r)$; $C = \frac{1}{2}(2)(3.14)(5.5) \approx 17.3$ centimeters. **See Lesson: Circles.**

39. B. The correct solution is 440. Substitute the values into the formula and simplify using the order of operations, $V = \frac{1}{3}Bh = \frac{1}{3}lwh = \frac{1}{3}(10)(11)12 = 440$ cubic inches. **See Lesson: Measurement and Dimension.**

40. B. The correct solution is 523.33 cubic inches. The radius is 5 inches. Substitute the values into the formula and simplify using the order of operations, $V = \frac{4}{3}\pi r^3 = \frac{4}{3}(3.14)5^3 = \frac{4}{3}(3.14)(125) = 523.33$ cubic inches. **See Lesson: Measurement and Dimension.**

41. B. The correct solution is 35. The data set in order is 31, 32, 33, 33, 34, 35, 35, 36, 37, 37, 38, 39, and the middle numbers are both 35. Therefore, the median is 35. **See Lesson: Interpreting Graphics.**

42. D. The correct solution is 38. The difference between the highest value of 65 and the lowest value of 27 is 38. **See Lesson: Interpreting Graphics.**

43. C. The correct solution is 42, 44, and 45. The modes are 42, 44, and 45 because these values appear four times in the data set. **See Lesson: Interpreting Graphics.**

44. B. The correct solution is ten-sided number cube and use multiples of 2 because there are 4 results out of 10 that would match the probability of the actual event. **See Lesson: Statistical Measures.**

45. D. The correct solution is convenience sampling because the group is at a mall asking shoppers at the mall for their opinions. **See Lesson: Statistical Measures.**

46. A. The correct solution is to ask how many fat calories patients eat and track patients' weight because the researcher is observing the number of fat calories eaten and the weight. **See Lesson: Statistical Measures.**

47. D. The correct solution is $\frac{1}{2}$. There are 3 S's and 2 T's in the word SUBTITUTE out of 10 letters. The probability is $\frac{3}{10} + \frac{2}{10} = \frac{5}{10} = \frac{1}{2}$. **See Lesson: Statistics & Probability: The Rules of Probability.**

48. C. The correct solution is $\frac{9}{20}$. There are six multiples of 3 and four multiples of 5. The overlap of 15 is subtracted from the probability, $\frac{6}{20} + \frac{4}{20} - \frac{1}{20} = \frac{9}{20}$. **See Lesson: Statistics & Probability: The Rules of Probability.**

49. D. The correct solution is more than half of the amount spent is between $110 and $170. There are 14 weeks where the amount spent is between $110 and $140 and 13 weeks where the amount spent is between $140 and $170. This is 27 weeks, which is more than half the data set. **See Lesson: Interpreting Categorical and Quantitative Data.**

50. B. The correct solution is minimum: 0.5, first quartile: 3, median: 4.5, third quartile: 7, maximum: 9, which are the values of the box plot. **See Lesson: Interpreting Categorical and Quantitative Data.**